Religion and Politics in the International System Today

This book proposes a post–Cold War paradigm based on the inter-action between the contemporary globalization of the political, eco-nomic, military, and communication systems and the increasing role of religion in influencing global politics. Rapid technological advances constantly recast politics, economics, armed conflict, and the media. These four systems are thus becoming not just more international each in themselves, but they are also rapidly integrating with each other. As a result, the four world systems constantly create new environments in which individuals and societies must make rapid choices on the basis of their perceived personal and communal identities. This book con-structs its new global paradigm by explaining the roles of Christian-ity, Islam, Judaism, Hinduism, Buddhism, Confucianism, and Maoist Marxism in world politics. Whereas secularism was the safe political bet for the modern West following the Thirty Years' War (1618–48), today's incredibly complicated global society can only escape its increas-ing economic stratification and global conflict with growing religious awareness, motivation, and public activity.

Eric O. Hanson is Patrick A. Donohoe S. J. Professor of Political Science at Santa Clara University. He studied in East Asia for five years, including graduate work at National Taiwan University, before receiv-ing his doctorate from Stanford University. He has been a Fellow at the Stanford University Center for International Security and Arms Control. He is the author of *Catholic Politics in China and Korea* and *The Catholic Church in World Politics*.

Religion and Politics in the International System Today

ERIC O. HANSON

Santa Clara University

CAMBRIDGE
UNIVERSITY PRESS

CAMBRIDGE UNIVERSITY PRESS
Cambridge, New York, Melbourne, Madrid, Cape Town, Singapore, São Paulo

Cambridge University Press
40 West 20th Street, New York, NY 10011-4211, USA

www.cambridge.org
Information on this title: www.cambridge.org/9780521852456

First published 2006

Printed in the United States of America

A catalog record for this publication is available from the British Library.

Library of Congress Cataloging in Publication Data

Hanson, Eric O.
Religion and politics in the international system today / Eric O. Hanson.
    p.   cm.
Includes bibliographical references and index.
ISBN 0-521-85245-5 (hardback) – ISBN 0-521-61781-2 (pbk.)
1. Religion and politics.   I. Title.
BL65.P7H36   2006
322′.1–dc22   2005008714

ISBN-13   978-0-521-85245-6 hardback
ISBN-10   0-521-85245-5 hardback

ISBN-13   978-0-521-61781-9 paperback
ISBN-10   0-521-61781-2 paperback

To *four generations of family for their love and support,*
Nana, Don, Jean, Kathleen, Erin Katharine, and
Kara Kathleen, and

To *family friend Padre Pascual Ramirez (1957–99), of*
Churintzio, Michoacán, the Mexican Highway Patrol,
and the Diocese of Oakland.

Padre Pascual exemplified his 3 Fs of faith, family, and festival
before a freeway accident (9/9/99) on his way to anoint the sick.

And to all those citizens of two nations who, like Padre Pascual,
must depend on coyotes for their lives and for the integrity of
their families.

Contents

Acknowledgments

A project like this demands more than the usual dependence on the expertise and personal assistance of friends and colleagues. First thanks go to the superb Santa Clara University students who have served as research assistants: Chris Van Meir, Shivani Chadra, Quinn Shean, Holly Bettencourt, Rahima Saratore, Casey O'Connor, and Richard Lumley. They not only found obscure sources, but they also suggested changes and offered sound critiques of both my ideas and my English. Second, Santa Clara is blessed with very fine departments in religious studies, political science, history, communication, and economics. I particularly appreciate the personal help of Gloria Hofer, Catherine Bell, Greg Corning, Paul Crowley, S.J., Paul Fitzgerald, S.J., Dennis Gordon, Leslie Gray, Ron Hansen, Kirk O. Hanson, Michael Kevane, Emile McAnany, Barbara Molony, Tim O'Keefe, Fred Parrella, David Pinault, Sita Raman, Joseph Sands, S.J., Paul Soukup, S.J., William Sundstrom, and Jiri Toman. May they accept my apologies for any misuse of their excellent ideas, and for forgetting anyone. As the process started to come to the end, both historian Bob Senkewicz and my wife Kathleen Hanson gave superb direction on the general fit of the ideas. Kathleen not only read and corrected the entire third and fourth drafts but also inspired many of the ideas as we discussed the lives of her ESL students. Administrative assistant Leslie Bethard handled many details with efficiency and dispatch. At Cambridge University Press, senior editor Lewis Bateman went out of his way to help craft a readable book out of what was originally twice as long a manuscript. Production and copy editor Laura Lawrie improved the manuscript significantly. Finally, many thanks to anonymous Reader B, who read the first three drafts and provided invaluable advice on how to cut and develop the book.

Religion and Politics in the International System Today

Introduction

The View from Silicon Valley

TECHNOLOGY AND THE GLOBAL ECONOMIC, MILITARY, AND COMMUNICATION SYSTEMS

The fall of the Berlin Wall and its aftermath have left both citizens and scholars grasping for ways to make sense of the new relations among nation states, multinational corporations, terrorist groups, and other global actors. This book proposes a post–Cold War paradigm based on the interaction between the contemporary globalization of the political, economic, military, and communication (political plus EMC) systems and the significant role of religion in influencing global politics. Indeed, current politics, be it local, national, or international, exists at this connection between the four rapidly integrating global systems and individual self-understandings based on particularistic, often religious, communal histories. Thus, Tip O'Neill and Thomas Friedman are both correct: all politics is both local *and* global at the same time.

Such dual approaches – local and global, religion and EMC systems – seem plausible when examining the reasons for the fall of the Berlin Wall itself. Any treatment of the November 1989 events in Eastern Europe that ignores the progressive weakening of the Soviet economy during the Soviet-American arms race, the political-economic *perestroika* [restructuring] of Mikhail Gorbachev, or the religious and popular communication role of John Paul II and Polish Catholicism misses significant parts of a complete political explanation. This book will expend most of its print discussing the lesser-studied religious causalities, but, hopefully, even the most spiritual factors will be situated within their political and EMC contexts. Ironically, rapid technological advances have made religion more relevant in the political and EMC systems.

Where, then, should the hunt for a new global paradigm start? From my perspective of living and teaching in California's Silicon Valley, the increasing rapidity of technological advances constitutes the most striking new phenomenon of the last two decades. Scientific innovation affects all areas of life, from biotechnology to entertainment. Technology most significantly influences world politics by fostering, in procedure and in product, the ever-tightening integration of the international economic system. And if any of us Americans have been tempted to ignore that global economic integration, the experience of the dislocation caused by the "Asian Flu" of the late 1990s should have cured us. What started as an obscure attack on the overvalued Thai Baht damaged whole regions. Friedman begins his 1999 book[1] by tracing the contagion: from Thailand to other Asian markets as both local and global investors sought currency stability; from Asia to Russia through lower worldwide commodity prices, especially for oil; from Russia to Brazil to the United States, where Hedge Funds like the Connecticut-based Long-Term Capital Management pulled their investments back into the "safe" American market and went belly up.

The contemporary international economic system thus demonstrates many of the dynamics described by Immanuel Wallerstein and other practitioners of world system theory, which seeks to explain the globe's gradual four-century development by focusing on the link between the dominant economic core and the exploited periphery, whose inhabitants have concentrated on low-productivity, low-wage tasks. Global production takes place from the Shannon Development Authority in Ireland to the Shenzhen Special Economic Zone in Guangdong. The U.S. market in beanie babies (Don't remove the Tyco label!), aided and abetted by the Home Shopping Channel, remains my personal favorite postmodern global commercial fad. Valley Fair, one of Silicon Valley's upscale malls, witnessed a mini-riot one Saturday morning when hundreds of rabid adult collectors descended on a small notions boutique rumored to be receiving a few Peace Bears.

Rapid urbanization has fostered great disparities within nations and regions, reflecting in almost all cases huge socioeconomic gaps between

---

[1] Thomas L. Friedman, *The Lexus and the Olive Tree: Understanding Globalization* (New York: Farrar, Straus, Giroux, 1999).

the cities and the rural areas. Shanties of tin and cardboard, bereft of water and electricity, exist on the edges of most developing world cities to absorb the constant population flow from the hinterland. The widespread knowledge about lifestyle disparities by many who live on the edge of starvation, plus a long string of regional wars, have fostered major immigration and refugee movements. Brutal authoritarian regimes on the periphery stimulate such flows, as does the desire for a better life. The return of Hong Kong to China in 1997 has not eliminated the great Sunday gatherings of Filipina maids in the center of the ex-colony. Their families at home continue to depend on their remittances, and Hong Kong bureaucrats feel secure that these guest workers, unlike their possible replacements from Sichuan, can always be sent home. In 2003, the Inter-American Development Bank reported that nearly one fifth of Mexico's population would receive remittances from relatives in the United States that year, a total of $14.5 billion.[2] That amount, which the bank estimates helps to feed, house, and educate twenty-five million Mexicans, exceeded both tourism and foreign investment. Only petroleum produced more foreign exchange for Mexico. The Iraq kidnapping of Filipino truck driver Angelo de la Cruz on July 8, 2004, made him a national hero, a symbol of the nearly seven million Filipinos who work overseas. While Mexican and Indian migrant workers sent home more money, the $7.6 billion in official bank transfers make up 7.5 percent of the Philippine gross national product, while untold millions or billions come through unofficial channels.[3] Public pressure forced President Arroyo to withdraw her country's fifty-one soldiers and police immediately, one month ahead of schedule, much to the displeasure of the United States.

The end of the Cold War increased the power of the international economic system by removing many of the political restraints to its operation. Thus, the international economy has become the most closely integrated and independent of the three EMC systems. The Al-Qaeda attack on New York's Twin Towers and the Pentagon, and the subsequent U.S. responses in Afghanistan and Iraq remind us, however, that sometimes a nation's military capacities trump all. The Nuclear Age began "the Day after Trinity" in July 1945 and has been extended and refined through the development of ever more sophisticated bombs and missiles

---

[2] *New York Times*, October 28, 2003 [date without further citation indicates the *New York Times*].

[3] August 1, 2004.

equipped with "smart" guidance systems. Like the international economy, thermonuclear bombs tie the world together as a system but in a less regulated and a more perverse way. However, the very devastation of the new weapons makes them awkward to employ successfully, aside from any moral considerations. Even India's most prominent nuclear advocate, K. Subrhmanyam, has commented, "[t]he world in which nuclear weapons could be used as a currency of power is gone forever."[4] The global projection of American conventional power proved sufficient for military victory in the Gulf War, Bosnia, Kosovo, Afghanistan, and Iraq.

Communication constitutes the third technologically driven system. The communication revolution, from the Internet to international mass distribution of Hollywood films, creates the possibility of a truly global culture. Such worldwide availability of *Siempre Coca-Cola, Terminator*, and Internet pornography terrifies many cultural nationalists and parents. The battle to restrict global communication access takes place in many forms, from "percent of content" laws to Internet filters and V-chips, to criminal prosecution of offenders. Communication remains, however, the least integrated of the three systems. There is no single unit for communication analysis, such as monetary value in the economic system. However, the religious-political issues probe more deeply than in the other two systems since communication inextricably involves personal and societal identities and values. During the last decade American and European media content has expanded throughout the world. Most of the global entertainment and advertising content seeks to project a fictitious "Main Street America with gangsters," but European conglomerates have become more serious rivals as they consolidate into larger commercial entities producing more regional programming. And China, India, and Nigeria have developed formidable film industries for specific niche markets. Communication alliances seek to promote as many tie-ins to advertising and merchandising as possible.

As indicated in the Kosovo and Iraq war examples, these three technology-driven systems are not just each becoming more international (horizontal integration), but they are progressively integrating with each other (vertical integration). Indeed, the September 11 attack illustrated global horizontal and vertical integration with its destruction of symbolic military and economic targets and the significance of communication

---

[4] David Cortright and Amitabhl Mattoo, eds., *India and the Bomb: Public Opinion and Nuclear Options* (Notre Dame: University of Notre Dame Press, 1996), 88.

media in its aftermath. Financial resources and costly satellites foster military might and media moguls. Armies protect oil fields and language schools. Television develops product demand and disposes domestic populations to support foreign military intervention with embedded reporters. Rather than "dual use," computer and satellite advances should be termed "triple use" in this context. Friedman states that "today, more than ever, the traditional boundaries between politics, culture, technology, finance, national security and ecology are disappearing."[5] From the theoretical perspective, the globe has become a truly horizontal and vertical world system, but with modern technological characteristics Wallerstein never dreamed of.

The Westphalian and Cold War paradigms derived their simplicity from the theoretical concentration of ideological and organizational legitimacy in the sovereign nation-state, even when that nation-state had allied with either Washington or Moscow. The current situation offers no such simplicity. Nation-states remain the principal military and political actors, but multinational corporations predominate in the economic and communication systems. Friedman even argues that the basic characteristic of contemporary economic markets is that no one is in charge. These three EMC systems change both within themselves and interactively. And driving technological innovations remain unpredictable, as any venture capitalist or purchaser of "vapor ware" will testify.

Faced with the impact of rapid technological changes in international EMC systems, has there been any systematic political response by any major global actor or groups of actors? Francis Fukuyama in *The End of History*[6] emphasized that this new world system offers by osmosis a single all-encompassing ideology, liberal democratic capitalism. Although this ideology has become progressively less attractive to the developing world, no unifying alternative ideology has arisen, whether from nationalist, imperialist, or internationalist sources. The cultural and political identities of people became more confused after the fall of the Berlin Wall. In summary, our contemporary world combines accelerating technological change with increasingly chaotic and fragmented ideological frameworks, the Valley Fair beanie baby riot writ globally. And this introduction hasn't even mentioned the impact of such an international system on global ecology. It is not a reassuring picture for us, our children, or our grandchildren.

---

[5] Friedman, *Lexus*, 15.
[6] Francis Fukuyama, *The End of History and the Last Man* (New York: Free Press, 1992).

RELIGION IN CULTURE AND POLITICS

Understanding the influences of the technologically driven, progressively integrating, global EMC systems on international politics has become the necessary starting point for any explanation of contemporary world politics, but such an understanding presents only half the picture. Macro explanations such as world system theory and its more ideological Latin relative, dependency theory, exhibit their Marxist roots. They constitute the leftover theories of the "losers" in the Cold War. More important, these theories generally favor economic explanations to the exclusion of almost every other factor. Sometimes military, cultural, or even specifically religious goals supersede every other motivation. For example, the restrained response of Egyptian public opinion to the 1981 assassination of Nobel Peace Prize winner and President Anwar Sadat shocked American citizens and policy makers. During the 1970s and 1980s, even the relatively mainstream Egyptian Muslim Brotherhood focused on a single religious motivation, defending Islamic values from both the secular West and the atheistic East. This religious motivation superseded any other economic or strategic consideration, with Sadat's government perceived as an irreligious collaborator.

World events since the Iranian revolution of 1979 have thus brought many to a realization that religion has become a major element in most national political systems, especially in the developing world. Religion constitutes an autonomous sphere of human activity but not an interactive system like the political and EMC systems. There is no global religious system because the religious characteristics of any two nations are not necessarily related as the economies of those nations are. All the disparate types of religions, however, have become increasingly significant political actors in the post–Cold War era. Ignoring religion or reducing it to politics, economics, military action, or media influence leads to grievous errors in world affairs. For example, in spring 2003, the U.S. Defense Department grossly underestimated the influence of religion in the political reconstruction of Iraq.

These trends have increased the global political impact of Islam and Christianity, and the growing national political impact of all religions. In contemporary political systems that have a predominant religion, those religions usually play two somewhat contradictory roles. First, the religion holds all social strata together in the name of a unified national culture. Second, it serves as the ideological cohesion for the poor and frustrated lower and middle classes to demand social justice. The political and social tensions in Latin American Catholicism and Middle Eastern Islam, for example, derive from these respective religions' attempts to mediate the national "common good" for all citizens, and at the same time, to exercise "a preferential option for the poor."

Scholars and diplomats still lack, however, a comprehensive synthetic theory to complement the myriad political-religious analyses limited to a single country, a single religion, or a single geographic region. In short, how are we to understand the post–Cold War relationship of religion and politics worldwide? And how does that relationship interact with the technology-driven international systems? Technological advances and the interpenetration of the EMC systems constantly create new environments in which individuals and societies are forced to make unforeseen political choices on the basis of their perceived personal and social identity (Who am I? Who are we?). In *Clash of Civilizations*,[7] Samuel Huntington shows that these cultural identities, based mainly on religion, play a significant role in defining the loyalties of the post–Cold War world. Huntington does not describe, however, the actual causal relationships of religion and politics in various cultures. In fact, current social science explains international economics, strategic doctrine, and communication theory much better than it does the global political system or the international relationships of religion and politics. This book hopes to fill that void and, by relating these political-religious relationships to the advances in technology-driven EMC systems, offer a new paradigm for understanding post–Cold War politics. The book will argue that the religious responses to these unforeseen political choices depend mainly on three factors: the level of political-religious interaction, from local to global; the nature of the religion, from religions of the book like Christianity to religions of meditative experience like Buddhism; and the regional or national culture of political-religious interaction, from the partially secularized West to Islamist Iran.

BOOK ORGANIZATION: THE NEW PARADIGM AND
CONTEMPORARY RELIGION AND POLITICS

The book is divided into two sections: Religion and Politics in the New Paradigm, and Religion in Contemporary World Politics. The first section, Chapters 1 through 4, presents the paradigm, defines religion, describes

7 Samuel P. Huntington, *The Clash of Civilizations and the Remaking of World Order* (New York: Simon & Schuster, 1996).

its practices, and explains its relationships to politics. The second section, Chapters 5 through 10, consists of five regional studies and a summary chapter. Each chapter compares the politics of the principal religions within the region: the West (Christianity, Islam, Judaism); East Asia (Buddhism, Christianity, Confucianism, Maoism); South Asia (Hinduism, Buddhism, Islam); the Middle East and North Africa (Judaism, Islam, Christianity); and Latin America (Indigenous Religions, Catholicism, Protestantism). Thus, this second section fosters the understanding of contemporary national, regional, and international politics.

The search for an overarching paradigm, of course, begs the question as to whether such a unified explanation exists. Maybe the insight, to borrow from the philosopher Bernard Lonergan,[8] is that there is no insight. Maybe the new international system defies explanation except as singular, unrelated problems and issues. Certainly the contemporary fragmentation of scholarly discourse would seem to suggest that even if such a paradigm existed, its elements would be so widely distributed in separate academic disciplines as to obscure it beyond comprehension. This academic fragmentation, however, has not prevented other political scientists from presenting grand designs. Those interested in excellent comparative discussions of the comprehensive theories of Ohmae, Furukawa, Barber, Kaplan, Huntington, Friedman, and others should consult the review articles by Drezner[9] and Hoffman.[10] To be successful, this book need not explain everything, but it must offer more insight than competing paradigms. This author might even settle for clarifying more than he obscures.

Such a book must be largely derivative for its local and national studies. Any mistakes in interpreting others' works, however, remain the sole responsibility of the author. Despite the author's attempt to take religion very seriously as a major determinant of political culture, this treatment remains political science, not theology or spirituality. The book's central methodological choice, to take religion seriously from the viewpoint of religious practitioners, highlights the significance of choosing some author to orient the text's general approach to spirituality. The book can follow well-known masters, theologians, and other academics for

---

[8] Bernard J. F. Lonergan, S.J., *Insight: A Study of Human Understanding* (New York: Longmans, 1957).

[9] Daniel Drezner, "Globalizers of the World United!" *Washington Quarterly* 21 (Winter 1998): 209–26.

[10] Stanley Hoffman, "The Clash of Globalizations," *Foreign Affairs* 81 (July/August 2002): 104–15.

each of the religions studied, but who will supply the general language for describing the spiritual life, even if all agree that no language suffices? I have settled on the spiritual writings of Trappist monk Thomas Merton (1915–68). Merton was born in France, had to leave Cambridge over involvement with a woman, and converted to Catholicism while studying the modernist canon under Mark Van Doren and other literary giants at Columbia University. From his Kentucky cloister, Merton later wrote a postwar best-seller, *The Seven Storey Mountain*,[11] which sold over six hundred thousand hardbacks. He liked beer. In the latter part of his life he became a friend of Beat poets, Civil Rights activists, and anti–Vietnam War protestors. When he went to Asia in 1968, Merton spent three days with the Dalai Lama at Dharamsala. Merton died shortly after of a heart attack resulting from electrocution by a defective fan at an ecumenical meeting of monks in Bangkok.

Merton seems to have had the relevant mystical experience, studied and prayed over the history of Christian spirituality all his religious life, and conducted significant dialogues with "great souls" in other traditions of Christianity, Buddhism, Hinduism, and Sufi Islam. In fact, when he was at Columbia, a Hindu ascetic from India first introduced him to the Christian spiritual classics, Augustine's *Confessions* and Thomas a Kempis's *The Imitation of Christ*. Merton also carried on a long friendship and writing projects with Daisetz T. Suzuki, the most important Zen master of early-twentieth-century America. Merton wrote one of his most revelatory spiritual letters to a Pakistani Sufi. No wonder, one month before his death, Merton wrote "I think we have now reached a stage of (long overdue) religious maturity at which it might be possible for someone to remain perfectly faithful to a Christian and Western monastic commitment and yet to learn in depth from, say, a Buddhist or Hindu discipline and experience. I believe some of us need to do this in order to improve the quality of our own monastic life and even to help in the task of monastic renewal which has been undertaken within the Western Church."[12]

We all start from our own religious traditions in seeking to link to those of others. If I were a Muslim, for example, I might follow the suggestion of Seyyed Hossein Nasr[13] to study the influence of the great Islamic philosopher Averroes (Ibn Rushd) on the equally great medieval

---

[11] Thomas Merton, *The Seven Storey Mountain* (New York: Garden City Books, 1948).

[12] Lawrence Cunningham, ed., *Thomas Merton: Spiritual Master: The Essential Writings* (Mahwah: Paulist Press, 1992), 24.

[13] Seyyed Hossein Nasr, *The Heart of Islam: Enduring Values for Humanity* (San Francisco: Harper, 2002), 82–83.

Jewish and Christian philosopher-theologians, Maimonides and Thomas Aquinas. Readers with a much deeper spirituality than mine can make their own adjustments to the religious sections of the text, but my political analysis relies on fairly simple spiritual insights often expressed in most religious traditions, for example, increasing gratitude as a sign of spiritual depth. No personal articles on spirituality are forthcoming, ever.

THE NEW MILLENNIUM: LINKING GLOBAL, NATIONAL, LOCAL, AND INDIVIDUAL PERSPECTIVES

The world's future has already arrived in Silicon Valley and other similar local societies. The inhabitants mirror the increasing rapidity of technological change in the increasing frenetic pace of contemporary life. Stepping back to take stock of our globe's total situation seems a luxury for academic *dilettantes*. Yet, never has there been a greater need to do so. It is not just that any worthwhile project, from reforming medical care to protecting the environment to preventing the proliferation of weapons of mass destruction, requires knowledge from multiple academic disciplines. Internationalization also progressively affects all local societies. In 1999 whites became a minority in this Santa Clara County. The 2000 Census showed that 45 percent of county residents spoke another language than English at home. That group included 18 percent Spanish and 19 percent Asian languages. The diversity of Silicon Valley's residents means that the local society constantly interacts with economic, political, and cultural events across the globe, from Belfast to Michoacán to Guangdong. For example, the Chinese Army Tiananmen massacre of June 4, 1989, resulted in an almost simultaneous flood of Hong Kong wire transfers seeking safe haven for money in San Francisco, Seattle, and Vancouver area banks. As soon as a nation experiences a political or economic crisis, my wife Kathleen begins teaching the area's refugees English as a Second Language at San Jose City College.

How much simpler this book would be if it were written one hundred years ago for the Paris World Exhibition of 1900 during an earlier phase of globalization that took place between the mid-nineteenth century and the Great Depression of the late 1920s. That 1900 Paris exhibition celebrated progress, technology, and the cultural and scientific ascendancy of Anglo-Europeans. Most European intellectuals, of course, remained skeptical about the possibilities of any cultural improvement of the rough, but obscenely rich, American "colonials." The elite of London, Berlin, Vienna, and Paris also assumed that Progress (capital P) soon would render religion unnecessary as humanity moved from one exciting scientific triumph to another. How naive that pre–World War I optimism seems from Silicon Valley at the beginning of the Third Millennium! Our grandmothers and fathers have experienced Verdun, the Rape of Nanking, the Holocaust, the Killing Fields, and the Vietnam War. We have experienced the Cuban Missile Crisis, the nuclear scare of the 1980s, arms proliferation, the Gulf War, Bosnia, Rwanda, and September 11. And neither Western nor Eastern religion in Silicon Valley has withered away, despite dizzying technological progress. In fact, immigration has strengthened and diversified local religious communities.

This late-nineteenth-century dismissal of religion is not limited to a historical curiosity. Many books that discuss contemporary politics reflect these intellectual antecedents. The late-nineteenth-century rise of social science in Germany accepted the positivist biases of the Enlightenment. This tradition also presupposed that as societies modernized, religion would become less relevant to politics. Because other parts of the globe would become modernized by accepting scientific Western values, non-Western religions could be relegated to arcane historical and anthropological studies. It was interesting to study Ottoman, Hindu, or Chinese religion, but not relevant to the future of world politics. Elsewhere I have pointed to the particular difficulties of the nineteenth-century American academic elite in studying the Catholic Church with its medieval roots and its unwashed and political ("Vote early and often") Irish and non-English-speaking immigrants. Jewish immigrants experienced even more problems having their religion taken seriously.

Attempting such a wide-ranging book in the current climate of academic fragmentation would be even more foolhardy than it is except that the project has arisen naturally from my job and from my academic and personal histories. First, many of the issues were first articulated by students in my Santa Clara University courses, especially an undergraduate capstone course entitled "Religion and Politics in the Developing World." I thank twenty years of students, many from non-Western parts of the world, for their penetrating observations. Teaching at the university also has privileged me to work closely with colleagues in many disciplines whose expertise on religion has fostered this work. In a further stroke of luck, the university focused its entire academic year, 2002–3, on globalization through a series of courses, lectures, and artistic presentations. We had a chance to benefit from speakers such as Thomas Friedman, Amartya Sen, Bryan Hehir, Douglass Irwin, Lori Wallach, and more than forty academics from Jesuit universities all over the globe.

The search for such a political-religious theory also derives from my background. I am a Lake Wobegon Lutheran culturally, with an academic specialty in Chinese political culture. My great-great-grandfather Osten was the first bishop of the Norwegian Lutheran Synod in the United States, his son Martin rector of Minnesota Redwing Seminary, and my late father Donald chairman of the Board of Trustees for Pasadena Presbyterian Church under Eugene Carson Blake, later head of the World Council of Churches. I also spent eleven years in the Catholic Jesuit Order, but readers with any religious expertise will easily discern that I never made it to theological studies. Lastly, five years were spent studying languages and politics in East Asia, with three semesters as a graduate student in political science at National Taiwan University in the late 1960s, a period of "more politics than science" amid the then heavy Nationalist party ideology.

The intended audience for this book is twofold. Hopefully, the book will be useful to academic scholars and diplomatic practitioners, as they seek to relate their own studies and policy initiatives to the rapidly changing contemporary international situation. This text argues that although secularism was the safe political bet for the modern West following the Thirty Years' War (1618–48), today's incredibly complicated global society can only escape its obscene economic stratification and the ever threatening Armageddon with growing religious awareness, motivation, and public activity, based on the individual sanctity of the true self (Thomas Merton), religious toleration, and interfaith dialogue. Political and religious leaders have separate and autonomous vocations, but, in the twenty-first century, their successes and failures have become inextricably linked. Western elites are poorly prepared for leadership in such a world because of their secular and compartmentalized educations. The text also faults the current largely unchecked powers of the EMC systems as leading to international political, religious, environmental, and societal disaster. It thus combines conventional liberal and conservative approaches to international affairs by advocating religious pluralism integrated into all four global systems as an alternative to the current compartmentalized, secular Western policy.

The book is also intended for the generally educated population such as Santa Clara University seniors who are about to enter the frenetic Silicon Valley lifestyle. The great challenge to them, as to my own two twenty-something children, is to bring some coherence to the "system overload" of modern life. For them and their friends, I chaired the Santa Clara University Core Curriculum Revision, 1992–97, and hope that this volume adds to the connective intelligibility that our committee sought to foster in their university studies, whatever the student's major. American and European graduates generally lack the requisite understanding of their own and non-Western religions that would make them more effective citizens, both nationally and internationally.

For this second group especially, I hope they catch some of my excitement about these topics. To do so, they might focus on how many Nobel Peace Prize winners naturally found their way into this text. Appendix 1 lists the winners for the last thirty years, 1975–2004. Selection of the recipient of "the world's highest honor" usually combines an individual's extraordinary series of actions for peace with an international context that supports choosing that particular recipient that year. In October 2002, for example, the committee chose former U.S. president Jimmy Carter for "his decades of untiring effort to find peaceful solutions to international conflicts, to advance democracy and human rights and to promote economic and social development."[14] The citation also mentioned the Camp David Accords ("in itself a great enough achievement to qualify"), conflict resolution, election monitoring, tropical disease, and socio-economic development. In terms of context, many felt Carter should have received the award after Camp David, and they worried that, like Gandhi, Carter would die before receiving it.

The Nobel Peace Prize thus offers a high-profile meeting place of often religious-based idealism, as in the case of Carter's Baptist faith, with *Realpolitik*. In contrast, the 1973 award went to Henry Kissinger and Le Duc Tho for the 1972 Vietnam Peace accord. Neither walked in the footsteps of Gandhi. By contrast most of the other recipients, like Andrei Sakharov, have demonstrated a high degree of idealism, with many coming from major religious traditions, from Martin Luther King (1964) to Mother Teresa (1979) to Lech Walesa (1983) to Desmond Tutu (1984) to Elie Wiesel (1986) to Aung San Suu Kyi (1991) to the Dalai Lama (1989) to Nelson Mandela (1993) to Bishop Carlos Filipe Ximenes Belo (1996) to John Hume (1998) to Kim Dae Jung (2000) to Shirin Ebadi (2003). Perhaps, in considering the extraordinary contributions of such great yet "ordinary" (as they themselves would insist) women and men, readers will find a little inspiration for their own lives.

---

[14] October 12, 2002.

PART I

RELIGION AND POLITICS IN THE NEW
GLOBAL PARADIGM

I

A New Paradigm for World Politics?

This book proposes a post–Cold War paradigm based on the interaction between the contemporary globalization of the political, economic, military, and communication (political plus EMC) systems and the significant role of religion in influencing politics. The first of the book's two sections, Chapters 1–4, explains the new paradigm. Chapter 1 presents the paradigm as a whole and then discusses each of the three EMC systems. Chapters 2–4 cover the second part of the paradigm, demonstrating the effect of the level of analysis and of the type of religion on the interaction between religion and politics.

THE NEW PARADIGM: POLITICS AND RELIGION WITHIN THE TECHNOLOGY-DRIVEN EMC SYSTEMS

From the Treaty of Westphalia (1648) international political analysts and diplomats have focused on the alliances and the conflicts of sovereign nation-states, each acting on the basis of "national interest," defined in various ways. Religion was thus relegated to the private individual and national ideological spheres. This Westphalian system hit bottom in the global, disproportionately European, debacle of World War I. At the end of World War II, the Cold War paradigm retained the centrality of the state system but modified it by aligning these sovereign states with one of the two ideological superpowers and by introducing a modicum of weak internationalism with the United Nations. In addition, transnationals like multinational corporations and global churches expanded their influence throughout the system by employing economic and expressive power. Superpowers, transnationals, and international organizations then all began to question the Westphalian principles of nonintervention in a nation's domestic affairs and the separation of religion and politics.

The post–Berlin Wall international system constitutes an expanded and much more complicated mix of relevant global actors including, among others, ethnic and tribal groupings, nation-states, terrorist groups, and transnational and international organizations. With the demise of the USSR, the major U.S. academic discussion has revolved around whether or not the preponderance of American military and economic power makes the system "unipolar," as it has been described by Charles Krauthammer. Huntington has called it "uni-multipolar" on the way to becoming multipolar, but all agree that the United States exercises a military and economic dominance unprecedented in history. Stephen Brooks and William Wohlforth term this dominance "American primacy" on the basis of overwhelming military, economic, and technological strength: "Today, in contrast [to former empires], the United States has no rival in any critical dimension of power. There has never been a system of sovereign states that contained one state with this degree of dominance."[1] The authors do end up counseling humility and cooperation for long-term national interest, but they don't see that the United States can be forced to adopt these virtues.

Joseph Nye's 2002 book, *The Paradox of American Power: Why the World's Only Superpower Can't Go It Alone*, emphasizes the necessity of such international cooperation, but does not deny the dominance of American power. From the American side, Nye warns against both isolationism and unilateral disregard for consultation with our allies: "Any retreat to a traditional policy focus on unipolarity, hegemony, sovereignty, and unilateralism will fail to produce the right outcomes, and its accompanying arrogance will erode the soft power that is often part of the solution. We must not let the illusion of empire blind us to the increasing importance of our soft power."[2] Nye classifies the sources of national power as military, economic, and "soft." Soft power includes national cultural power and government-championed values like democracy and human rights that attract the citizens of other nations. This text calls the latter "expressive power," and analyzes the global communication system

---

[1] Stephen Brooks and William Wohlforth, "American Primacy," *Foreign Affairs* 81 (July/August 2002): 23.
[2] Joseph F. Nye Jr., *The Paradox of American Power: Why the World's Only Superpower Can't Go It Alone* (Oxford: Oxford University Press, 2002), xvi.

for national cultural influences. The United States dominates the global communication system at about the same level as the economic system. What even Nye's focus on "hard" and "soft" power misses, however, is the second part of this book's paradigm, the relationship of religion and politics at the local, national, regional, and global levels.

The unipolarity-multipolarity debate obscures some very necessary distinctions based on answers to the question, "power for what?" Different types of power accomplish different objectives: economic power purchases goods; military power kills, maims, and destroys; communication power makes others listen to your message. None of these EMC powers, however, guarantees a specific human response. Some people, mostly for religious-political motivations, even choose death or the risk of death rather than compliance. In general, those who currently argue for unipolarity focus on the military system, unipolarity-multipolarity on technology and on the military and economic systems, and multipolarity on the residual "soft" areas of culture, communication, and political ideology, approached from various perspectives.

Faced with such a complicated set of global influences, is there a relatively simple, and therefore useful, way to imagine such a fluid, multifaceted new global political environment for analysis and long-range planning? Any such model, of course, constitutes only the first step toward full understanding. It derives its usefulness from its simplicity and from its superior accuracy to competing models. This book offers its paradigm as the intersection of two planes.

A. First, imagine one plane of the paradigm as four (political, economic, military, and communication) autonomous systems overlapping like two-dimensional sets. This provides fifteen possible types of events and causalities as is illustrated in Appendix 2. Each of the four systems exists independently and has its own set of rules for integration. Although it is difficult to name any human event that cannot be related to all four systems at least tenuously, it is possible to specify issues and events where decisions can and are made primarily within one, two, three, or all four systems. The visual model in Appendix 2 presents all systems as having the same size, but, of course, the nature of the event or of the question to be decided expands or shrinks the general influence of each of the four systems for that decision or event. The political and EMC systems of the first plane intersect at all four geographical levels of the second plane. In the twenty-first century, no region, no nation-state, no locality can escape this great complexity of global political, economic, military, and communication opportunities and constraints.

B. The second plane divides the world into local, national, regional, and international geographic sets of religious-political interactions. The resulting environments demand an answer to the questions of personal and societal identity (Who am I? Who are We?) before any consistent responses to these opportunities and constraints become possible. The relationships of religion and politics in the second plane strongly influence those identities, and religions affect politics in many other ways discussed in the next three chapters. Religion is an autonomous sphere of human activity, not a system. The various religions thus project different ideological and organizational patterns, no more related than Arabic, Basque, and Chinese are linguistically.

The paradigm thus encourages scholars, diplomats, and citizens to ask three questions about every political event and decision: Plane One: How does the event or decision relate to the global political and EMC system? Plane Two: What are the relevant political-religious considerations, judged from the level of interaction, the nature of the religion, and the regional or national political-religious forms? Intersection of Planes: How do these two answers relate to each other?

Each of the two planes introduces an unpredictable nonsystematic element, technology for the first plane and religious inspiration for the second. Predicting scientific discoveries and their technological applications remains impossible. Predicting religious inspiration is equally baffling. In both science and technology and in religious experience, the breakthroughs constitute random events. Religious breakthroughs tend to influence political and communication systems more directly, whereas technological ones tend to influence primarily the EMC systems. These breakthroughs, of course, interact with the preexisting cultures as they find their local, national, or regional expressions. Even the neighboring Arab Muslim countries of Egypt, Syria, Jordan, and Saudi Arabia adopted the Internet through four different bureaucratic processes.[3] In the case of religion, the Buddha's enlightenment led to very different religious traditions in Thailand, Tibet, and Japan. Science and technology as insight and systematic application and religion as ideology and organization also

---

[3] Jon W. Anderson, "Alternative Trajectories of IT Development: Shaping Arab and Muslim Cyberspace," Santa Clara University Center for Science, Technology, and Society, October 23, 2003.

affect each other reciprocally, especially at the level of general world-views. The Catholic Church, for example, finally accepted the scientific discoveries of Galileo and apologized for its earlier recalcitrance. The Chinese Falun Gong succeeded in its early period by claiming scientific competency.

Scientific and technological breakthroughs have their primary impact in the EMC systems, often influencing multiple systems at the same time. For example, the 1991 launch of Star TV in Asia began the contemporary global communication age. The enormous economic barriers to market entry have led to the concentration of all stages of communication delivery, from content production to satellite and cable broadcasting, in larger and fewer international conglomerates. In conflicts such as Yugoslavia and Iraq, furthermore, managing the media has been as important as managing the military. Media and advertising also play significant roles in national politics, especially as Western leaders such as Germany's Schröder mimicked American campaign politics. Sections 2–4 of this chapter treat the contemporary global economic, military, and communication systems. In each section, the three EMC systems influence politics and each other, demonstrating the vertical integration among all four systems alluded to in this book's Introduction. Section 5 summarizes the impact of this first part of the paradigm on the growth and decline of religious belief and organization.

THE GLOBAL ECONOMIC SYSTEM

This section discusses the international economic system from three perspectives: (a) the entire world economy as an integrated system; (b) the global competition among various regions of unequal economic clout; and (c) the relations among the economically advanced countries, mid-level nations such as Brazil and India, and the desperately poor countries. First, the global economy truly constitutes a system because of the international flow of goods, money, and people. The 1997–98 "Asian flu" global economic crisis illustrated the causality between economic events in Asia, Europe, South America, and North America. Modern technologies, from computer networks to huge cargo ships, facilitate the almost instantaneous transfer of money and the rapid transfer of goods and people. Stock markets in every region affect each other as do global trade and immigration patterns.

This modern period for the global economic system began at Bretton Woods (1944) shortly before the end of World War II. Allied leaders, seeking to design an economic regime that would foster peace and prosperity, pledged themselves to unfettered free trade. They founded both the World Bank and the International Monetary Fund (IMF). The policy mistakes of 1997–98 have resulted in a general consensus that the IMF should specialize in monitoring global and national economies, acting as a lender of last resort, and that the World Bank should focus on fighting poverty. In setting the rules for world trade, the General Agreement on Trade and Tariffs (GATT) evolved into the World Trade Organization (WTO) in 1995. The latter organization fosters negotiations, administers trade agreements, and serves as a court for handling trade disputes. Many hailed the 2001 entrance of China into the WTO as a milestone, but Russia still remains outside because of its low energy prices and its protection of fiscal and telecommunications industries. When Friedman describes the world as "flat" in his 2005 book,[4] he focuses on the wiring of the world by global communication giants that has greatly mitigated the geographical barriers to business activity. Now intelligent people all over the world can compete for the same contracts.

So far, the post–Cold War free trade leverage has privileged developed world corporations vis-à-vis labor, agriculture, the environment, and any country whose economy remains highly dependent on the global market for basic commodities. These less powerful economic players flourish best when they can form cartels that at least partially control supply, as in the case of OPEC setting guidelines for oil production. The relationship between the international system and the economic superpower, the United States, remains ambiguous. Although the U.S. government professes ideological fealty to free trade and exercises considerable political muscle in fostering and directing the global system, even Republican governments sometimes make decisions that undercut this free trade and conservative fiscal stance. For example, at its fall 2002 Washington meeting, the IMF criticized the United States for running huge trade deficits that threatened the devaluation of the dollar and for maintaining trade barriers through agricultural subsidies and import quotas. The IMF also singled out the European Union for the latter charge.

A truly international work force has also developed, which is far more inclusive than just Indian telephone customer service representatives for U.S. corporations. By the end of the American decade of prosperity in the 1990s, U.S. Bureau of Labor statistics showed that the number of

---

4 Thomas Friedman, *The World is Flat: A Brief History of the Twenty-First Century* (New York: Farrar, Straus, Giroux, 2005).

immigrant laborers rose to 15.7 million, 12 percent of all U.S. workers. Approximately one third remained undocumented, keeping wages low for meat packers, maids, gardeners, restaurant and hotel workers, and fruit and vegetable pickers. Not surprisingly, the trade associations in these industries have lobbied strongly for increased immigration. Likewise, Silicon Valley high-tech companies ask for more foreign engineers. Conversely, labor organizations such as the United Farm Workers and the AFL-CIO have fought such temporary worker proposals. AFL-CIO President John Sweeney, however, has softened his objections to undocumented workers already in the United States as he has attempted to unionize service industries. Countries on the economic rise such as China also have become major sources of immigrant labor in the West. Nations as diverse as Mexico, the Philippines, and Egypt rely on remittances to maintain the national economy. One tenth of Filipino wage-earners work overseas, for example, as Hong Kong maids, Japanese entertainment workers, and U.S. nurses.

The second topic of this section concerns regional economic competition. Technically, North America is represented by the North American Free Trade Agreement (NAFTA), but the United States in itself exercises disproportionate size and influence on the whole global system. This is reflected in the sensitivity of other stock markets to the New York Stock Exchange and the dependence of many nations on the U.S. market for selling their goods. When the American economy slowed down in late 2000, for example, many other nations felt the impact. During the global stock slide of June 28–July 24, 2002, the NYSE declined 14.8 percent, whereas British, German, Brazilian, Mexican, Japanese, and Hong Kong indices dropped 18.9, 17.1, 10.8, 7.0, 6.9, and 5.9 percent, respectively. "The die is cast in America,"[5] stated Sir Martin Sorrell, chief executive of London's WPP advertising group. Washington also maintains the largest national influence on transnational financial institutions like the World Bank and the IMF, and intergovernmental policy groups such as the Organization for Economic Cooperation and Development (OECD) and the Group of 8 (G8) economic powers.

The European Union as a whole, however, comes closest to having the power to rival the United States in its various sources. Even prior to the 2004 E.U. expansion, Nye commented that "the economy of the European Union is roughly equal to the United States; its population is considerably larger, as is its share of world exports.... Europe spends

---

[5] July 25, 2002.

about two-thirds of what the United States does on defense, has more men under arms, and includes two countries that possess nuclear arsenals."[6] Most Europeans rejoiced when the euro finally reached parity with the dollar on July 15, 2002, after trailing it for most of its first three and one half years of existence. Nye also noted that European culture and politics, like its American counterparts, exercise significant attraction throughout the world.

East Asia constitutes the third regional grouping in economic size. Japan has long been the world's second largest national economy. However, most economists predict that China will replace Japan within twenty-five years. On the negative side, both Japan and China worry international investors because of their large nonperforming debt ratios. The Japanese problem has worsened as the government has forced banks to use more realistic criteria for classification. In April 2002, for example, government-mandated auditors, who were assigned when the Tokyo Stock Market hit an eighteen-year low in the preceding year, found an additional $10.6 billion in nonperforming loans.[7] One month later, Standard & Poor's estimated that half of Chinese banks' outstanding loans were nonperforming.[8] China also remains dependent on the U.S. market for its large trade surpluses as Japan did in earlier decades.

Despite enthusiasm for joining the WTO, the Chinese government has long sought to protect national markets from the worst features of the global system, as it did during the Asian flu. At the end of September 1998, for instance, Chinese authorities initiated a series of price controls, currency restrictions, and limits on the sale of state-owned companies that represented a slowdown in the nation's effort to shift from a planned to a market economy. The Asian economic flu reminded all Asian political leaderships of the very real dangers of total integration into the global market. Chinese President Hu Jintao and his "fourth generation" leadership seek to retain the authoritarian political controls of a Leninist party with the gradual decentralization and rationalization of the economy within the international market. This neo-Conservative approach also targets the growing gap between rich and poor and between the coastal and the inland provinces. Conspicuous consumption and corruption, such leaders point out, appear in Guangdong Province as well as on Rodeo Drive in Beverly Hills. Transparency International's 2004

[6] Nye, *American Power*, 29–30.
[7] April 13, 2002.
[8] May 10, 2002.

Corruption Perception Index[9] gave China a low honesty rating of 3.4 out of 10 compared with Taiwan's 5.6 and South Korea's 4.5.

Third, what can be said about economic relations among advanced nations, the mid-level countries, and developing nations – a crucial issue for both religious and political leaders? The 2004 UN *Human Development Report* divides 175 nations into high human development (fifty-five nations in 2004), medium human development (eighty-six), and low human development (thirty-three).[10] Many analysts, including Nobel laureate Joseph Stiglitz in his 2002 book,[11] have criticized the World Bank and the IMF for their mismanagement of economic and financial crises in the developing countries during the 1990s. Stiglitz backs his central thesis with case examples from, among others, Mexico, Russia, Asia, and Latin America. This criticism documents IMF errors throughout the decade, principally in forcing the developing nations to raise interest rates and tighten fiscal policy when slow growth, not inflation, was the problem. Paul Blustein[12] also focuses on the yawning gap between this "economic priesthood's" exalted view of its own mathematically based expertise and the haphazard way it approached these new types of crises in which political calculations remained as important as economic ones. Eventually, even its sister institution, the World Bank, criticized both the IMF and itself. In May 2000, the World Bank issued a thick report on Africa that blamed itself and other aid donors for ill-conceived projects. World Bank data on the continent was appalling: the GNP of all forty-eight sub-Saharan African states did not surpass Belgium. They had fewer roads than Poland, less than 2 percent of world trade, and more than 70 percent of the new AIDS cases.[13] "In 1970, the poverty rate of Africa was virtually identical to Asia's. Today, the percentage of Africans living on less than a dollar a day has nearly doubled, to about 40%."[14] Such a dire situation led the World Bank and the IMF in January 2005 to recommend doubling development aid to poor countries within five years.[15] That recommendation

---

[9] http://www.transparency.org.

[10] United Nations Development Programme, *Human Development Report 2004* (Oxford: Oxford University Press, 2004).

[11] Joseph E. Stiglitz, *Globalization and Its Discontents* (New York: W.W. Norton, 2002).

[12] Paul Blustein, *The Chastening: Inside the Crisis That Rocked the Global Financial System and Humbled the IMF* (New York: Public Affairs, 2001).

[13] June 1, 2000.

[14] William Sundstrom, "Addressing Disparities in Income and Wealth," Santa Clara University Markkula Center for Applied Ethics, October 23, 2003, 2.

[15] January 13, 2005.

seconded earlier ones by the Blair Commission and by the U.N.'s Millennium Project headed by economist Jeffery Sachs.[16]

Such disparities rocked the WTO. At Cancun in October 2003, the mid-level group of twenty-plus nations led by Brazil and India walked out over the question of American and European agricultural subsidies. These subsidies hurt mid-level countries like Brazil, but they more seriously damage African and Caribbean countries that depend almost completely on their agricultural exports. After all, Brazil also produces Embraer jets that it has sold to India and to the United States in competition with Boeing and Airbus. Franz Fischler, the miffed E.U. agricultural commissioner, responded to the walkout, "The improvised articulation led by Brazil is something from another planet. They need to come back to earth quickly."[17] But the new group held firm. In August 2004, an agreement was reached at the WTO that eliminated the E.U.'s export subsidies and cut back on U.S. export subsidies and some of its cotton subsidies. U.S. negotiator Robert Zoellick also agreed to make a 20 percent reduction in the $19 billion-dollar subsidies of corn, wheat, rice, and soybeans during the first year of the pact. Brazil had just won WTO judgments against the United States over cotton subsidies and the EU over sugar subsidies.[18] WTO officials are again hoping for the successful conclusion of the new round of talks in 2006.

In attempting to predict the future of the global economic system, issues of population growth and environmental impact remain crucial. The U.N. predicts that in the next fifty years the population of the more developed countries will remain at 1.2 billion whereas the population of the less developed countries will grow from 4.9 billion in 2000 to 8.2 billion in 2050.[19] In 1950 developed nations made up half of the top ten countries in population. In 2000, the United States, Japan, and Russia remained in the top ten. In 2050, only the United States, whose higher fertility rates and larger intake of immigrants increase population, will rank in the top ten. The bottom quintile of nations suffers great deprivation, and population growth will increase in these areas. In 2050, according to U.N. projections, the top ten most populous nations will be in this order: India, China, the United States, Pakistan, Indonesia, Nigeria, Brazil, Bangladesh, Ethiopia,

---

[16] For the 2000 Millennium Declaration and Goals, see Jeffery D. Sachs, *The End of Poverty: Economic Possibilities for Our Time* (New York: Penguin, 2005), 210–14.

[17] November 11, 2003.

[18] August 2, 2004.

[19] February 28, 2002.

and the Democratic Republic of the Congo. In the economic disaster zone of Africa, population will increase by 152 percent.

The environmental impact of the Bretton Woods system can be viewed from multiple angles. First, the fostering of increased international trade adds greatly to the impact of transportation and fuel consumption for airplanes, container ships, and trucks. These carriers also spread non-native plant forms to new countries in bilge water and packing materials. Second, the rapid mobility of people increases the rate of transmission of diseases such as AIDS and SARS. A CIA report warned that by 2010 five countries (China, Ethiopia, India, Nigeria, and Russia) will have 40 percent of the world's AIDS population and more HIV-infected people (fifty to seventy-five million each) than any other five countries put together.[20] Third, the global demand for basic commodities has led to massive destruction of native habitats, for example, the Amazon rainforest for timber and beef. Rapid economic growth in both China and India has fostered a greater race for energy sources, even in pariah countries such as Sudan and Myanmar. Fourth, as a country moves up the economic ladder, it uses more energy and contributes more to global warming. China has embarked on a transportation strategy that more and more emphasizes private cars, with the resulting increased demand for fossil fuel. The World Bank offers a chilling overview of the impact environmental issues such as urban crowding, housing on fragile land, and access to fresh water, fish stocks, and forest cover have on economic growth.[21] The 2004 Nobel committee stressed the link between the environment and peace by awarding the Peace Prize to Kenyan environmental activist Wangari Maathai. In February 2005, Brazilian President Luiz Inácio Lula da Silva formed two vast preserves in the Amazon after gunmen shot the over-seventy-year-old American Catholic nun and Brazilian citizen Dorothy Stang. Stang had fought both for the poor and landless and for the environment.

Finally, global economic stratification will most likely influence a decline in political democratization. The 2002 *United Nations Human Development Report* notes that 140 of the roughly 200 nations have had multiparty elections, and 81 countries have become democracies since 1980. Many of these countries, however, have not constructed democratic cultures (political opposition, free press, active citizen's groups) so

[20] October 1, 2002.
[21] World Bank, *Sustainable Development in a Dynamic World: Transforming Institution, Growth, and Quality of Life* (Oxford: Oxford University Press, 2003).

that people in the developing world are losing faith that democracy can improve their lives. Almost half of the world's people still live on less than $2 per day, and 3.6 billion have died in civil wars since 1980. More than sixty countries have lower per capita incomes than they did in 1990. Indeed, the aggregate world growth of the first decade after the Cold War did not benefit all, or even most, of the globe's inhabitants, even in "economic success stories" like India. Since the 1997–98 crisis, capital flows have reversed from the developing countries to the United States, making probably only the United States and China current major beneficiaries of the Bretton Woods system. The financier George Soros stated, "The U.S. government view is that markets are always right. My view is that markets are almost always wrong, and they have to be made right."[22] The World Bank offered the following more bureaucratically nuanced economic statement on the societal effects of free trade:

Avoiding inflation and protecting investors, ensuring labor and service delivery, maintaining environmental assets and systems for using them, preventing crimes and maintaining peace are all coordination problems. Markets work well for addressing some kinds of coordination problems – matching suppliers and demanders of goods, services, and physical assets – if supporting institutions such as property rights are in place. Mechanisms for other kinds of coordination problems, especially those in the social and environmental sphere, are often lacking, undeveloped, faulty, or weak.[23]

THE GLOBAL MILITARY SYSTEM

With the fall of the Berlin Wall the greatest military threat to the world comes from the proliferation of nuclear, chemical, and biological weapons. Indeed, a high-level American government report in July 1999 identified Russia, beset with political and economic instability, as the most likely unwitting source of such proliferation. It then listed China, North Korea, and other states with the capability to manufacture such weapons, and pointed to the instability of the Middle East and South and Central Asia as areas of likely use. In June 1999, the United States and Russia renewed for another seven years their Cooperative Threat Reduction Program. That initiative had cost $2.7 billion in the preceding seven years assisting political, military, and commercial institutions of the former Soviet Union to reduce the threat of global proliferation.

---

[22] March 21, 2002.
[23] World Bank, *Sustainable Development*, xiv. For this general argument, see especially the last half of Sachs, *The End of Poverty*.

In January 1994, the Ukraine agreed to give up the nuclear weapons it inherited from the USSR. Very few analysts, however, remain optimistic about global success in the long run. The nuclear, chemical, and biological genies are out of the bag. Possession of such weapons has become linked to national and religious pride, as in India's "Hindu bomb" matched by Pakistan's "Islamic bomb" during spring 1998. When representatives of 189 nations met at the United Nations in May 2005 for the five-year review of the Nuclear Nonproliferation Treaty, the nuclear powers and Iran, for different reasons, both opposed a five-year moratorium on the enrichment of uranium and the reprocessing of plutonium.[24]

Conflicts since 1989 are much more likely to be civil wars or terrorist attacks rather than the nuclear Armageddon or Warsaw Pact tank attack feared during the Cold War period. The Kosovo conflict constituted NATO's first war, and the first war fought since the Berlin Wall for primarily humanitarian reasons. That NATO held its unity, and that air power accomplished as much as it did in the ex-Yugoslavia surprised many analysts. Kosovo and Iraq also illustrated the integration of economics, military affairs, and communication factors in the modern world. The television pictures of Serbian paramilitaries loading Albanians into refugee trains for expulsion constituted Milosevic's major diplomatic mistake. Western public opinion then supported the bombing of Serbia to prevent "a new Holocaust" similar to Europe's original portrayed in that year's Oscar-winning Italian film, *Life Is Beautiful*. The war to topple Saddam Hussein in petroleum-rich Iraq introduced global television viewers to "real time" action described by reporters "embedded" with fighting units.

The two Cold War superpowers gained their preeminent status precisely from their military capability. What is called the Cold War paradigm depended most fundamentally on what came to be referred to as Mutual Assured Destruction (MAD) between the White House and the Kremlin. Although Japan followed Article Nine of its "Peace Constitution," Britain, France, and China deployed smaller nuclear forces whose usefulness depended on the limited American and Soviet defensive capabilities constrained by the Anti-Ballistic Missile (ABM) Treaty and the limited number of nuclear-weapon states constrained by the Nuclear Non-Proliferation Treaty. The ABM Treaty also fostered offensive reductions because by the time of the treaty both superpowers possessed many thousands of missiles more than needed to overwhelm such puny defenses.

[24] May 1, 2005.

During the Cold War, American conservative strategists periodically called for the consideration of more limited nuclear use. Yet, until the George W. Bush ("Bush 43," for the forty-third president) Administration, both Democratic and Republican presidents opted for the stability of MAD over the strategic uncertainties and the political costs of proceeding down the road to what critics such as W. K. H. Panofsky and S. M. Keeny Jr. called NUTS (Nuclear Utilization Target Selection). Bush 43 directly challenged the ABM Treaty by offering a new architecture that would include a National Missile Shield (NMS), whose principal use would be to protect Americans from the threat from "rogue nations" like North Korea. By this time, North Korea had already traded "delivery" technology to Pakistan for nuclear technology. *The New York Times* details the story of that exchange, which began with a visit of Benazir Bhutto to a frozen Pyongyang in winter 1993. She left with the plans for the DPRK's one-thousand-mile Nodong missile, and by April 1998 Pakistan flight tested its Ghauri missile.[25] Pakistani scientist A. Q. Khan, who had earlier stolen Dutch engineering plans for gas centrifuges, visited North Korea several times after Kim Jong II decided to pursue his enriched uranium project in 1997 or 1998.

In September 2002 the Bush Administration released its theoretical basis for responding to foreign threats in the thirty-three-page "National Security Strategy of the United States." This document took a markedly different stand from previous iterations, stating that the United States would not hesitate to act alone and "preemptively" against states and terrorist groups that threatened to use or to acquire weapons of mass destruction. The most controversial section, dubbed "The Hertz Doctrine" ("We're No. 1") declared that the world's strongest power "will never again allow its military supremacy to be challenged as it was during the cold war." In October 1999, the Senate had already turned down ratification of the Comprehensive Test Ban Treaty. The vote, fifty-one to forty-eight with two thirds needed, largely followed party lines. That vote constituted the first U.S. rejection of an international security treaty since the defeat of the Versailles Treaty in 1919. According to the Congressional Research Service, the United States proved the clear leader in global arms sales for the year 2000, marketing about half of all arms sold for just below $18.6 billion. Sixty-eight percent of U.S. weapons were bought by developing countries. Russian sales followed with 7.7 billion, France with 4.1 billion, Germany with 1.1 billion, Britain with 600 million, China with

[25] November 24, 2002.

400 million, and Italy with 100 million. Russia's principal buyers were India and China, but its sales to Iran and Iraq raised more concern.[26] For most of the world, war means the low-tech, "dirty" struggles of civil wars like those of Sri Lanka and Africa's "First World War" in the area around the Congo.

The military system took a much greater role in Bush 43's foreign policy because of that policy's emphasis on forceful unilateral action to solve world problems. Foreign policy experts Ivo H. Daalder and James M. Lindsey state that the younger Bush's worldview "has its roots in a strain of realist political thinking best labeled hegemonist." They offer five principles of this worldview: (1) the U.S. lives in a dangerous, almost Hobbesian, world; (2) self-interested nation states remain the key actors in world politics; (3) the United States should exercise power in its self-interest; (4) multilateral agreements are neither essential nor necessary; and (5) others recognize the United States as a unique great power. Finally, the authors offer a representational image. "Most of Bush's advisers accepted this billiard-ball view of the world, where the United States was the biggest (and most virtuous) ball on the table and could move every other ball when and where it wanted."[27]

When the United States announced that it would unilaterally pursue Iraq's disarmament, and maybe even regime change, the issue took center stage in global public opinion, at the United Nations, and even within the Bush Administration itself. After no compromise was possible within the American time frame, the United States attacked Iraq in March 2003. Military victory came swiftly, so that on May 1, forty-three days after the initial attack, Bush 43 could land on the aircraft carrier Abraham Lincoln off the California coast and declare the Iraqi conflict "one victory in a war on terror that began on September 11, 2001, and still goes on."[28] As the president landed on the flight deck, a post–Cold War paradigm which emphasized the United States as the unilateral military superpower seemed sufficient. Although the war proved relatively easy, however, internal police security and political-economic reconstruction have not. The political, economic, and communication systems have daily become more important, as have the relationships of religion and politics in both Iraq and the United States.

---

[26] August 20, 2001.
[27] Ivo Daalder and James Lindsay, *America Unbound: The Bush Revolution in Foreign Policy* (Washington, DC: The Brookings Institution, 2003), 45.
[28] May 2, 2003.

So what does the international military system look like at the present time? United States military power enjoys a strategic advantage never enjoyed before in history, even by the British Empire at its zenith. If U.S. power is extraordinary, however, so are the current global challenges. Not even the sole military and economic superpower can afford simultaneously to pursue all three members of "the Axis of Evil." Yet, there is no secondary global rival to the United States on the horizon. Russia still is "Avis," number two, in weapons of mass destruction, but Moscow threatens world stability mainly as a source of proliferation to other countries. The United States wants the European Union to spend more, not less, on its military programs, and encourages individual NATO allies to specialize, for example, the Czech Republic in chemical warfare. Britain and France remain nuclear powers. China has become a significant regional military power but at the present time lacks the military-industrial complex to support greater ambitions. Japan has softened its "nuclear allergy" but only sent support personnel for Iraqi reconstruction after much national soul searching. Although the United States and Russia continue to possess over 95 percent of the world's nuclear weapons, countries with only a few of these weapons pose a significant challenge to any military influence from Washington or Moscow.

THE GLOBAL COMMUNICATION SYSTEM

In his July 2003 inaugural address to the Strasbourg parliament, the new six-month president of the European Union, Italian Prime Minister Silvio Berlusconi, starkly illustrated the mutual influence of the political, economic, military, and communication systems. The prime minister is Europe's richest man. His family owns Italy's three main commercial television networks, its largest publishing house, its main advertising agency, and a food conglomerate. In 2002 Forbes ranked him the third most powerful billionaire in the entire world. On this July day, a German Socialist, Martin Schulz, publicly questioned Berlusconi's suitability for the rotating presidency. Berlusconi countered, "Mr. Schulz, I know there is a man in Italy producing a film on the Nazi concentration camps. I would like to suggest you for the role of leader. You would be perfect."[29] Raising the historic specter of Nazism seemed perfect for fragmenting the European Union as it approached its 2004 expansion.

[29] July 3, 2003.

Emile McAnany sets the late 1991 satellite launch of the Hong Kong-based Star TV as the beginning of the most recent age in the global communication system.[30] The twentieth century had already seen the diffusion of telephones, movies, radio, and "the Golden Age of television," but the current expanding use of communication satellites fosters global cable television, mobile phones, and the Internet. If CBS stood for the earlier age, Rupert Murdoch's Star TV or Finland's Nokia, which has less than 2 percent of its sales and 10 percent of its investment in the home country, both serve as apt symbols of this new communication era. The Star TV satellite broadcasts to 2.5 billion Asians without the permission of the peoples or the governments involved. Murdoch's News Corporation purchased Star TV for $950 million two years after its initial launch, but it was not until the News Corporation spent an additional $850 million during the following eight years that it began to turn a profit. By 2001 it had forty of the top fifty programs in the rapidly fragmenting Indian cable market. That year's big hit was an Indian version of *Who Wants to be a Millionaire* in Hindi. Star TV's strategy of producing for the domestic market in the "language of advantage," Hindi for India and Mandarin for China, began to pay off. But India still approximates the "Wild West" growth time of U.S. cable in the 1980s. The country offers a market of 70 million homes with television, 28.5 million with cable.[31] Thirty to fifty thousand cable companies operate in the country, leading to fierce competition with each other and with Bollywood.

The astronomical (pun intended) sums necessary for participating in the global communication market have led to major conglomerates such as News Corporation-Fox, AOL-Time-Warner, ABC Disney, NBC-General Electric, and Viacom-CBS. These media corporations seek to control both content and distribution systems, and "bundle" (sell various services as a package) and "window" (show the same program in multiple time slots) their services to meet the needs of upscale global consumers at a reduced price. The development of the television industries in India and China offer competing models with regard to economic and political influence on media content. In India, economic advantage determines the content of programming from MTV India to soft porn French fashion shows. In China, the political content of programming dominates, and cable generally means CNN for foreigners and the Chinese elite.

---

[30] Emile McAnany, "Globalization and Localization" *Explore* 6 (Fall 2002): 5–11.
[31] HSBC Securities in March 23, 2001.

U.S. government regulators have also been much kinder to this type of integration than in former eras. In 1995, the U.S. Federal Communication System (FCC) began to permit networks to own and to profit from programming. In February 2002, the FCC reversed the rulings of the 1940s and expanded the rights of networks to own the extremely profitable local stations. On June 2, 2003, for example, the FCC voted three to two on straight party lines to increase the power of broadcast and newspaper conglomerates. Media groups could now own television stations that reach up to 45 percent, increased from 35 percent, of the market, and in markets with five stations, it could own two. In markets with nine or more TV stations, a company could own both a newspaper and a TV outlet. The clear winners were companies such as News Corporation and Viacom, with the protests coming from interest groups on both the right and the left, from the National Rifle Association to the National Organization for Women. Conservative columnist William Safire termed the FCC action "the takeover of America's local press, television, and radio by a handful of mega-corporations."[32] Safire noted that his own paper, the *New York Times*, gave the story full coverage in contrast to little coverage in the broadcast media.

This section will touch on three specific questions with regard to media in the post–Cold War period. The first two concern recent global political-military crises. First, what impact did the communication media have in the disintegration and war in the ex-Yugoslavia? Russia's intervention in Chechnya will serve as a comparison. Second, what has been the media role in the international crisis resulting from September 11, 2001? The third section will treat the more general question about the different impacts of the old (telephones, movies, radio, television) and the new (Internet, satellite television, cell phones) communication technologies. This latter issue influences significantly the view of religious leaders toward the global communication system.

In contemporary international conflicts such as Yugoslavia, managing the media is every bit as important as managing the military. In the early 1990s, when General Colin Powell and other military leaders faced the decision of whether or not to intervene against Milosevic, the advances of modern technology affected that decision in two contradictory ways. On the one hand, the United States had achieved high accuracy with precision guided munitions (PGM), as had just been demonstrated in the first Gulf War. On the other hand, the generals could all remember their experience

---

[32] June 26, 2003.

in Vietnam ("the first living room war") when television undercut home support as the war dragged on. Halberstam comments that:

They [the generals] had a visceral sense that the technology of modern communications had more than kept up with the technology of modern armaments and had made the sustaining of war and the taking of casualties in distant places far harder for civilian politicians in ways that they discovered too late. A number of ratios had changed in modern warfare, especially in wars in distant lands. Not the least of these changes was the coming of instantaneous communications, which gave politicians something they did not always comprehend at first, a ticking clock, transforming a military equation into a more political one in which a critical factor would be our innate national impatience that eventually undercut the military.[33]

With the elder Bush and Clinton not wanting to know how bad Serb aggression had become because it might force them to act, it took a few print reporters (Blaine Harden of the *Washington Post*, Roy Gutman of *Newsday*, and John Burns of the *New York Times*) and CNN's Christiane Amanpour to alert the American people to the horrendous ethnic cleansing of the Bosnian villages. It was not an accident that CNN provided the television link, because, as both Halberstam and Haynes Johnson[34] demonstrate conclusively, the large networks had become less and less focused on international news as they were swallowed up by large corporations much more intent on the bottom line than on journalistic prizes for investigative reporting. The heyday of television reporting giants such as Edward R. Murrow, Walter Cronkite, and John Chancellor had disappeared, replaced by the era of "anchor stars" making millions of dollars. Johnson details this blurring of entertainment and news in the new "Era of Celebrity" (aka "Era of Scandal"). The first great show trial of the 1990s featured O. J. Simpson and the second Bill Clinton. These celebrity events led to unprecedented acrimony between blacks and whites in the first instance, and between Democrats and Republicans in the second. The entire process has weakened the independence of the political leaders of both parties, who have become extremely sensitive to the winds of fickle public opinion. Halberstram notes: "The cycle seemed to build on itself. Because of modern technology, the two most important developments in American politics were the use of polling and television advertising, both of them joined together in zeroing in on and then manipulating what the

---

[33] David Halberstam, *War in a Time of Peace: Bush, Clinton and the Generals* (New York: Scribner, 2001), 35–36.

[34] Haynes Johnson, *The Best of Times: America in the Clinton Years* (New York: Harcourt, Inc., 2001).

voting public thought at a given moment. . . . Politicians had to be nimble and more poll-driven, and because they were nimble, they seemed less grounded. It was a dynamic that at the core created little in the way of traction between politician and voter and held a great potential for cynicism and mutual distrust."[35]

From the time of the Vietnam War and the Iranian Revolution, with their daily reminders of body counts and days in captivity, the global communication system has played a major role in all global crises. The national elite may be influenced by the print media like the *New York Times*, the *Washington Post*, the *Wall Street Journal*, and the *Los Angeles Times*, but television pictures ("if it bleeds, it leads") exercise predominant influence on the American public's perception of war. And the twenty-four-hour news cycle, with viewership fragmented by cable television, produces an unremitting demand for more arresting images and more radical and combative talking heads, the better to draw audience share. One fiasco in Somalia, covered again and again in the media and later the subject of a major motion picture, *Black Hawk Down*, led to American withdrawal. Afterward, the U.S. negotiator Richard C. Holbrooke termed this phenomenon "Vietmalia" and kept reporters and demonstrators as far as he could from the Bosnian negotiators at the fenced-in Dayton Air Base.[36] On the other side, control of television could greatly assist dictators like Milosevic to stir up hatred against rival ethnic groups. From the late 1980s Milosevic used state television to denigrate Croats and Muslims almost as Hitler had employed film propaganda against the Jews. Roger Cohen described the societal parallels as follows: "The Serbia that I encountered in the early 1990s was a society unmoored, much like the Germany that proved susceptible to Nazism. Its Communist ideology had disintegrated. Its economy was in tatters, its memory of Croat crimes against Serbs during World War II had awakened and its thirst for scapegoats was consuming."[37]

The Russian communication dynamic on the Chechen War constituted a hybrid of the American and Serbian ones. Vladimir Putin gained control of the national communication system to assure the public that the

---

[35] Halberstam, *War*, 208.

[36] Halberstam, *War*, 265.

[37] July 15, 2001. Whether or not Serbia continues to see itself as the victim in the Yugoslavian conflicts may depend on how the nation processes a video, released in 2005, of Serbian forces killing six unarmed Muslims at Srebrenica. This video has been called "the most significant piece of evidence to shape Serbian public opinion since the end of the Balkan wars of the 1990's." June 12, 2005.

war was over. Putin's media challenge was not generalized expectations of press freedom and a fragmented system seeking ratings as in the United States, but networks controlled by his political enemies, rich Russian businessmen supporting other politicians. About 75 percent of the powerful TV-6 was owned by Boris A. Berezovsky, who fled to London after being charged with criminal dealings. In 2001, the Russian government engineered a state gas company takeover of NTV from millionaire Vladimir A. Gusinsky. Ms. Amanpour's Yugoslavian role was played by reporter Anna Politkovskaya in Chechnya, but without the same political or individual effect. Politkovskaya, the author of *A Dirty War: A Russian Reporter in Chechnya*, received death threats, and her television appearances were cancelled. In her twenty-six trips to Chechnya since 1999, Politkovskaya had sought to present both sides of the conflict, primarily from the angle of unknown and nonpolitical suffering people, such as the residents of an old-age home in Grozny who became political pawns of both sides.[38] In February 2005, the Russian Defense Ministry began broadcasting on its own national television channel, and the Russian Orthodox Church has sought its own channel.

What about the technological components of the U.S. response to the September 11 attack? The U.S. campaign against Al-Qaeda and the Taliban featured high precision bombing and a significant role for the international media. Unlike Yugoslavia, however, the most important global media audience in the fall of 2001 was the skeptical Muslim "street," not U.S. public opinion that at that time solidly supported American military action. In the Afghanistan case, the leaders of Islamic nations who had joined the U.S.-led coalition needed protection from the further radicalization of their own publics. Just as its first Gulf War coverage of the Baghdad skyline enhanced CNN's reputation, so the Qatar station Al-Jazeera ("the Peninsular") became a major political-communication player by having the sole TV bureau in Kabul and by using its connections to Al-Qaeda. Middle Easterners from many political slants felt that they needed an independent Arab station. After all, Iraq's invasion of Kuwait in August 1990 was not reported for three days by local government-backed media outlets while their political elites decided on a course of action. Al-Jazeera dared to criticize political leadership in Tunisia, Libya, Saudi Arabia, and other Arab states, and even interview Israeli leaders such as Ehud Barak and Simon Peres. In terms of promoting Arab democracy, the United States and Al-Jazeera have been unwitting allies since the station

[38] December 15, 2001.

has featured recent Middle East elections, with or without state approval. The station has also been a major force in keeping the images of the Palestinian-Israeli conflict in the minds of Arabs across the Middle East.

Despite Al-Jazeera's anti-American slant, however, Colin Powell, Donald Rumsfeld, and Condelezza Rice all gave interviews to the Arab station during the fall, even as the U.S. government warned American networks about airing Al-Qaeda tapes that, it said, might contain secret terrorist instructions in code. From the Arab side, Saudi political leaders complained about American media bias. For example, Defense Minister Prince Sultan and his son and ambassador to Washington, Prince Bandar bin Sultan, attacked the American media for blaming the Saudis for not doing enough to counter the roots of terrorism in their own country. "We don't expect Zionism [which many Saudis believe control the United States media] to be our friends unless we are enemies of ourselves and friends of Jews."[39] In early 2003 the Saudi TV pioneer MBC, Lebanon's Hariri Group, and others launched the Dubai-based Al-Arabiya, which by November had been banned from Iraq by the Governing Council for "incitement to murder" for broadcasting a tape of Saddam. There are also many religious channels, mainly Sunni out of Saudi Arabia, featuring religious education and interpretation of the Qur'an. For example, should *jihadis* attack American troops?[40]

The media war began as soon as the first bombs fell on Afganistan. Indeed, Al-Queda had provided the first bin Laden tape to Al-Jazeera with instructions to air it as soon as the fighting began. A few days later, British Prime Minister Tony Blair accepted an Al-Jazeera interview at his official residence to assure Muslim viewers that "This is not about the West versus Islam.... Decent Muslims, millions of them in European countries, have condemned these acts of terrorism in New York and elsewhere in America with every bit as much force as the rest of us."[41]

The Bush Administration learned from U.S. difficulties in the Afghanistan War, so it prepared for the propaganda war during the Iraq Conflict. The U.S. government decided to woo Al-Jazeera, assigning a top media liaison, whose regular job was running the Pentagon's television and film office in Hollywood, and offering it four choice posts for embedding reporters. The experiment of assigning reporters from all news organizations to specific American units proved a huge success in

---

[39] The Saudi Press Agency in December 21, 2001.
[40] February 6, 2005.
[41] October 9, 2001.

getting favorable coverage during the quick war. During the later, messier reconstruction period, however, the images of rioting, looting, and attacks on American troops became increasingly troublesome for Bush Administration political management.

Media coverage of terrorism and war makes its strongest impact by the visual images employed to represent an event in the viewer's minds. On September 11, the crash of the airliners into the Twin Towers and the many montages of firemen and policemen rescuing victims became the dominant American television pictures, including those of CNN in the United States. All fall, the U.S. media repeated these images, often merged with American flags. The following winter Super Bowl XXXVI trumpeted the theme "Heroes, Hope, and Homeland," reemphasizing the traditional link between U.S. patriotism and American sports. CNN International, however, combined such images with those of the bombing damage to Afghani houses and children. Al-Jazeera slighted United States suffering to focus on the Afghan bombing damage and the anger of the Muslim "street" in cities like Kandahar and Karachi. Each outlet knew the images most welcome to its audience.

Does the type of media, old or new, make any difference in its political and religious impact? Soukup et al. state that "[p]ast research has shown how communication systems connect with cognitive practices, human relationships and interactions, educational systems, entertainment, business, trade, intercultural influences, power arrangements, political systems, and religious practices."[42] Readers probably already know that the printing press was essential to the Reformation and television to the rise of the Religious Right. In fact, most people still live in a communication world defined by "the old media" of print, radio (especially "talk radio" for cars and for workers and peasants in rural Africa and Asia), television, and film. For these people, according to Soukup, "This knowledge is real, but it *is* mediated and hence filtered through reporters, camera operators, news organizations and other intermediaries. These mass media shape world views, probably as powerfully through entertainment as through news and information."[43] This mediation places significant power in the hands of the global communication corporations that provide news,

---

[42] Paul Soukup, S.J., Francis J. Buckley, S.J., and David C. Robinson, S.J., "The Influence of Information Technologies on Theology," *Theological Studies* 62 (2001): 367. Soukup, a scholar of the late Walter Ong, S.J., brings together the literature of media ecology with the psychological and social development of self. See, for example, Paul A. Soukup, "Media echoes in the development of the self," *Explorations in Media Ecology* 1: 119–33.

[43] Soukup et al., 368.

entertainment, and advertising, and increasingly blend the three for maximum economic profit.

Such power, of course, depends on the penetration of the market more prevalent in more economically developed countries. Ellis and ter Haar stress the importance of oral rumor in African religion and politics. "Information in Africa has always been transmitted largely by word of mouth, sometimes accompanied by forms of ritual activity that are of great effect in communicating meaning. . . . *Radio trottoir* properly consists of stories recounted in public, such that anyone present can question the accuracy of what is said or add embellishments of their own to correct or complement the story. *Radio trottoir* is a feature of societies in which many people do not earn salaries and can count on no bureaucratic form of social welfare, and where even policing and punishment are often not undertaken by organized bureaucracies."[44]

The "new media" of Internet, satellite television, cell phones, and so on offer many more choices to the consumer, and less quality control. Anyone can set up a Web site and purvey any nonsense, however implausible. For example, although the nearly universal Muslim Internet reaction to September 11 was condemnation, thanks to the Internet it was "common knowledge" across the Islamic world that over four thousand Jews stayed home from work in the Twin Towers that day. In exchange for this lack of quality control, the educated public with computer access receives almost instantaneous information and contact. The new media also empower political and religious dissidents in forming new movements. For example, China's Falun Gong and Mexico's Zapatistas both used the Internet against the repression of their governments. The former also subverted state-controlled satellite and cable television. Even in democratic countries, satellite and cable television have greatly lowered access costs for ethnic and public interest groups. Residents of Silicon Valley, for example, can watch television in over twenty different languages for at least a couple of hours per week. Thus, all sorts of intermediary groups, from the public-spirited to the lunatic and dangerous, can form without public checks and balances.

Eickelman and Anderson argue that mass education and the Internet have significantly changed Muslim politics, leading to an emerging public, nongovernmental sphere, analogous to the growth of voluntary organizations in the West. They point to its influence in three layers of social

---

[44] Stephen Ellis and Gerrie ter Haar, *Worlds of Power: Religious Thought and Political Practice in Africa* (New York: Oxford, 2004), 42–43.

infrastructure: (a) the interpretation of Islam in the world of Muslim religious opinion; (b) the examination of local Islamic political and social forms in Muslim-majority societies when they learn of other very different Islamic forms in other societies; and (c) the creation of virtual Muslim communities by sustaining contact between Diaspora and homelands.[45] The Muslim Internet began with engineers, who then started to use it privately for religious objectives. Next, religious professionals and opinion makers joined the engineers. Finally, the beneficiaries of mass education entered the conversation. Eickelmann comments: "The frontier between banned words and images and those that are tolerated in the Middle East has never been fixed, but access to new technologies has multiplied the channels through which ideas and information can be circulated and has enlarged the scope of what can be said and to whom."[46]

That the Internet does not always work for democratization can be seen in Robert Hefner's study of the Indonesian Islamist group, the Laskar Jihad. The Laskar Jihad combined the new media, face-to-face proselytizing of predominantly science and engineering students, and secret army financial backing to escalate Christian-Muslim conflict in Maluku during the presidency of the moderate Muslim Abdurrahman Wahid.[47] The second part of this book offers further discussion of politics and the media in almost every case study, for example, in the war in the ex-Yugoslavia in Chapter 5, the Falun Gong in Chapter 6, Los Angeles Persian-language TV stations sparking Iranian student protest in Chapter 7, Muslim use of TV and the Internet in Chapter 8, and Latin American televangelism in Chapter 9.

Are there any broad observations about the relationships of the EMC systems to political decision making? The specific political issue determines the exact mix of economic, military, and communication causalities, but, in general, absent the extreme case of a global or major regional war, the world economy remains more influential than the military or communication systems. Until the Iraq War of spring 2003 at least, the end of the Cold War increased the significance of the economy vis-à-vis military affairs because of the loss of a competing superpower and the limited potential for actually using weapons of mass destruction. Global

---

[45] Dale F. Eickelman and Jon W. Anderson, eds., *New Media in the Muslim World: The Emerging Public Sphere*, 2nd ed. (Bloomington: University of Indiana Press, 2003), x–xi.

[46] Dale F. Eickelman, "Communication and Control in the Middle East: Publication and Its Discontents," in Eickelman and Anderson, *New Media*, 33.

[47] Robert Hefner, "Civic Pluralism Denied? The New Media and *Jihadi* Violence in Indonesia," in Eickleman and Anderson, *New Media*, 158–79.

economic integration retains more political significance than the global communication revolution partly because the financial clout of the former more significantly influences the latter, and partly because it is much more difficult to opt out of the international economy than to escape being subjected to the latest movie or sitcom. Even if a person does watch globally based entertainment and advertising content, local cultural viewpoints always mediate the meaning of such cultural artifacts. And even within the United States, cable and satellite television is progressively fragmenting the audience along racial, generational, gender, and political lines. People often choose their cable news channels, for example, to reinforce their own prior opinions. U.S. media, from talk radio to best-sellers, often reinforce ideological divisions among the American population.

THE EMC SYSTEMS AND THE FUTURE OF RELIGION

The above three sections have demonstrated the crucial significance of the economic, military, and communication systems for contemporary politics. These EMC systems, internationally integrated in themselves, exercise mutual influence on each other and on the global political system. Sometimes the same technology drives innovation in all three systems. For example, satellites have fostered the instantaneous transfer of money, precision-guided munitions, and Direct TV, all of which influence politics and each other.

Often religious leaders and believers object primarily not to the influence of various levels of the political system, but to the impact of the EMC systems in their lives and in the lives of their families. These believers judge that they must influence the local or national political system to block the secular or antireligious impact of one or more of the global EMC systems, whether the issue is lifetime unemployment, a marauding army, or child pornography. In articulating a new paradigm, it would be extraordinarily helpful for analysts to know whether or not, or the degree to which, such efforts will be successful. For that answer, we need to understand the relationships of religion and politics from the individual to the global level. Will the secularization of the last five hundred years continue in the West? Will it extend to non-Western civilizations?

During the three hundred years between 1600 and 1900, the political, social, and cultural influence of Western religion weakened so significantly that scholars began to anticipate the total demise of religion in modern society, or at least its relegation to the private sphere of personal choice and sectarian life. Twentieth-century politics, especially since World War II, offered a more mixed picture. Western European documentation of the phenomenon of "believing, but not belonging" and recent American emphasis on "spirituality, but not religion" have supported the thesis of institutional ecclesiastical decline. The North American and global growth of evangelism does not. As of 2006, no determination is yet possible for Middle and Eastern Europe. After the Islamic and Hindu political resurgences, the developing world data argues against secularization.

The mixed nature of this twentieth-century data on religion results partly from the mixed impact of the contemporary communication system, the major cultural difference between personal life in the nineteenth and personal life in the twentieth century. The new communication system can discourage religion. Radical Catholic political economist Michael Budde[48] contends that "the global culture industries" rob humanity of its religious symbolism, making widespread religious conversion and practice improbable. With every movie and TV star wearing a cross, how can that symbol represent the crucifixion of Jesus? The thousands of commercial ads daily negate solitude. The average of sixteen thousand outside messages that each of us receives each day convinces Budde that Americans at least will gradually lose their ability to stand in the presence of the Sacred and make the serious conversions that such presence should foster. Solitude does not cause religious experiences or conversions of life, but it does seem to be a prerequisite for depth in all religions. Therefore, Budde's principal objection to the contemporary communication system does not concern content, but the psychological totalitarianism of the process. From this perspective, even Christians who spent their entire day listening to Vatican Radio or watching the Christian Broadcast Network would lose their souls from lack of prayerful solitude.

Other public figures, from Tipper Gore to Dr. Rowan Williams, the Archbishop of Canterbury, have made the content argument. In 2003, for example, the nonprofit Kaiser Family Foundation (Menlo Park, CA.) found that two thirds of American shows airing between 7 A.M. and 11 P.M. had some sexual content. About one in seven portrayed sexual intercourse, either in reality or strongly implied.[49] Research also shows that contemporary media are not successful in determining what people think, but that they are extraordinarily successful in limiting what people think about. Religion is rarely treated seriously in the mainstream media.

---

[48] Michael Budde, *The (Magic) Kingdom of God: Christianity and the Global Culture Industries* (Boulder, CO: Westview Press, 1997).
[49] July 27, 2003.

If religious conversions and practice occur, however, the international communication system can magnify the influence of even those who hold no formal political, economic, or military position. The movie *Gandhi* won an Oscar. *Time* Magazine placed both Nobel laureate Mother Teresa and 1980 "Man of the Year" Ayatollah Khomeini on its covers. Khomeini used audio cassettes to speak to the Iranian people from his Paris exile. Global television broadcast Mother Teresa's funeral in English, Hindi, and Bengali, even in a week when those rites had to compete for coverage with the death of Princess Diana. Muslim and Christian preachers proclaim their religious message in both old and new media. For example, thirty-four-year-old Amr Khalid of Egypt has become a very popular Islamic televangelist with his ordinary background, vernacular Arabic, and moderate message. The Saudi-owned ART satellite network broadcasts his Ramadan sermons live across the Arab world, Europe, and North America. Cairo's Islam-Online.net provides news articles, discussion of Islamic issues, discussion groups, and a "fatwa corner" where readers can ask questions about law and interpretations – in both Arabic and English. Conservative Catholics in the United States have attempted to compete with Protestant televangelists by forming their own radio network, Catholic Family Radio, and Mother Angelica of Alabama directs the even more conservative Eternal Word Television Network. The Catholic Redemptorist Order operates Poland's top-rated radio station, which challenges both the bishops and the state. Radio Maryja has thus served as a primary outlet for the popular fear that any new political-economic situation brings to the disadvantaged, a la Detroit's Father Coughlin in the Depression. The trips of the late John Paul II and the Dalai Lama have produced the expanded media coverage that their respective religious institutions could not afford to purchase.

In addition to the issue of secularization at the level of individual belief, a parallel organizational discussion targets the possible role and strategies for religious organizations in the rapidly globalizing international system. The social challenge for religious institutions, as Peter Beyer articulates it, is that over the last five hundred years religion has progressively lost its various social functions such as education and health care. Western society's functional differentiation has thus made religion less relevant socially and culturally as religious organizations have gradually lost their customary niches in public life. In the face of such public loss of social legitimacy, Beyer states, ecclesiastical institutions can choose one of two strategies. Conservative religious movements attempt "to gain control over a limited geographic area and then control pluralism within it,"[50] thus locking the prime source of relativism and disbelief outside the community. The contrasting liberal religious strategy stresses ecumenical cooperation and interfaith dialogue with all. This liberal approach, states Beyer, makes it difficult to specify what is unique about one's organization, and to prevent other religious and secular organizations, especially praiseworthy ones like Amnesty International and the Nature Conservatory, from coopting one's *raison d'etre* and personnel. From a purely institutional maintenance perspective, the best general strategy would be a combination of conservative and liberal elements.

On the individual, national, and global levels, then, the data supports neither continued global secularization nor its opposite in any conclusive way. The sociologist José Casanova divides secularism into three currents: societal differentiation, the lessening of belief, and the privatization of religion.[51] The first trend still holds, he asserts, but the other two propositions are in doubt. This text would amend Casanova's conclusion, however, by questioning even the future certainty of increased global societal differentiation. On point of fact, many contemporary religious-based organizations, from Hezbollah to the RSS, do provide more and more social goods as national and local political systems fail in the developing world. In addition, this author judges that all three EMC systems remain monopolistic in the sense that they seek to reduce the power of the other two EMC systems, and of the political system. Religion and politics thus constitute an integrating "united front" against the EMC systems. In a mature civil society, religious and political leaders should not only serve as checks on each other, but together they should seek to defend the society from EMC monopoly practices. The EMC systems must be limited by the political system in the first part of the paradigm and by religious experience in the second.

The World Bank approaches the same issues of EMC autonomy from an economic development viewpoint. Its report denominates three sets

---

[50] Peter Beyer, *Religion and Globalization* (London: Sage Publications, 1994), 92.

[51] José Casanova, *Public Religions in the Modern World* (Chicago: University of Chicago Press, 1994). Pippa Norris and Ronald Inglehart affirm the modern secularization thesis, provided the people in the societies involved, that is, advanced industrial societies, experience human security at both the societal and the personal levels. In the contemporary world, However, *"due to demographic trends in poorer societies, the world as a whole as a whole now has more people with traditional religious views than ever before* [italics in original] – and they constitute a growing proportion of the world's population." Norris and Inglehart, *Sacred and Secular: Religion and Politics Worldwide* (Cambridge: Cambridge University Press, 2004), 25.

of assets: economic assets such as agricultural output; environmental assets such as fresh water; and social assets such as trust. It concludes that "these assets are not perfectly substitutable," and offers the "lose-lose-lose" example of Madagascar deforestation harming all three sets of assets. Even the persistent failure to adopt economic "win-win" policies, states the report, does not derive from a failure in economic rationality, but "is most often a result of distributional problems and society's inability to make credible long term commitments." This World Bank report thus advocates the universal adoption of a political-economic principle, greater inclusiveness in decision-making made possible by a broader distribution of income: "Groups that lack assets tend also to lack voice, security, and a stake in the larger society, hampering institutions' ability to perform needed coordination functions. The result is a vicious cycle in which biased institutions implement policies that lead to an increase in polarization and unequal asset distribution."[52]

From a World Bank perspective, the rest of this book focuses on "social assets," not just as they are related to rational "coordinating functions," but as they are lived as religious experience, political participation, poverty and wealth, war and peace, and human communication. Chapters 2–4 treat the second part of the paradigm, the various relationships of religion and politics. Chapter 2 takes the political perspective and Chapter 3 the religious one. Chapter 4 then presents seven major global religious traditions and their characteristic political effects.

[52] World Bank, *Sustainable Development*, xiii–xv.

2

A Political Perspective on Religion and Politics

A fundamental understanding of the relationships between politics and religion demands analysis from both political and religious viewpoints. Chapter 2 presents the political perspective and Chapter 3 the religious one. Each viewpoint provides one of the principal three factors (level of interaction, nature of religion, regional or national cultural form) in describing these political-religious interactions for the second geographical plane of the paradigm. This second chapter examines the political impact of religion at the local, national, regional, and global levels. In doing so, it provides examples that have been chosen for their later usefulness in contemporary political-religious analysis. It is no accident that the political influence of Christian, Hindu, Jewish, and Muslim "fundamentalisms" receives treatment.

RELIGION IN LOCAL POLITICS: DIFFUSED RELIGION

Traditional religion has played a major role in local politics by constituting a civilization's basic unit, thus setting the parameters and rules for political competition for material and psychic resources and determining legitimacy in the use of force for common ends. Such diffused religion remains dominant at the local level in much of the developing world. "The religion of the village is the life of the village," making it very difficult to separate what professional academics call the political and religious aspects of life, either in rural village or urbanized neighborhood settings. The principal local political-religious issues are: (1) the individual's ability to maintain or to create a satisfactory personal identity within a static or changing worldview; and (2) the distribution of political and economic power within the fused local political-religious system. Anthropologists, using the methodology of participant observation, often best analyze these situations. Anita Chan, Richard Madsen, and Jonathan Unger combine anthropological investigative methods with sociological theory in their treatment of the interaction of Confucian and Communist ideologies and organizations in Guangdong's Chen village. The struggle for local political-religious supremacy between Chen Qingfa and Chen Longyong, "local emperor" Communist cadres, reflected the mutation of personal identities within the village as the leaders reacted to both local and national events. Despite their personal and ideological differences, however, both men demonstrated their primary loyalty to the village over the national system.[1]

The population of Israel's Ultraorthodox [*haredim*], both in numbers and in percent of the population, has increased greatly since the foundation of the nation, and especially since the Six-Day War of 1967. The Ultraorthodox continue to form new and to expand former enclaves throughout the country, but especially in Jerusalem. Kenneth Wald notes that this expansion has been accompanied by a change in culture and lifestyle. "What was once something of a folk religion, relying on informal transmission of tradition and custom, has become highly institutionalized. Leadership has passed from rabbis and community elders to Torah scholars who head the great and influential academies of Jewish learning known as *yeshivot* (singular *yeshivah*)."[2] These new local religious elites capitalize on all the instruments of modern technology, from VCRs to the Internet, to spread their message. Many scholars have also highlighted the crucial importance of "Islamized spaces," created by Middle Eastern Islamist movements for their social and educational projects. For example, Egypt's Hosni Mubarak has directly attacked radical Islamist groups and continued his country's ban on religious political parties, yet he has allowed moderate Islamist groups to expand their local spaces. Such local autonomy makes these latter groups much stronger, both religiously and politically.

In sub-Saharan Africa, according to Ellis and ter Haar, "communication with the spirit world is a key concern of African politicians.... In African societies, power is widely thought to originate in the spirit world.

---

[1] Anita Chan, Richard Madsen, and Jonathan Ungar, *Chen Village Under Mao and Deng,* expanded and updated (Berkeley: University of California Press, 1992).

[2] Kenneth Wald, "The Religious Dimensions of Israeli Political Life," Ted Gerald Jelen and Clyde Wilcox, eds., *Religion and Politics in Comparative Perspective: The One, the Few, and the Many* (Cambridge: Cambridge University Press, 2002), 108.

Spiritual power is regarded as ambivalent in the sense that it can be used for either good or ill. In recent years there has been a growing sense among Africans that power is increasingly deployed for destructive purposes, leading to a widespread feeling of the omnipresence of evil."[3] Their entire book (2004) documents the interpenetration of the material and the spiritual worlds in the African world view of religion and politics. Indeed, they assert, religious relationships through Christianity, Islam, and indigenous religions now constitute the most significant way Africans relate to their local environment and to the entire world.

These Chinese, Israeli, Egyptian, and African examples show religious groups that create a local political-religious community that provides the primary identification for its members by enlisting them in a cause greater than themselves. In revolutionary situations, the local ideology may change drastically, whereas the religion, in the following example, Shiite Islam, remains constant. The anthropologist Mary Hegland reports on a small Iranian village where the people's primary ideological referent changed from "Imam Husain as Intercessor" to "Imam Husain as Example" during the revolution against the Shah.[4] This transformation in religious mentality coincided with the changed social and economic conditions that fostered the national political success of Ayatollah Khomeini. Many of the village's new religious and social perspectives came from the nearby city of Shiraz. This village-city local dynamic constitutes one of the major areas of religious change in contemporary society. Local religious identity (Shiite) can remain constant while the specific religious-political content of the identity changes.

As the rural inhabitants move to the city, they tend to form little urban "villages" for mutual support and psychological comfort. In Nigeria, for example, a city can bring together more than two hundred ethnic groups. Such urban dwellers identify with their ethnic or tribal group, not with the nation. Berkeley emphasizes that such ethnic or tribal "kinship corporations" are not just a throwback to primitive African society, but just as they "were strengthened as a means of protection against a predatory state during the slave trade, the predatory nature of postcolonial or 'neocolonial' states provoked self-defense by means of kinship ties and their bureaucratic equivalents, and with this, a corresponding subversion of the

[3] Stephen Ellis and Gerrie ter Haar, *Worlds of Power: Religious Thought and Political Practice in Africa* (New York: Oxford, 2004), 2.

[4] Mary Hegland, "Two Images of Husain: Accommodation and Revolution in an Iranian Village," Nikki R. Kedde, ed. *Religion and Politics in Iran: Shi'ism from Quietism to Revolution* (New Haven, CT: Yale University Press, 1983), 218–35.

state by smuggling, and related kinds of economic crime."[5] The presence in the capital Lagos of so many competitors for scarce local resources fosters the Nigerian state's use of coercion to maintain political stability while making that distribution.

Sometimes immigrants create double identities as they locate their sense of home in, for example, both Jalisco and Los Angeles, or Hong Kong and Vancouver, or Manila and San Francisco, or San Juan and New York, or Kingston and Boston. These dual identities have been made possible in the last decades by improved air and bus transportation that allows the immigrants to return often to their original homes. Churches, synagogues, and mosques served as the central meeting points for the new ethnic ghetto in earlier immigration to North America and Europe. In recent cases of such "back and forth immigration," the same religious affiliation in both localities helps these immigrants to harmonize their dual identities. This book is dedicated to the late Padre Pascual Ramirez, whose self-identity derived from both a small Michoacán village and Oakland, California.

RELIGION IN NATIONAL POLITICS: CHURCH-STATE CONFLICT AND THE RISE OF FUNDAMENTALISM

At the national level, this book groups relationships between religion and politics under four headings: (1) dominant religions can offer a "sacred canopy" legitimizing state power, as in traditional Christian, Islamic, Hindu, Confucian, and Buddhist empires, and civil religion in the United States; (2) governmental and religious organizations can battle for institutional and expressive power within the national society, as in Communist Poland or contemporary Iran; (3) various religions can compete for influence within the nation, as in contemporary India or Guatemala; and (4) religious groups can seek to control the national culture or to defend their group from a threatening national or global culture, as the Religious Right in the United States or Islamist movements in Egypt. National systems, of course, can exhibit political-religious conflicts that combine the last three of the above dynamics. In such cases these aspects reinforce each other as they do in the contemporary politics of India, Iran, and Israel. Such movements often call for the return to an earlier confessional era of imagined political-religious unity.

[5] Bill Berkeley, *The Graves Are Not Yet Full: Race, Tribe and Power in the Heart of Africa* (New York: Basic Books, 2002), 12–13.

In the first national type, the legitimacy of the state depends upon a specific religious ideology, for example, neo-Confucianism in imperial China, or the more generalized "secular Protestantism" of American civil religion. Contemporary American civil religion has retained its Protestant themes, but it no longer excludes Catholics and Jews. Presidents such as Eisenhower, Nixon, Reagan, and both Bushes have attended church and employed very general religious sentiments in their political discourse. The religious historian Martin Marty stresses that the revolutionary separation of church and state in the United States opened the way for, nay demanded, such a generalized cultural form not tied to any specific denomination. The French philosopher Rousseau, no friend of institutional religion, first employed the term "civil religion" to name those religious sentiments such as the existence of God, personal immortality, and the sanctity of obedience to national laws that would support social order. In the American case, this cultural nationalism drew its themes from the dominant Protestant ethos: Americans are God's Chosen People, whose manifest destiny is to settle the wilderness continent and thereby produce a righteous republic as a living sign of God's Providence for the nation and the world.

Both the nineteenth-century French social commentator Alexis de Tocqueville and the early-twentieth-century British thinker G. K. Chesterton emphasized the peculiar nature of the United States relationship to religion. Chesterton stated, "America is the only nation in the world that is founded on a creed."[6] Bellah presents the individualistic American "cultural code" as deriving from the secularization of two religious ideas: Calvinist predestination and the evangelical emphasis on the individual acceptance of Jesus Christ as one's Lord and Savior. This religious individualism, says Bellah, merges with strong economic individualism to produce the American cultural worldview.[7]

In the second national type of political-religious institutional competition, both religious and political leaders have sought to control the other's sphere of power, or at least the disputed area between spheres, even where a common political-religious worldview like Christendom found common acceptance. The two classical cases are the eleventh-century investiture

---

[6] Cited in David Chidester, *Patterns of Power: Religion and Politics in American Culture* (Englewood Cliffs, NJ: Prentice Hall, 1988), 87.

[7] Robert N. Bellah, "Religion and the Shape of National Culture," *America* 181 (July 31, 1999): 9–14. For a fine chapter on "Religion and American Political Culture," see Kenneth D. Wald, *Religion and Politics in the United States*, 4th ed. (Latham, MD: Rowman & Littlefield, 2003), 40–68.

controversy in which the Holy Roman Emperor and the Pope sought to control the appointment of Catholic bishops, and that of Orthodox empires, from the Second Rome of Constantinople to the Third Rome of Moscow, in which the Emperor or Czar generally exercised more influence than the patriarch. Four twentieth-century examples of such conflict between religious and political leaders come from Poland, the Philippines, South Africa, and Iran.

In cases such as postwar Communist Poland, states and churches battle for "instrumental" and "expressive" power. "Instrumental power" denotes control of the possible instruments of coercion – the national political, military, and economic systems. "Expressive power" refers to the national articulation of collective identity and norms, and the representation of national symbols. My book on Catholic world politics employed the June 1983 Warsaw photo (*New York Times*, front page, June 18, 1983) of Party Secretary General Wojciech Jaruzelski and Pope John Paul II face to face as its thematic image. Rarely has a person like Jaruzelski so purely represented the "instrumental" coercive power of army, party, and state versus another like the Polish pope representing the legitimizing "expressive" power of the Polish national church. The general had declared martial law, but he could not command popular legitimacy. Neither leader could shake the other's source of power at the time of the photo, but Communist instrumental power did not last the decade.[8]

Such political-religious dynamics remained relevant for struggles against twentieth-century authoritarian regimes. Filipino Cardinal Jaime Sin battled President Ferdinand Marcos in the February Revolution of 1986 that led to the election of Cory Aquino. In the battle against apartheid in South Africa, the ecumenical South African Council of Churches, led by Anglican Archbishop Desmond Tutu, played a similar role of "primary ethical broker," that person or organization that society recognizes as the legitimate arbiter of national ethical issues. The presence of such a broker, religious or not, constitutes a first step toward solving any grave societal crisis. In the end, with international economic and athletic sanctions, the South African Council of Churches' ethical judgment against apartheid prevailed.

Iran provides another classic twentieth-century case of political-religious conflict over instrumental and expressive power. The supreme religious leader seeks to control the entire country, both politically

---

[8] Eric O. Hanson, *The Catholic Church in World Politics* (Princeton, NJ: Princeton University Press, 1987), 2–3.

and religiously, against what he terms illegitimate political and religious opposition. Khomeini crafted the new religious-political doctrine of *velayat-e faqih* [the leadership of the Jurisprudent], which proposed a supreme guide as the only legitimate successor to the Prophet and the Imams. According to Article 109 of the new Constitution, he had to be a *marja' al-taqlid* [source of emulation], possess leadership qualities, and be accepted by the majority of the population. The state president, the moderate Muslim layman Banisadr, functioned almost as a leader of an opposition party until his 1981 demise. Ayatollah Khomeini also attacked some of the clerical establishment, evidenced in 1982 when he defrocked the senior Ayatollah Shariatmadari, who had suggested rejecting the new Constitution by boycotting the December 1979 vote. Indeed, the Constitution of 1979 "left out a large part of the *ulama*, including all of the highest authorities except Khomeini." Yet Chehabi argues that two basic trends in Iran impeded the establishment of a true theocracy. First, Iran had a long Constitutional tradition. Second, the constant claim that Islam answered all modern problems "precluded any too blatant backtracking on the achievements of the constitutional revision."[9]

The third national type for religion and politics concerns the struggle of competing religious groups for power and influence within a multireligious state, especially where the popular commitment to religious liberty is suspect. Despite its secular Constitution and Gandhian tradition, India has illustrated this dynamic since independence in the conflict between Hindus and Muslims. The Bharatiya Janata Party (BJP) leader Lai Krishna Advani fostered Hindu fundamentalist fervor by instigating the destruction of the Muslim mosque at Ayodhya in December 1992. In nations with a multiplicity of religions, opposition religions such as Islam and Christianity in India support the establishment and maintenance of a secular state. In the Nigerian case, Catholic bishops protested the full enrollment of the country in the Organization of the Islamic Conference (OIC), lest that membership affect the secularism of the state. Nigerian President Babangida had secretly enrolled Nigeria as a full member in 1985 in an attempt to increase personal political support in the Islamic north. The same religion, of course, can play contrasting roles in different geographic regions. Whereas Catholics in northern Nigeria were persecuted, their fellow Catholics in Latin America used state power to limit Pentecostal expansion. Islam may have attacked Catholics in Nigeria, but minority Muslims support the secularity of the state in both India and Israel.

[9] H. E. Chehabi, "Religion and Politics in Iran: How Theocratic Is the Iranian Republic?" *Daedalus* 120 (Summer 1991): 77–78.

The fourth national type concerns religious attempts to control or to influence national culture on moral issues. Here the book narrates as its main example the fundamentalist attack on modernism. The term "fundamentalism" first described those American Protestants who originated in the evangelical revivalist tradition, but reacted strongly against certain modernizing trends such as biblical criticism, the influence of science, and emphasis on the social gospel. Historian George Marsden defines U.S. Protestant fundamentalism as a "twentieth-century movement closely tied to the revivalist tradition of mainstream evangelical Protestantism that militantly opposed modernist theology and the cultural change associated with it."[10] The movement began in 1909 when two Union Oil executives, Lyman and Milton Stewart, financed the publishing of twelve pamphlets, *Fundamentals: A Testimony of Truth*. U.S. fundamentalists solidified their theological position in the first two decades of the twentieth century, but they suffered defeat after defeat politically and legally. The most famous early case, the Scopes Monkey Trial (1925), pitted the literal interpretation of the Bible against the scientific theory of evolution. William Jennings Bryan won a monetary judgment against biology teacher John Scopes, but the trial proved to be a public relations debacle for fundamentalists. The American public generally accepted the independence of scientific authority in such questions, and religious conservatives withdrew from public confrontation for a time. Fundamentalists then focused on strengthening their own institutions separate from the larger society before returning to the cultural battle.

Following World War II, many fundamentalist preachers such as Carl McIntire, Billy James Hargis, and Frederick C. Schwarz combined their religious beliefs with virulent anti-Communism and thus found more public acceptance. In the next decades, televangelists such as Oral Roberts, Jimmy Swaggert, Pat Robertson, and Jim Bakker found that communication technology had provided them with the perfect media to oppose what they perceived as the moral irresponsibility of 1960s values. Indeed, that strategy became enormously profitable. By 1986, all four were grossing at least $130 million per year. This reenergized Religious Right reentered national politics in the 1980 campaign of Ronald Reagan. However, the televangelists' political vision did not always resonate with the evangelical community at large. Many evangelicals, for example, voted for Democrat and fellow Southern Baptist Jimmy Carter in both 1976 and 1980. Robertson ran unsuccessfully for president in 1988.

[10] Cited in Chidester, *Patterns*, 260.

Especially after the 1979 Iranian revolution, some commentators employed the same term of "fundamentalism" to describe Jewish and Islamic attacks on modernism. Lawrence, for example, chronicles the three phases of Islamic Revivalism (Anti-Colonial Revolt), Islamic Reform (Secular Nationalism), and Islamic Fundamentalism (Religious National-ism) as the Islamic world reacted to the colonialist penetration of the West. Other commentators on Israeli and Islamic politics found difficulties in using the term. Wald observes that Israeli Modern Orthodox "are much more likely than the Haredim to act in the manner we usually associate with fundamentalism,"[11] calling into question whether either of the two groups deserves the term. Mehran Tamadonfar[12] finds the term very mis-leading for Islam, and with many others, proposes the still inadequate "Islamist" [*Islamiyyun*] instead. This book will follow his suggestion.

In terms of late-twentieth-century Islamism, Scott Appleby[13] points to Egyptian Sayyid Qutb (1906–65), Indian Maulana Sayyid Abul Ala Maududi (1903–79), and Lebanese Sheik Mohammed Hussein Fadlallah (1935–) as particularly influential in promoting religious-based revolu-tionary violence. In his 1960 treatise *Milestones*,[14] Qutb extended the traditional concept of *Jahiliyyah* [state of ignorance of guidance from God] from pagans to even Muslims such as Nasser who, Qutb claimed, had abandoned Islam. Maududi developed an entire system of Islamic politics, economics, and religion from his key concept of *iqamat-I-deen* [the establishment of religion]. All institutions of the state and civil society, according to this theory, must be subordinated to divine law as revealed in the Qur'an and in the life of Mohammed. Finally, Fadlallah, the Shiite founder of the Hezbollah [the Party of God], blamed the poverty and the powerlessness of his people on the abandonment of Islam by so many. Backed by Shiite Iran, he sought to establish a worldwide Islamic state that would lead to the coming of the *Mahdi*, long awaited in Shiite the-ology. This global state could serve as an exemplar of virtue that would

---

[11] Wald, "Israeli Political Life," 119.

[12] Mehran Tamadonfar, "Islamism in Contemporary Arab Politics: Lessons in Authoritar-ianism and Democratization," Jelen and Wilcox, *Comparative Perspective*, 142.

[13] R. Scott Appleby, *The Ambivalence of the Sacred: Religion, Violence, and Reconcilia-tion* (New York: Rowman & Littlefield, 1999), 91–101. Marty E. Marty and Appleby directed the Fundamentalism Project, 1987–95, which eventually studied fundamental-ism in twenty-three different religions. The University of Chicago Press published five volumes, 1991–95. For a 2003 perspective, see the excellent Gabriel A. Almond, R. Scott Appleby, and Emmanuel Sivan, *Strong Religion: The Rise of Fundamentalisms around the World* (Chicago: University of Chicago Press, 2003).

[14] Sayyid Qutb, *Milestones* (Indianapolis: American Trust, 1990).

accomplish this, Fadlallah argued in *Islam and the Logic of Power*,[15] and thus violence in the service of the creation of this state was justified. Yet this violence, in having a religious purpose, needed to be conducted in accordance with religious law. Often, Hezbollah fighters have sought sanction from Islamic scholars for particular clandestine military operations.

Political analysts also have sought to locate such Islamic trends in various social classes. Huntington points out that the new religious movements come disproportionately from two groups, both very mobile: migrants to the cities, and the new middle class, who embody Dore's "second generation industrialization phenomenon."[16] Such groups fear the loss of their traditional religious culture. In discussing Egypt, Lawrence points to the rise of a new class that is both educated and un- or under-employed. Each year, he remarks, 375,000 new people enter a workforce that already has 40 percent unemployment.[17] The Muslim Brotherhood of Egypt, however, has viewed the basic global contest as cultural, not economic. In the 1970s and 1980s they feared that "[t]he powerful cultures of both the secular West and the atheistic East threatened Egypt's Islamic heritage."[18] Each Cold War bloc sought to dissolve the character of the other culture – its thought, religion, language, and heritage. The cultural battle thus took primacy over social goals such as development, revolution, or democracy, which other Egyptians thought essential. The Muslim Brotherhood constituted an autonomous political actor because it reacted to the Cold War according to its pan-Islamic interpretation of events. It identified domestic and foreign threats different from those identified by its two main competitors, Nasser's pan-Arabic movement and the Westernized elites surrounding Sadat and Mubarak.

REGIONAL RELIGION IN THE GLOBALIZATION OF THE CONTEMPORARY INTERNATIONAL SYSTEM

The globalization theory of Samuel Huntington highlights the influence of religion on regional political identity. Huntington states that "culture and

---

[15] For Hezbollah, see Appleby, *Ambivalence*, 95–101.

[16] Samuel P. Huntington, *The Clash of Civilizations and the Remaking of World Order* (New York: Simon & Schuster, 1996), 101.

[17] Bruce B. Lawrence, *Shattering the Myth: Islam Beyond Violence* (Princeton, NJ: Princeton University Press, 1998), 122.

[18] Raymond William Baker, "Afraid for Islam: Egypt's Muslim Centrists between Pharaohs and Fundamentalists," *Daedalus* 120 (Summer 1991): 92. For the importance of the Muslim Brotherhood in the development of Islamism, see Gilles Kepel, *The War for Muslim Minds: Islam and the West* (Cambridge, MA: Belnap, 2004).

cultural identities, which at the broadest level are civilization identities, are shaping the patterns of cohesion, disintegration, and conflict in the post–Cold War period."[19] Huntington describes post–Cold War international politics as a multipolar system consisting of nine civilizations: Western, Latin American, African, Islamic, Sinic [Chinese], Hindu, Orthodox, Buddhist, and Japanese. The current balance of power, according to Huntington, is shifting from the West, thus bringing the West's universalistic pretensions into conflict with other civilizations, most notably with Islam and China. "Religion is a central defining characteristic of civilizations, and, as Christopher Dawson said, 'the great religions are the foundations on which the great civilizations rest.'"[20] Civilizations are led by core states, and wars occur along the fault lines between civilizations. This book agrees with Huntington on the centrality of religion in holding together regional civilizations. In fact, Huntington's text constitutes a devastating critique in describing *La Revanche de Dieu* [The Revenge of God] against those who would disregard the role of religion in world politics.

Huntington's analysis, however, does not coincide with current world affairs on several significant points. First, important parts of world system theory and *Realpolitik* must also be adopted since global politics takes place as a result of the interaction between Huntington's culture, Wallerstein's economics, and "national interest" alliances like those between the United States and Saudi Arabia. Second, both Huntington and this book focus on "politics of identity," but the nature of the identities are different. Whereas Huntington defines cultural identity by choosing the most inclusive descriptor, the civilization, the most strongly held personal and local identity is far more crucial. A much more detailed and differentiated analysis of religion produces different descriptions, explanations, and proscriptions for different levels of the political system. According to Huntington, "Since religion, however, is the principal defining characteristic of civilizations, fault line wars are almost always between people of different religions."[21] There is no question that the breakup of the ex-Yugoslavia is the great example of Huntington's splitting of a country along the fault lines of three civilizations: Western, Orthodox, and Islamic. However, most conflicts do not fit this dynamic. Bruce Russett and John O'Neal[22] devote an entire chapter to a large-scale statistical

---

[19] Huntington, *Clash*, 20.
[20] Huntington, *Clash*, 20.
[21] Huntington, *Clash*, 253.
[22] Bruce Russett and John Oneal, *Triangulating Peace: Democracy, Interdependence, and International Organization* (New York: W.W. Norton & Co., 2001), 239–69.

analysis of global interstate conflict, 1950–92. They find the traditional realist and liberal theories of international relations better explain the aggregate data. Such a result emphasizes the complicated nature of the elements grouped under "civilization" by Huntington. For example, Errol Henderson found that a common religion reduces the frequency of such wars, but common ethnicity and language increase it.[23] Jonathan Fox also concludes that "In all, as is the case with previous quantitative studies, the preponderance of the evidence examined here contradicts Huntington's 'clash of civilizations' theory."[24]

The Iran-Iraq conflict of 1980–89, which occurred within Islamic Civilization, was just as brutal and resulted in many more casualties than the Yugoslavian conflict. One might escape this theoretical problem by classifying Sunni Islam and Shiite Islam as different religious civilizations, but Iraqi Shiites fought for Saddam Hussein against Shiite Iran. The accuracy of Huntington's treatment of Islam lies at the heart of subsequent discussions, so the criticism of Roy P. Mottahedeh,[25] chairman of Harvard's Committee on Islamic Studies, demands serious consideration. Mottahedeh appreciates Huntington's reemphasis on the influence of culture and the significance of "identity politics," but he disagrees both with Huntington's analysis of Islamic civilization and with the theoretical links between Huntington's description of Islam and actual political events. For the former, Mottahedeh introduces many counterexamples and highlights the ambiguities of the examples used, with traditional Islamic support for free markets the centerpiece of his argument. For the latter, Mottahedeh asserts that even if a normative stance can be demonstrated, it does not guarantee that people will act according to that norm, with the many adaptations of Islam in various national contexts the proof. Bernard Lewis wrote an entire book, *What Went Wrong?*,[26] about the process of change in Islam during the last five hundred years. Middle Eastern nations adopted the idea of patriotism from Western Europe and the idea of nationalism from Central and Eastern Europe. No longer were a person's primary loyalties to his local religious community and his empire.

[23] Russett and Oneal, *Triangulating Peace*, 247.

[24] Jonathan Fox, "State Failure and the Clash of Civilizations: An Examination of the Magnitude and Extent of Domestic Civilisational Conflict from 1950 to 1996," *Australian Journal of Political Science* 38 (July 2003): 209.

[25] Roy P. Mottahedeh, "The Clash of Civilizations: An Islamicist's Critique," *Harvard Middle Eastern and Islamic Review* 2 (1995): 1–26.

[26] Bernard Lewis, *What Went Wrong? Western Impact and Middle Eastern Response* (Oxford: Oxford University Press, 2002).

The most basic objection to Huntington's approach, however, derives from his failure to analyze *how* religion and politics affect each other in contemporary international affairs, the material for this book's Chapters 2–4. For this reason, this author does not agree with Huntington's general political proscriptions in what he sees as the West and Latin America in alliance versus Sinic and Islamic civilizations, with Japanese, Orthodox, and Hindu civilizations as the "swing votes." That does not deny that the religious card is often available for politicians to play, whether it be in northern Nigeria, in Northern Ireland, or in the first Gulf War of 1990. As Mottahedeh pointed out, the very secular Saddam Hussein disingenuously called for a *jihad* against the infidels and their Muslim collaborators. In short, the current world remains much more complicated than the Huntington thesis suggests.

What further modifications do we need to make after the September 11, 2001, attacks? The Introduction referred to a *Foreign Affairs* article by Harvard professor Stanley Hoffman. Hoffman argues that none of four recent approaches (Fukuyama, Huntington, realists such as Kissinger, and Friedman) have satisfactorily explained the new international system, especially the relationship between nation states and globalization. Some of their conceptual problems antedate September 11: the residual great power rivalries, the increasing civil wars, and the uncertain mixture of foreign and domestic considerations in the framing of foreign policy. "Globalism," Hoffman writes, "seems to foster conflicts and resentments. The lowering of various barriers celebrated by Friedman, especially the spread of global media, makes it possible for the most deprived and oppressed to compare their fate with that of the free and well-off. These dispossessed then ask for help from others with common resentments, ethnic origin, or religious faith."[27] Both the terrorism itself and the war against it limit globalization by impeding the free flow of people, money, and trade. And the great powers, especially the superpower the United States, focus more specifically on their own national good rather than on the health of the international systems.

To summarize, the interpretations of the interactions of religion and politics at the regional level depend very heavily on the analysts' underlying global paradigm and on the political-religious cultures of the regions. Therefore, this author's final judgments on such interactions need to wait for Chapter 10, after the text has covered the crucial regional cases in

---

[27] Stanley Hoffman, "The Clash of Globalizations," *Foreign Affairs* 81 (July/August 2002): 111–12.

Chapters 5–9. In fact, religion plays very different political roles in the West, East Asia, South and Central Asia, the Middle East and North Africa, and Latin America, respectively.

RELIGION IN WORLD POLITICS: THE FOUR GLOBAL SYSTEMS AND THEIR FOUR POLITICAL-RELIGIOUS ISSUES

This initial discussion of political-religious issues in global politics will focus on four major themes, one emerging from each of the economic, military, communication, and political systems, respectively. The international economic system with its enormous income stratification cries out for social justice. The global military system poses issues of war and peace – between nations, within nations, and between nations and nonstate groups. The international communication system threatens traditional personal and communal identities and values. Religious actors naturally focus on human rights in the global political system. Indeed, the individual's right to religious belief and activity combines altruistic orientation with the religious organization's institutional good.

Social Justice in the Economic System. Global equity is the primary political-religious issue for the next one hundred years. The United Nations rightly characterizes the level of worldwide inequality as "grotesque."[28] The world's richest 1 percent of the population receive as much income as the poorest 57 percent. The income of the richest twenty-five million Americans approximates that of two billion of the poorest citizens globally. In a global comparison of equality among nations since 1970, there are both positive and negative trends. The major positive factors for equality during that period have been rapid growth in China since 1980 and in India since the late 1980s, and the catching up of the European countries with the United States until the 1990s. The principal negative factors have been the economic expansion of the OECD countries versus the rest of the world, the slow growth on the Indian subcontinent until the late twentieth century, and stagnation in Africa. Population expansion will continue to be concentrated in the less developed sections of the world. In response to this situation, some have directed their critiques at the economic regulators of the system, the IMF and the World Bank, whereas other protestors have focused on multinationals such as

---

[28] United Nations Development Programme, *Human Development Report 2002* (Oxford: Oxford University Press, 2002), 29.

Nestlé for its promotion of baby formula in the developing world, Nike for sweatshop conditions in countries such as Vietnam, and McDonalds for fostering the depletion of the Amazon rain forest to raise beef. It is in protest against global social inequity that religion, labor, and the environmental movement sometimes find common cause. International groups based on relevant occupational background, such as the Nobel Peace Prize–winning *Médecins sans Frontières*, provide indispensable medical and relief work.

To get a feel for the cultural nuances to such criticism, one could start with *Eyes of the Heart*, a very small book (2000) by the ex-priest and ex-president of Haiti, Jean-Bertrand Aristide. Aristide recounts many of the policy errors of international regulators that have hurt the Haitian poor, from the sale of the state-owned flour mill to the replacement of the small, native garbage-eating Creole pigs by poorer-tasting U.S. "four-footed princes" requiring unavailable and expensive clean drinking water, foreign feed, and special roof top pens. U.S. agricultural subsidies especially hurt Haitian rice farmers. Aristide uses the theme of "the water of life" to tie together environmental damage, the lack of clean water for 80 percent of Haiti's population, and the spiritual dignity of all through Christian baptism. This argument leads to the last chapter entitled "Material Questions, Theological Answers?" Aristide professes a dual faith in God and in the poor.[29] But the poor must receive a chance to chart their own course. Eighty-five percent of Haitians cannot read and write. The literate 15 percent speak French instead of the commonly spoken Creole, and for two hundred years all laws, justice, and the educational system have been conducted in French.

The issue of fresh drinking and agricultural water not only affects Haiti but also causes serious political tensions all over the world. By 2015, at least 40 percent of the world's population will experience difficulty in obtaining fresh water to satisfy basic needs. For example, Turkey has developed a series of dams on the upper Euphrates that threaten both Syria's and Iraq's water supplies. The Turkish villages on one side of the border flourish while Syrian villages on the other side bake in the sun. It is difficult to quantify the impact of environmental degradation on the world economic system since most of nature's goods and services are considered "free" in accounting practice. Efforts to clean up pollution are even considered a positive asset. Clear-cutting of forests, for example,

[29] Jean-Bertrand Aristide, *Eyes of the Heart: Seeking a Path for the Poor in the Age of Globalization* (Monroe: Common Courage Press, 2000), 56.

does not show up as a negative economic charge against future increases in wood prices, but the cleaning up of clear cutting is calculated as positive economic activity. If global warming is taking place, and the evidence grows stronger and stronger that it is, that warming will benefit some locales and hurt others. But from a general perspective, the potential for social dislocation and increased climatic variability paints a frightening picture, especially for the poorer countries of the developing world. All of these issues stand at the center of any religious consideration of current politics and society.

No religion can ignore the central global reality of increased socio-economic stratification between the richest and the poorest and still maintain any spiritual legitimacy with its adherents, either the poor or the rich. Almost all world citizens know that others have better or worse lives than themselves, and that some live horrendous lives through no fault of their own. They experience this socioeconomic disparity daily through radio, television, film, and the Internet. Rapid technological change also increases the value of the latest education, which divides the world's winners and losers on their possibilities for educational access, another quasi-monopoly of the developed world.

Peace in the Military System. During the Cold War, the international peace movement focused on the military buildup between the two Super-powers, especially in the early 1960s surrounding the Cuban Missile Crisis and in the early 1980s during the Euromissile debate. Many still remember Pope Paul VI's stirring speech, and he was rarely a stirring speaker, to the General Assembly in 1965 in which he cried "War. Never Again!" During the Euromissile crisis, many national churches and bishops' conferences wrote letters on peace, but the Holy See also campaigned at the United Nations, especially through the Pontifical Academy of Sciences. National episcopal statements such as *The Challenge of Peace* by the American Catholic bishops[30] combined traditional Just War Theory with a new Catholic appreciation of the pacifist tradition of the "peace churches" such as the Quakers,[31] the Church of the Brethren, and the

---

[30] National Conference of Catholic Bishops, *Challenge of Peace: God's Promise and Our Response* (Boston: St. Paul Editions, 1983). The process of drafting this document resulted in a major change in American Catholic opinion about the ethics of nuclear war.

[31] See, for example, Cynthia Sampson, "'To Make Real the Bond Between Us All': Quaker Conciliation During the Nigerian Civil War," in Douglass Johnston and Cynthia Sampson, eds., *Religion, The Missing Dimension of Statecraft* (New York: Oxford, 1995), 88–118. Johnston founded the International Center for Religion & Diplomacy to focus

Mennonites.[32] Traditional Just War Theory divides its analysis into those elements that affect whether waging war is permissible [*jus ad bellum*] and those elements that affect the conduct of the war [*jus in bello*]. The former include just cause, competent authority, comparative justice, right intention, last resort, probability of success, and proportionality. The latter uses the two criteria of proportionality of means, and discrimination between combatants and noncombatants. Both latter conditions remain very difficult hurdles when the use of weapons of mass destruction is contemplated.

In the September–October 2002 debate over a potential war in Iraq, the vast majority of religious leaders and ethicists lined up against a preemptive strike. Opposition came from traditionally pacifist churches and from "Just War" practitioners who had supported American intervention in Afghanistan, Bosnia, and the first Gulf War. In September, one hundred Christian ethicists, from all sides of the political spectrum, signed a one-sentence declaration against preemption. African-American Bishop Wilton Gregory, president of the United States Catholic Conference, handed a letter to Condoleezza Rice with the same message. Robert Edgar, general secretary of the National Council of Churches and an ex-member of Congress, brought forty-eight leaders of member denominations to Washington to lobby. Jewish opinion split, but Muslim leader Sharifa Alkhateeb, said, "It will be a war not just against Saddam Hussein and the small group who support him, but against the people of Iraq, who are already suffering."[33] Support for the preemptive strike came from Dr. Richard D. Land, president of the Ethics and Religious Liberty Commission of the Southern Baptist Convention, who argued that it would be permissible as a "Just War" defensive action against Iraq's presumed weapons of mass destruction. Evangelical leaders Bill Bright, Charles Colson, D. James Kennedy, and Carl Herbster signed his statement.

---

on religion in conflict resolution. Recent work from the Center on Kashmir, Sri Lanka, the Balkans, Sudan, and the Middle East is covered in Douglass Johnston, ed., *Faith-Based Diplomacy: Trumping Realpolitik* (New York: Oxford, 2003).

[32] For an appreciation of the impact of theology on a basic orientation toward U.S. foreign policy, see the contrast of American "classic" theologians Reinhold Neibuhr and John Countney Murray in J. Bryan Hehir, "Religion, Realism, and Just Intervention" E. J. Dionne, Jr., Jean Bethke Elshtain, and Kayla Drogosz, eds., *Liberty and Power: A Dialogue on Religion & U.S. Foreign Policy in an Unjust World* (Washington, DC: Brookings Institution, 2004), 15–17.

[33] October 5, 2002. For a religious proposal that made it to Blair, see the story of the six-point plan of Sojourners' Jim Wallis, Episcopal Bishop John Bryson Chane, and other church leaders. Jim Wallis, *God's Politics: Why the Right Get It Wrong and Left Doesn't Get It* (San Francisco: HarperCollins, 2005), 43–55.

In the contemporary military system, civil wars or terrorist attacks are much more likely than the Warsaw Pact tank attack feared during the Cold War. This changed strategic environment has produced different emphases in religious peace activities. Even among the Mennonites, for example, there has been movement from seeking to withdraw from conflict to a very active campaign for conflict resolution. The Mennonite Central Committee (MCC) broadened its relief work to set up an International Conciliation Service (ICS) to deal with conflicts such as the tension between the Nicaraguan Sandinista government and the Miskito Indians.[34] The MCC's relief presence throughout the world assists the ICS by providing the mediators with local contacts and prior legitimacy. Single-issue international NGOs such as Jody William's International Campaign to Ban Landmines can be particularly effective in removing conventional weapons such as small arms from chaotic low-level scenarios in developing countries. The 1997 international treaty prohibiting land mines represented the "the most significant abolition of a weapons system since the use of poison gas in wartime was banned in 1925" (Nobel citation).

The toughest ethical questions about the legitimacy of violence usually arise in situations where a revolutionary force faces an unjust dictatorial government, such as with the African National Congress (ANC) struggle against apartheid in South Africa. This struggle generated a long argument between two prestigious black churchmen, Anglican Archbishop Desmond Tutu, president of the South African Council of Churches, and Alan Boesak, president of the World Alliance of Reformed Churches. When Tutu rejected all political violence, Boesak replied that the revolutionaries did not face a legitimate police force, but that they were engaged in a civil war. Thus Boesak argued for "a prophetic – and selectively violent – liberationist stance."[35] Similar to certain strands in Catholic Liberation Theology, Boesak advocated using something like traditional Catholic Just War Theory to decide when violence was legitimate in this quasi–civil war.

Compared with Islam, both Lawrence and Jame Turners Johnson have identified Christianity's over two-hundred-year tension with the Roman Empire as the crucial historical difference on war ethics. That experience of state persecution of Christians produced a minority strain of pacifism

---

[34] See also Bruce Nichols, "Religious Conciliation Between the Sandinistas and the East Coast Indians of Nicaragua," in Johnson and Sampson, *Missing Dimension*, 64–87.

[35] Cited in Appleby, *Ambivalence*, 35.

and questioning of state power, which has endured to modern times. In emphasizing the Islamic believer's primary personal identification with the united community of Islam, the 'Abbasid jurists developed the theory of competition between the world of Islam [*dar al-Islam*] and the world of conflict [*dar al-harb*]. Whereas practical statecraft required further refinements such as "the territory of peaceful arrangement or covenant" [*dar al-sulh* or *dar al-'ahd*] introduced by Shafi'i jurists, the classical formulation provided the foundation and language for *jihad* against both infidels and heretics, thus suiting the political needs of the 'Abbasid caliphs.[36] Johnson analyzes a three-step process in the progressive relation of Islam and war: (1) the above 'Abbasid formulation; (2) the use of defensive *jihad* by Saladin to justify the retaking of any land previously held by Islam; and (3) the *ghaza* war for the faith of the Ottomans whose legitimacy came from victory.

Many examples of cooperation among religious groups in the pursuit of peace also exist. Muslim politicians from many Algerian opposition groups formed a common political position in the Rome platform of 1995, under the mediation of the Italian Catholic NGO Sant'Egidio. Only the Algerian secular military government rejected the platform. The lay-led Sant'Egidio illustrates the role of religious NGOs in mediating conflicts. Sant'Egidio has a long tradition of "friendship" (the group's specific hallmark virtue) with Islam. It has worked with Islamic immigrants in Europe and Muslims in Africa and Yugoslavia. It joined with the Mozambican Christian Council, which represented seventeen Protestant churches, to succeed in mediating a General Peace Accord in Mozambique in 1992. Another example of developing world ecumenical peace work took place in Cambodia in the spring of 1993, when the sixty-eight-year-old Buddhist primate Samdech Preah Maha Ghosananda led a month-long Peace March, entitled a *Dhammayietra* [Pilgrimage of Truth], with support from Jesuit priest Bob Maat, Jewish human rights activist Liz Bernstein, and the Mennonites, among others. This countrywide march in the midst of active military engagements inspired Cambodians to take part in the first U.N.-sponsored elections. Ghosananda, "Cambodia's Gandhi," used a traditional Buddhist pilgrimage ritual stressing the traditional Buddhist virtues of *panja* [wisdom], *metta* [loving-kindness], *karuna* [compassion], and *sati* [mindfulness].[37]

---

[36] James Turner Johnson, *The Holy War Idea in Western and Islamic Traditions* (University Park: Pennsylvania State University Press, 1997), 144.

[37] For a fuller treatment of these examples, see Appleby, *Ambivalence*.

Personal and Communal Values in the Communication System. Rapid internationalization of communication has resulted in larger and larger multinational media conglomerates producing the same entertainment and advertising content for an increasingly similar world market. Many religious leaders, not just conservatives, perceive the messages of the world communication networks, from liquor advertisements to pornography to runaway commercialism, as disruptive of their religious way of life. Michael Budde warns that, "[t]he language of faith, unless brought more fully and intensively into people's hearts and minds, will become as dead as Latin in our world of jingles, spectacles, and nonstop sales pitches."[38] It is on this point that technological change poses its greatest threat to religion by robbing believers of the possibility of any permanent set of narratives and symbols. Even a runaway best-seller such as the sensational *Da Vinci Code* makes religious people of both the left and the right nervous about spiritual formation. The facts about Leonardo and the Dead Sea Scrolls don't matter if Doubleday continues to run full-page ads in the *New York Times* one year after publication to suggest the book as a Father's Day gift.

Family values remain particularly sensitive to religious groups. For example, the United Nations held global conferences on population and development in Cairo in 1994[39] and on women in Beijing in 1995. Both conferences fostered intense lobbying by both states and nongovernmental organizations (NGOs), secular and religious, over the wording of the final draft recommendations. The first draft of the Cairo program presented a sophisticated analytical framework that focused on sustainable development, empowerment for women, and women's reproductive health concerns. Many Catholic and Islamic leaders, although comfortable with most of the general language, feared that the draft could be used to promote abortion as a method of family planning, or that a universal right to an abortion would be recognized. John Paul II met with the conference Secretary General, Pakistani gynecologist Dr. Nafis Sadik of the U.N. Population Fund, and wrote to U.S. President Clinton, Argentine President Carlos Menem, and other state leaders. In the end, when the final statement included the text "in no case should abortion be promoted as a method of family planning," the Vatican supported most of the final program.

For the 1995 meeting on women, the Vatican named Harvard law professor Mary Ann Glendon to head its delegation. Similar policy

---

[38] Michael Budde, *The (Magic) Kingdom of God: Christianity and the Global Culture Industries* (Boulder, CO: Westview Press, 1997), 129.

[39] See Mary A. Segers, "The Catholic Church as a Transnational Actor: The Case of the 1994 Cairo Conference on Population and Development," paper for APSA, September 1998.

disagreements arose with Glendon supporting the basic provisions of the program, but objecting to the "selective use of rights language" to promote "an emphasis on formal equality at the expense of motherhood's special claim to protection, and by the elimination of most references to religion and parental rights."[40] Sadik's successor as head of the U.N. Population Fund was Saudi Thoraya Obaid, a graduate of Cairo's American College for Girls, Mills College in California, and Wayne State University in Detroit. She worked with Cairo's Al-Azhar University to create materials that use a Muslim perspective to address reproductive health issues. In a June 2001 interview, Mrs. Obaid stressed the necessity of cross-cultural understanding in approaching these issues and work against the spread of AIDS. "If you offend the cultural environment, you really lose rather than win."[41] Although Obaid continues the Fund's positions on women's rights to control their sexual lives and against female genital mutilation, she recommends that sexual presentations eschew Western bluntness and respect non-Western preferences for vaguer language.

Human Rights in the Political System. J. Bryan Hehir describes the "Westphalian synthesis" as built on "two explicit propositions and a third implicit idea": state sovereignty, nonintervention, and the secularization of world politics.[42] All three principles militated against the internationalization of human rights. The human rights era of international diplomacy began on December 10, 1948, when the United Nations adopted the Universal Declaration of Human Rights. The Declaration established thirty principles, which were concretized in the two treaties of the International Covenant on Civil and Political Rights and the International Covenant on Economic, Social, and Cultural Rights. If we add the Nuremberg and Tokyo War Trials and the 1948 Genocide Convention, the basic outline of the global human rights regime appears. Such a regime challenges the absolute sovereignty of nation states since these states are obligated to abide by the above human rights documents even in their domestic politics. Since 1948, religious groups have become more and more supportive of human rights, especially the right to religious belief and activity, which is also supported by the 1981 U.N. Declaration on the Elimination of All Forms of Intolerance and Discrimination Based on Religion or Belief. As the world has developed more sophisticated international political and legal organizations, many religious figures have called for intervention in

---

[40] Cited in Appleby, *Ambivalence*, 252.
[41] June 20, 2001.
[42] J. Bryan Hehir, "Religion, Realism, and Just Intervention," 12–14.

national human rights issues, from punishing genocide in Bosnia, to a boycott of South Africa during apartheid, to religious freedom in Tibet.

David Rieff calls the 1990s the height of the international human rights movement.[43] The United States fought a war in the Balkans principally for this reason. Human Rights Watch, thanks to funding from the Ford Foundation, George Soros, and others, had a yearly budget of $15 million. The movement's "signature strategies, releasing shocking reports detailing abuses, exploiting the media to shame Western leaders into action" seemed to be working. Reiff credited both the human rights orientation of the Carter Administration and, indirectly, the insistence of the Reagan Administration on the democratic nature of the United States in the Cold War. The very undemocratic activity of the U.S. client, the Salvadoran right, became a shameful international political embarrassment. Since the September 11 attacks, the difficulties in promoting global human rights have increased. For now, national security trumps human rights in almost every case, as illustrated in China, Russia, Australia, Egypt, and Zimbabwe. And the Iraq War has given U.S. unilateral intervention, for whatever reason, a bad name.

Despite the obvious advantages of such strictures against intolerance, the universality of the rights enumerated in the above documents has come under attack from some non-Western representatives, including religious leaders. Such concepts, they argue, derive from post-Enlightenment political theory, thus constituting a more modern form of Western cultural imperialism. Some Buddhists and Muslims, for example, object to the emphasis on a personal autonomy that does not find a strong basis in their own cultures and religions, which put more emphasis on responsibilities to the group. In 1992 Hassan al-Turabi, the Sudanese lay leader of the National Islamic Front, for example, stated that Muslim-majority countries will continue to draw the content of such human rights terms from the sacred sources of Islam.[44]

The future role of the United Nations remains a crucial global ethical issue. In September 2005, over 170 world leaders met to consider the progress on the Millennial Draft Goals and the future direction of the world body. The U.N. High-Level Panel on Threats, Challenges and Change had produced *A More Secure World: Our Shared Responsibility*, which had recommended significant changes, from the composition of the Security Council to implementation of "the right to protect" those suffering from genocide. The United States presented another thoughtful

---

[43] David Rieff, *The New York Times Magazine* (August 8, 1999): 37–41.
[44] Cited in Appleby, *Ambivalence*, 249.

report from a panel of foreign policy experts cochaired by George Mitchell and Newt Gingrich. The new U.S. ambassador John Bolton had his own list of changes. In the end, the General Assembly unanimously approved a compromise document, which, although weakened, offered some hope for action.

This chapter has used the political perspective to analyze the interaction of religion and politics at the local, national, regional, and global levels. Definitions of politics run a broad gamut. This chapter emphasized the competition for scarce resources and the legitimate use of coercion. For an observational definition of politics, in 1936, the political science pioneer Harold Laswell defined politics as *Who Gets What, When, How*, thus emphasizing competition for scarce resources. Most contemporary political scientists would add the question "Who gets to participate?" as many categories of persons, for example, peasants, blacks, women, lower castes, have been systematically excluded from political participation during certain periods. For a second definition of politics that relies on judgment, we can ask about the right constitution of authority, the legitimate use of coercion, and pursuit of the common good. This political philosophy approach asserts that we can judge the difference between good and bad politics. Some governments are legitimate and some that claim to be governments are not. There is a difference between Thomas Jefferson and Idi Amin as presidents. Legitimate coercion takes place in the implementation of just laws and finds its basis in popular acceptance of government authority in the promotion of the common good. This book thus approaches politics from the twin perspectives of the distribution of resources and of the political meaning of our common life. In between these boundary definitions lie questions of public policy, party and election politics, and other topics dealt with in political science and government departments.

The central methodological principle of the paradigm affirms that both politics and religion are independent variables, neither reducible to the other. Religion raises the stakes for politics, but it does not change the nature of political decision making. Political events continue to pull prophets and hermits back into society from their solitude in the desert or on a mountain top, but these prophets and hermits use religious, not political, principles to decide whether or not or when to return. Chapter 3, therefore, offers a parallel discussion of political-religious issues from the religious perspective. What are the religious categories of analysis? First, and even most basically, what is religion? Section 1 of the next chapter begins by discussing parallel observational and judgmental definitions of religion and then compares them to the above political definitions.

3

A Religious Perspective on Religion and Politics

The second plane of the book's paradigm focuses on the political and on the religious contributions to personal and social identity. But what is religion? The exact meanings of "religion" change as the discussion moves from civilization to civilization, from nation to nation, even from locality to locality. This book's worldwide analysis, however, requires, first, a general definition of religion and, second, general categories of religious practice relevant for the description and the explanation of the influence of religion on politics. Therefore, this chapter begins by employing three separate books to examine three very different types of religion: Roman Catholicism, the most complex institution of "the religions of the book" (Judaism, Christianity, Islam); Zen Buddhism, the least doctrinally focused of "the religions of meditative experience" (Hinduism, Buddhism); and Maoist Marxism, the most militant and far-reaching of the twentieth-century "religions of public life" (Confucianism, Maoist Marxism).

Because these three cases constitute such disparate phenomena, a definition of religion and categorization of religious practices that covers all three cases would seem to be a good starting point for a general theory of religious influence on politics. A book on global politics must discuss at least what are generally listed as the world's major and most numerous religious traditions. Primarily national religious traditions such as Mormonism, Sikhism, and Jainism that may be more important from other perspectives will be discussed in their regional contexts. Of the "universal religions," Roman Catholicism and Zen Buddhism set the outlying

poles of what is usually considered "religious." A narrower Western definition that included "God," for example, might classify the latter as a
natural philosophy. Radical ideology during the Chinese Cultural Revolution is also generally not considered a religion in the West, but this book
follows C. K. Yang's classic *Religion in Chinese Society* and terms Maoist
Marxism a "nontheistic faith" because of the adherents' "ultimate ideological concern" for Chinese nationalism and material progress.[1] From
this more inclusive theoretical perspective, of course, secularism, nationalism, or even atheistic materialism could also constitute religions if adherents practiced them as nontheistic faiths of "ultimate concern" and held
them so strongly (we usually say "religiously") that people were willing
to live and to die for them on principle. The faith some Germans placed
in Hitler during the 1930s and 1940s best exemplifies this phenomenon in
the twentieth-century West. Nazism developed its own spirituality, ritual,
worldview, and organizations. No wonder Hitler attacked Protestant and
Catholic churches as competing religions, even apart from their resistance
to his racial policies.

For each of the above three boundary religions, I chose a particular
book that emphasizes a distinct character of the religion without reducing the religion to that characteristic. *Inside the Vatican* by Jesuit political
scientist Thomas Reese focuses on the central bureaucratic organization
of Roman Catholicism.[2] Reese's balanced analysis combines the multiple organizational charts so dear to business sociologists with a treatment of the "corporate culture" (business term) of those who work at
the Vatican. Reese's book retains its judicious balance because the author
never forgets that spiritual choices and values motivate those who inhabit
this complicated ecclesiastical structure of "saints and sinners." Indeed,
scholars can become so fascinated with the Catholic organization that
they miss the spiritual motivations of ecclesiastics. Critical reviewers have
pointed out, for example, that sociologist Ivan Vallier's otherwise seminal
paper on "The Catholic Church as a Transnational Organization"[3] did
not even discuss the Second Vatican Council, Catholicism's major event
of the twentieth century. Reese's book also retains the historical sense

[1] C. K. Yang, *Religion in Chinese Society* (Berkeley: University of California Press, 1961),
381–85.
[2] Thomas Reese, *Inside the Vatican: The Politics and Organization of the Catholic Church*
(Cambridge, MA: Harvard University Press, 1996).
[3] Ivan Vallier, "The Catholic Church as a Transnational Organization," Robert O. Keohane
and Joseph F. Nye, Jr., eds., *Transnational Relations and World Politics* (Cambridge, MA:
Harvard University Press, 1972), 129–52.

that the Roman Curia, like its Chinese Mandarin bureaucratic counterpart, has evolved over its long history, and that it will continue to
evolve.

The Three Pillars of Zen by ex-Tokyo War Crimes court reporter Philip
Kapleau[4] presents a record of spiritual practice under Zen masters, not
a more systematic treatise like most works on Zen. Even these more systematic treatises, however, do not constitute Western-style theology, for
as Merton comments in his dialogue with Suzuki, "any attempt to handle
Zen in theological language is bound to miss the point."[5] Kapleau's Zen
masters guide their disciples both before and after the defining experience of *satori* [enlightenment]. Although the book is not a doctrinal or
a cultural treatment, it does serve cross-cultural dialogue by discrediting
various Western "beat" stereotypes about Zen. Practice does not focus on
a Western-style "God," but requires faith [*daishinkon*]. Buddhism is "not
merely philosophy," says the Zen Master Yasutani, "and what makes it
one [religion] is this element of faith. . . . Our supreme faith, therefore,
is in the Buddha's enlightenment experience, the substance of which he
proclaimed to be that human nature, all existence, is intrinsically whole,
flawless, omnipotent – in a word, perfect."[6] The adherent focuses on
his/her own effort, but the fitting response to the "success" of *satori* is
not self-satisfaction, but of gratitude and humility. One Zen adherent
who attains enlightenment reports experiencing a "consciousness which
is neither myself nor not myself, which is protecting or leading me into
directions helpful to my proper growth and maturity . . ."[7]

In *Religion in Chinese Society*, C. K. Yang titles Chapter Fourteen
"Communism as the New Faith." Yang then chronicles the historical experience of the Chinese people beginning with the Opium War (1839–42)
as they seek "national salvation" from foreign exploitation and domestic oppression. Chinese nationalism and material progress become the
"ultimate concern" for the Chinese, intellectuals and peasants alike.
Thus, says Yang, we observe that Chinese Marxism exhibits characteristics we usually associate with religion. It inspires personal conversion
(*metanoia* in Christian terms) and provides its adherents with absolute
ideological certainty. For example, Fukien Radio (1971) reported a propaganda example of Maoist conversion by an intellectual sent down to the

---

4 Philip Kapleau, *The Three Pillars of Zen: Teaching, Practice, and Enlightenment* (New
York: Harper and Row, 1966).
5 Thomas Merton, *Zen and the Birds of Appetite* (New York: New Directions, 1968), 139.
6 Kapleau, *Three Pillars*, 59.
7 Kapleau, *Three Pillars*, 268.

countryside. Faced with the personal crisis of pigs fighting in his bunk, he stood in front of Chairman Mao's portrait and pledged: "Although thousands of mountains are between me and Beijing, I shall follow you closely and advance resolutely along the road of integrating with workers, peasants, and soldiers."[8] His wife conveniently arrived from the city to visit him at just that moment and he converted her to tending pigs also. The veracity of the account is not as significant as the general religious form. Nevertheless, Maoist Marxism peaked in the religious-political revivalism of the 1960s. In addition, Marxism never built up the extensive culture of spiritual practices associated with traditional Confucianism, the central focus of Yang's book on Chinese religion.

Taking into account these three cases, this book defines religion as "that pattern of beliefs and activities that expresses ultimate meaning in a person's life." Religion constitutes the fundamental orientation to the questions, "Who am I? Who are we?" and "Why do I [verb]? Why do we [verb]?" when others – usually annoying small children, old people with too much time on their hands, or ourselves in our most reflective moments – keep asking "Why?" to deeper and deeper questions. A good indicator of this "ultimate meaning" is the person's willingness to die for his belief, which is why all religions honor their martyrs. The term "martyr" comes from the Greek "to witness." Ultimate meaning echoes Paul Tillich's "ultimate concern." It also matches the fifth of five meanings for religion by French theologian Michel Meslin.[9] Using an anthropological approach, Meslin begins by listing some of the many approaches to defining religion, and emphasizes that the initial meanings remain strongly tied to specific cultures.

Meslin's first meaning focuses on the separation between the sacred and the profane in Western culture. The second sense is complementary, adding the notion of truth to one's own religious system and denying it to others. The third meaning derives from sociology. Religion constitutes all human activities informed by a faith. Meslin comments that the fourth definition is more spiritual in that it includes not only devotion to God, but also altruistic service of other people. Finally, the most existential definition comes from Bishop F. F. Barry, "Religion is what a man lives for; a man may live for whiskey or dividends, for his wife and children,

---

[8] Cited in Donald E. MacInnis, *Religion in China Today: Policy and Practice* (Maryknoll, NY: Orbis Books, 1989), 364.

[9] Michel Meslin, *L'experience humaine du divin – Foundaments d'une anthropologie religieuse* (Paris: Cerf, 1988).

or for the New Jerusalem, and that is his religion."[10] This latter meaning approximates the definition used in this book.

None of Meslin's definitions are false, just more or less useful for various discussions. Certainly the person's faith, in the experience of Mohammed or Buddha or in Mao's leadership, plays a significant role in binding together the religious community. And even the most solitary hermit speaks in terms of serving the community at large by his/her example. Most of us would criticize the priest who passes by the injured traveler in the parable of the Good Samaritan. The apostle James (I, 27) stated that point strongly when he wrote, "Looking after widows and orphans in distress and keeping oneself unspotted by the world make for pure worship without stain before our God and Father." One excellent way of judging a religious tree is by the fruit of its works. So the great popular suffering during the Great Leap Forward and the Cultural Revolution remains a black mark against Maoist Communism. The first two definitions, the distinction between the sacred and the profane and the truth of one's religion find their place in this book by focusing on what defines a specifically religious experience. Spiritual masters of all religions speak of extraordinary religious experience, sometimes called mystical, which will ever remain impossible to describe adequately in human language.

What can be said in general about this extraordinary personal experience that is at the center of what is called "religion"? The text has already introduced the twentieth-century monk Thomas Merton as its "expert" on spirituality. Merton calls this experience "contemplation." "In fact," says Merton, "Contemplation is man's highest and most essential spiritual activity." Solitude prepares for the experience, but does not guarantee it. "[T]he contemplative is ... simply he who has risked his mind in the desert beyond language and beyond ideas where God is encountered in the nakedness of pure trust, that is to say in the surrender of our own poverty and incompleteness in order no longer to clench our minds in a cramp upon themselves, as if thinking made us exist."[11] The knowledge, then, constitutes a "knowledge in darkness." Merton states that, "the spirit sees God precisely by understanding that He is utterly invisible to it."[12] If this deep spiritual experience cannot be earned or guaranteed,

---

[10] Meslin, *L'experience*, 115.
[11] Lawrence Cunningham, ed., *Thomas Merton: Spiritual Master: The Essential Writings* (Mahwah, NJ: Paulist Press, 1992), 426.
[12] Cunningham, *Merton*, 356.

then the proper response must be gratitude. Spiritual masters all agree that a religious person who takes pride in this gift is an abomination and a threat. The Old Testament archetype of such pride is Satan.

Merton speaks of God or the Trinity as the object of Christian mysticism, but studies in comparative mysticism have produced no agreement on whether "the object" of such experience is the same for masters in all religions. What is the same is the dual characteristic that "the object" is both Other and in unity with the person. "For it is surely in the Trinity of Persons that God appears to us most clearly as the 'wholly other', and, at the same time, as closer to us than any being."[13] This text will therefore use the term "the Other" for the subject/object of extraordinary religious experience in its discussion across religious boundaries, again acknowledging that no language suffices. The scholar of Islamic politics Bruce Lawrence uses the same term for "the Subject/Object of [religious] imagination: Yahweh, God, Allah, Other. Let us call it Other. Other is a transtemporal force; exceeding time, it also exceeds all other human beings."[14] In addition, this experience of the transtemporal Other is joined to experience of the unity of others who share life with us. The Dutch spiritual writer Henri J. M. Nouwen wrote that "intimacy with God and solidarity with all people are two aspects of dwelling in the present moment that can never be separated."[15]

Finally, Merton distinguishes between true and false religious experience on the basis of whether it involves the person's "true inner self" or the person's "false interior self." The latter is linked to the believer's desire to manipulate the world by magic. False mysticism, according to Merton leads to social and political disaster:

The relation between this false inner self and external reality is entirely colored and perverted by a heavy and quasi-magical compulsivity.... The highest form of religious worship finds its issue and fulfillment in contemplative awakening and in transcendent spiritual peace – in the quasi experiential union of its members with God, beyond sense and beyond ecstasy. The lowest form is fulfilled in numinous and magic sense of power which has been "produced" by rites and gives one momentarily the chance to wring a magical effect from the placated deity.[16]

---

[13] "Contemplatives and the Crisis of Faith," letter of monks to October 1967 Bishops' Synod, Cunningham, *Merton*, 431.

[14] Bruce Lawrence, *Shattering the Myth: Islam Beyond Violence* (Princeton, NJ: Princeton University Press, 1998), 21.

[15] Henri J. M. Nouwen, *The Only Necessary Thing: Living a Prayerful Life* (New York: Crossroads, 1999), 144.

[16] Cunningham, *Merton*, 316–17.

Merton links medieval anti-Semitism to a false external approach to religion when many in the German Catholic Church accepted "the Carolingian suggestion [of imperial political-religious unity]." "The consciousness of Germanic Christianity in the eighth to the eleventh centuries," states Merton "was increasingly levitical and military. The God of Charlemagne is the Lord of Hosts who anointed him emperor. . . . In this aggressive, solemn, dark, and feudal Christianity . . . there grows up the hatred and contempt of the Jew, whose role is more and more that of the theological Christ-killer on whom the curse has fallen."[17] The practice of religion can thus lead to both good and evil in politics. The two definitions of religion in this chapter are parallel to the two definitions of politics discussed in Chapter 2. The first definitions are based on observation and fit a broader range of phenomena, and the second rely on experiential judgments that can distinguish between good and bad political and religious actions.

Religion	Politics
OBSERVATION	
"pattern of beliefs and activities that expresses ultimate meaning in a person's life and death"	"pattern of beliefs and activities that determines who gets what, when, how" plus "who gets to participate"
JUDGMENT	
"pattern of beliefs and activities that predispose and accompany the person's contact with the Other in which one accepts one's inmost self"	"pattern of beliefs and activities in which rightly constituted authority exercises legitimate coercion for the common good"

RELIGIOUS PRACTICES RELEVANT TO POLITICS

Examining the very disparate Catholicism, Zen Buddhism, and Maoist Marxism also provides useful descriptive categories of religious practice. Which religious practices are most likely to influence politics? This book discusses seven practices: spirituality, ritual, scripture and prophecy, cultural worldview, doctrine, organization, and morality and law. For the political analyst, these practices generate interest precisely because they do have political impacts. However, in almost all cases the religious leader or adherent initiates these practices for religious, not for political reasons. The political side effects are sometimes intended, sometimes endured.

---

[17] Cunningham, *Merton*, 124.

These seven practices can be analyzed separately, but they are experienced by the adherent and by the society as a continuum. For example, spirituality constitutes both the ordinary and the extraordinary personal experience of the Other. Such experience often takes place in public ritual, at which scripture, the public record of the historical community's relationship to the Other and to humanity, is proclaimed.

Spirituality. Spirituality, the experience of the Other, grounds personal identity and community solidarity. The word "spirituality," according to the theologians Denise and John Carmody, "is lived, experienced philosophy, theology, wisdom, or whatever else one wants to call people's outlook, *Weltanschauung*, way of proceeding in the world. It is comprehensive because it is deep. It touches all aspects of the person's life, including the person's contribution to the religious or civic community, because it colors if not determines the person's core."[18] In spirituality, adherents experience the Other of their "ultimate concern" in both extraordinary and ordinary ways. Records of extraordinary experience are found in the various mystical traditions. The ordinary experience manifests itself in individual prayer and communal ritual. In response to these extraordinary and ordinary meetings with the Other, the adherent is called to change his/her life. In fact, continual conversion, gratitude, and an appreciation of holiness as "ordinary" seem to mark all great religious figures. These personal meetings and responses are termed spirituality in this book.

Spirituality underlies all other religious expressions. It nourishes the believer's dedication to persevere through difficult periods when such dedication does not seem at all "cost effective" in any worldly calculus. In political terms, spirituality provides the basis for the legitimacy of all religious movements and organizations. In the twentieth century, great political figures such as Mahatma Gandhi, Nelson Mandela, and Kim Dae Jung faced death with equanimity and lived lives of personal and civic integrity, even though most of the time these leaders had little hope of political success. Extraordinary meetings with the Other especially inspire founders, reformers, and saints. Authentic spiritual experiences often involve a deep perception of the unity of the human community, thus grounding the person for a life of communal service against great political odds.

---

[18] Denise Lardner Carmody and John Tully Carmody, *In the Path of the Masters: Understanding the Spirituality of Buddha, Confucius, Jesus, and Muhammad* (Armonk, NY: M. E. Sharpe, 1996), 9.

Ritual. Catherine Bell uses six categories of religious rituals: rites of passage such as baptism, bar mitzvah, and funeral customs; calendrical rites such as Easter and the spring offering of the Confucian emperor; rites of exchange and communion like the mass and the Hindu _puja_ [showing reverence to a god, a spirit, or another aspect of the divine]; rites of affliction like those performed by Korean shaman to exorcise evil influences; rites of feasting, fasting, and festivals like Ramadan and Carnival; and political rites.[19] These latter accomplish the two goals of, first, depicting "a group of people as a coherent and ordered community based on shared values and goals"; and, second, of demonstrating "the legitimacy of these values and goals by establishing their iconicity with the perceived values and order of the cosmos."[20] Bell discusses the international diplomatic arguments surrounding the 1990 coronation of Emperor Akihito of Japan to show the contemporary political impact of what appears to be arcane traditional ritual.

People naturally wish to express their individual spirituality in communal ritual. Aristotle observed that human beings are "political animals" whose full development depends upon social and political interaction. Even the most solitary religious hermits have often left their huts or caves once a day to meet for common liturgy. Ritual not only provides a complementary venue for meeting the Other, but it also offers the spiritual encouragement of a communal religious experience. Adherents are strengthened when they realize that hundreds, thousands, or even millions affirm a religious experience similar to their own. Ritual also can constitute the sacramental meeting place with the Other when the rite affects what it signifies, as in the Christian Eucharist.

With regard to the political impact of religious ritual, ritual also can join "ultimate meaning" to political events. For example, millions of Iranians took to the streets on Shiite Islam's holiest feast of Ashura in 1978 to protest against the government of the "new Yazid," the Shah. The Protestant funeral of Steve Biko constituted an early turning point in the battle against apartheid in South Africa. In authoritarian regimes of the right and the left, ritual can provide "sanctuary" for events that would not otherwise be tolerated by the government. For example, in the 1970s, Islamic prayer gatherings of more that 250,000 believers shut down central Cairo, reminding the Sadat government of the organizational strength

---

[19] Catherine Bell, _Ritual: Perspectives and Dimensions_ (Oxford: Oxford University Press, 1997), 91–137.
[20] Bell, _Ritual_, 129.

of the Muslim Brotherhood. When John Paul II visited martial law Poland in 1983, one-fourth of the nation's citizenry attended one of his masses. The pope's and the crowd's use of the word "solidarity" and the distinctive Solidarity script invoked both religious and political meanings.

Scripture and Prophecy. Almost all religions hold certain writings sacred, either as the revealed Word of God, or as the description of the experiences of the Other by revered coreligious. Scripture can also present commentary on that experience privileged by the religious community. Scripture often forms the common language of prayer for the religious community, whose liturgy proclaims select passages for common recitation and hearing. Therefore, the interpretations of scriptures demand not just the study of the original languages but also the knowledge of the history and beliefs of the various religious traditions. The principal duty of Jewish and Muslim religious professionals, rabbis and ulama, remains the study and the commentary on the Torah and the Prophets or the Qur'an, applying these holy books to life situations. This central significance of Jewish and Muslim scripture can be further appreciated by Christians when Islamic scholars such as Nasr compare the Qur'an not to the Christian Bible but to the more central Body of Christ in Christianity.[21] Yale Professor Lamin Sanneh from Gambia adds that, unlike Islam, Christianity was a "translated faith right from the start.... Where it was undertaken, Bible translation became the vehicle of indigenous cultural development and the basis of establishing churches."[22] In discussing the four types of biblical interpretation available to Christians and Jews, the Jewish scholar Michael Signer states that he believes that scholars from both religions have and can continue to cooperate best in elucidating the literal and the ethical sense of scripture. Dialogues on the allegorical and the mystical senses "will not yield a similar consensus or agreement, but, nonetheless, they can provide an important link between the Jewish and the Christian communities."[23]

[21] Seyyed Hossein Nasr, *The Heart of Islam: Enduring Values for Humanity* (San Francisco: Harper, 2002), 23.
[22] Lamin Sanneh, "Conclusion: The Current Transformation of Christianity," in Lamin Sannah and Joel A. Carpenter, eds., *The Changing Face of Christianity: Africa, the West, and the World* (New York: Oxford, 2005), 214.
[23] Michael A. Signer, "Searching the Scriptures: Jews, Christians, and the Book," Tikva Frymer-Kensky, David Novak, Peter Ochs, David Fox Sandmel, and Michael A. Signer, *Christianity in Jewish Terms* (Boulder, CO: Westview Press, 2000), 98. For an excellent comparative history of Jewish and Christian interpretation, see Jaroslav Pelikan, *Whose Bible Is It? A History of the Scriptures Through the Ages* (New York: Penguin, 2005).

In the late eighth century, Muslims who held that the Qur'an was the "uncreated" and eternal world of God disputed with those who held that the Qur'an, like all of God's works, had come forth in time. The latter position remained acceptable for a time in the ninth century, but by the end of the tenth century, the *I'jaz* [inimitability] of the Qur'an became the norm. As in Christianity and Judaism, a vast body of exegetical and historical literature has arisen to interpret the Islamic scripture. The most important of these works are the *hadith*, the collected sayings and deeds of Mohammed; the *sunna*, the body of Islamic social and legislative custom; the *sira*, the biographies of the Prophet; and the *tafsir*, Qur'anic commentary and explication. The central Islamic domestic political question thus has always concerned the relationship of *shari'a* [religious law] to society as a whole. Hourani states that "it [Islamic law] was both more and less than what now is usually regarded as [Western] law."[24] Islamic law is more because it regulates private acts that concern neither a man's neighbor nor his ruler. Islamic law is less because some of its provisions remain only theoretical, and it ignores whole fields of action that would be included in other legal codes.

Although Christ is the premier Word of God in Christianity, both Old and New Testaments maintain their great significance in narrating the story of God's intervention in human history. All three religions of the book define exactly which writings are inspired and which writings are only associated historically with these works. The latter are termed apocryphal by Jews and Protestants and deuterocanonical by Catholics and most Orthodox. Mainline Protestants and Catholics, however, have long since used the tools of nineteenth- and twentieth-century literary criticism to interpret their scriptures. This movement has not generally taken place in evangelical Protestantism or in Islam. Those Muslims who have attempted to practice it, for example, Egyptian professor Nasr Abu Zaid, have been attacked vigorously. Abu Zaid was branded an apostate and had his marriage dissolved by Egypt's highest court in 1996. Certainly, interpretations of the Bible or the Qur'an that stress the historical evolution or the literary genres of the books can become incredibly sensitive politics for Christians and Muslims.

Buddhist sutras chronicle the spiritual experience of Buddhas and Bodhisatvas, but the exact content and approach to these writings differ with the type of Buddhism. Sutras remain in the original Pali and Sanskrit, even though this may obscure some of the meaning to later adherents.

---

[24] Albert Hourani, *A History of the Arab Peoples* (Cambridge, MA: Belnap, 1991), 160.

The Hindu *Upanishads* constitute some of humanity's oldest recorded prayers. Most Hindus, however, remain more familiar with the *Bhagavad-Gita*, sometimes called "the layman's *Upanishads*," and the Ramayana. The Confucian tradition used the Four Books to test the worthiness of hundreds of generations of Mandarin officials in an elaborate three-stage examination system that culminated in the Forbidden City. During the Cultural Revolution, Maoists tirelessly chanted the short pithy sayings of the Little Red Book, even on air flights.

Illustrating a specific single-factor political effect of scripture remains difficult, precisely because holy writings usually exist in an organizational or cultural context, not by themselves. However, the discovery of a translation of the Protestant Bible by Taiping Rebellion (1850–64) founder Hong Xiuquan led to his self-proclamation as "Jesus Christ's Younger Brother." The syncretist Taiping very nearly toppled the Qing Dynasty. The call to return to the simplicity of biblical religion also formed the heart of the Protestant Reformation. Indeed, disagreements over biblical interpretation still raise legal, political, and educational issues. Controversies surrounding creation science still bedevil local school boards in the United States.

Prophecy constitutes one of the common literary genres across many scriptural traditions. In its narrowest sense, prophecy means the actual prediction of future events. In its broadest sense, the word refers to scriptural statements about the spiritual nature of the world in highly imaginative language. The Christian *Book of Revelation* has been read in both senses. Yang discusses the functional role of prophecy in Chinese sectarian rebellion against the state. He lists six general characteristics of such prophecy: a basic theory explaining dynamic world changes; an account of mythological and historical events as proof of the theory; explanation of the transition of one phase of the world to another; deliverance of believers and extermination of the wicked; obscure and general language; and immense stretches of time.[25] The first four characteristics make the prophecies useful politically, and the last two protect the sects from being proved wrong. When *Revelation* is read as strict prediction, the analyst could apply these Chinese characteristics to Christian apocalyptic writings. In both civilizations, prophecy as strict religious prediction usually occurs at the nexus between fringe religion and fringe politics, as in the case of Jerusalem sects as the Millennium approached.

[25] Yang, *China*, 232–39.

Cultural Worldview. Sacred writings contribute to the establishment of the cultural worldviews of major civilizations. Religious worldviews can nourish the individual's faith and practice so that one integrates religion into one's entire life. These worldviews can also frame the intellectual and social states of the question so that certain solutions of intellectual and political questions are indicated even before the questions are posed. Both thought and art remain essential to the long preservation of religious traditions since all people naturally relate their religious experience to their life experience. In the sixteenth-century Reformation, radical Protestants and Calvinists sometimes destroyed Catholic statues and stained-glass windows because these artistic artifacts were perceived to be "idolatrous." Catholics defended such practices, whereas Lutherans took a middle position. Iconoclastic disputes have punctuated many religious disputes, down to the Talibans' 2001 dynamiting of two great Buddhist statues in Afghanistan.

Doctrine. When intellectuals reflect on the mystery of the Other and the Other's relationship to the world, they formulate rational explanations that help adherents understand their religion, for just as each person seeks to locate his faith experience within his life experience, intellectuals especially seek to understand and to justify their beliefs within the context of reason. The Catholic tradition terms this activity, more important in Western than Eastern religion, "faith seeking intelligibility" [*fidens quarens intellectum*]. Such intellectual activity produces theology, the science of God. If an ecclesiastical or state organization codifies official theological and moral doctrine, adherence to that doctrine separates the "orthodox" (those having right doctrine) from the "heterodox" or "heretics." Relations with "heretics" can sometimes exhibit more venom than relations with "infidels." Whether or not the understanding of doctrine can develop over time, and in what ways, becomes a central theological question in such traditions.[26]

Organization. Adherents of a religion not only meet sporadically or regularly for liturgy, but they also form permanent structured organizations to maintain and to propagate their faith. Indeed, the nature of ecclesiastical organizations, in which the leadership roles remain a significant variable,

---

[26] See, for example, John T. Noonan, Jr., *A Church That Can and Cannot Change: The Development of Catholic Moral Teaching* (Notre Dame, In.: University of Notre Dame Press, 2005).

constitutes one of the most important indicators of a religion's political influence. Once formed, religious organizations can play both religious and political roles. In Western sociology, scholars have traditionally distinguished between broad-based and inclusive "churches" and narrower and more doctrinally rigid "sects," but the distinction becomes blurred when applied to specific religious organizations.

When analyzing the political impact of ecclesiastical organizations, scholars can focus on either the internal politics of the religious organization or on the political interaction between ecclesiastical organizations and external societal, especially state organizations. However, these two types of organizational politics almost always affect each other. Internal Catholic discipline prevailed so strongly in the late nineteenth and early twentieth century partially because such a tight organizational structure proved extremely useful to local and national Catholics in their battles with national governments that persecuted or discriminated against them. The same disciplinary emphasis exists today in developing countries where churches battle authoritarian states over human rights.

Monastic organization has appeared in both the East and the West. If the adherent's experience of the Other is to become the central focus of one's life, it seems reasonable that organizations should arise whose primary purpose is to facilitate that experience. The monastic order, the Sangha, appeared among the early followers of Buddha who sought to follow his prescriptions in search of Enlightenment. Over time Buddha and his followers gave more formal structure to these groups and set their rules.

The Christian monastic form originated with hermits in the Egyptian desert who sought to witness Christ by a life of contemplation as the martyrs had witnessed Christ during Roman state persecution. As in the East, Western monastic foundations demonstrated the special gifts of their founders. Benedict, Dominic, and Francis each promulgated monastic rules that expressed their distinct spiritualities. It is no accident that the most fruitful Buddhist-Christian dialogues have come from the discussions of monks, who face some of the same issues of spirituality and organization.

Morality and Law. Law and morality teach righteous living. Religions of the book emphasize morality, and generally relate righteous living very closely to scriptural warrants, the most famous of which is the Ten Commandments. Justice and taking care of the *anawim* [poor] are prominent themes in Hebrew social thought, but what impresses scholar J. David

Pleins is the diversity of the ethical perspectives found in the Hebrew scriptures. According to Pleins, [t]he legal material points the way toward an ethics of obligation." The prophetic tradition fosters "an ethics of conscience and advocacy for society in its brokenness." The narrative voice presents "an ethics of scrutiny" focused on the institution of monarchy. The wisdom voice "offers an ethics of consequence," and the voice of worship "an ethics of disposition." The very diversity of these ethical voices and the diversity of perspectives within each voice calls for the continued appropriation of the text by religious scholars and communities. "It is the flexibility of the biblical tradition, this ability to draw the biblical record into dialogue with the present, which not only illumines our understanding of the political depths of the biblical materials but also urges us to unpack the theological depths of the contemporary political moment."[27]

In Christianity, Islam, and Buddhism, the life of the religion's founder sets the ultimate ethical norm: "What would Jesus [WWJD movement] or Mohammed or Buddha do? However, it is often difficult to apply that norm to complicated contemporary ethical dilemmas like those of bioethics. And believers face the temptation of falsifying the understanding of the founder by their own biased reading of scripture. For example, the U.S. religious ethicist William Spohn comments, "The sentimental Jesus of middle-class piety hides the cross of poverty and oppression; the Jesus of Western imperialism is refuted by the nonviolence of the passion accounts; the Jesus of patriarchal tradition wilts under the evidence that the Nazarene chose the powerless and the marginal to share his table."[28]

Although Christianity points to Christ as the norm, Gananath Obeyesekere argues that the sources of Buddhist morality are much more problematic because, for the Theravada Buddhist, the operation of the world is for the most part due to karma. Obeyesedere does emphasize, however, how important to the formation of the Buddhist conscience are the *jakata*, stories about the Buddha in lives prior to the one in which he reached nirvana.[29]

Within this difficult interpretation, however, there remains another complicated question. Mohammed, in establishing the Muslim community, led a much more varied life than Jesus or the Buddha. Nasr

[27] J. David Pleins, *The Social Visions of the Hebrew Bible: A Theological Introduction* (Louisville, KY: Westminster John Knox, 2000), 530–32.
[28] William Spohn, *Go and Do Likewise: Jesus and Ethics* (New York: Continuum, 2000), 11.
[29] Gananath Obeyesekere, "Buddhism and Conscience," *Daedalus* 120 (Summer 1991): 219–39.

approaches the same question from another angle when he comments that the founders of great religions fall into two categories: those like the Buddha and Christ "who preach detachment from the world and a spiritual life that does not become entangled with ordinary worldly matters with all their ambiguities and complexities"; and those such as Moses, Krishna, and Mohammed who "entered into the complexity of the ordinary human order to transform and sanctify it."[30]

Ethical judgments, however, do not depend on religion alone. Both the East and the West have developed moral philosophies that purport to proscribe good acts on nonreligious bases. Three types of such philosophical approaches are virtue or character ethics, an ethics of obligation, and an ethics of consequences. Western Christianity has often sought to combine its religious ethical warrants with philosophical argumentation. Spohn advocates combining the New Testament, spirituality, and the ethics of virtue or character. He argues both that the ethics of virtue are superior to those of obligation and consequences, and that they fit the nature of the scriptural narrative whereas the ethics of obligation and consequences do not. Employing the New Testament, spirituality, and the ethics of virtue as independent sources guards against "the common tendency to use spirituality as an instrument for self-enhancement."[31] Here Spohn supports the warning of Merton against the "false exterior self."

It is obvious from the above discussions of the definitions of religion and spirituality, and from the interaction of all religious expressions, that there can be almost as many concrete types of religious contexts as there are adherents. Spiritualities, rituals, sacred writings, cultural worldviews, doctrines, organizations, and ethical systems exist in more or less developed forms in all religions. Although this book classifies Buddhism as a religion of meditative experience, for example, Buddhism has developed monastic organization. Therefore, the above characterizations of the various world religions indicate emphases within the traditions, not the complete lack of complementary elements. Finally, although this complexity remains a significant challenge to scholarly analysis, it is precisely this complexity that makes possible comparative political-religious analysis and interreligious dialogue. It helps the student to note continuities in a single tradition that might not appear if s/he focused on rivalries within the religion. For example, any casual observer can distinguish the Protestant and Islamic traditions in general, even while appreciating the

---

[30] Nasr, *Islam*, 33–34.
[31] Spohn, *Jesus and Ethics*, 13.

differences between mainline and evangelical Protestants and Sunni and Shiite Muslims.

RELIGION AND IDENTITY: RADICAL OTHERNESS AND THREE TYPES OF RELIGION

The most significant political statement about religion is that the religious adherent orients herself toward a radical Other that has the potential to challenge every political legitimacy, organization, and moral command. From the religious perspective, then, even the person herself does not control this relationship with the Other. Rather, she freely responds to the free initiative of the Other. Contact with the Other is always a gift, a "grace." Adherents wait for the Other, as the psalmist waits for the dawn. True spirituality is like true love, which is never earned.

In community life, the experience of the Other judges all political and religious institutions, especially those governments, those churches, and those political and religious gurus who seek totalitarian control. The personal experience of the Other thus radically anchors the autonomous religious influence on politics. Such an individualistic approach, however, would seem to fragment religious influence so that it would be difficult to make more general conclusions useful for systematic political analysis. To meet this challenge, this text offers a general typology of world religions. It seeks to organize the incredible diversity of global religious phenomena by employing three general categories.

The religions of the book constitute the first general world type. Judaism, Christianity, and Islam share reverence for the initial call of Abraham. The same monotheistic God inspired their sacred writings and their moral imperatives. These religions take their central focus from specific revelations to specific persons at specific times in specific places. Their emphases on history as progress, the material world, and the equality of all believers underlie many common Western civil values. These religions have developed significant ecclesiastical organizations and significant traditions of political-religious relations in which law and morality constitute major issues. Religious leaders tend to receive their legitimacy from their organizational posts. When comparing the religions of the book to world religion in general, political analysts should focus on the scriptures and prophecy, doctrines, organizations, and law and morality of the religions of the book. The purpose of this statement is to distinguish among the three types, so that naming four expressions disproportionately found in the religions of the book is in comparison with the other two types. Not selecting spirituality, ritual, and worldview does not deny the central religious significance, for example, of the mysticism of St. John of the Cross, Greek Orthodox worship, or Islamic architecture.

The religions of meditative experience constitute the second general world type. These religions emphasize personal spirituality and the subsidiary reality of the material world. Time is cyclical. Religious leaders receive their legitimacy less from organizational positions and more from a reputation for holiness. Religions of meditative experience tend to be most active politically when the religion's cultural worldview fuses with Western-style nationalism. Obeyesekere argues, for example, that one cannot understand the terrible violence between the Sinhala Buddhists and the Tamil Hindus without "an understanding of the processes that led to this dismantling of the [traditional Eastern-style] Buddhist conscience."[32] In contemporary India even casual observers are shocked by the huge disconnect between the traditional tolerance and inclusiveness of Hindu spirituality and the social exclusiveness of the Hindu Bharatiya Janata Party (BJP). Compared with world religion in general, analysts should focus on spiritualities, scriptures, rituals (both elite and popular), and cultural worldviews when analyzing the religions of meditative experience.

The religions of public life constitute the third general type. Confucianism and Maoist Marxism arose in China. Chinese political elites have only welcomed foreign religions such as Buddhism and Christianity during times of social and political crisis. In organizational terms, religions of public life seek to provide the ideological component for state systems. As such, these religions serve as bases of legitimacy and as gatekeepers for their state-based "clergy," Mandarin officials and Communist cadres. The combination of a native ideology (Confucianism) with a Western-style Marxist nationalism allows the Chinese, as it did the Sri Lankans mentioned earlier to view themselves as both indigenous and modern, while at the same time reacting to the threat of Western colonialism. Also, like religions of meditative experience, Confucianism and Maoist Marxism have sought to establish the national cultural worldview, both elite and folk, through popular art and literature, from puppet shows to regional opera. Compared with religion in general, political analysts should focus on rituals, cultural worldviews, joint religious-state organizations, and morality and law when examining religions of public life.

---

[32] Obeyesekere, "Conscience," 237.

This chapter has approached the relationship of religion and politics from the perspective of the categories of religious practice. It does not demand that the reader believe in a specific religion, or even in the societal usefulness of a more generalized combination of various religious values. The reader could, for example, appreciate the revolutionary military influence of the Taiping Rebellion without taking a position on whether or not its leader was truly "Jesus Christ's younger brother" when the Taiping captured over six hundred walled cities in eighteen provinces. However, the book's dialectic of politics at the intersection of religion and the EMC systems does ask the reader to consider religion as an autonomous sphere, an independent variable in a world in which adherents act at least in part for the self-articulated religious motivations described in this chapter.

COMBINING POLITICAL AND RELIGIOUS CATEGORIES OF ANALYSIS

Chapters 2 and 3 have presented the political and religious perspectives for the analysis of the interaction between religion and politics. From the political viewpoint, Chapter 2 treats religion and politics at the local, the national, the regional, and the international level. From the religious viewpoint, Chapter 3 shows how spirituality, ritual, scripture and prophecy, cultural worldview, doctrine, organization, and law and morality influence politics. This section demonstrates how the two perspectives can be integrated by applying the religious practices of Chapter 3 to the geographical settings of Chapter 2. At the local level, all types of religions operate with equal political clout in setting the local cultural worldview on the basis of spirituality, scripture and prophecy, and communal ritual. It is through the experience of this lived totality that individuals find and express their identity and values in relationship to their family, their community, and nature. Their face to face dealings with priests, ministers, rabbis, ulama, mullahs, sadhus, monks, mandarins, and cadres all demonstrate the basic dynamics of human interaction. The source of the local religious leaders' legitimacy may be different theoretically, but its location in the cultural worldview and the empathy and skills needed to perform the local pastoral task remain very similar. At this local level, religion and politics often fuse, and the anthropologist does the best scholarship. Traditionally, religions of the book and religions of public life demonstrate stronger links between the village and the major city, region, or nation.

Chapter 2's discussion of the national level offered four cases. The traditional "sacred canopy" reproduces the local dynamic at the state level, and like the local dynamic, finds all religions equally adept at providing a national religious worldview. We can notice the strong political impact of combining religious legitimacy and military power in Christian (Catholic, Orthodox, and Protestant) and Islamic crusades and holy wars. For example, Appleby begins his first chapter with the Hamas coffin-centered ritual preparing young Muslims for suicide bombing and for awakening in the Gardens of Delight where they will experience all good things.[33] Confucian states and Communist parties have also fought ideologically based wars, and Buddhism has had its warrior monks, but the ambiance differs.

The second and third cases, in which state and church compete and religions compete, place more emphasis on religious organization, so that independent religious links among the capital city, regional market towns, and the villages matter. Catholicism has developed the strongest linkages, and Hinduism the weakest. Hindu politicians have sought to solve this problem through a political party, the BJP, which combines political and religious legitimacy. Although both the Philippine Catholic Church and the BJP strive for "expressive power" in their societies, the BJP wants to capture the state apparatus, not function as "primary ethical broker." Religions with a cardinal primate, a patriarch, or an ayatollah, who personify the religious legitimacy of an entire political entity, can more easily challenge the political ruler. The Chinese and Roman emperors claimed both religious and political national legitimacy, thus making religious heterodoxy automatic political treason. It has been much harder, therefore, to launch a political or religious rebellion in these states, and the religious rebels had to topple the political authority to survive.

In the fourth case of politics at the national level, in which protecting one's group from outside cultural influences is the objective, fundamentalist Protestantism, the Jewish Ultraorthodox, and Islamist movements have demonstrated the most effective approach. This cultural autonomy derives from strong local and national organizations, directed from a doctrine and an understanding of morality and law that clearly delineate good and evil, friends and enemies. These groups seek to protect believers from an outside society that challenges its values. In doing so, fundamentalist

---

[33] R. Scott Appleby, *The Ambivalence of the Sacred: Religion, Violence, and Reconciliation* (New York: Rowman & Littlefield, 1999), 25–26.

leaders will often use politics to defend the religiously elect from the autonomous economic and communication systems, but they often espouse a crusade mentality that makes them supportive of the "right" military initiatives.

At the global level, this chapter has presented four issues (social justice, peace, identity and values, human rights) deriving from the four different international systems. On all four issues in general, one finds significantly different viewpoints from the more secular developed world to the more religious developing world. The former emphasizes individual legal and political equality and stability for "the pursuit of happiness" in a free market. The latter stresses the religious and cultural sources that call for development of the community, traditional family values, and a more religious morality.

In analyzing the political-religious interactions of the second plane of the paradigm, the above general comments should be helpful, but they are insufficient in two major senses. First, categories such as "religions of the book" remain exceedingly general. Not only do Christianity, Judaism, and Islam contain a multitude of general political-religious differences among themselves, but the three religions must at least be analyzed as Catholic, Orthodox, and Protestant; Ashkenazi and Sephardic; and Sunni, Shiite, and Sufi, respectively. Chapter 4 will offer that discussion.

Second, the geographic plane of the paradigm designated three general factors for political-religious analysis: the level of political-religious inter-action, from local to global; the nature of the religion, from religions of the book like Christianity to religions of meditative experience like Buddhism; and the regional or national culture of political-religious interaction, from the partially secularized West to Islamist Iran. At the end of Chapter 4, the text will have covered the first two factors. The third will have to wait for the regional analyses of Chapters 5–9. Then we will be able to understand, for example, the political-religious impact of figures like the great sixteenth-century Jesuit Mateo Ricci who worked: (a) at the national level, trying to convert Ming Dynasty mandarin scholars and the emperor (factor one); (b) within the ideological and organizational framework of Catholicism (factor two); and (c) within the Chinese imperial framework which sought to destroy any politically autonomous religious organiza-tion (factor three). Harmonizing these three factors proved extremely dif-ficult for one of the great intellectuals of sixteenth-century Europe, despite his extraordinary linguistic, scientific, and mnemonic abilities. Whenever a religion leaves one regional or national culture to locate itself in another, the political-religious impact becomes very complicated. For example, we will probably never completely understand the global political-religious influences of the Afghan war against the Soviets as *mujahidin* [Muslim warriors engaged in *jihad*] returned to their countries of origin across the Muslim world. Moreover, the technological advances of the twentieth century accelerated such processes a thousand fold.

4

The Religions of the Book, Meditative Experience, and Public Life

Students of religion and politics must know their history. Much of the religious influence on politics takes place over long time periods. People do not change their basic identities in a split second. Even when they think they do, the resulting identity is formed in reference to the former one. This chapter briefly presents the relevant histories of the seven world religions treated in this book. This historical knowledge will be crucial to understanding contemporary politics in Chapters 5–10. The religions of the book receive more coverage for two reasons: history makes a bigger difference to these religions; and the majority of humanity belongs to them.

RELIGIONS OF THE BOOK: HISTORICAL REVELATION, SCRIPTURE, LAW, AND WORLDVIEW

Shortly after the beginning of the second millennium B.C.E., God called a rich Semitic trader to leave his culturally advanced city on the fertile crescent and to take his family and his belongings to the less developed hinterland. And Abram, later Abraham, went. Roughly six hundred years later the same Yahweh, who then tells the Israelites his name, commanded Moses to lead the descendants of Abraham out of Egypt, where they had fled to escape famine during the time of the patriarch Joseph. Moses led the Israelites through the Red Sea and into forty years of wandering in the desert. Moses's successor, Joshua, led the people into Canaan, the land promised to Abraham and his descendants. The Jews had become a people defined by their covenant with Yahweh.

The Jewish people lived under judges for several generations, but then they asked God for a king "like the other nations." God chose Saul through the prophet Samuel. In 1000 B.C.E., Saul's successor David captured the Jebusite citadel of Jerusalem situated between, and thus perfect for uniting, the ten tribes of the north with the two tribes of the south. David's son Solomon established a great kingdom from this capital, and the fame of his wisdom brought courtiers and trade from far away. Solomon also built the first Temple. Subsequent Jewish kings, however, did not continue Solomon's wise governance, and the northern tribes broke off to form a separate kingdom. The Assyrians defeated this northern kingdom, and its inhabitants disappeared from history. Later, the Babylonians captured Jerusalem and took many of its inhabitants to their capital. From the reign of David through the Babylonian captivity (597–38 B.C.E.), the Jews slowly came to a realization of who this God was who had called them, and what it meant to be God's Chosen People. Slowly, through the preaching of the prophets and the meditations of wise men, the Hebrew tribal and ethnic worldview became purified into a more spiritual vision. No longer did the Jews believe that God would punish sons for the sins of their fathers.

The call of Abraham began the story of the intervention of God in human events, thus giving direction and meaning to history. The Israelites first codified the narratives of the callings of Abraham and of Moses in Genesis and Exodus, the first two of what became the five books of the Torah. The Jewish *Tanakh* (the Torah, the Prophets, and the Writings), gradually formed the Hebrew scriptural canon.[1] The great threat to Jewish identity in the following years came from Hellenic culture, which advocated a life focused on the gymnasium, not on the synagogue. In 164 B.C.E., the Maccabee Brothers purified the second Jewish Temple from the Hellenic "abomination of desolation." In the next century, Herod the Great, emulating his hero Solomon, rebuilt and enlarged the Temple and supported the numerous Jewish communities throughout the Roman world.

The Romans put down the Jewish revolt of 66 C.E. and destroyed that Temple. The last Jewish defenders committed mass suicide at the fortress rock of Masada rather than surrender to Caesar's legions. Today on that spot Israeli soldiers take an oath: "Masada shall not fall again." In 132 C.E., the military hero Simon bar Kochba led the last Jewish rebellion against Rome with the support of the great Rabbi Akiva. Each year at Yom Kippur, the Day of Atonement, Jews commemorate Akiva's and nine

---

[1] For the formation of the Jewish canon, see Jaroslav Pelikan, *Whose Bible Is It? A History of Scripture Through the Ages* (New York: Penguin, 2005), 45–47.

other sages' torture and death by the Romans. With these two great defeats within seventy years, the Jewish people began their nearly two-thousand-year Diaspora, the sojourn of living in small communities throughout the pagan, Christian, and Muslim worlds.

The Jewish prophet, John the Baptist, appeared in Roman Palestine, preaching repentance for the forgiveness of sins. What became known as Christianity began with the call of Jesus as he waited for the baptism of John. Throughout his public life Jesus followed the direction of His Father, even to crucifixion. Soon after Jesus's death, his apostles testified to his resurrection and preached to the Jewish community. Indeed, both Jesus and Christianity's first great preacher, Paul, were Jews, but the primitive Christian community quickly spread throughout the Roman Empire and beyond. This community accepted the Jewish Tanakh as its Old Testament, and added the "Good News" [Gospel] of Jesus as the New Testament. By the fourth century the Christian Church had established its scriptural canon. The Roman Emperor Constantine's edict of toleration at Milan in 313 allowed Christians to have a secure public life for the first time, but at the price of government interference in their communities.

The third religion of the book, Islam, began with the call of the Arabian trader Mohammed in the first years of the seventh century C.E. When he was about forty years old, on a night later known as the Night of Power or Destiny, Mohammed received what became a series of revelations from Allah, the name God gave Himself. These revelations, which became the Qur'an, created tension with the polytheistic townspeople, and in 622, Mohammed and his followers left Mecca for the oasis of Madina. After a series of wars, Mohammed's followers returned on pilgrimage to Mecca in 629, and the following year, the city surrendered to Mohammed. The final form of God's revelations to Mohammed was established during the next two centuries, mainly in the Baghdad intellectual circles of the 'Abbasid Dynasty, thus producing the definitive text of the Qur'an and classical juridical commentaries in Arabic. The Islamic community reveres many of the same prophets as Judaism and Christianity and traces its lineage back to Abraham through Ishmael, his second son.

Judaism, Christianity, and Islam all base themselves on specific historical calls and revelations by God. The communities codified these revelations in sacred scriptures, whose exact form was established in the centuries following the revelations. God's law, initially given to Moses on Mount Sinai, fostered a strong ethical orientation in all three faiths. Despite their similarities, of course, the three religions of the book are divided by the foundational claims of Christianity that Jesus is "true God and true Man," and of Islam that Mohammed is "the Seal of the Prophets."

JUDAISM AND THE DIASPORA

Judaism's uniqueness lies not only in its religious vision but also in its political and social experience. For nearly two millennia, Judaism ceased to exist as a state religion but survived in small, predominantly urban communities scattered throughout the Roman, and later the Christian and Islamic worlds. The destruction of the Temple negated the possibility of the Jewish national political and religious organizations, the State and the Sanhedrin, so Jews instead focused on the Torah as their fortress of mind and spirit. Judaism thus developed its potential as a "congregationalist faith" based on the community synagogue led by the rabbi as the revered interpreter of the Law. Johnson terms the resulting social form an urban "cathedocracy." Under the Justinian (Emperor, 527–65 C.E.) code in Byzantium, synagogues became legally protected places of worship and Jewish courts of law enforced their social and religious decisions among Jews. These urban communities, however, constantly faced political pressure. Their survival demanded the development of interurban trading and financial networks which then served as the historical link between the urban communities of the Roman Empire and the new cities of Medieval Europe and Islam.

As these new cities developed, Jews regained some lost political leverage. In Medieval Europe, nobles and higher clergy tended to protect Jews for their own purposes, and folk revivalist movements often targeted the impiety of Jews first and the corruption of Catholic higher clergy second. From the first and second centuries, however, Christian apologists manifested what Jewish scholar Jules Isaac has termed the tradition of "the teaching of contempt," the polemical attempt to show Christianity's superiority to the rabbinical interpretation of common texts.[2] The theologian Eugene Fisher, however, distinguishes the general impact of Christian anti-Jewish movements during the first and second millennia: "While the teaching of contempt against Judaism was by the end of the third century so well developed and so widespread as to be uncontested

---

[2] Christian use of the Greek Septuagint text of the *Tanakh*, for example, made later Jews leery of translations from the original text. Pelikan, *Whose Bible*, 63–66.

among subsequent fathers of the church, it did not (save in far-away out-posts like the Iberian peninsula) result in any large-scale violence or even forced conversions of Jews until the eleventh century."[3]

In 1096, however, the third wave of the First Crusade, in disregard of both ecclesiastical and political leadership, became a mob that massacred thousands of Jews in the Rhineland. The Jewish historian Robert Chazan notes that in the wake of the First Crusade, Catholic leaders such as the monk Bernard of Clairvaux opposed vigorously the idea that God was punishing the Jews for the crucifixion, "and, so, too, did ecclesiastical authorities generally reject the ritual murder allegation, the host dese-cration charge, the blood libel, and the anti-Jewishness they spawned."[4] However, the majority of the population did not prove to be as rational. By the end of the thirteenth century, these imaginative embellishments of traditional Christian notions of Jewish enmity and malevolence began to take a considerable toll on Jewish life. Waves of anti-Jewish violence swept northern Europe in the 1290s, the 1330s, and then in the 1340s. By 1391, the violence reached Spain as well, costing tens of thousands of Jewish lives and forcing large numbers of Jews to the baptismal font.

From the fourteenth century, the two Jewish groups most relevant to contemporary intellectual and political life can be clearly delineated. The first, the Sephardi (from a corruption of the Hebrew term for Spain), had their roots in the Iberian Christian-Islamic battlefield of the seventh to the fifteenth centuries. Johnson describes Spanish Jews as "learned, liter-ary, rich, immensely proud of their lineage, worldly-wise, often pleasure-loving and not over-strict."[5] When the Spanish Catholic monarchs Ferdinand and Isabella finally united the Iberian peninsula and attacked the Jewish community at the end of the fifteenth century, Sephardic Jews dispersed all over the Mediterranean and Muslim world. Hebrew consti-tuted the common language of this highly literate tradition.

The second group, the Ashkenazi, spoke Yiddish as their community language. They left their Western European ghettoes and expanded into Germany, Poland, and Russia as these states developed agriculturally from the fifteenth to the eighteenth centuries. The most significant cultural inter-action for Ashkenazi Jews came when they participated in the German

[3] Eugene J. Fisher, "Catholics and Jews Confront the Holocaust and Each Other," *America* (September 11, 1999): 12.

[4] Robert Chazen, "Christian-Jewish Interactions Over the Ages," Tikva Frymer-Kensky, David Novak, Peter Ochs, David Fox Sandmel, and Michael A. Signer, *Christianity in Jewish Terms* (Boulder, CO: Westview, 2000), 17.

[5] Paul Johnson, *A History of the Jews* (London: Weidenfield and Nicolson, 1987), 230.

Enlightenment. Central and Eastern Europe presented a stark contrast, especially in the Russian Empire. Russian Jews became alarmed by the anti-Semitism and pogroms of the 1870s, and even more so by the acceptance of such anti-Semitism in the following decade by their erstwhile allies, the Russian liberals. After World War I and the fall of Czarist Russia, "[e]verywhere explicitly anti-Semitic, fascist-style organizations emerged; not only did they harass Jews on the streets and railways, in the universities, and even in their own stores and shops, but in the 1930s they gained power over government in Austria, Hungary, Poland, and Rumania, either directly or through anti-Semitism engaged in by other, ruling parties. Hitler's rise to the German chancellorship in 1933 climaxed a trend that was equally apparent elsewhere."[6]

Anyone who has seen the Broadway musical *Fiddler on the Roof* or Steven Spielberg's cartoon movie, *An American Tale*, featuring Fievel Mousekiwitz, knows that in the late nineteenth and early twentieth centuries many Ashkenazi Jews, aided by their Western European brethren, migrated out of Eastern Europe, primarily to the United States. With the passage of new American immigration laws aimed at restricting immigration of mainly Jews and Catholics from Southern and Eastern Europe in 1924, the percentage of European Jewish immigrants to the United States dropped from 70 percent in 1920–23 to 27 percent in 1924–25. A remnant of Jewish settlement had existed in Palestine under the Ottomans, but new waves of immigrants resulted from the Russian pogroms. Zionism, the political-religious ideology, which advocated a Jewish national homeland, combined many different movements and various reasons for settling in Palestine. Halpern and Reinharz comment: "In addition to the goal of popular sovereignty, Zionists proclaimed the following specific aims: to develop Hebrew as a spoken language and the foundation of a national consensus; to transfer to Palestine all Jews who could not or did not wish to live in Diaspora countries; to establish a community in Palestine free from the peculiar social, economic, and cultural problems that beset the Jewish status as dispersed minority people."[7]

In 1896, Theodor Herzl published *Der Judenstaat* [The Jewish State], and the First Zionist Congress met in 1897. Herzl himself believed that Jews would attain emancipation by financial power and imaginative diplomacy. However, Herzl's somewhat amateurish diplomatic attempts in

---

[6] Ben Halpern and Jehuda Reinharz, *Zionism and the Creation of a New Society* (Oxford: Oxford University Press, 1998), 229.

[7] Halpern and Reinharz, *Zionism*, 9–10.

Ottoman capital Istanbul failed, so that the World Zionist Organization (WZO) became his most lasting legacy. According to Halpern and Reinharz, "Jewish tradition, the patterns of Western society, and the dynamic ideologies of Zionism and socialism" constitute the three major formative pressures which shaped the communal structure of the *Yishuv* [Palestine Jewish community] and also the organization of the leading labor institutions."[8]

Labor Zionists, largely the product of the Russian radical environment between the twin revolutions of 1905 and 1917, gradually gained control of the Jewish movement in Palestine and of the WZO. These labor Zionists led Histadrut [General Federation of Jewish Workers in the Land of Israel] and Mapai [Erez Israel Workers' Party], formed in 1929 by the union of the two largest labor parties. Their most influential radical social experiment, the agricultural *kibbutz*, exercised a much greater influence than its numbers, since many of the Histadrut and Mapai leaders spent some of their formative years as *kibbutzim*. The tragedy of the Holocaust increased global perception of the need for Jewish security, and Britain and the United States supported the establishment of the state of Israel on May 14, 1948. Ashkenazi Jews provided the leadership for the secular founding Mapai Party. The distinguishing characteristic of all Zionist factions, however, was their strong belief that whatever function or approach they emphasized, that activity constituted the one key to the solution of the Jewish problem, and would eventually be embraced by all Palestinian Jews.

WESTERN CHRISTIANITY AND THE BYZANTINE EMPIRE

It was with some difficulty that first-century Christians accepted gentiles into their faith without requiring that they convert to Judaism. However, the Council of Jerusalem (50 C.E.) ruled that gentiles did not have to adopt circumcision and other Jewish practices. The new faith thus became more and more Hellenized (Greek) as it spread throughout the Empire. During the first three centuries Christianity existed as a mostly tolerated, sometimes persecuted, religion within the pagan Roman Empire.

All this changed when the Emperor Constantine issued the edict of Milan tolerating Christianity in 313 C.E. Constantine then converted to the new faith and sought to establish it as the state-sponsored equivalent of the old cult. For example, the emperor presided over the Council of

---

[8] Halpern and Reinharz, *Zionism*, 239.

Nicaea in 325. This form of the tight connection of church and state survived in the East after the emperor moved his capital to Byzantium. In the West, Rome fell to the barbarians. Patrick, a Romanized British boy captured by Celtic raiders, initiated Celtic Christianity. After escaping back to Britain, Patrick studied in France and returned to Ireland to preach Christianity. He adopted many of the cultural forms of the receiving society and thus fostered both the first non-Roman Christian civilization and the first one focused on the rural inhabitants (*pagani* to the Romans) of the countryside. Much of Roman literature and culture, and Greek thought through Latin texts, were preserved by Celtic monks copying manuscripts on the island edge of civilization. When urban Europe decayed in the following centuries, Celtic missionaries went forth to found monasteries and to evangelize the new barbarians.

The Irish monk John Scotus Eriugena exercised strong influence at the court of the illiterate barbarian Charlemagne. Christendom, the new form of church-state relations in the West, emerged when the pope crowned this shrewd King of the Franks on Christmas Day in 800. Following a century of chaos, 850–950, in which all Western European civilization nearly disappeared from the twin attacks of the pagan Norsemen and Islam, the West found political stability under the German emperors, who sent missionaries to the Vikings and crusaders to the Holy Land. The new Europe combined elements of the Roman Empire, the Catholic Church, and the classical literary and philosophical tradition. And it would survive, no matter how rude and underdeveloped in comparison with the other civilizations. The new Western political-religious form also differed from the more advanced Byzantine civilization in its more independent ecclesiastical organization. Although both political and religious authorities in the West recognized the basic legitimacy of the other, they fought over disputed areas like the right to appoint bishops.

During the Dark Ages in the West, a high Christian civilization existed in the East. Medieval historian Christopher Dawson pointed to the significance of this development by commenting "the Byzantine culture . . . is a new creation, which forms the background of the whole development of medieval culture, and to some extent, even that of Islam."[9] Dawson states that the Byzantium should be approached intellectually as a combination of the Roman Empire and the influence of the East: "The Holy Roman Empire – *sancta respublica romana* – was the creation, not of Charlemagne, but of Constantine and Theodosius. By the fifth century

---

[9] Christopher Dawson, *The Making of Europe* (Cleveland: Meridian, 1956), 103–4.

it had become a veritable church-state, and the emperor was a kind of priest-king whose rule was regarded as the earthly counterpart and representative of the sovereignty of the Divine Word."[10]

The paths for social advancement in such an empire were the church, the army, and the civil service. However, unlike in the West, urban life survived and Byzantine cities became great trading centers. The creative genius of the era can be appreciated in its architecture and art, especially in the magnificent cathedral of Holy Wisdom. Throughout this period, oriental and Greek influences fought for the soul of Byzantine Christianity. In his struggle with Islam and his attempt to convert Jews and Montanists, the Byzantine Emperor Leo III inaugurated a policy of iconoclastic reform, thus beginning a struggle with the Church that lasted until 843. The historian Richard Fletcher states that the Byzantine Empire "experienced its gravest peril between about 650 and 850, symbolized by the two bruising sieges of Constantinople in 674–78 and 716–18.... As late as 838 Islamic armies invaded Asia Minor: the Emperor Theophilus lost a battle and nearly his life."[11]

With security from Islam and the western section of the Byzantium Empire's victory over the iconoclasts of the East, Constantinople again turned its face to the West, but it encountered the newly formed Carolingian Empire of Charlemagne's successors. Dawson concludes, "The real cause of the schism [between Rome and Constantinople] was not the dispute between [Byzantine patriarch] Michael Cerularius and Leo IX, or even the theological controversy concerning the Procession of the Holy Spirit which had arisen in the time of Photius; it was the growing cultural divergence between East and West."[12]

The foundation of Slavic Christianity derives from the missionaries Ss. Cyril and Methodius, who devoted themselves to the conversion of Moravia. Throughout the second half of the tenth century, the Russian state, founded by companies of Scandinavian adventurers (Ros), extended south toward Constantinople. In 988, Vladimir the Great (980–1015) made a treaty with the Byzantine Emperor Basil II to accept baptism and furnish six thousand troops to the empire, provided he received the hand of the emperor's sister Anna in marriage. Indeed, at the beginning of the eleventh century the Byzantine Empire seemed destined for the leadership

---

[10] Dawson, *Europe*, 104–5.

[11] Richard Fletcher, *The Cross and the Crescent: Christianity and Islam from Muhammad to the Reformation* (London: Penguin Press, 2003), 41–42.

[12] Dawson, *Europe*, 161.

of the Christian world. Dawson comments: "It far surpassed Western Europe in wealth and civilization, and the conquest of Bulgaria and the conversion of Russia offered fresh opportunities of cultural expansion. The foundations had been laid for the development of a new Byzantine-Slavonic culture in Eastern Europe which seemed to contain no less promise for the future than the corresponding Roman-Germanic development in the West."[13] However, from the seventh century both the West and the Christian Empire of the East had to deal not only with the growing cultural division between Rome and Constantinople but also with the strong military and cultural pressure of Islam from the south and east.

THE EXPANSION OF ISLAM

As Islam expanded rapidly, it began to split into its two major groupings of Sunni (*sunna* [custom]) and Shiite (*shi'at 'ali* [the Party of 'Ali]) after Mohammed's death. The issue of leadership succession surfaced immediately. The former argued for an election among advisers and community leaders, whereas the latter supported family leadership, specifically 'Ali ibn Abi Talib, Mohammed's cousin and son-in-law who was married to his daughter Fatima. The first group gained control on the prophet's death and the first three caliphs [political guides] were elected by Sunni community leaders. Meanwhile, the Shiite community held 'Ali as their Imam [righteous leader]. 'Ali finally assumed the position of caliph as the fourth after the death of the Prophet.

In 661, Sunni supporters of Mu'awiyya, who became the first Umayyad Dynasty caliph, murdered 'Ali and seized permanent control of the Muslim political organization for those outside of Mohammed's family. Mu'awiyya forced Fatima's eldest son, Hasan, to go into retirement in Madina, where Shiite sources say he was poisoned. When Mu'awiyya died, the caliphate was passed to his corrupt son Yazid. The Shiite stronghold of Kufa then sent a message to 'Ali's second son Husain asking him to lead a revolt against Yazid. Husain and two hundred of his close followers set off for the Umayyad capital Baghdad, but they were surrounded by Yazid's forces at Karbala in Iraq. From the second to the tenth day of the month of Muharram, Husain and his followers withstood the siege, but finally Yazid's forces slaughtered the men and captured the women.

The tragedy of Husain's martyrdom at Karbala sets the tone for contemporary Shiite spirituality. In scholarship treating places as diverse as

[13] Dawson, *Europe*, 164.

Hyderabad, Darjeeling, and Ladakh, David Pinault[14] demonstrates the strength of such community commemorations of Ashura, the tenth of Muharram. In each locale Shiites scourge themselves in ritual *matam* both to demonstrate their love for Husain and his companions and to obtain favors through the intercessory powers [*shafa*] that Husain was granted because of his martyrdom on the banks of the Euphrates. One of the most moving tableaus is the return to the Shiite camp of the riderless horse Zuljenah, which signaled the certain death of Husain. Now the women's full grief begins. From the defeat of Husain, the Shiites survived mainly by practicing *taqiyya* [precautionary dissimulation] under Sunni caliphate rule, but they never recognized Sunni leaders as their religious instructors.

Today, the difference of opinion concerning succession to the Prophet continues to divide Sunnis and Shiites. Shiites believe that religious inspiration and leadership is held by the twelve Holy Imams, 'Ali and his successors. These Imams are infallible and contain a special knowledge and quality of soul that enables them to interpret correctly the Qur'an. The Shiites also believe that the twelfth Imam, al-Mahdi, disappeared near Baghdad in 873. Shiites await the return of this *Imam ul Zaman* [the Imam of all time] to ensure justice throughout the world.

Nasr divides the Shiites according to their belief about the correct number of Imams. The main branch believes in all twelve. The second most important branch, the Ismailis, disagree over the identity of the seventh Imam. The third branch, the Zaydis, chose Zayd, the son of the fourth Imam as its leader. Nasr also discusses various Islamic sects, often rejected as heterodox: the Khawarij, the Druze of Lebanon, the Alawites of Turkey and Syria, the Taliban of Afghanistan, the Bahai of Iran, the Ahmadyyahs of Pakistan, and various leaders claiming to be the Mahdi. Nasr offers a spectrum of Muslim tendencies, from left to right: Shiite extremism, Ismailism, Zaydism, Twelve-Imam Shiism, the Four Schools of Sunnism, Ibadism, Wahhabism, old Khawarij, and Sunni extremism.[15]

Nasr interprets Sufism as the unifying link between the Shiite and the Sunni traditions on the basis of its superior depth. Sunnism and Shiism do mark a formal division on the formal and legal levels, asserts Nasr, but they come together at the level of the Path to God [*tariqah*] visualized as the radii of a circle: "one must first stand on the circumference, that is, practice the *Shariah*, and then follow the *Tariqah*, or Path to God, whose end is the

[14] David Pinault, *House of Karbala: Muslim Devotional Life in India* (New York: Palgrave, 2001).

[15] Seyyed Hossin Nasr, *The Heart of Islam: Enduring Values for Humanity* (San Francisco: Harper, 2002), 111.

Center, God Himself, or the *Haqiqah* [from *al-Haqq*, the truth]."[16] Karen Armstrong places the beginnings of Sufism in the asceticism that developed in reaction to the growing worldliness in both the Umayyad and 'Abassid societies. The mark of Sufism, she states, is that "it did not develop an overtly political philosophy. Instead, it seemed to have turned its back on history, and Sufis sought God in the depths of their being rather than in current events."[17] In its semihidden tradition, Sufism shows more affinity for Shiism than Sunnism. Pinault[18] also shows how the language and images of Sufi groups have been incorporated into the religious poetry of the Shiite groups he studies. In another example, the Mogul Emperor Akbar the Great's predilection for Sufism fit well with his religious toleration. Sufism, according to Said Amir Arjomand, thus serves as the antithesis of the pattern of institutionalization of Islam through the rigid application of the *shari'a*, as in the Hanbalite legal tradition. Sufism, he asserts, proved much better adapted to penetrating deeply into society: "The mission to convert the population of the frontier and rural areas increasingly fell upon a new mass movement, Sufism (Islamic mysticism)."[19]

The majority Sunni tradition, as mentioned earlier, supported the line of caliphs beginning with Abu Bakr. The first four caliphs (Abu Bakr, 'Umar, 'Uthman, and 'Ali) are called "rightly guided" caliphs, the Rashidum. They are credited with special religious guidance, whereas subsequent Sunni caliphs exercised only political power, except the duty to rule "their followers so as to promote Islamic life." The Sunni solution of the church-state question thus employed Islamic law in customary questions, but adopted laws from pre-Islamic Byzantine and Persian Empires as the primary source of imperial legislation. This combination of religious and secular sources fostered the practical priority of the ruler's decree, though his decree was not supposed to contravene Islamic law. Zubaida remarks that, "Middle Eastern polities were in practice as Islamic as their European counterparts were Christian."[20]

The historian Albert Hourani explains Islam's rapid expansion during its first century by various factors.[21] First, the Mediterranean world

---

[16] Nasr, *Islam*, 60.

[17] Karen Armstrong, *Islam: A Short History* (New York: Random House, 2000), 73.

[18] Pinault, *Karbala*, 33–51.

[19] Said Amir Arjomand, "Islam," Mark Juergensmeyer, ed., *Global Religions: An Introduction* (Oxford: Oxford University Press, 2003), 31.

[20] Sami Zubaida, *Islam, the People and the State: Essays on Political Ideas and Movements in the Middle East* (London: I. B. Tauris & Co., 1993), 42.

[21] Albert Hourani, *A History of the Arab Peoples* (Cambridge, MA: Belnap Press, 1991), 23–24.

had declined because of barbarian invasions and the failure of both the Byzantine and Sasanian (Persian) Empires to maintain agricultural systems and urban markets. Second, the Arabs constituted an organized and experienced military force. They had both the military advantage of camel transport and the religious conviction that they were doing God's will. Third, with the exception of officials and the classes tied to them, most of the conquered people did not care who ruled them, Persian, Greek, or Arab. Muslims captured Jerusalem in 648 C.E. and established the Umayyad Dynasty (650–750) in Damascus soon thereafter. The second Islamic Dynasty, the 'Abbasids, lasted from 749 to 1258. Baghdad became a great capital and center of learning tied to other parts of the world by pilgrimage and trade. The political and cultural center of Islamic civilization thus left the Arabian Desert for the cosmopolitan capital of Mesopotamian civilization where they faced political-religious problems similar to those faced by the new barbarian kings in Western Europe.

Both Christian and Islamic ruling groups borrowed from preexisting political forms, but the Catholic Church developed a stronger and more independent religious institution than Islam. In 1095 Pope Urban II proclaimed the Crusades to win back lands lost to Islam since the seventh century. The Crusaders failed to hold the Holy Land when the Islamic warrior Saladin proclaimed a *jihad* to retake the new Christian principalities in Palestine. In the same geographic area, the Byzantine Empire came under pressure from the Muslim Ottoman Turks who eventually captured Constantinople in 1453, driving Orthodox Christianity north.

The Ottomans, however, soon faced a heretical competitor on the east, the Shiite Safavids of Persia. In the west, the seven-century Catholic *Reconquista* [Reconquest] gradually replaced Islam on the Iberian peninsula. Ferdinand and Isabella expelled the Moors from Granada with its beautiful Alhambra fortress in 1492. The Ottomans failed to take Vienna twice, in 1529 and 1683, but they did capture Iraq from the Safavids in that latter year. Polish Catholic King Jon Sobieski, "the Lion of the North" (1629–96), rode to Vienna's rescue in 1683.

Scholars like Marsden, Hourani, Huband, and Lawrence all point to late-nineteenth-century and early-twentieth-century Islamist thought in Egypt as central to the global development of political Islam. Napolean's invasion of Egypt in 1798 particularly alarmed Arab opinion. The main challenge, according to such Cairo thinkers as the Persian Sayyid Jamal al-Din al-Afghani (1839–97), the Egyptian Mohammed Abduh (1849–1905), and the Syrian Rashid Rida (1865–1935), was to cope with the decline of Islam in the face of Western imperialism. In 1928 the Egyptian

school teacher Hassan al-Banna (1906–49) founded the Muslim Brotherhood, a radical Islamic organization focused on expelling Western imperial influence from the Muslim world. As early as 1929 the Egyptian
Brotherhood adopted the slogan, "The Qur'an is our constitution. The
Prophet is our Guide; Death for the glory of Allah is our greatest ambi-
tion." The Brotherhood quickly developed into a mass movement with a
network of mosques, schools, and other institutions, thus demonstrating
that Islam could legitimately encompass every aspect of the economic,
political, and cultural life of the believer. In this movement, *jihad* could
be interpreted as the striving for social and economic development, and
zakat [almsgiving] collections could be used for the same ideal.

Since 1970, however, there has been an intellectual revival of Liberal
Islam in a very changed political climate, with Liberal scholars often suffering physically for their beliefs. Charles Kurzman[22] divides the current
Liberal movement into three tendencies with regard to its position on
the relationship of liberalism to the Qur'an, the traditions of the Prophet
Mohammed, and the law. The first group of scholars argue that all three
explicitly sanction liberalism. The second group states that Muslims may
adopt liberal positions on subjects that the law leaves open to human inge-
nuity. The third position states that the law is divinely inspired, but that it
must be interpreted by humans. Each of the three liberal positions, termed
by Kurzman as "liberal," "silent," and "interpretive," offers its own problems in debate. The first and most influential "liberal" stance draws both
its strength and its weakness from fundamental exegesis, opening itself
up for a strong scriptural counterattack from Islamic conservatives. The
second position relies on Qur'anic interpretation to establish its main
point, that the Islamic tradition remains silent on many points. Finally,
the third position, with its divinely inspired scripture and fallible human
interpretations, must navigate the charge of relativism.

THE PROTESTANT REFORMATION, WARS OF RELIGION, AND SECULARISM

The Protestant Reformation began in 1517. The Protestant historian
Martin Marty emphasizes how quickly the change occurred. "One might
say that while the Christian Church is twenty centuries old, only twenty
to fifty years of these ages were given over to development of the new

---

[22] Introduction to Charles Kurzman, ed. *Liberal Islam: A Sourcebook* (Oxford: Oxford
University Press, 1998), 3–26.

Christian atlas within the Western churches."[23] German monk Martin Luther nailed his ninety-five theses to the Wittenberg church door in an attempt to reform the Catholic Church, and twelve years later "Protestants" were so labeled at the Diet of Speyer. The Peace of Augsburg (1555) resulted in the basic religious boundaries for continental Europe: Protestant in the north, Catholic in the south, and Orthodox in the East, with Catholic national outliers in Poland and Ireland. The Catholic Church partially retreated from modern European civilization with its reform initiated at the Council of Trent (1545–63).

Marty divides the early Reformation into what became three of the movement's great branches: Lutheranism as the largest continental faith; the Reformed-Presbyterian churches influenced theologically by Zwingli and Calvin; and the English Anglican tradition that maintained its apostolic succession. In addition, radical Protestants such as the early Anabaptists suffered persecution from both Catholic and other Protestant authorities, leading groups such as the Mennonites and the Swiss Brethren to adopt organizational forms that separated them from society. In England, Anglicanism generated reaction from the movements of the Congregationalists (1560), the Baptists (1606), the Quakers (1647), and the Methodists (1729). Historically, the Lutheran and Anglican traditions developed in tandem with the rising nation states, and retained episcopal ecclesiastical forms, whereas the Calvinist tradition, based in Geneva and later Scotland, tended to attack the state establishment, Catholic or Protestant. It also fostered religious individualism and congregational control. The new nation-states introduced themselves into the great imperial rivalries, but not always according to religious lines. For example, the Catholic King of France allied with the Ottoman Sultan and the Protestant German princes against the Catholic Holy Roman Emperor in the brutal Thirty Years War.

When compared with the religions of meditative experience and the religions of public life, the similarities among Judaism, Christianity, and Islam remain evident. But the historical and institutional differences also stand out. The Islamic scholar Bernard Lewis explains the absence of secularism in the Islamic tradition from these differences. Islam never endured early periods of separation from political authority the way Judaism and Christianity did. "Muhammad was, so to speak, his own Constantine. In the religiously conceived polity that he founded and headed in Medina, the Prophet and his successors confronted the realities of the state and, before very long, of a vast and expanding empire.... Such terms as clergy

---

[23] Martin E. Marty, *Protestantism* (New York: Holt, Rinehart, and Winston, 1972), 21.

or ecclesiastic cannot properly be applied to Muslim men of religion. These were in time, and in defiance of early tradition and precept, professionalized, and thus became a clergy in a sociological sense. They did not become a clergy in the theological sense."[24]

The West chose secularism in response to religious war within the society. Islam did not have a Thirty Years War. As long as Jews and Christians paid their poll tax, did not bear arms, and remained within their religious community for matters of personal status, these fellow adherents to the religions of the book maintained a tolerable secondary place within society, superior to that of Jews in medieval Europe. However, in response to the expansion of the West during the last five hundred years, "The old pluralistic order, multidenominational and polyethnic, was breaking down, and the tacit social contract on which it was based was violated on both sides."[25] Christians would no longer accept less than full equality, and Muslims would no longer extend the old toleration. Internally, Islam seemed to have been influenced by Christian forms in developing some elements of a hierarchical clergy. Lewis focuses on the Ottoman system of muftis of place culminating in the Chief Mufti of Istanbul, and the recent rise of the position of ayatollah in Iran.

OUT OF INDIA: HINDUISM AND BUDDHISM

Judaism, Christianity, and Islam began in the deserts of the Middle East, and, even in their later Western, African, and Asian forms, reflect the historical worldviews of that region. For the spiritual descendants of Abraham, Hinduism remains the most difficult religious system to understand. The Hindu scholar Kim Knott comments:

Comparing Hinduism to Christianity, we see that it does indeed have a God – one ultimate reality and many gods and goddesses, in fact. But it has no founder, a multitude of scriptures rather than one book, brahmins but no priests in the Christian sense, and no central institution like a church. Ritual, myth, and ethics are important, but belief is of less significance, there being no core creed and few common teachings. But there might also be things intrinsic to Hinduism that just don't show up in a comparison with Christianity. For example, Hinduism extends into the complex socio-religious system of caste and the varied popular practices which, in Christian terms, constitute magic and superstition rather than religion.[26]

---

[24] Bernard Lewis, *What Went Wrong? Western Impact and Middle East Response* (Oxford: Oxford University Press, 2002), 98–99.

[25] Lewis, *Middle East Response*, 115.

[26] Kim Knott, *Hinduism: A Very Short Introduction* (Oxford: Oxford University Press, 1998), 109.

The complex history of India has contributed to the enormous variety of religious concepts and experiences associated with Hinduism. Around the beginning of the second millennium B.C.E. nomadic peoples from the northwest invaded India's northern half. These Aryans (their term for themselves means "nobles") brought their gods associated with heavenly phenomena – the sun, wind, storm, stars, rain, moon. The native darker-skinned inhabitants, the Dravidians, remained more devoted to their preexisting earthly pantheon – vegetation, animal life, rivers, and mountains. Recent excavations in the Indus valley have demonstrated the advanced level of the Dravidian civilization, so this was not a case of a more advanced people subjugating a culturally inferior one. The Aryans, however, did employ the more advanced military technology.

Both groups accepted elements of the other's beliefs and gradually they formed an uneven and highly diffuse system, composed of millions of gods, each an imperfect representation of ultimate reality. The favorite term for the supreme ultimate was Brahman, who is also known under the three forms of Brahman the creator, Vishnu the preserver, and Shiva the destroyer. Vishnu takes form in numerous *avatars* [incarnations], the most famous of which are Rama, Sita, and Krishna. The reader can thus appreciate how theologically inclusive Hinduism can be. Hinduism also differs from the religions of the book in that it has accepted the prevailing caste system that divides Indians into four social groups: priests, warriors/rulers, merchants, and ordinary laborers. Later, a lower fifth group of "untouchables" was added. Historically, caste reflects the traditional Indian divisions of labor and the social supremacy of the Aryan Brahmin priests, with the colors white, red, brown, and black associated with the four castes. The Dravidians were dark-skinned.

The Vedas, Hinduism's most revered scriptures, also reflect the dominance of the Aryans. The roles the Aryan gods, *Agni* [sun, fire], *Varuna* [sky, cosmic order], and *Indra* [storm], predominate. At the end of the Veda period, other anonymous authors crafted the *Upanishads*, which seek to add a more human element to the impersonal and terrifying aspects of traditional Hindu religion. Both the Vedas and the *Upanishads* are classed as revealed [*shruti*]. This revelation was internal, not external. Among those scriptures handed down [*smriti*] are the Epics such as the *Mahabharata* and the *Ramayana*, the *purana*, and the *sutras*. The Indian classic *Bhagavad-Gita*, which is part of the *Mahabharata*, offers the narrative of Krishna's instruction of the warrior prince Arjuna that the prince must above all follow his *dharma* [duty, law, teaching, order] in fighting his brothers. The *Bhagavad-Gita* and the *Ramayana* definitely constitute the best-loved expositions of the Hindu tradition. In 1987, every Sunday morning more than eighty million Indians watched a television production of the latter story of Ram. Hindu scholar T. N. Madan states that the *Gita* "has acquired in modern times the status of a central scripture, comparable to the Bible and the Qur'an. It is believed by many Hindus to be the word of God."[27]

Even if Hinduism did not develop a large ecclesiastical organization, the above traditions were passed down by three types of religious figures: the storyteller [*pandit*], the spiritual guide [*guru*], and the ascetic [*sannyasis, sadhu*]. A *shankara-acharya* [leader, master] had to be both a brahmin by caste and experienced as a guru. Hindus seek *moksha* [release] from *samsara* [the endless cycle of rebirth] through one of the three paths of intellect [*jnana yoga*], of action [*karma yoga*], or of devotion [*bhakti yoga*]. The key insight of the Vedic tradition and the *Upanishads* is the Sanskrit *tat tvam asi* [thou art that one], or that *Brahman* [the ultimate reality] and *atman* [the self] are one. But even this basic principle of the Shankara philosophical system is questioned by some later Hindu systems. Both Hinduism and Buddhism assert that yogistic discipline is the best method for liberation, hence this book's category of religion of meditative experience.

Traditional Hindu religious forms do not explain the current "church-state" relationship between the Hindu political party, the Bharatiya Janata Party (BJP), and the Indian state. The BJP emerged as a function of twentieth-century nationalism and modern advances in communication technology. The BJP ideology of *Hindutva* ["Hinduness"] took its first cue from early British scholarly treatments of Hinduism that limited it to the religious traditions of the Aryan people. The 1925 founder of the *Rashtriya Svayamsevak Sangh* [National Volunteer Association] (RSS), K. B. Hedgewar, left the Congress Party. He adopted the theories of V. D. Savarkar who had formulated his Hindu nationalist ideology in response to both an ideology of Muslim nationalism advocated by Sir Mohammed Iqbal and Congress's secular nationalism. In his *Essentials of Hinduism* (1922) Hedgewar based Indian nationhood on the cultural heritage of Aryan Hinduism.

Buddhism came out of the Hindu tradition. It was the Hindu problem of suffering, disease, and death through endless rebirths according to a person's *karma* [the results of good and bad actions] that the prince Guatama (c. 563–486) solved under the pipal tree. Gautama grew

---

[27] T. N. Madan, "Hinduism," Juergensmeyer, *Global*, 55.

up privileged and happy, but when he left his palace, he discovered death, disease, and physical decline. How could he enjoy any peace when faced with these imperfections in life? In an attempt to get an answer, he turned first to yoga teachers, then to extreme asceticism. Neither satisfied him. Finally, he vowed to sit under a certain pipal tree until he had the solution. The resulting enlightenment experience convinced him of Buddhism's noble truths: that all life is suffering, that suffering comes from desire, that removing desire removes suffering, and that the right way to remove desire is the Eightfold Path of right views, right intention, right speech, right conduct, right livelihood, right effort, right mindfulness, and right concentration. Guatama had become the Buddha (the Enlightened One), and he spent the rest of his life wandering through India preaching the "Middle Way" (neither extreme asceticism nor self-indulgence) of the Eightfold Path. Others came to join him and they formed the Buddhist monastic community, the *Sangha*, by taking vows of chastity, non-violence, and poverty.

Bimbisara (c. 540–490), king of North India's richest and most powerful state of Magadha, became Buddhism's great patron, and by 200 B.C.E. Buddhists were widespread in India. Like Christianity and Islam, but unlike the more amorphous Hinduism that is conceptualized as including a myriad of religious practices, Buddhism split into two separate ecclesiastical forms. The roots of this division can be found in the Buddhist monastic community within one hundred years after Buddha's death. One set of general names for these two groups were given by the adherents of the Mahayana [greater vehicle], who perceived that the Hinayana [lesser vehicle] focused too much on the individual's own spiritual advancement. The latter group calls itself Theravada [Way of the Elders]. In general, Theravadists tend to be more conservative theologically, insisting that Buddha was merely a saintly human being. Their spiritual practice fits more closely the spiritual needs of monks and nuns. Mahayanists allowed for much greater theological development in which the Buddha took on more and more supernatural qualities. They also focused their teaching on the laity, in Buddhist terms "the householder." These two Buddhist traditions coexisted in India for almost one thousand years before Buddhism declined on the subcontinent. Theravada devotees relocated to South Asian countries like Sri Lanka and Thailand, where that tradition remains a strong constituent of national politics. The Mahayana tradition went to East Asia along the Silk Road and ended up in China, Japan, Korea, and Vietnam.

CHINA AND JAPAN: CONFUCIANISM, BUDDHISM, AND MAOISM

Confucius (551–479 B.C.E.) lived at the same time as the Buddha. He grew up in an agricultural society whose religious moorings were anchored in a peasant society's appreciation for the power of nature and for the necessity of conforming one's life to the natural Way [*Dao*]. In Confucius's time, China experienced great warfare and duplicity from its nobles. Confucius asserted that the individual, perfected by moral education, could make a political difference, and substantiated this contention by pointing to the example of the past sages, who practiced wise government. Such an orientation to a past "Golden Age" is conservative, but Confucius's insistence on the natural nobility of ethics also contained the seeds for a social critique. The emperor ruled with the mandate of Heaven, but Heaven had bestowed the mandate conditionally. If the emperor failed to take care of the people, he theoretically forfeited the mandate. Heaven then bestowed that mandate on another dynasty, usually established by peasant rebellion. Such a theoretical framework allowed the Chinese to rationalize "the changing of the mandate" ["revolution" in Chinese]. In practice, starving peasants tend to rebel more than satisfied ones.

Confucius did not produce stirring and poetic religious documents like the Hindu Vedas, the Buddhist sutras, or the Qur'an. However, subsequent generations did possess a short book of his sayings, the *Analects*, collated from the notes of his disciples. These pithy sayings are striking for their originality, but they are open to considerable interpretation depending on the perspective of the reader. The major interpretive issue concerns the balance of control and inspiration needed to form the moral individual. Confucius's two greatest disciples, Mencius and Hsun Tzu, disagreed over whether human nature was good or bad. Hsun Tzu took the latter position, which led to the necessity of government control to inculcate moral discipline in the people. Some of the followers of this tendency formed the separate Legalist School. Its great exponent, Han Fei Tzu, advocated controlling politics by the two handles of favor and punishment alone, emphasizing clear laws and automatic sentences. Legalism formed the ideological foundation of the unification of China under the Qin Dynasty in the third century B.C.E., but it also fostered the dynasty's speedy collapse.

Confucianism and Legalism operated within the general cultural context of the various traditions of preexisting native Chinese religion, generally grouped as Daoism. Daoism, like Hinduism, includes a myriad of local practices. Creel[28] divides his treatment of Daoism into four general orientations: philosophical speculation, religious practices such as breathing, the study of *yin* and *yang*, and special practices such as trips to the Isles of the Blessed. All these approaches presuppose harmony in nature and seek to teach the adherent how to grasp immortality. Daoism exercised its greatest influence on Chinese politics through rebellion. Peasant sectarians employed a syncretist blend of various political, religious, and philosophical systems to attack the Neo-Confucian orthodoxy. Scholars often list four historical examples. First, the Yellow Turbans built their rural political-religious network on a nine-day confession ritual. It took the Han over twenty years to suppress the rebellion. Second, the White Lotus owed their five-hundred-year revolutionary legitimacy to the leadership of a "fairy fox" (shaman) family from Stone Buddha Village. Finally, Qing officials discovered a list of adherents and destroyed the group, beheading the men and sending the women to work on the Great Wall. Third, Chapter 3 has already mentioned the Taiping rebellion led by "Jesus Christ's younger brother." And fourth, in 1900, the Empress Dowager Cixi encouraged another secret society, the Boxers, to attempt to drive the foreigners out of China. The Boxers believed they were impervious to enemy bullets.

Confucianism developed into a national ideology over the centuries by adding insights from other traditions. Its most significant political form, called Neo-Confucianism, arose during the Sung Dynasty (960–1279 C.E.). In 1190 the scholar Chu Hsi published the *Analects*, the *Great Learning*, the *Doctrine of the Mean*, and *Mencius* as the official Four Books of Confucian study. This compilation and Chu Hsi's commentaries served as the required texts for the public examinations of the official scholar class for six hundred years, from 1313 to 1906. This gave Neo-Confucianism enormous political and social influence as this three-tiered (county, province, empire) examination process controlled all upward mobility in Chinese society. In philosophical terms, Neo-Confucianism added cosmological speculation, meditation for individual development, and a special concern with death to the original Confucian message of the *Analects*. It thus responded to the challenge of Mahayana Buddhist metaphysics and spirituality for the Chinese soul.

For adherents of the religions of the book, the Confucian tradition seems closer to a moral philosophy than a religion. Indeed, at first glance, religion does not seem to be particularly important in Chinese society.

---

[28] H. G. Creel, *What Is Taoism?* (Chicago: University of Chicago Press, 1970).

In responding to this objection, C. K. Yang points to the diffused rather than the independent nature of Chinese religion. Like Hinduism in India, Chinese religion is "a religion having its theology, cultus, and personnel so intimately diffused into one or more secular social institutions that they become a part of the concept, rituals, and structure of the latter, thus having no significant independent existence."[29] Yang's book demonstrates that Chinese religion interpenetrates every Chinese institution, from the family through social and economic organizations to the state and rebellious political sects.

Buddhism came to China both from Vietnam in the south and along the Silk Road in the west, probably first with traders. The exposure heightened when Indian missionaries came, and finally when Chinese students of Buddhism made the arduous trip to India. A similar process took place throughout Asia. Indeed, Reischauer and Fairbank term the period from the mid-fourth century to the ninth century as "the Buddhist age of Asian history, or perhaps of world history. . . . It [Buddhism] blanketed the whole of the Asian continent, except for Siberia and the Near East, giving this vast area a degree of cultural unity that has never been matched since then."[30] At the beginning of this period the Chinese state had fallen apart. Buddhism attracted the upper classes because of its high moral and intellectual plane, noble literature, and aesthetic ceremonies. Monastic life also offered an oasis of peace in a troubled era. Furthermore, Mahayana Buddhism appealed to many East Asians because it tended to add supernatural characteristics to the historical Buddha. It also revered Buddhist saints or *bodhisattvas* such as the motherly Guanyin, much venerated by the Chinese. Thus, when Buddhism reached Chinese intellectual circles, it impressed scholars with its affinities to native Chinese Daoism.

Some Japanese began to adopt Buddhism as their first conscious borrowing of Chinese civilization that resulted in the wholesale copying from China in the Taika Reform of 646. Reischauer points out that "Buddhism first came to Japan in the sixth century and played much the same role as Christianity in northern Europe as the vehicle for the transmission of a whole higher culture."[31] Buddhism appealed to the political elite because it could provide a unifying higher theology absent in the native Shinto [the

[29] C. K. Yang, *Religion in Chinese Society* (Berkeley: University of California Press, 1961), 295.

[30] Edwin O. Reischauer and John K. Fairbank, *East Asia: The Great Tradition* (Boston: Houghton Mifflin, 1960), 147–48.

[31] Edwin Reischaur, *The Japanese Today: Change and Continuity* (Cambridge, MA: Belnap, 1988), 206.

way of the gods]. From the beginning, the Japanese mixed Buddhism and Shinto, but until the Tokugawa period, Buddhism remained the stronger element. Reischauer then lists three additional emphases in Mahayana Buddhism and locates their coming to Japan in three periods. First, "esoteric" Buddhism with its magical formulas, ritual, and arts arrived in the ninth century. One century later, the Japanese focused on salvation through faith, particularly in Amida Buddha of the "pure land" of the Western paradise. Finally, the various types of Zen stressed self-reliance and self-discipline in meditation. This mix of Buddhism and Daoism that became Ch'an [Zen in Japanese] Buddhism in China, found a special resonance with the Japanese military class. Zen came to Japan in the warlike Kamakura period (1185–1336).

This spiritual amalgamation, plus the social emphasis on clans, reinforced the role of the group versus that of the individual in Japanese society. Not much of Buddhist influence survives in contemporary Japan, however, "after the savage destruction of the political power of Buddhist institutions by the unifiers of Japan in the late sixteenth century, the three centuries of the progressive secularization of society that followed, and a ruthless attack by the early Meiji government on Buddhism as an element of the discredited past that stood in the way of the creation of an emperor-centered new political system."[32] But things got even worse. When the Meiji reformers attacked institutional Buddhism, its leaders, as did those of the newly enfranchised Christians, sought to prove their worth by an exaggerated patriotism and support for Japan's expansion into East Asia. "By the end of the 1920s," states the Soto Zen priest Victoria, "institutional Buddhism had firmly locked itself into ideological support for Japan's ongoing military efforts, wherever and whenever they might occur."[33]

In his two books (1997, 2003), Victoria documents the long tortured reasoning of those leaders as they sought to marry a tradition strongly biased against taking life to an imperial war effort. Zen Buddhism, with its emphasis on meditation and its long association with Bushido [the way of the warrior] had an advantage over the other sects in articulating "imperial way Buddhism." Buddhist leaders proposed their religion as the core of what made the various countries of the East Asia Co-Prosperity Sphere united in their opposition to the Western powers. From this perspective, the invasion of China became "an act of Buddhist compassion

[32] Reischauer, Japanese Today, 206.
[33] Brian Victoria, Zen at War (Tokyo: Weatherhill, Inc., 1997), 63.

which benefited the Chinese." All Japanese Buddhist sects sent missionaries with the Japanese troops who served as chaplains, promoters of Japanese culture, and even espionage agents. No wonder that in January 1992, the Soto Zen sect issued a statement of repentance, which included the following: "We forthrightly confess the serious mistakes we committed in the past history of our overseas missionary work, and we wish to deeply apologize and express our repentance to the peoples of Asia and the world.... Moreover, these actions are not merely the responsibility of those people who were directly involved in overseas missionary work. Needless to say, the responsibility of the entire sect must be questioned inasmuch as we applauded Japan's overseas aggression and attempted to justify it."[34] Some of the subsequent Buddhist apologies, for example, that of Secretary General Keiitsu Hosokawa of the Zen headquarters temple Myoshin-ji in September 2002, have stated that Victoria's research "provided the impetus" for their actions.[35]

Whether or not Buddhism will further develop social ethics and social organizations will greatly influence future political roles. Chapter 2 referred to the ecumenical peace work of the Cambodian Buddhist primate Ghosananda as an example of "Engaged Buddhism." Buddhist leaders from this point of view have formed the International Network of Engaged Buddhists (INEB) and the Buddhist Peace Fellowship (BPF). In the 1970s and 1980s, the BPF focused on the arms race, but now both organizations have developed interests in the environment, human rights, and conflict resolution. The Vietnamese monk Thich Nhat Hanh, who left Vietnam in 1966, has worked with American veterans to encourage them to foster a public awareness of the cruelty of war. Now he encourages the victims of AIDS to an analogous task, to "be nourished by the bodhisattva idea," to advocate compassion for those who have the condition.[36]

Unlike Buddhism, Confucianism starts with social ethics, so the central political dynamic is both ideological and organizational. The ideological issue focuses on the balance between state support and state criticism. Both currents exist in the *Analects*, but subsequent state-sponsored Neo-Confucianism sought to lessen the critical element. The Chinese state found its ideal organizational form by making access to officialdom depend upon studying the designated Four Books along with the approved

[34] Victoria, *War*, 154–55.
[35] January 11, 2003.
[36] December 2, 2000.

commentaries. The Mandarin scholar class thus constituted the sole governmental leadership by combining both ideological and organizational functions. Foreign independent religions such as Buddhism, Catholicism, and Protestantism all found initial acceptance in periods of social and political crisis, but no long-term roles as autonomous organizations.

Because religion was diffused throughout Chinese society, both the Chinese State and rebellious organizations such as the Yellow Turbans, the White Lotus, and the Taiping constituted political-religious entities. To be heterodox religiously was to be heterodox politically, and vice versa. That meant that the Chinese state always sought to penetrate, regulate, and control Chinese religion.[37] For example, the Confucian state reserved the right to worship Heaven to the emperor and limited the number of Buddhist monks to be ordained. It even established a Daoist pope to facilitate controlling those habitually pesky Daoist monks with their idiosyncratic religious practices. The more the Confucian state failed to provide security and sustenance, the more both scholars and peasants were disposed to accept world religions and native heterodox sects. Both world religions and heretical sects tended to survive best in the rural areas and in politically marginal areas where the people had already experienced alternative forms of political-religious legitimacy, plus elite betrayal and suppression of peasants. Mao came from just such an area in Hunan Province.

The Confucian state failed to meet the challenge of the late nineteenth and early twentieth-century West. As the Qing dynasty expired of its own corruption and inefficiency under Chinese reactionaries such as the Empress Dowager Cixi, reformers such as the Mandarin scholar Kang Youwei, and revolutionaries such as the Westernized doctor Sun Yat-sen failed to find a satisfactory Chinese response to the expansion of the West. For most educated Chinese, the searing national question remained: "Where will China find salvation from imperialist exploitation?" The Hunanese peasant Mao Zedong, operating in and assisted by the political chaos of China during the first half of the twentieth century, finally found the answer. Mao adapted the Marxist-Leninist ideology and organization of the Soviet Communist Party to the Chinese situation. His seminal insight, gleaned from the Hunan Peasant Uprising of 1926, was that the peasants could be the major force in revolutionary struggle.

---

[37] Supporting this thesis for Chinese, Korean, and Vietnamese politics is Eric O. Hanson, *Catholic Politics in China and Korea* (Maryknoll, NY: Orbis Books, 1980).

When Mao proclaimed the new People's Republic of China (PRC) from the rostrum of Tiananmen on October 1, 1949, he followed in the tradition of previous Chinese dynasties that claimed both organizational and ideological hegemony. All religious groups must actively support the party and the government. CCP religious policy followed the fluctuations of general state policy. For example, the government demonstrated the least tolerance during the radical periods of the Great Leap Forward (1957–59) and the Cultural Revolution (1966–76). But, no matter what the policy, the Chinese state sought to penetrate, regulate, and control religion. During moderate times, the state Religious Affairs Bureau (RAB) accomplished this penetration, regulation, and control. In radical periods, the government used all its institutions to attack religion in all its forms, driving both world religions and native sectarians underground.

Party ideological policy, based on Mao's personality cult, most approximated revivalist religion during the Cultural Revolution. In the fall of 1966, more than eleven million youth met in Tiananmen Square liturgies to cheer the godlike Chairman Mao before spreading out over the entire country to purify the nation of the "four olds": old ideas, old culture, old habits, and old customs. State radio broadcast new Communist-style marriages and funerals. A sixtieth birthday celebration that, analogous to the Jewish Seder's remembrance of the exile in Egypt, recalled the bitter days before Mao's victory. The Red Guards targeted the heretical "Capitalist Roaders" of the party and state bureaucracies. State president Liu Shaoqi was vilified as China's "Capitalist Roader No. 1" and "China's Khrushchev." In this populist attack on the Chinese establishment, Mao relied on the idealism of the students and the firepower of the national army, symbolized by the Little Red Book's preface written by Minister of Defense Lin Biao. But the army and the students failed Mao in important ways. His "Closest Comrade in Arms" Lin Biao morphed into a traitor and died in a plane crash while fleeing to the Soviet Union in 1971. The announcement of Lin's fall from grace constituted the death knell of popular belief in Maoist ideology. In commenting on Mao's failure as a political leader after 1957, Stuart Schram states:

Mao's tragedy is that of a man who has striven all his life to adapt to new and strange conditions and ideas, who had succeeded in doing this far better than most of his contemporaries, and who then discovers that the world with which he has sought to come to terms for half a century no longer exists, or in any case has been so profoundly modified that old formulas and old ideas are no longer applicable. Having begun life as a tradition-oriented Hunanese nationalist, he soon acquired the radically untraditional goal of breaking the grip of superstition, custom, and hierarchical social structure on the lives of his compatriots, so that they might freely turn their energies to building a new China.[38]

Unlike the Soviet Union's emphasis on the urban proletariat, the Marxist revolution in China succeeded and failed at the village level. Richard Madsen characterizes the revolution's eventual failure in this rural milieu as the result of Mao and the CCP's inability to combine the strengths of various Chinese leadership styles, both traditional and modern. Madsen's four competing styles all had something to offer the Chinese village, but when used exclusively, led to disaster. "When Maoism exploded into absurdity, the moral basis of Chinese culture disintegrated into its diverse themes. The Communist gentry, the Communist rebel, the moralistic revolutionary, and the peasant technocrat emerged in all their one-sided, incompatible purity. Being thus one-dimensionally moral as persons, they became immoral as politicians. And thus Chinese political culture became demoralized – an ironic, tragic end for Mao's attempt at moral revolution."[39]

As a result the Chinese nation suffered a crisis of faith, and embraced the new materialism offered by Mao's successor, Deng Xiaoping, at the beginning of the 1980s. The moral, ethical, and spiritual vacuums expanded as the traditional networks of *guanxi* [connections] returned as the principal informal structure for Chinese society. In crafting the successful Chinese revolution, Mao both directly attacked and borrowed from Confucianism. Mao sought to erase the decadent vestiges of Confucian ideology, for example, the separation of the work of the mind from the work of the body symbolized by the long fingernails of the elite. Communist cadres, however, reproduced the Mandarin scholar's dual ideological and organizational legitimacy.

The Chinese Cultural Revolution constituted the strongest example of religion diffused in radical politics. Mao and his successors also have offered the people a true Communist saint in Lei Feng, a heroically altruistic orphan soldier who supposedly died by being crushed by a telephone pole in 1962. Such populist "model worker" hagiography has been tried in all Marxist states, but it especially fits China's traditional Confucian moralism. Each time the Chinese people face new suffering, as in the current social dislocations from unbridled capitalism, "Learn from Lei Feng"

---

[38] Stuart Schram, *The Political Thought of Mao Tse-tung*, rev. ed. (New York: Praeger, 1969), 139.

[39] Richard Madsen, *Morality and Power in a Chinese Village* (Berkeley: University of California Press, 1984), 262.

campaigns surface again, this time on posters next to Sony billboards. According to a recent article sent out by the New China News Agency, there is "something in Lei Feng's spirit that can help solve some of the most pressing problems in modern China, like the reform of state-owned enterprises, which has led to massive layoffs of redundant workers."[40]

[40] April 16, 2000.

PART II

RELIGION IN CONTEMPORARY
WORLD POLITICS

5

The West

Christianity, Secularization, and Immigration

This book proposes a post–Cold War paradigm based on the interaction between the contemporary globalizations of the political and EMC systems and the political role of religion at the local, national, regional, and global levels. The political and EMC systems constantly create new, and very complicated, environments in which individuals and societies must make rapid choices on the basis of their perceived personal and communal identities (Who am I? Who are we?). The religious response to political choices depends mainly on three factors: the level of political-religious interaction, from local to global; the nature of the religion, from religions of the book like Christianity to religions of meditative experience like Buddhism; and the regional or national form of political-religious interaction, from the partially secularized West to Islamist Iran. Religion constitutes an autonomous sphere of human activity, but not a system.

This second half of the book, Chapters 5–10, examines religion and politics in the contemporary world to demonstrate the usefulness of the proposed paradigm for understanding international affairs. The reader will grasp that usefulness by focusing on two factors: the horizontal and vertical integration of the four global systems; and the response of the disparate types of political-religious ideologies and organizations to those globalizations. Each of these chapters, then, emphasizes the regional interaction of the political and EMC systems with the major characteristic impacts of religion at the various levels of politics. Chapter 5 begins this analysis with the West because Europe and the Anglo countries, for better or for ill, currently exercise disproportionate global influence. For that reason, Chapter 1 employed examples like Yugoslavia, Chechnya, and the

Iraq War to demonstrate contemporary U.S. primacy in all four global systems and the supporting interaction among these systems. That chapter also emphasized the current tensions between American and European interests and viewpoints that threaten the unity of the West.

Since World War II, the U.S. president has been the instrumental leader of the West, while the pope has been its expressive leader. U.S. Presidents Ronald Reagan and George H. Bush cooperated with John Paul II in ending the Cold War, but George W. Bush and the same pope split over the U.S. attack on Iraq. When Bush 43 visited John Paul II in June 2004, the pope reminded him of "the unequivocal position" of the Vatican in opposing the war. The pope added that "In the past weeks, certain deplorable events [Abu Ghraib prison] have come to light which have troubled the civic and religious conscience of all, and made difficult a serene and resolute commitment to shared human values." That the pope and the great majority of Western religious leaders opposed the war should have given the president pause. The president had requested the meeting, partially at least, because he hoped his photos with John Paul II would help his campaign against Catholic Democrat John Kerry in crucial electoral states such as Florida, Ohio, and Pennsylvania. The pope did praise the president for "[his] commitment to the promotion of moral values in American society."[1]

THE RISE OF THE RELIGIOUS RIGHT IN THE UNITED STATES

The precipitous rise of the political influence of the Religious Right has constituted the most significant religious trend in American politics over the last three decades. *Roe v. Wade* and other Supreme Court decisions roused fundamentalists to enter national politics in defense of "traditional moral values." The increasing use of direct mail, pioneered by New Right leader Richard Viguerie, augmented the financial power of televangelism. The Religious Right threw its full power behind Ronald Reagan in the election of 1980. That year the director of the Committee for the Survival of a Free Congress, Paul Weyrich, joined Viguerie and Jerry Falwell in the formation of the Moral Majority to promote conservative virtue in public life. Although Falwell insisted that such

---

[1] June 5, 2004. "The Vatican," of course, judged that involvement with the "concrete aspects" of U.S. politics was "not our business," especially with major objections to both candidates. Vatican watcher John L. Allen, however, estimated that a slight majority of Vatican prelates would support Kerry "At the end of the day the Vatican is a European institution." October 24, 2004.

political initiatives remained separate from his religious and educational activities, it was often hard to separate the themes of Christianity and patriotism in both. After all, evangelicals felt that the United States had always drawn its main social and political strength from dissenting Protestantism. The relationship of evangelical Protestantism to other religions, however, has remained ambivalent. Although Weyrich and Viguerie were conservative Catholics, many members of the Moral Majority had a long history of tense relations with "Roman papists." Direct mailing put a premium on highlighting moral issues in the most alarming rhetoric to maximize donations, thus working against temperate language, let alone ecumenism.

When Ronald Reagan finished his two terms, the 1988 presidential campaign presented an almost perfect referendum on the three general types of American Protestantism. The candidates included Walter Mondale, representing Minnesota mainline Protestant virtue, Jesse Jackson from the black evangelical tradition, and the televangelist Pat Robertson. When the secular Yankee aristocrat George H. Bush won the presidency, Robertson came to understand that the Moral Majority lacked sufficient numbers to elect a president. The movement, he decided, must reach out to other groups concerned with traditional values, most importantly Catholics and blacks. He then formed the Christian Coalition, which eventually targeted programs to both constituencies. This fundamentalist hope of American moral reform reached its zenith in the Congressional elections of 1994 when Newt Gingrich led the Republicans to victory in the House of Representatives. Gingrich's Contract with America did support traditional morality, but, as with Reagan, conservative political leaders delivered more on speech rhetoric rather than on policy substance. Four years later Gary Bauer, president of the Family Research Council and presidential candidate in 2000, commented that, "There is virtually nothing to show for an 18-year commitment [of religious fundamentalists to the Republican party]."[2]

Gingrich and other party politicians did embrace the most popular religious issues such as the ending of late-term abortions, the $500-a-child tax credit, and the Freedom From Religious Persecution Act, but in general, Republican leaders have restricted their actions on social issues such as abortion, school prayer, and Gay Marriage to energizing their base. Conservative Christian spokespersons Cal Thomas and Ed Dobson detailed the spiritual complications resulting from the politicization of

[2] March 23, 1998.

religion in *Blinded by Might: Can the Religious Right Save America?*[3]
Their conclusions coincided with the deepest wellsprings of the dissenter
tradition that has always eschewed the close identification of religious
faith with the government and its works. By 1999, the Christian Coalition
had a $2.5 million debt. Almost all of its senior leadership had resigned,
divulging questionable practices used to inflate the number of Coalition
supporters, including moving the same employees around to different
offices to fool visiting newspaper reporters.[4] When Ralph Reed left the
organization in 1997, his successor was stunned to find that he had inherited a $3 million debt. Jerry Falwell responded by contributing $1 million,
and the organization had to close its outreach to Catholics and blacks in
the "Christmas massacre" at the end of the year.

In the 2000 election, 40 percent of George Bush's votes came from
evangelical Christians. This gave the Religious Right enhanced entrée to
the White House, especially through political adviser Karl Rove. Such
influence raised the profile of issues like the Sudanese civil war, persecution of Christians, sex trafficking, and AIDs that already had general
backing from both religious conservatives and religious liberals. The perfect spokesman for such issues was U.N. ambassador John C. Danforth,
Anglican priest and ex-Republican senator from Missouri. The Ralston
Purina heir had already served as Bush's special envoy to Sudan, and his
appointment in July 2003 signaled the administration's desire to patch up
its relations with the world body in the wake of Iraq. Richard Cizik, vice
president for governmental affairs for the National Association of Evangelicals, commented on his group's current openness to broader coalitions.
"Evangelicals have thought historically, 'Well, we'll do politics the way
we do faith – we'll just convert the opposition.' But you can't do politics
the same way you do religion."[5]

Contentious national political debate between the Religious Right and
liberals, both secular and religious, peaked over the impeachment of Bill
Clinton. Haynes Johnson chronicles both the bitterness of the debate
and the fundamentalist pressure for maintaining the attack in the face
of national popular disapproval. For example, Johnson observes that
Jerry Falwell's TV program showed two patently biased videos, *Circle*

[3] Cal Thomas and Ed Dobson, *Blinded by Might: Can the Religious Right Save America?*
(Grand Rapids, MI: Zondervan, 1999).
[4] August 2, 1999.
[5] October 26, 2003.

of Power and *The Clinton Chronicles*, thus introducing these films to the Moral Majority and evangelical churches at large. Both conspiratorial videos highlighted the mysterious deaths of countless people who had opposed Clinton in Arkansas.[6] The Clinton investigation generated enormous political-religious controversy as ministers and intellectuals waded into the fray on both sides. For example, the entire third section of the 2000 Brookings book *What's God Got To Do With the American Experiment?* consists of such pieces by professors Patrick Glynn, Alan Wolfe, Max Stackhouse, Jean Bethke Elshtain, and the president's personal minister, Tony Campolo, who ruefully reports on receiving angry criticism from many of his fellow evangelists.[7]

Although the U.S. public is the most polarized it has been since Pew began such polling in 1987, the American public takes much more centrist and nuanced moral positions than do the political and religious elites. On the most contentious issue of abortion, for example, the *Wall Street Journal* found that opinion segments into five separate positions with at least 10 percent support, from "favor abortion in all instances" (27 percent) to "oppose abortion in all instances" (17 percent). The plurality (36 percent) favors the most centrist position "oppose abortion, except under special circumstances [rape, incest, and the mother's health]."[8] Many analysts have recently attempted to explain the increasingly polarizing role of U.S. political leadership, from Florida 2000 electoral bitterness and September 11, to the impact of the shrill media (The O'Reilly Factor versus Al Franken), to "professionals" versus "managers,"[9] to "the God Gulf."[10] In *The Diminishing Divide: Religion's Changing Role in American Politics* (2000), Pew survey researchers document both the public's more centrist orientation on issues than that of the elite and the traditional influence of religious affiliation on voting patterns. Andrew Kohut states: "In the 1990s, evangelical and mainline Protestants – particularly the most committed members of these groups – tended to be Republicans, while less committed white Protestants, black Protestants, Jews, and seculars tended to be Democrats. Catholics were divided, with the committed tending

---

[6] Haynes Johnson, *The Best of Times: America in the Clinton Years* (New York: Harcourt, Inc., 2001), 258.

[7] E. J. Dionne Jr. and John J. DiJulio, eds., *What's God Got To Do With the American Experiment?* (Washington, DC: Brookings Institution Press), 106–11.

[8] *Wall Street Journal*, May 6, 2004.

[9] David Brooks, "Bitter At The Top," June 15, 2004.

[10] Nicholas D. Kristof, "Hold The Vitriol," July 3, 2004.

toward the GOP and the less committed toward the Democrats."[11] Because no religion-based political majority exists, we would expect both political parties to seek to craft majority coalitions. They have not disappointed us.

The ideal Republican religious coalition would combine evangelicals and Catholics to secure an electoral majority. It is precisely this coalition that George W. Bush, despite his campaign debacle at traditionally anti-Catholic Bob Jones University, pursued vigorously. Bush 43's Texas roots help foster links with the traditionally Democratic constituency of socially conservative Hispanic Catholics, which in 2004 he only lost 39/59.[12] "Old ethnic" White Catholics of European Descent (WCED) like the Irish and the Italians present a separate political challenge. At the 2001 University of Notre Dame's graduation ceremony, Bush delivered what *The New York Times* religion editor and centrist Catholic intellectual Peter Steinfels described as "a superbly crafted address, clear, eloquent and filled, like some of his other speeches, with sentiments about both personal and governmental responsibility to combat poverty that could have won as much agreement on the left of the political spectrum as on the right."[13] Bush even quoted the Catholic pacifist Dorothy Day. In fact, Bush's "compassionate conservatism," including its advocacy for Faith Based Organizations (FBO), has often adopted themes from Catholic neo-conservative intellectuals like Richard John Neuhaus and Michael Novak. The FBO initiative was originally led by Catholic Penn professor John DiJulio, who had experienced an "epiphany – a conversion of heart, a conversion of mind" at Mass on Palm Sunday 1996.[14] In 1994 Father Neuhaus and former Nixon

[11] Andrew Kohut, John C. Green, Scott Keeter, and Robert C. Toth, *The Diminishing Divide: Religion's Changing Role in American Politics* (Washington, DC: The Brookings Institution, 2000), 123–24. For the most sophisticated U.S. grouping of religions, see John C. Green's "The American Religious Landscape and Political Attitutes: A Baseline for 2004." It lists multiple groups and their percentage of the population: White Evangelical Protestants (26.3), White Mainline Protestants (16), White Roman Catholics (17.5), Black Protestants (9.6), Latino Protestants (2.8), Latino Catholics (4.5), Other Christians (2.7), Other Faiths (2.7), Jews (1.9), Unaffiliated Believers (5.3), Unaffiliated Seculars (7.5), and Unaffiliated Atheists and Agnostics (3.2). Then he divides Evangelical Protestants, Mainline Protestants, and Catholics into Traditionalists, Centrist and Modernists. Reported by Peter Steinfels, October 9, 2004.

[12] Percentages for the 2004 presidential election come from the Edison/Mitofsky national exit surveys commissioned by the National Election Pool, a consortium of ABC News, Associated Press, CBS News, CNN, Fox News, and NBC News. See November 4, 5, 7, 2004.

[13] May 26, 2001.

[14] February 9, 2001.

aide Charles Colson started a joint evangelical-Catholic group of religious leaders and theologians that included Campus Crusade for Christ's Bill Bright, Pat Robertson, Cardinal John O'Connor, and theologian Avery Dulles. In the communication system, Catholics and evangelicals both flocked to Mel Gibson's *The Passion of the Christ*, but the best-selling evangelical book series *Left Behind* features a dastardly Catholic cardinal assistant to the Antichrist in the older evangelical tradition.

For their "moral values" campaign, Bush strategists vigorously pursued campaign connections with religious leaders. The above Bush visit to the Vatican aimed at causing problems for Kerry by encouraging Catholic bishops to focus Catholic voters on personal moral issues, not the war or the economy. These bishops, it was hoped, might even completely under-cut the legitimacy of pro-choice Catholic candidates by withholding Com-munion. In late 2003, Archbishop Raymond L. Burke, then of La Crosse, Wisconsin and now of St. Louis, announced such a policy for his dio-cese. Few bishops followed suit, however, and the issue became more and more contentious in the months that followed. The Pope even warned the U.S. bishops about forming factions. In May, forty-eight Catholic Demo-cratic members of Congress, including those who opposed abortion, sent a strongly critical letter to Cardinal Archbishop Theodore McCarrick of Washington, DC. Finally, in June the bishops met and passed a compro-mise declaration that reaffirmed the individual bishop's right to make such regulations, but neither endorsed nor criticized withholding Com-munion.[15] As in the pedophile crisis, the entire interaction demonstrated Catholic near autonomy at the local diocesan level, and its fragmentation at the national level. In the 2004 election WCEDs voted 56/43 for Bush, with Hispanic Catholics voting 58/39 for Kerry. The Catholic total (27 percent of the voters) was 52/47 for Bush, exactly the same ratio as the second Reagan vote. In the meantime, Democratic presidential candidates had won the 1992 (44/35), 1996 (53/37), and 2000 (49/47) Catholic votes. In 2004 Catholic votes became particularly significant in Pennsylvania, Florida, and the crucial decision-state, Ohio (Bush 55/43). Kerry visited many black churches, but the Democrats failed to mount an effective religious counterattack to churches in general.

In the case of evangelicals (23 percent of voters), the Bush campaign's attempt to use "friendly congregations" as an organizational base fostered public controversy. Bush strategists like the former head of the Chris-tian Coalition, Ralph Reed, viewed the Southern Baptist Convention as

---

[15] June 19, 2004.

friendly territory. At the SBC's 2004 meeting in Indianapolis, Mr. Reed sponsored a Bush "pastors reception." Dr. Jack Graham stated that he did not host the reception as the outgoing SBC president, but as "Jack Graham the person."[16] White evangelicals voted 78/21 for Bush, Hispanic evangelicals 60/39 for Bush, and black evangelicals 83/16 for Kerry. Even white evangelicals, however, do not constitute automatic Republicans, as fellow SBC member Jimmy Carter demonstrated in his 1976 campaign. The current primary spokesperson for such evangelicals is Jim Wallis, whose 2005 book *God's Politics: Why the Right Gets It Wrong and the Left Doesn't Get It*, is endorsed on the back cover by Bono, Bill Moyers, Desmond Tutu, E. J. Dionne Jr., and Cornell West. The above survey data does suggest, however, that a "God gulf" could continue to be lethal to a Democratic Party run by too secular a national leadership, especially in the former confederacy where Bush won by roughly five million votes, thus influencing many Congressional races. Bush also improved his showing among Jewish voters (three percent of electorate), to 25 percent of the vote. With California and New York ceded to Kerry, Jewish voters remained disproportionately crucial in Florida, Ohio, and Missouri. Republican pollster Frank Luntz found that the president got two-thirds of the Orthodox vote.[17]

Kohut's polling showed that "Americans have grown increasingly tolerant of closer links between religion and politics" and that "the new connections between religion and politics are a product of increased political activity among religious people."[18] How, then, can we account for the active role of religion in current United States politics? In addition to the prior treatments of the impact of American civil religion and fundamentalist outrage over Court decisions, Jelen and Wilcox focus institutionally on the "porous, undisciplined nature of American [political] parties" that greatly increases the significance of all interest groups, not just religious ones. U.S. political parties remain less structured and doctrinal than those of Europe. Candidates often must compete against members of the same party in primaries, thus leading to highly individual coalitions of interest groups. In addition, the federal system of national, state, and local politics gives religious groups and social movements multiple entry points to advocate particular issues.[19]

---

[16] June 18, 2004.
[17] November 5, 2004.
[18] Kohut, *Diminishing Divide*, 123–25.
[19] Ted Jelen and Clyde Wilcox, *Religion and Politics in Comparative Perspective: The One, the Few, and the Many* (Cambridge: Cambridge University Press), 300–01.

ANGLO SOCIETIES: PROTESTANT, CATHOLIC, JEWISH, AND THE NEW IMMIGRANTS

U.S. church attendance, while falling, remains strong. For many scholars, this American religiousness has always constituted the bedrock of "American exceptionalism," those characteristics that make the United States radically different from Europe. Over 90 percent of Americans believe in God. Continued immigration will gradually raise the percentages of Catholics, Pentecostals, and non-Christians, the latter well described by Diana Eck in her study of *A New Religious America*.[20] The social parameters of American religion have also changed greatly during the postwar period. The Princeton sociologist Robert Wuthrow grounds his analysis of the changing nature of American spirituality since the 1950s on the progressive urbanization of the country. In 1950, when half of the U.S. population lived on farms or in cities of less than ten thousand, Americans belonged to small churches and practiced "dwelling-oriented spirituality" that focused on affirming their relationships to the "sacred space" of the churches and to home. Twenty years later, life had become much more mobile and urban, and families less stable. Many Americans, describing themselves as "spiritual, not religious," have rejected the stability of denominational membership for a "seeker-oriented spirituality" emphasizing individual choice from a multitude of "religious retailers." In reaction, the 1980s saw a vigorous return to their religious past for a minority who realized the difficulties and superficialities ("spirituality lite") of constructing spirituality on their own. Others joined New Age religions or focused on miraculous experiences with angels. And the number of secularists and nonreligious people increased.[21]

Although earlier tensions existed primarily between religions, the subsequent tensions have more and more pitted members of the same religion against each other. For example, in October 2000 Jimmy Carter, in what he termed "a painful decision," severed ties with the Southern Baptist Convention because its "increasingly rigid" doctrine violated the "basic premises of my Christian faith." Carter's letter reached seventy-five thousand Baptists four months after the SBC had declared its opposition to female pastors. The Convention's president, fellow Georgian Rev. James G. Merritt responded that, "We felt the need to turn our denomination

---

[20] Diana L. Eck, *A New Religious America: How a "Christian Country" Has Become the World's Most Religiously Diverse Nation* (San Francisco: Harper, 2001).

[21] Robert Wuthrow, *The Restructuring of American Religion* (Princeton, NJ: Princeton University Press, 1988), 44–45.

back to a more conservative theology, and for whatever reason, the president did not agree with that."[22]

Since the 1960s, the mainline Protestant churches, then the establishment majority, have weakened in numbers as fundamentalist ones have strengthened. Mainline churches advocated the social gospel at that time of cultural upheaval, and subsequently suffered some loss of activists to civil rights and other progressive organizations. Indeed, mainline congregations like the United Methodist Church have continued to advocate liberal social values in their doctrinal statements. Richard Parker summarizes as follows: "Even a cursory reading of this [statement of "Social Principles"] and similar Methodist resolutions indicates that the Methodists' vision is much more progressive than anything emanating from Democratic Party platforms or policies in the past thirty years – and represents claims that are meant to serve as core social teachings for more than 10 million Americans."[23]

The most significant religious trend among mainline Protestantism has been the ecumenical joining of various denominations. In August 1999, the country's largest Lutheran denomination, the Evangelical Lutheran Church in America (ECLA), voted to enter into "full communion" with the Episcopal Church, forming a body of nearly eight million Christians. The agreement means that the two denominations fully recognize each other's members and sacraments, exchange clergy if appropriate, and cooperate in social service projects. Two years earlier, the ELCA had signed similar agreements with three churches in the Reformed tradition: the Presbyterian Church (U.S.A.), the United Church of Christ, and the Reformed Church in America.[24] Such ecumenical agreements, however, have not been embraced by all the clergy and laity. Just as some Anglicans have converted to Catholicism over their church's ordination of women, others have refused to accept the Lutheran-Anglican compromise statement on the role of bishops. A few Anglican priests have also placed themselves under more conservative African bishops, thus exhibiting a conservative religious facet of globalization.

U.S. Catholicism also constitutes a hybrid of religious influences as it digests its national rise to social and economic prominence and the many religious changes of the Second Vatican Council. Weekly church

[22] October 21, 2000.
[23] Richard Parker, "Progressive Politics and Visions," Dionne and DiJulio, *American Experiment*, 61.
[24] August 20, 1999.

attendance decreased from 1968 to 1975, but that decline has mitigated. WCEDs who were going to leave the church over birth control have left. The majority stayed for community and sacramental values, but not to embrace completely episcopal positions on sexual and ecclesiastical matters. The shortage of clerics also has put major strains on the ecclesiastical organization, and the recent pedophilia crisis has weakened both the moral stature and the financial position of the American bishops.

During the late 1960s to the mid-1980s, Catholics spread out along the entire political spectrum, while retaining a slight bias for the center-left. William Prendergast points out that the Catholic voter began to leave the Democratic Party at three junctures during the twentieth century: the early 1920s, the Eisenhower years, and the Reagan years. In the first two cases, the candidacies of Al Smith (reinforced by Catholic identification with FDR's New Deal) and Jack Kennedy saved Catholic Democratic loyalty for their times. The Reagan-Bush years, however, left a permanent adjustment among WCED Catholics, many of them Reagan Democrats. They returned to support Clinton and Gore, but not with the same percentages of previous eras.[25] As the United States enters the twenty-first century, to be religiously Catholic is to be politically schizophrenic. Both Republicans and Democrats can legitimately claim that their party represents Catholic values. The Republican Party benefits from the rising socioeconomic position of the WCEDs, from the party's support for parochial school funding, and from its opposition to "nonnegotiable" issues like abortion and Gay Marriage. Democrats benefit from Catholic social and labor theory, a more internationalist foreign policy, and Hispanic and Asian Catholic immigration.

American Labor, spurred by the increased social stratification of the 1990s, has sought to refurbish its links with American churches. For example, at a Labor-Church meeting just prior to the October 1999 Labor Convention in Los Angeles, AFL-CIO President and Catholic John Sweeney linked family, faith, and work as "sacred." Those attending included Roman Catholic Cardinal Roger Mahony of Los Angeles and United Methodist Bishop Jesse DeWitt, president of the National Interfaith Committee for Worker Justice. In late January 2003, the U.S. and Mexican bishops issued a joint pastoral letter calling on both governments to ameliorate the plight of undocumented workers.

[25] William B. Prendergast, *The Catholic Voter in American Politics: The Passing of the Democratic Monolith* (Washington, DC: Georgetown University Press, 1999).

American Judaism continues to experience high rates of intermarriage with gentiles and a political focus on the viability of Israel. In November 1999, Jews joined Hindus in protesting recent conversion attempts by the SBC. Sixty Jewish groups across the spectrum wrote "Our quarrel with the Southern Baptist Convention is not over their right to proselytize. Rather, the Jewish community is deeply offended that the SBC has formally embraced a strategy that attempts to deceive Jews into believing that one can be both a Jew and a Christian."[26] Jewish relationships with Islam, of course, have been further strained by the September 11 attacks. Immediately after the attacks, Jewish and Muslim leaders shared a common concern about civil liberties in defending Arab and Muslim citizens from unprovoked attacks. But as events progressed and both sides connected statements on terrorism to the Palestinian conflict, the Jewish-Muslim gulf widened.

Jews across the religious spectrum also express concern about the loss of Jewish religious identity in American life. For example, in May 1999, the liberal Reform Central Conference of American Rabbis voted 324 to 68 for guiding principles that for the first time encouraged traditional observances like wearing skullcaps, keeping kosher, and using Hebrew.[27] Reformed Judaism also has tightened its rules for interreligious marriage. Jewish population patterns render them powerful in New York, Florida, and California politics. Jews have traditionally formed alliances with Catholics on labor issues and with African Americans on civil rights, and have voted Democratic.

Progressive social positions are thus largely shared by the leadership of Jews, Catholics, United Methodists, Presbyterians, Episcopalians, United Church of Christ, American Baptists, Evangelical Lutherans, Unitarians, and Quakers. These denominations constitute the Religious Left on social policy. Such churches also have naturally formed alliances with traditionally black churches like the African Methodist Episcopal Church in the Civil Rights Movement. African Americans themselves have continued to vote overwhelmingly for the Democratic Party. In 2004, it was 88/11 for Kerry despite significant outreach efforts by the Bush campaign. Black churches that took socially progressive positions during the Civil Rights Movement formed the Congress of National Black Churches (CNBC). This organization of sixty-five thousand churches and twenty million members is comprised of the African Methodist Episcopal Church, the

---

[26] November 9, 1999.
[27] May 27, 1999.

African Methodist Episcopal Zion Church, the Church of God in Christ, the Christian Methodist Episcopal Church, the National Baptist Convention of America, the National Baptist Convention of the USA, the National Missionary Baptist Convention of America, and the Progressive National Baptist Convention. The CNBC hopes to revivify the black church as the center of community social and political organization.[28] In this endeavor they have both competed and sometimes cooperated with twentieth-century black Islamic congregations such as the Moorish Science Community (1913), the Indian-missionary Ahmadiyyah Movement, and the Nation of Islam (1930). After his pilgrimage to Mecca, Malcolm X left the Nation and embraced the *umma* [global community] of Orthodox Sunnis, taking the name of El Hajj Malik El-Shabazz. In 1977 Louis Farrakhan became the leader of the Nation and supported Jesse Jackson in his 1984 campaign for the Democratic presidential nomination.

Public education, the legal system, and the mass media constitute the triple bases of secularity in the United States. None of these three systems advocates agnosticism per se, but the general absence of religion in elite public discussions has fostered a secular society with religion relegated to the private sphere. For this reason, most conservative Protestant and "politically mixed," for example, Jewish and Catholic, religions operate at least a small number of their own schools. Nineteenth-century Catholic immigrants built their large parochial system because they felt that public education promulgated a Protestant civil religion that undermined their faith. Catholic universities, largely built near commuter immigrants in urban settings, for example, Boston College, the University of San Francisco, St. Louis University, Seattle University, Georgetown University of Washington, DC, and Fordham University of New York have provided an excellent avenue for Catholics into United States professional life, if less distinguished doctoral programs. The postwar GI Bill enabled many Catholics and Jews to become the first college-educated members of their families. Evangelical Protestants and Jews also established elementary, secondary, and post-secondary institutions, for example, Oral Roberts University, Liberty Baptist College, and Brandeis University.

The contemporary spiritual descendents of Thomas Jefferson who advocate law as the defense of American religious liberty focus on the phrase "wall of separation [between church and state]" used by Jefferson in a letter to Connecticut Baptists in 1802. When the Constitutional

---

[28] Thanks to Santa Clara senior Kendra Boyd whose fine paper provided materials and helped me think about these issues.

Congress itself faced the issue of the public role of religion, it adopted an ambiguous compromise in the First Amendment that states, "Congress shall make no law respecting an establishment of religion." The most important Supreme Court decision of the last half of the twentieth century was *Lemon v. Kurtzman* (1972), which set forth three tests for deciding when a statute could legally involve religion: the statute must have a secular purpose; the statute's primary effect must neither advance nor inhibit religion; and the statute must not foster an excessive entanglement with religion. The changing nature of U.S. society and its opinions about the proper relations of church and state, of course, complicate the judicial interpretation of such political-religious decisions and their impact on American life.

The Anglo countries of Canada, Australia, and New Zealand offer a possible bridge of understanding between the United States and continental Europe on this issue. Anglo countries are legally less secular than the United States and more observant religiously than continental Europe. Despite many recent changes in the Canadian political party system, religion continues to be a reliable predictive variable in voter party preference. The traditional major parties, the Liberals and the Conservatives, have been joined by the Reform Party (1987) and the Bloc Québecois (BQ), whereas the New Democratic Party (NDP) has persisted and the Progressive Conservatives have declined. Guth and Fraser demonstrate that Canadian religious variables indicate political partisanship much better than the socioeconomic, attitudinal, or organizational variables that would do better in an analysis of American voters. They document "the ties between Mainline Protestants and the Conservatives, and between Catholics – especially English speakers and devout French speakers – and the Liberals. Other connections are new on the federal scene, reflecting changes in both Canadian religion and politics: the strong Evangelical constituency for the Reform Party, the growing secularist constituency with the NDP, and nominal Catholicism of the BQ."[29]

The evangelical base of the Reform Party introduces comparative questions concerning the role of evangelism in American and Canadian conservative politics. At first glance, the Canadian system differs in that it includes six political parties, and evangelicals make up only 10–12 percent of the Canadian population compared to 23–33 percent (it depends on the definition and the methodology) of the American populace, and

---

[29] James L. Guth and Cleveland R. Fraser, "Religion and Partisanship in Canada," *Journal for the Scientific Study of Religion* 40 (March 2001): 62–63.

Canadian evangelicals have no regional base comparable to the U.S. South. Hoover et al. found that "Canadian evangelicals' attitudes about [economic] redistribution are similar to Canadian non-evangelicals' attitudes, and both are, on average less opposed to big government than are U.S. non-evangelicals or Catholics. U.S. evangelicals are even more opposed.... Evangelicals in both countries have moralist national priorities, and are opposed to abortion rights and equal rights for homosexuals, but U.S. evangelicals are distinctive in their disdain for big government."[30] In short, Canadian evangelicals have adopted American evangelical moral positions but not socioeconomic ones. Canadian evangelicals also have attached themselves to new political parties.

In social terms, Canada thus remains the great Blue State to the North, with a political culture much closer to Europe than to the United States. Liberals have ruled the country for 73 of the last 103 years, and for the last 11. Liberals do lose votes, however, during periods of corruption and mismanagement, as at present. In the June 2004 election, they took 36.7 percent of the vote, which translated into 135 of the parliament's three hundred seats. Their partners, the NDP, won nineteen seats, which made a coalition government possible. The reunited Conservatives garnered ninety-nine seats and the *Bloc Québecquois* fifty-four. Liberal Party scandals continued, and in May 2005 Paul Martin's government survived by a single vote. Both opposition parties played down their differences with the pervasive liberal culture that is supportive of national health care, tolerant of marijuana and gay marriage, and opposed to the Iraq War and an American missile defense. BQ leader Gilles Duceppe even strongly embraced later, mostly non-European immigrants by having himself photographed surrounded by Muslim, Chinese, and Russian voters. He stated, "There's no difference between Quebecers who are immigrants and *Québecois de souche* [French settlers before the eighteenth-century British conquest]."[31] National values of multiculturalism and equality, however, have contradicted each other in proposals like that of some Canadian Muslims to use *shari'a* to settle their civil disputes over marriage, inheritance, and property.

New Zealand history professor Peter Lineham terms that country's church-state relationship as "unequal co-dependency" because of the

---

[30] Dennis R. Hoover, Michael D. Martinez, Samuel H. Reimer, Kenneth D. Wald, "Evangelicalism Meets the Continental Divide: Moral and Economic Conservatism in the United States and Canada," *Political Research Quarterly* 55 (June 2002): 363.

[31] June 25, 2004.

state's prominence in a nation where "rigorous separation of church and state has never been a dogma."[32] New Zealand has even produced two religious political parties within the last twenty years, the Christian Heritage Party (July 1989) and the Christian Democratic Party (May 1995). Although neither threatens the major Labour or National Parties, their existence indicates that New Zealand's religious-political culture sits between U.S. and European models. In 1998 the Anglican Church organized a Hikoi of Hope, a nationwide protest march, to focus attention of the needs of native Maori who make up 15 percent of the population. Policies toward Maori will continue to play a political-religious role in New Zealand analogous to immigration in other Anglo countries.

Across the Anglo world, non-Western immigration has remained a salient political issue. Asians currently make up 5 percent of Australia's nineteen million people. These new immigrants have followed the path of Orthodox and Catholic Greeks, Italians, and other southern Europeans following World War II. Immigration issues and the U.S. military response to the Twin Towers overshadowed other issues in the Australian election of November 2001. Conservative Prime Minister John Howard, who had trailed in polls until the last week of August, saw his popularity surge when he denied entry to 433 refugees, mostly Afghan, who had been rescued by a Norwegian freighter. Muslims have thus replaced Asians, currently half of Australia's immigrants, as the main object of Australia's fear. The October 2002 Islamist terror attack on Bali pubs frequented by Australians and the September 2004 bombing of the Australian embassy in Jakarta have increased this perception. Australians reelected Howard in an October 2004 campaign in which the vibrant economy overshadowed any opposition to the Iraq War. Australian special forces played an important role in the first attack, but Howard pulled them out as soon as the main conventional fighting ended in May 2003.

RELIGION IN CONTEMPORARY EUROPE AND THE EXPANSION OF THE EUROPEAN UNION

If U.S. religious practice is said to constitute the bedrock of "exceptionalism," what do we know about religion in contemporary Europe? The

---

[32] Peter Lineham, "Government Support of the Churches in the Modern Era," Rex Ahdar and John Stenhouse, *God and Government: The New Zealand Experience* (Dunedin: University of Otago Press, 2000), 53.

quantitative scholar and novelist Andrew M. Greeley examined the European Values Surveys and the International Social Surveys and found very complicated data: "Europe is hardly godless. [...] However, the quality of belief in God varies from measure to measure and from country to country. Fervent faith exists only among a minority. Faith is, on the average, strongest in Catholic countries except France. Faith is weakest in Eastern Europe (excepting Slovakia, Latvia, and Poland) and in Scandinavia and the Netherlands."[33] Greeley also demonstrates that the majority of the data does not fit any current social model nor does that data suggest the future disappearance of religion.

The British sociologist Grace Davie also emphasizes the complicated nature of current European religious practice in terms of historical culture and Enlightenment secularism. Everywhere, she writes, postwar surveys document declining church attendance, weakening institutional attachment, and the lessening of traditional belief. However, the degree of religious decline varies across cultures: "The most obvious is the difference between the notably more religious and Catholic countries of southern Europe and the less religious countries of the Protestant north. This variation holds across almost every indicator. Levels of practice, for example, remain markedly higher in Italy, Spain, Belgium, and Ireland (closer in its religious life to continental Europe than to Britain) than elsewhere. Not surprisingly, one effect of regular Mass attendance has been a strength in the traditional orthodoxies through most of Catholic Europe."[34]

Among Catholic countries France represents the great exception, so other scholars offer a more differentiated typology. The sociologist Jean Stoetzel, for example, delineates four European religious-cultural settings: (1) Protestant north; (2) Catholic south; (3) mixed Protestant-Catholic, for example, Germany; and (4) a *région laïque* (France, Belgium, the Netherlands, and, possibly, England) where large numbers of people identify with no religion.[35]

Ex-British diplomat Michael Emerson presents the most inclusive picture of Europe. He divides the greater Europe of eight hundred million into geographic quadrants based on culture, religion and language. The quadrants correspond to the watersheds of the Rhine, Rhone, Volga, and

---

[33] Andrew M. Greeley, *Religion in Europe at the End of the Second Millennium: A Sociological Profile* (New Brunswick, NJ: Transaction Publishers, 2003), 19.

[34] Grace Davie, *Religion in Modern Europe: A Memory Mutates* (Oxford: Oxford University Press, 2000), 70–71.

[35] Davie, *Memory*, 12.

Danube Rivers, all flowing in separate directions (his use of caps shows relative importance):

Rhine: the North-West as GERMANIC, Latin; and PROTESTANT, Catholic;
Rhone: the South-West as LATIN and CATHOLIC;
Volga: the North-East as SLAVONIC, Turkic; and ORTHODOX, Islamic;
Danube: the South-East as TURKIC, Slavonic, Latin; and ISLAMIC, Orthodox, Catholic.[36]

If immigration provides the initial negative definition ("not those non-Westerners") of what it means to be a European, what more can be said? When the British novelist A. S. Byatt queried Europeans as to whether they were Europeans and of what their "Europeaness" consisted, many responded that they were "not Americans." Byatt's French interlocutors most strongly proclaimed their Europeaness, which, he suspected, meant that in their minds the E.U. was somehow becoming a socio-cultural extension of elite bureaucratic France.[37] If the United States provides a negative definition for a pan-European consciousness, how do these two entities differ in their approaches to the world? The German novelist Peter Schneider[38] starts with the obvious differences over religion. In addition, Schneider says, that although the United States should be justly proud of "the world's most varied and integrative" multicultural society, "the only one to have a worldwide appeal," this achievement has caused Americans to believe that they can truly understand foreign societies without learning their languages, histories, and cultures. Neo-con strategic planner Robert Kagan[39] adds that the current disparity in military power causes Americans and Europeans to take significantly different approaches to world affairs. The United States possesses overwhelming military power, Kagan says, and focuses on "threats" in a Hobbesian world. Europe perceives the "challenges" of a global unification that depends on economic

[36] Michael Emerson, *Redrawing the Map of Europe* (London and New York: Macmillan and St. Martin's, 1998), 13.
[37] A. S. Byatt, "What Is a European?" *The New York Times Magazine* (October 13, 2002): 46–51. For an excellent discussion of various approaches to this issue, see the second chapter ("Europe as Not-America") in Timothy Garton Ash, *Free World: America, Europe, and the Surprising Future of the West* (New York: Random House, 2004), 46–83.
[38] March 13, 2004.
[39] Robert Kagan, *Of Paradise and Power: America and Europe in the New World Order* (New York: Knopf, 2003).

integration and on the rule of international law for security. The reciprocal swear words are, according to Schneider, "cowboy nation" and "axis of weasels."

Whatever the content, being European isn't like belonging to "a United States of Europe." Europeans balance their relationships with continent, nation, and region, for example, the European Union, Spain, and Catalonia for Barcelona's residents. On the Irish question, John Hume, David Trimble, and Gerry Adams could not have reached their limited cooperation without residents of Northern Ireland identifying simultaneously with Northern Ireland, either Ireland or the United Kingdom, and the European Union.[40] Post–Cold War Western and Middle Europe also have embraced democracy, human rights, and the mixed economy.

The modern push for European unity came out of Christian Democratic politics with the major early roles being played by Catholic thinkers and politicians like France's Robert Schuman and the culturally Catholic Jean Monnet, Germany's Konrad Adenauer, and Italy's Alcide de Gaspari.[41] The Vatican is even considering the beatification of Schuman. The postwar popes have strongly supported European Unification as when in November 1982, John Paul II joined King Juan Carlos, European Nobel Prize winners, and the leaders of the European Common Market and the Council of Europe at a "European Act" ceremony in the traditional continental pilgrimage site of Compostela. Individual Catholics have also been disproportionately supportive. After examining the Eurobarometer's data, Nelsen, Guth and Fraser concluded:

Roman Catholics are warmest toward the Union, while Protestants tend to be less supportive than secular citizens are, although their position may depend on

---

[40] Northern Ireland, however, remains a work in progress. In the May 2005 parliamentary elections, Paisley's DUP won nine seats, while Trimble's UUP won one. Adams's more extreme Sinn Fein bested Hume's SDPL five seats to three among Catholics. On July 28, 2005, the IRA declared an end of violence in their campaign to unite Northern Ireland with the Irish Republic, raising hopes that the conflict had entered a political phase.

[41] For this history, see Thomas Kselman and Joseph A. Buttigieg, eds., *European Christian Democracy: Historical Legacies and Comparative Perspectives* (Notre Dame: University of Notre Dame Press, 2003). See also Edward Luttwak, "Franco-German Reconciliation: The Overlooked Role of the Moral Re-Armament Movement," and Douglass Steele, "Appendix: The Role of Other Religious Networks in Franco-German Reconciliation," in Douglas Johnston and Cynthia Sampson, eds., *Religion, The Mission Dimension of Statecraft* (New York: Oxford University Press, 1995), 37–63. The August 2005 assassination of the Swiss Protestant monk-theologian Brother Roger reminded many of how much his ecumenical community of Taizé, founded in Burgundy in 1940, has contributed to the unity and spiritual life of Europe.

national circumstances. Sectarian Protestants are the least fond of the European Union, although examination of their attitudes is limited by the Eurobarometer's inadequate identification of religious groups.... [R]eligious commitment also plays a solid role. Among Catholics (and perhaps among some Protestants), high commitment "internationalizes," making attendees more sympathetic to integration projects. But among sectarian Protestants the opposite effect appears, with observant members least pro-Union.[42]

The initial steps toward European unity were economic, but the ultimate motivations remained political-religious. On May 9 (now Europe Day), 1950, Schuman proposed that France, Germany, and other interested countries combine their steel and coal industries under an independent European entity. Thus, France, Germany, Italy, and the Benelux countries formed the European Coal and Steel Community (ECSC) with the Treaty of Paris in 1951. The next major step occurred when these same six countries agreed on the Treaty of Rome (1957), which set up a customs union to eliminate barriers to trade. Denmark, Ireland, and the United Kingdom extended the European Economic Community (EEC) to the English-speaking northwest of Europe in 1973. In 1981 Greece became the first Orthodox nation to join. Then Portugal and Spain joined in 1986, accepted by EEC members principally for the political reason that such integration would guarantee the democratization of these crucial Western European nations after earlier decades of authoritarianism.

The Single European Act (SEA) of 1986 brought the nearly exclusively economic phase to an end, lessening the national veto of any single country, and dedicated the EEC to a single market for the free movement of goods, capital, and services by the end of 1992. The EEC changed its name to the European Union (E.U.) in 1992 since its focus became more political. That year's Treaty of Maastricht divided the organization into three pillars. The first pillar, containing the EC, ECSC, Euratom, and most of the functions of the European Central Bank, belonged to united European control. The second pillar, a common foreign policy and defense (CFSP), by contrast, was subject to intergovernmental cooperation. The third pillar, areas covered by the Justice and Home Affairs Department, remained a mix of the two types of control. Maastricht also established a European citizenship and called for a single currency by 2002. Austria, Finland, and Sweden joined the European Union in 1995.

[42] Brent F. Nelsen, James L. Guth, and Cleveland R. Fraser, "Does Religion Matter? Christianity and Public Support for the European Union," *European Union Politics* 2 (2001): 210.

The Treaty of Amsterdam (1997) established the form of the E.U.'s "agreed common values" [*acquis communitaire*], strengthened the pooled sovereignty structure of the third pillar, and established conditions for applicant countries to join the European Union. Amsterdam also strengthened the European Parliament by giving it the right of "co-decision." The subsequent meeting at Nice in 2000 attempted to reform the E.U. structure, because of widespread anticipation that its current structure would prove unworkable if many new countries were added. On January 1, 2002, all E.U. countries except Britain, Sweden, and Denmark introduced euro bills and coins without much difficulty.

In October 2002 the fifteen members of the European Union, then a population 378 million, voted to add ten new nations (population seventy-five million) in 2004 and perhaps admit two more (population thirty million) in 2007. The ten were Poland, Hungary, the Czech Republic, Slovakia, Slovenia, Estonia, Lithuania, Latvia, Malta, and Cyprus. The two were Bulgaria and Romania. Despite U.S. lobbying for its NATO ally Turkey, membership or conditional status was not extended to Ankara at that time. The E.U.'s Foreign Affairs representative, Javier Solana, lambasted the American lobbying, "Turkey is not ready. The United States must understand that putting Turkey into the European Union is not like putting Mexico into a free trade agreement. We treat Turkey far better than you treat Mexico."[43]

In June 2003 the 105-member Convention on the Future of Europe, headed by ex-French president Valéry Giscard d'Estaing, released its draft constitution. This task constituted the world's most complicated legal challenge since the document had to summarize five decades of treaties among existing members and provide a context for the addition of ten new members. The draft stipulated that more legislative powers would reside in the European Parliament. Public opinion polls constantly show that Europeans take pride in the accomplishments of the entire continent since World War II, but that they have little affection for the E.U. bureaucratic institutions that have made that progress and unification possible. National governments have not helped as these E.U. bureaucrats remain handy political scapegoats for any unpopular policy. The draft had to be ratified individually by the twenty-five nations, so public opinion became crucial. Negative popular sentiment reflects the great gap between elite and popular perceptions of unification. The left fears the mythical "Polish plumber" who will take French jobs and the right fears future Turkish

---

[43] October 25, 2002.

immigration. All fear the loss of the European social safety net and farm subsidies. The French political elite united in supporting ratification in the May 29, 2005, referendum, but it lost 55/45. The unpopular President Chirac then replaced his more unpopular prime minister Jean-Pierre Raffarin with his protege Dominique de Villepin, and even appointed his rival Nicolas Sarkozy as party head. On June 1, the Dutch defeated the referendum 62/38 even though the main political parties, the labor unions, and most of the press supported it. The Dutch prime minister Jan Peter Balkenende, who campaigned for the document, attributed the loss to public concerns about a "loss of sovereignty, about the speed of the changes and about our [the Dutch] financial contribution."[44]

The drafting committee did not mention God or Christianity in the document, despite lobbying by the pope, the patriarch of the Greek Orthodox Church, and delegates from several nation states like Germany, Italy, Portugal, Poland, and Malta. The original draft of the preamble took its historical orientation from French secularism [*laïcité*] by mentioning that Europe was "nourished first by the civilizations of Greece and Rome, characterized by spiritual impulse always present in its heritage and later by the philosophical currents of the Enlightenment." After this religious lobbying this section became "inspiration from the cultural, religious and humanist inheritance of Europe" without any historical details.

The Christian churches have been represented in the drafting by the Commission of the Bishops' Conferences of the European Community for Catholics, and by the Church and Society Commission of the Conference of European Churches for 126 member churches from the Anglican Communion and the Orthodox and Reformed traditions. Article 51 gives such institutions public status in the following words: "The Union respects and does not prejudice the status under national law of churches and religious associations and communities in the Member States. . . . Recognizing their identity and their specific contribution, the Union shall maintain an open, transparent and regular dialogue with these churches and organizations.[45] The governments signed the treaty in Rome on October 29, 2004, initiating a period of state and popular ratification. John Paul II praised "the promotion of a united Europe on the basis of those values that are a part of its history."[46] The European Union in its growth has combined the

---

[44] June 2, 2005
[45] John Coughlan, "God and Caesar in the New Europe," *America* 189 (August 4–11, 2003): 20–23.
[46] November 7, 2004.

support of the continent's elite with religious, especially Christian Democratic, backing. Nine countries ratified the Constitution before its French and Dutch defeats. These latter votes show that the European masses feel some anxiety about the speed of a process they do not understand. Parties and politicians of the far left and of the far right stand ready to attack the center establishment on this issue.

NATIONAL EUROPE: POLITICS, IMMIGRATION, AND EDUCATION

J. Christopher Soper and Joel Fetzer point out that religion affects Western European national politics in at least three ways: party identification, immigration, and education. On coalitions, they state "religion remains important in political party coalitions in ways that secularization theory could not have predicted, and political-religious conflicts have not disappeared from contemporary conflicts."[47] In terms of voting, for example, "[I]n France and England, those who actively practice the majority faith are more likely to support the right than are nominal affiliates."[48] This phenomenon parallels U.S. political party dynamics.

Soper and Fetzer also focus on the two often-entwined issues of Muslim immigration and religious education. Almost fifteen million Muslims from Africa and the Middle East reside within the E.U. Although Muslims constitute less than 5 percent of the Western European population, and many second-generation European Muslims have become as secular as their "unchurched" Christian brethren, the attack on the World Trade Center heightened European fears, especially as planning for the attack had taken place on the continent. Like the United States, both Muslim and non-Muslim immigrants to Europe remain much more likely to be jobless, uneducated, harassed by police, and residing in ghettos.[49]

Muslims in France make up a community of five million, eight percent of the population. France, with its doctrinaire secularism derived from Revolutionary ideology, faces the most difficult relationship with its Muslim minority, mainly from its former colonies in North Africa. In September 2003, the government certified the first Muslim *lycée* in Lille. As in all nine thousand private, mostly Catholic, schools in France,

---

[47] J. Christopher Soper and Joel Fetzer, "Religion and Politics in a Secular Europe: Cutting Against the Grain," in Jelen and Wilcox, *Comparative Perspective*, 187.

[48] Soper and Fetzer, "Europe," 177.

[49] For analysis of the Muslim experience in Europe, see Brigitee Maréchal, Stefano Allievi, Felice Dassetto, and Jørgen Nielsen, eds. *Muslims in the Enlarged Europe* (Leiden: Koninklijke Brill, 2003).

the government provides 80 percent of the financing and determines the required curriculum. Courses such as Arabic, Islamic history and culture, and the Qu'ran remain electives. Students may wear head scarves at this school. Head scarves and other "conspicuous" religious symbols have been banned in public schools according to a February 2004 law. In supporting the law, Prime Minister Jean-Pierre Raffarin argued strongly that such symbols "were taking on a political meaning."[50] The (Catholic, Orthodox, and Protestant) Council of Christian Churches criticized the ban as "discriminatory," as did the Sikh community.

Many Catholics who do not attend Mass regularly, if at all, still feel strongly attached to Catholic schools. François Mitterand and the French Socialist Party, like the German Social Democrats, have built their political victories on the ideology and the cadre of the 1960s social movements. Mitterand, however, gradually reached an understanding on Catholic schools that antagonized his secular base while preserving his government. France also battles periodic incidents of anti-Semitism. In July 2004, Israeli Prime Minister Ariel Sharon infuriated the Paris government and French Jewish leaders when he commented to American Jewish leaders that, "If I have to advise our brothers in France, I'll tell them one thing: Move to Israel as soon as possible."[51] French Islamic leaders also denounced the kidnapping of French journalists in the Middle East to protest the ban on head scarves. The kidnappers unwittingly had done that implementation of *laïcité* a favor.

Austria retains the highest percentage of Muslims (17 percent) in the European Union, and thus faces a strong internal political debate. Jorg Haider from the Freedom Party (FPÖ), who had earlier spoken sympathetically of Hitler, criticized *Uberfremdung* [overforeignization] and advocated that only European asylum seekers should reside in Austria while their petitions were being processed. Non-Europeans, he asserted, should go to "safe third countries" on their own continents. When Mr. Haider's FPÖ joined the ruling coalition in February 2000, it set off a crisis in Austria's relations with other European nations as the European Union had demanded that Austria keep the FPÖ out of the government or European diplomatic ties would be kept to a "technical level." A majority of European politicians, press, and population supported this E.U. position.[52] Haider overreached himself, however, in the November 2002

---

[50] February 4, 2004.
[51] July 20, 2004.
[52] February 2, 2000.

campaign with several polarizing incidents, for example, his visits to Saddam Hussein. The FPÖ vote set a postwar record by dropping from 27 percent to 10 percent. The center-right Christian Democratic People's Party won the plurality with 43 percent. Christians least observant in religious practices are the most xenophobic. Soper and Fetzer state that "Among French Catholics and German *Evangelishch* [Lutherans], those who attend church at least once a week are significantly less nativist."[53] Thus, practicing members of the national majority religion get their political party from family socialization, but their stand on immigration from the pulpit. In France, the nativist Le Pen's support comes disproportionately from the tribal feelings of unchurched Catholicism, whereas nonreligious, members of minority religions, and active Catholics are more welcoming of Islamic immigration.

In terms of education, secularization, and the traditional anticlerical/ clerical split in politics, Soper and Fetzer offer a comparative religious-political analysis of Britain, Germany (West and East as separate political-religious cultures), and France. Despite inheriting an established religion, Britain retains much less religious tension in its politics than France. The Church of England has joined with nonconformists, Catholics, and Jews to support common religious values and religious schools for all. Thirty-five percent of primary and 16 percent of secondary schools are church-related. The great majority of Britain's Muslims prefer this to France's "fundamentalist secularism,"[54] but this did not protect the country from the London bombings of July 7, 2005. In 1997, the British Labour government for the first time approved the state financing of two Muslim schools.

Germany exhibits two distinct religious cultures in the former West and East. The West has pluralistic religions of Catholics and Lutherans at about 35 percent each and a postwar tradition of collecting the *Kirchensteuer* to support the church of the taxpayer. This provides a majority of the churches' budgets – including social, health, and cultural activities – as well as overseas missionary works. The ex-GDR East has a majority of nonbelievers, with Lutherans the largest religious group. In general, Catholics in West Germany remain moderately more likely to vote center-right. West German members of other religions tend to vote for the Social Democrats or the Greens. In the East, Catholics and Lutherans are more likely to support the right and liberalization, with the nonreligious

---

[53] Soper and Fetzer, "Europe," 181.
[54] This term was used by Dr. Thomas Milcent, a Strasbourg physician and convert to Islam.

majority voting for the Social Democrats or the ex-Communists (PDS). Catholics and Lutherans offer most of the religion classes in schools, but other religions also have access, leading to a much less tense situation than in France.[55] The parliamentary election of September 2005 showed Schröder a formidable campaigner and Christian Democrat Angela Merkel, the daughter of a Lutheran minister in East Germany, a weaker one, but it produced no policy direction for the country. The vote fragmented into Christian Democrats 35.2 percent, Social Democrats 34.3 percent, Free Democrats 9.8 percent, New Left 8.7 percent, and Greens 8.1 percent.

The previous section referred to the role of the Christian Democrats in promoting a unified Europe. However, this huge and complex project required more than the support of the continent's leading political party in the immediate postwar era. Germany's second major political party, the Social Democrats, also backed unification. Nelsen et al. state "Socialist parties often participated in the task of building the Union and producing a supportive public, influencing many outside the Catholic Church and countering a universal suspicion among working-class Europeans and left ideologues that the European Union would harm their interests."[56] National elections, especially in Germany and France, could have derailed the E.U. process if radical parties had gained control of national policy, even for a short period of time, or if major parties had developed intense political antagonisms over foreign policy. The 2002 French presidential contest drew little interest until the nativist Le Pen eliminated the Socialist Jospin in the first round by a whisker with 17.02 percent of the vote. With France shamed at having Le Pen running for president, all the parties, even the Communists, called for a victory for Chirac. In the second round, Chirac took over 82 percent of the vote. In that year's parliamentary elections Chirac's center-right coalition, the Union for a Presidential Majority, won 399 of the 577 seats. Le Pen's party failed to win a single seat.

With the far right diminished in the continent's two leading nations, that political tendency was growing in other countries. In 2001 Denmark's People's Party gained 12 percent and Norway's Progress Party 14.7 percent of their respective parliamentary votes. In 2002 Portugal's

---

[55] In November 2002, Gerhard Schröder announced that the Central Committee of German Jews would receive equal standing for funding of schools and social institutions. That announcement came on the fiftieth anniversary of the Luxembourg Accords, which have provided $90 billion in restitution for Holocaust survivors. November 15, 2002.

[56] Nelsen, "Religion," 210.

anti-immigrant Popular Party took 8.8 percent of the vote and became part of the ruling coalition. Belgium's Vlaams Belang [Flemish Interest] has grown from ten percent of the electorate in 1999 to nearly a quarter in 2005, with nearly one-third of the voters in cosmopolitan Antwerp where Hasidic diamond traders uneasily coexist with unemployed Muslim youths.[57]

After the assassination of right-wing anti-immigrant populist Pim Fortuyn by an environmental activist, the Dutch electorate moved to the right by giving his disciples and the Christian Democrats control of the parliament in May 2002. Fortuyn's inexperienced followers self-destructed, and the government fell in October. Fortuyn's assassination, however, has strongly affected the style of discourse in what has long been Europe's most tolerant nation. MP Ayaan Hirsi Ali and Dutch filmmaker Theo Van Gogh made a movie condemning sexual abuse of Muslim women that employed Qur'anic verses written on the model's bare skin. Ms. Hirsi Ali referred to Mohammed as a "pervert" and a "tyrant," and Mr. Van Gogh used an epithet for conservative Muslims that referred to bestiality with a goat.[58] Seven non-Dutch militants assassinated Mr. Van Gogh in November 2004, which resulted in the counter burnings of Muslim schools and Protestant churches. The Amsterdam Council of Churches placed paid advertisements in Dutch newspapers pledging solidarity with the country's nine hundred thousand Muslims, only about 20 percent of whom are practicing. The above elections and incidents illustrate that 10–15 percent of the population in most European countries have reacted strongly against immigration, crime, and the loss of sovereignty to the European Union by voting for the nationalist right. Some of this urban-based support had voted Communist in previous elections.

As soon as the analyst crosses the Alps or the Pyrenees into the Latin traditions of Italy, Spain, and Portugal, s/he enters traditionally Catholic countries that present a different set of questions regarding the political role of religion. The institutional church became linked early to the monarchy, so revolutionary movements took on an anticlerical cast. In the eighteenth century, the Church, seeking to escape the control of anticlerical or regalist states, identified with the petit bougeoisie. Only in Italy did the Christian Democratic Party play a major role, through the early 1980s. But the death of "the Christian Democratic pope" Pope Paul VI after the

---

[57] February 12, 2005.
[58] November 10, 2004.

assassination of his close friend prime minister Aldo Moro brought an end to that era of close cooperation between the papacy and the Italian Christian Democrats. In February 1984 Socialist Prime Minister Bettino Craxi and Vatican Secretary of State Casaroli signed a concordat that settled most outstanding issues. As a fitting close to vibrant traditional Italian anticlericalism, the frail Pole John Paul II became the first pope to address the Italian parliament in November 2002.

ORTHODOX EUROPE IN THE POST-COMMUNIST PERIOD

With the collapse of the USSR at the end of 1991, the nature of the succeeding Russian governments, Russia's relations with the rest of Europe, and the handling of the Soviet nuclear threat became global political concerns. The Orthodox Church has played a significant role in the first two. Gorbachev visited the pope at the beginning of December 1991, a few weeks before the USSR fell. Catholic-Orthodox relations under Boris Yeltsin became more complicated because Yeltsin projected himself as a worldwide promoter of Orthodoxy as illustrated in his pilgrimage to the Orthodox shrines in Jerusalem. State relations with all churches remain tense under Othodox believer Vladimir Putin, who meets often with Patriarch Aleksey II, but who also distrusts the strident nationalism of the Russian right wing. Some church radicals like have formed alliances with the ultraright, for example, fifteen Rodina party representatives sent a letter to the prosecutor general in January 2005 asking for a ban on Jewish ethnic and religious organizations as "extremist." And some Russian political elites, especially Army and Police, see Orthodoxy as the answer to what they perceive as the lack of morality and discipline in society. Followers of the priest Alexander Shagunov, founder of the Committee for the Moral Revival of the Fatherland, have defaced "blasphemous" artistic exhibitions and commercial billboards that offend their religious sentiments.[59]

In addition to Orthodox-Catholic tensions, post-Soviet religious controversies have included the coming of Protestant foreign missionaries and the attempt to reach closure on the relationships of the church and the government during the Soviet era. Russians demonstrated the most interest in new Protestant churches during the U.S. euphoria of the early

---

[59] *Wall Street Journal*, March 29, 2005, covers the trial verdict on the "Caution, Religion!" exhibition in Moscow.

1990s, but that interest had waned by the end of the decade. In May 2000, Professor Sharon Linzey and Russian journalist Iakov Krotov published survey data and an analysis of the future of religion and religious freedom in the Moscow journal *Kontinent*.[60] Linzey and Krotov conclude that the Russian Orthodox Church remains a symbol of national and cultural unity, but that the maximum number of churchgoers on any feast can only be 28 percent of the population. With regard to registered church groups:

> In 1997 there were 54 registered denominations or confessions in Russia. The Moscow Patriarchate brand of Russian Orthodoxy had the most churches at 7,195. Alternative Russian Orthodox confessions included the Old Believers with 164 churches, The Russian Orthodox Free Church with 98 churches, and The Only True Russian Orthodox Church, 26 churches. The Roman Catholic Church had 183 congregations, and The All-Russian Union of Baptists was the fastest growing Protestant denomination with 677 groups. The Union of Evangelicals had 248 groups, Pentecostals: 351, and Apostolic Pentecostals: 22. Seventh-day Adventists had 222 congregations, Presbyterians: 129; non-denominational Protestants: 213, and Charismatic: 136.
>
> Non-Christian groups included the Buddhists with 124 groups, Jews with 80, and Muslim with 2,494.[61]

Patriarch Aleksey II has claimed that 90 percent of Russians are Orthodox, but yearly state survey figures for 1993–97 gave 50, 56, 44, and 48 percent for Orthodox, and 40, 39, 43, and 37 percent for unbelievers. It is true that these unbelievers may be part of what sociologist Sergei Filatov calls "uninformed" Orthodox, or culturally religious. The article concludes that after 1995 the growth of religiosity seems to have abated, and that 10 percent are atheists and 30 percent are unsure what they believe. The Moscow Patriarchate's vision of religious reform focuses on the participation of the full Russian population in Orthodox religious institutions. The reader can thus appreciate the Patriarch's distrust of Protestants, especially foreigners with their financial and media advantages, Catholics with their age-old competition with Orthodoxy, and splinter Orthodox churches who challenge the institutional framework. Patriarch Aleksey II assisted the Russian census of fall 2002 by assuring believers

---

[60] Sharon Linzey and Iakov Krotov, "The Future of Religion and Religious Future in Russia," *Kontinent* (May 2000), translated in *Religion in Eastern Europe* 21 (October 2001): 26–47.
[61] Linzey and Krotov, "Russia," 32.

that it was not "a sign of the end of the world," but he blocked a survey question on religious affiliation lest it discover too many non-Orthodox.[62]

The December 2003 parliamentary and March 2004 presidential elections formalized the new post-Soviet system under Putin. Before becoming president, Putin directed the Federal Security Service, Russia's successor to the domestic operations of the KGB. His *siloviki* [root word is "power"] bring together ex-KGB, army, law enforcement, and tax police to control the oligarchs and the mafia. Just prior to the December election the *siloviki* arrested Russia's richest man, Mikhail Khodorkovsky, the forty year-old chief executive of Russia's richest company, Yukos Oil, for embezzlement, fraud and tax evasion. In 1995 Yeltsin had given over the country's most valuable assets to the oligarchs in return for their bankrolling his 1996 presidential election. After Putin's election in 1999, the oligarchs contributed campaign funds and stayed out of politics. "Open Mike" Khodorkovsky, however, reinvented himself as a "socially responsible" capitalist, protecting himself with foreign, especially American and Israeli, connections. In 2001 he formed Open Russia, a philanthropic and political organization that donated to the Library of Congress, Washington think tanks, and Laura Bush's National Book Festival. Khodorkovsky's growing international prominence and speeches extolling corporate transparency attracted foreign investment and interest in mergers from Exxon Mobil and Chevron Texaco. But Putin's men took no chance on the parliamentary elections and arrested Khodorkovsky in October. They also completely domesticated the television industry, the major news source for Russians, granting a little more independence to newspapers, radio, and the Internet.

Putin came to power in 1999 with patriotic support for sending Russian troops to Chechnya to battle the separatists. Despite the decimation of the Chechen capital Grozny and many thousands of Russian military deaths, Putin has maintained that support. Chechen Islamist fighters, however, struck back. For example, in October 2002, fifty fighters took seven hundred Moscovites hostage in a theatre three miles from the Kremlin. The Russian security forces stormed the theater and killed the Chechens, but over one hundred hostages died. An even more horrible massacre occurred in September 2004 when terrorists captured Beslan's Middle School Number One on the first day of class. Hundreds of children died.

Russian politicians have to deal with both the national symbolism of Orthodoxy and with the institutional clout of the Moscow Patriarchate.

---

[62] September 29, 2002.

The Religious Freedom Act of October 1997, which replaced the more democratic law of 1990, mandated that only religious groups that had been in Russia for fifteen years could be registered. It further divided those groups into those that could own property and those that could not. Formal and informal religious policy can be summarized in five tendencies. First, the Moscow Patriarchate is not yet a state church, but it is privileged vis-à-vis other religious institutions. Second, the state prefers those churches that support its foreign policy, for example, supporting Serbia during the Balkan war. Islam remains the most suspect religion for its foreign connections. Third, considering traditional Soviet fear of religious espionage, more indigenous and less foreign religions are likely to be treated better. Fourth, world religions will be better treated than groups like the Jehovah's Witnesses and the Unification Church which are classified as sects [*sekt*]. Fifth, in the government application of somewhat ambiguous laws, local decisions often take precedence. Orthodox Belarus also passed its new religious law in November 2002 with similar results: Orthodoxy playing "a determining role" in national culture and government, discrimination against Pentecostalism with its 450 registered churches, and repression against sects. In October 2004 Belarus President Aleksandr G. Lukashenko won a referendum removing a two-term limit to his office amid dubious electoral practices. Lukashenko thus consolidated authoritarian power, even closing the liberal European Humanities University established by professors and elements of the Belarussian Orthodox Church that sponsored its theology department.

The conflict between the Vatican and the Moscow Patriarch heated up in February 2002 when the Vatican upgraded four geographical areas – Moscow, Saratov, Novosibirsk, and Irkutsk – to permanent dioceses. Because many Orthodox leaders had viewed these four jurisdictions as temporary apostolic administrations until all Russian Christians united under Orthodox leadership, they accused the Vatican of "an unfriendly act." The Vatican replied that these changes were merely normal post–Cold War ecclesiastical adjustments, and that any Roman Catholic converts came from nonbelievers. In July 2004, the pope announced that in August a Catholic delegation would return the revered Mother of God of Kazan icon, bought by Catholics in the 1970s and later given to the pope, to Patriarch Aleksy II in the hope that it would "contribute to the unity so longed for between the Catholic and Orthodox churches."[63] There are only six hundred thousand Catholics in Russia, so

[63] July 12, 2004.

Orthodox-Catholic relations remain more significant in European than in Russian politics. Putin visited John Paul II in October 2003, but the Polish pope died before he could visit Russia. Benedict XVI reaffirmed his desire to end the split with the Orthodox in his first official papal trip, to Bari, Italy, the home of the relics of St. Nicholas, venerated by both churches.[64]

The Ukraine sits on the fault line between political-religious spheres. The Orthodox eastern half of the country was ruled by the Russians, the western more Catholic half by the Poles and the Austrians. The Greek Catholic Church began in 1596 when many Orthodox were pressured by the Polish rulers into allegiance to Rome but were allowed to keep their non-Latin liturgy. Today, there are five million Greek Catholics and one million Roman Catholics among the fifty million Ukrainians. Orthodox number 7.5 million in union with the Moscow patriarchy, and two million not. The latter autocephalis ["self-headed" or "independent"] Ukrainian church had been active in the 1920s before Stalin suppressed them as separatists. They reappeared during German occupation, but were suppressed again after the war as "collaborators." Finally, on October 22, 1989, Orthodox Bishop Ioann (Bodnarchuk) of Zhitomir proclaimed the reestablishment of the Autocephalis Orthodox Church throughout the Ukraine and was immediately excommunicated by the Russian Orthodox Holy Synod. Later the autocephalis church split into two groups, the larger one led by Metropolitan Filaret of Kiev, and the smaller Ukrainian Orthodox Church.

Pope John Paul II sought to bring about reconciliation among Roman Catholics, Ukrainian Orthodox, and Russian Orthodox when he visited the Ukraine in June 2001. The Ukrainian Orthodox Metropolitan Filaret welcomed the pope, but Russian Orthodox Patriarch Aleksey II, the Russian Orthodox Metropolitan Vladimir, and the Russian ambassador to the Ukraine opposed the visit. Ukrainian President Leonid Kuchma, under fire for corruption and lack of economic progress, invited the pope to emphasize the Ukraine's desire to join Europe. The pope tried to steer his way through all these political-religious complications, balancing the pastoral nature of his visit to Greek Catholics who had suffered under Communist persecution with trying not to offend the Orthodox in union with Moscow. The Vatican pleased neither side, for example, when it named the head of the Greek Catholics, Lubomyr Husar, as cardinal in February, but not patriarch as his followers desired. The pope met with Filaret, but canceled a visit to St. Sophia, an ancient Orthodox monastery that is now

[64] May 30, 2005.

a museum. John Paul II did visit both Bykovnia, where the Soviet secret police shot nearly two hundred thousand Ukrainian nationalists during Stalin's terror, and Babi Yar, the notorious death camp near Lvov where the Nazis executed two hundred thousand Jews and other regime enemies. The pope called for the Ukraine to be accepted as part of Europe, President Kuchma's primary foreign policy goal at the time.

The two distinct halves of the country are also evident in politics and in visions of the Ukraine's future. When Kuchma decided not to pursue a third term, the two candidates, Viktor A. Yushchenko and Viktor F. Yanukovich, conducted a particularly virulent campaign focused on the country's future. The former criticized Kuchma's corruption and advocated a balanced position between the E.U. and the Ukraine's largest trading partner, Russia. The latter, endorsed by both Kuchma and Putin, depicted the former as a tool of the United States. Both polled roughly forty percent of the vote in the first round. In the November runoff, Yanukovich won by a slight margin in a tainted election that demonstrated the great cultural split between the two halves of the country, and the antagonism between the West and Russia over the results. Then Ukrainians demonstrated in Kiev until the election was overturned. Despite having been poisoned, Yushchenko won the reelection, but made his first visit to Putin to try to maintain Russian goodwill as he sought the Ukraine's entry into the E.U.

Although John Paul II's visit to the Ukraine remained controversial, the pope's first visit to an overwhelmingly Orthodox country, Romania in May 1999, resulted in a much more pleasant dialogue. The pope attended the Orthodox mass of Patriarch Cristian Andrei, and the patriarch attended the papal mass that afternoon. Romanians perceived the pope's visit as a positive link to the West, and a boost for its application to join the European Union, now a possibility in 2007. After September 11, the United States started to court Romania because of its strategic geographical position across the Black Sea from Central Asia. Romania responded by "playing the American card" in sending troops to Afghanistan to help in guarding Kabul and military bases. NATO welcomed Romania in November 2002, despite the country's status as the lowest and least reformed economy of all the nations so invited.

RELIGION AND POLITICS IN THE CONTEMPORARY WEST

At the beginning of the twenty-first century, some observers write as if "the West" has a single definition, that this West has always been united, and that it will continue permanently as a prominent civilization. But this chapter has already demonstrated the increasing polarization of American society and the tenuousness of "Europe" in this post–Cold War period, let alone united action by these two entities. Even a strong West remains a historically recent phenomenon. Only in the last three or four hundred years have the European social and scientific revolutions, exported through colonial expansion, begun to create the contemporary global balance of power. This recent modern West seemed to hit a dead end in the first half of the twentieth century. The destruction of World War I, the global depression, and the rise of Communism and Nazism turned the 1930s into a dismal decade. The overseas Anglo ex-colonies rescued Europe, both in World War II and afterward, with economic assistance from the Marshall Plan and the military protection of NATO. Western Europe then recreated itself in democracy, peace, and prosperity. The fall of the Berlin Wall presents the significant challenge of extending that democracy, peace, and prosperity to Middle and Eastern Europe.

Social stratification in the American economic system and shrill partisanship in the political and communication systems have increasingly divided Americans into Red and Blue states of consciousness. The weakening and politicizing of institutional religion became obvious in the 2004 presidential campaign as stronger political, economic, and communication forces used the churches for their own purposes. Only increased dialogue and mutual understanding among secular elites, the Religious Right, and the Religious Left can save the United States from this increasing cultural fragmentation.

Postwar European political and religious leaders have fostered and maintained a general consensus that the continent's increased economic cooperation has necessitated further economic and political integration. This linkage is sometimes referred to as "disequilibrium dynamics" or "the bicycle theory of integration." A bicycle will fall if it does not keep moving forward, as, for example, a common currency will fail without a central bank that sets common monetary policy. No consensus exists, however, on what form further political integration might take. The major debate has occurred between those who favor "deepening" the European Union, greater economic and political integration among present members, and those who favor "widening" the European Union by admitting more members. This division exemplifies the split between those Western continental countries dedicated to the Christian Democratic vision of reunification and those northern culturally Protestant nations who joined afterwards: Britain, Denmark, Finland, and Sweden. Sociologist Davie states: "The complexities are evident as a historically Protestant, and in some ways increasingly fragmented, group of nations seeks to come to terms with a primarily Catholic Europe.... Europe as a whole is invited to think again about what it has in common rather than what pulls it apart."[65]

The reunification of Europe, like the nineteenth-century Meiji Restoration in Japan, has resulted from a bureaucratic revolution from above, albeit with popular consent in countries with full democratic processes. This popular support has derived both from economic success and from an almost "stealth" Christian Democratic and Socialist ideological backing. Nelsen et al. worry that if religion in Europe is ebbing, "a prime source of Europeanist sentiment may be eroding."[66] After all, in more tolerant times the mythical "Polish plumber" who so spooked France's referendum on the E.U. Constitution would have been viewed as a fellow Catholic.

Recent treaties have strengthened the European parliament, but it still remains weaker than either the European Commission or the Council of Ministers, whose representatives are named by the respective governments. Finally, the centerpiece and strongest symbol of "deepening" would be a common foreign and defense policy (CFSP). The difficulty in crafting a CFSP became obvious in the principal foreign policy and military challenge to Europe in the 1990s, the disintegration of Yugoslavia. In the heady days following the fall of the Berlin Wall and the reunification of Germany, many leaders took their cue from the pronouncement of Jacques Poos of Luxembourg, then the six-month E.U. Chairman, that "the age of Europe has dawned."[67] "Letting Europe do it" also appealed to the American political leadership that had just completed fighting Saddam in the Gulf, to the U.S. military leadership like Colin Powell who feared a repeat of the disastrous Vietnam War, and especially to the American people who felt that they deserved "a decade of vacation" from international affairs after "winning the Cold War." Halberstram describes the American psyche at this time: "It was the most schizophrenic of nations, a monopoly superpower that did not want to be an imperial power, and

---

[65] Davie, *Memory*, 183.
[66] Nelsen, "Religion," 210.
[67] David Halberstam, *War in the Time of Peace: Bush, Clinton and the Generals* (New York: Harcourt, Inc.), 85.

whose soul, except in financial and economic matters, seemed to be more and more isolationist."[68]

When Milosevic attacked the Croats and the Bosnians, the principal E.U. members fragmented over a response. Germany, with traditional links to Catholic Slovenia and Croatia, supported their independence, and then pulled back to concentrate on Russian economic development and German unification. Since World War I, Britain and France had backed Serbia, and Russia also supported its fellow Orthodox. France under Socialist President Mitterand became particularly pro-Serb. Indeed, united European-American action against Milosevic had to wait for Mitterand's replacement by Chirac, an ex-French army officer in colonial Algeria. Tony Blair's victory over John Major in Great Britain also helped facilitate joint action, as Blair has fostered a foreign-policy "bridge project" linking the United States with Europe. In May 2005 Blair's support for America's Iraq War resulted in a reduced Labor majority in parliament, and probably hastened the day when more traditionally Laborite Gordon Brown will be prime minister. Timothy Garton Ash has described the four possible British alliance strategies as "(1) regain independence; (2) choose America; (3) choose Europe; and (4) try to make the best of our intimate relations with both America and Europe."[69] The British media have overwhelmingly supported the Euroskeptics, with TV talk-show host Robert Kilroy-Silk,[70] the best-known member of the United Kingdom Independence Party, which in June 2004 took twelve of the U.K.'s seventy-eight seats in the European parliament.

In the end, NATO did not split over the bombing of Belgrade as Boris Yeltsin had expected. Russian Prime Minister Viktor Chernomyrdin met with Clinton's fellow student at Oxford, Strobe Talbott, and Vice President Al Gore to work out a peace mission to Milosevic. Talbott and Chernomyrdin added the neutral President Martti Ahtisaari of Finland. NATO even blocked the use of Russian peacekeeping troops. It was "a singular victory for the use of modern air power."[71] On June 15, 1999, the Orthodox Patriarch Pavle and the Holy Synod called for Milosevic's resignation and new elections. Thirteen days later the patriarch and the senior Orthodox Bishop Artemije of Kosovo denounced Milosevic's policies.

---

[68] Halberstam, *War*, 75.

[69] Garton Ash, *Free World*, 24. The book offers a riveting history and analysis of the U.S.-Europe split.

[70] Christopher Caldwell, "The Anti-Europeanist," *New York Times Magazine*, January 9, 2005.

[71] Halberstam, *War*, 478.

Pavle said, "If the only way to create a greater Serbia is by crime, then I do not accept that, and let Serbia disappear. And also if a lesser Serbia can only survive by crime, let it also disappear."[72]

Even after the Yugoslavian crisis the relationship of the West with Eastern Europe remains tenuous. Michael Emerson states that the West must include not only the Orthodox states, but also Ankara to find permanent stability. It is extremely dangerous, Emerson asserts, to leave the three big outsiders (Russia, Turkey, Ukraine) without a connection to Europe. The most dangerous situations for military escalation are those, primarily, in Middle and Eastern Europe where, "the [ethnic-nationalist] minority is concentrated on the frontier of an irredentist power. In practice such circumstances are virtually sure to be the result of an earlier war and may well represent deep historical enmities and unresolved grievances."[73] Emerson offers a table of thirty-one cases. Efforts should be made during the first decades of the twenty-first century for "both a widening of the deep Europe and a deepening of the wide Europe, with the two processes deliberately converging. Whether the two would ultimately merge together into one would remain a mystery for the future to reveal."[74] But at the end of September 2005, the United States, Germany, and France are all saddled with weak political leaders distrusted by their electorates.

Chapter 1 documented the current divisive influences of the global economic, military, and communication systems: social stratification, regional wars, and communication imperialism. These influences have made even rudimentary global political democratization difficult in most of the post–Cold War world. Each of the autonomous EMC systems can block political initiatives so that, as in the Palestinian case, only one solution exists, with the most probable outcome of all political crises being gridlock. At each stage of political, military, and economic unity, the political and social leadership also must define at least a quasi-religious vision both domestically and internationally that can inspire new generations to sacrifice their narrow personal and national interests for a broader

---

[72] June 29, 1999. For a detailed analysis of the role of religion in the ex-Yugoslavia, see David A. Steele, "Christianity in Bosnia-Herzegovina and Kosovo: From Ethnic Captive to Reconciling Agent," in Douglas Johnston, ed., *Faith-Based Diplomacy: Trumping Realpolitik* (New York: Oxford, 2003), 124–77. For "Interreligious Dialogue Toward Reconciliation in Macedonia and Bosnia," see the *Journal of Ecumenical Studies 39,* Vol. 1–2 (Winter–Spring 2002). Experienced ecumenical theologians and mediators Paul Mojzes and Leonard Swidler wrote the preface to this collection of over thirty contributions.

[73] Emerson, *Map*, 61.

[74] Emerson, *Map*, xxi.

common good. Does the West have a political-religious ideological and organizational answer to this challenge? This chapter has discussed secularization to determine if and in what ways religion might be relevant. It has treated immigration to determine whether Anglo and European countries will be able to integrate new immigrants into their national unities. It has documented the current political-religious polarization in the United States.

What general roles then do Western religions, which both unite and divide, play in contemporary European and Anglo political dynamics? Religions remain important for personal and social identity at the Western, the European, and the national levels. They correlate strongly with political voting in almost all countries, thus influencing national policy. The E.U. Constitution, although not mentioning God, gives religious organizations legal status and pledges a continuing dialogue with them. Europe's Protestant-Catholic split has largely been bridged religiously by ecumenical dialogue, but the remnants of that division still color even secular worldviews about the E.U.'s future. Cooperation between the Catholic Commission of the Bishops' Conferences of the European Community and the Anglican-Reformed-Orthodox Church and Society Commission of the Conference of European Churches remains particularly important at the continental level. Orthodox-Catholic and Orthodox-Protestant tensions remain, as do Jewish-Christian and Muslim-Christian ones. These latter tensions make the accession of Russia, the Ukraine, and Turkey to the European Union more difficult. Dialogue and cooperation between Christians and Orthodox, and Christians and Muslims remain crucial for the further expansion of the European Union and the national integration of immigrants.

Catholic interventions for a united Europe have both strengths and weaknesses. As Timothy Byrnes has pointed out, "bishops in postcommunist countries by and large share the Pope's vision of a new European community animated by religion, and they share his devotion to the idea that the Catholic Church must play a central role in making that new Europe a reality."[75] However, that effort in South and Eastern Europe is still limited by two national factors: (a) "idiosyncratic state political structures," as in the Polish case; and (b) preexisting Catholic nationalisms, as in the Slovak and Croat cases.[76]

---

[75] Timothy A. Byrnes, *Transnational Catholicism in Postcommunist Europe* (Lanham, MD: Rowman & Littlefield, 2001), 138.

[76] Byrnes, *Postcommunist Europe*, 136.

At the national level, most majority religious organizations tend to support immigration and national unity, while "unchurched" Catholics (France), Protestants (Germany), and Orthodox (Russia) have taken more nativist positions. The same pattern can be seen in Catholic voting for the Liberals and the BQ in Quebec. Institutional religions have thus joined with the major political parties in helping limit the dangers of anti-immigrant "tribal religion" and small-party xenophobic politics on the extreme left and right. The weakening of institutional religion, therefore, makes the "widening" and the "deepening" of Europe less likely, and the xenophobic use of ethnic-based religion more likely.

France, the E.U.'s most stridently secular state facing Western Europe's largest Muslim population, has proved to be the most difficult national case. France's civil religion will not even allow Muslim headscarves to be worn in public schools. However, Prime Minister Raffarin called for ideological adjustments, saying that "we need to invent a new *laïcité* for the twenty-first century, a *laïcité* which is not negative [read antireligious], but which expresses the intrinsic freedom of each person."[77] From the other side, the clerical leadership of French Muslims remains overwhelmingly foreign born. According to the Interior Ministry, only about 10 percent of the imams are French citizens and half do not even speak French.[78] The French government has deported dozens of Muslim clerics since 2001 for advocating actions not in accord with national and E.U. democratic values. On Bastille Day 2004, Chirac admitted that France's effort to integrate people of different religious and ethnic backgrounds "doesn't work well."[79] For this reason, Paris fears the early integration of seventy million Turks into the European Union, despite the fact that Erdogan's politics embody Islam's closest approximation to Christian Democracy. In October 2004, however, the twenty-five E.U. heads of state unanimously gave what Romano Prodi called a "qualified yes"[80] to begin negotiations over Turkey's entrance.

Catholic leaders like the late John Paul II include Russia in Europe, and see a special relationship between Poland and Russia. For the Polish pope, and for his countryman and Nobel laureate Czeslaw Milosz, the new direction for conceptualizing a continental spiritual mission could come from cities such as Krakow, Vienna, and Prague. The people of

---

[77] *Le Point*, March 21, 2003.
[78] April 30, 2004.
[79] July 15, 2004.
[80] October 7, 2004.

Mittel Europa, such Poles assert, have come to wisdom through suffering the horrible ravages of both Marxism and Fascism. Milosz quotes Russian writer Dmitri Merezhkovsky, "Russia is a woman, but she never had a husband. She was merely raped by Tartars, Czars, and Bolsheviks. The only husband for Russia was Poland. But Poland was too weak."[81] Indeed, many Poles feared that their country was not strong enough spiritually or economically to enter into the European Union. But the Polish bishops visited Brussels in November 1997 and endorsed voting to ratify their nation's entrance to the European Union.

In June 1999 Pope John Paul II made his sixth papal trip to Poland, his longest at thirteen days. Ten million Poles attended events, and another twenty million watched on television. The pope reiterated his message that Poland remain true to its traditional religious values so that it could serve as a spiritual focus for European unity. The pope was deeply disappointed by the rush of some of his countrymen to materialism as the Poles themselves have been disillusioned by the darker aspects of Western capitalism such as corruption, low wages, rising unemployment, and the crisis of the peasantry. The resulting economic stratification fosters the return to power of former Communists and a potent blend of nationalism and populism as tapped by Andrzej Lepper in his Self-Defense movement and party. Solidarity as a political party has disintegrated, and the former Communists of the Democratic Left took over in the September 2001 elections, but only in coalition with Self-Defense.

American leaders have also cautiously identified Russia with the new Europe. On June 3, 2000, President Clinton, standing in the courtyard of the Aachen cathedral where Charlemagne is buried, called for the inclusion of Russia in the European expansion. Since 1994 Russia has been a member of the interim Partnership for Peace, a quasi-junior NATO, and in 1997 signed an additional agreement for further cooperation with NATO. Following September 11, the United States dropped its threat to cut aid for Russian disarmament and has not objected to increased contacts between Russia and the Ukraine and Russia and Poland. However, Secretaries of State Powell and Rice have commented critically on the lack of democratic transparency in Russian elections, Russian media, and Russian business practices. Putin has turned his attention to forming an economic bloc from the core of the old USSR: Russia, Belarus, Ukraine, and Kazakhstan. So as Turkey's E.U. membership has progressed, that

---

[81] Czeslaw Milosz, *Native Realm: A Search for Self-Definition*, trans. Catherine S. Leach (Garden City, NY: Doubleday, 1968), 147.

of Russia has received less emphasis. French and Dutch rejections of the E.U. Constitution, however, will slow down both.

If the war in the ex-Yugoslavia posed the first major challenge to the unity of the West, the Iraq War has posed the second, with France, Germany, and Russia opposing the U.S. initiative. After the difficulties in political reconstruction, however, both Bush and Chirac put the best possible face on relations between Washington and Paris. By the following spring Bush was willing to give the U.N. a more prominent role and to transfer sovereignty to the Iraqis. Within the single month of June Western leaders met in ceremonial, economic, and military settings: D-Day at Normandy; G-8 at Sea Island; NATO in Istanbul. The different compositions of each group allowed some sophistication in attempting to bring the West together. Bush, for example, used the latter meeting to mend fences with NATO member Turkey. In the end, however, Chirac and Schröder would not give Bush the diplomatic cover he sought for reelection. They also feared their publics. After all, Spanish Prime Minister José Maria Aznar had been defeated in March, partly for his backing of the Iraq War opposed by 90 percent of his fellow citizens. Aznar's government also had used its control of state media to suggest Basque involvement in the Madrid train bombing just before the election. Before the bombing, Spain had had one of the continent's best relationships with its Muslim immigrants, mainly from Morocco. The election of the Socialist government under José Luis Rodriguez Zapatero reintroduced state-church tension over issues like same-sex marriage and adoption, abortion, and religious education.

What analogy shall we employ, then, in thinking about the future of the West? Instead of the image of a bicycle in disequilibrium as is commonly used for the European Union, recent technological advances applied to the economic, military, and communication systems have made the Western political-religious dynamic analogous to that of riding a motorcycle at full throttle without brakes or helmets while the two riders (U.S., E.U.), each arguing with themselves, jostle for control of the handlebars. The West owes its political-religious coherence to a synthesis of its classical and religious traditions with those of the Enlightenment. Without serious dialogue between people who take both their belief and their unbelief seriously, the motorcycle will crash and likely destroy all the motorcycles, bicycles, and pedestrians, the rest of the world, with it. Chapter 6 describes the current political-religious situation of the globe's second fastest motorcycle, East Asia.

6

East Asia

Modernization and Ideology

Following the Cold War, East Asia (China, Japan, Korea) has become the globe's second most powerful region economically, militarily, and politically. Unlike Western Europe (France, Germany, Great Britain), North America (Canada, Mexico, the United States), and South America (Argentina, Brazil, Chile), these three East Asian countries have legitimately harbored little trust for each other, resulting in high militarization throughout the region. The Korean peninsula constitutes one of the world's four major flashpoints for a nuclear war. East Asia also contains the second, the Taiwan Strait, with Kashmir and the Middle East located in South and West Asia respectively. East Asia has thus become an area of great hope and great danger.

Despite the traditional antipathy between the Koreans and the Japanese and the unique tension-filled relationship between the Chinese and the Japanese, historical and cultural links do remain. Whereas autonomous and politically engaged religious and secular institutions characterize the West, East Asia has experienced the unified political-religious legitimacies of the state in Confucian and Maoist forms, and the separate tradition of Mahayana Buddhism. Korea and Taiwan have produced strong indigenous Buddhist and Christian traditions. Although their cultures and spoken languages preexisted the borrowing, the Koreans and the Japanese did adopt the Chinese writing system and facets of Chinese art and literature. Buddhism and Confucianism profoundly influenced all three countries, with neo-Confucianism eventually winning out among the political elite in ninth-century China, fifteenth-century Korea, and seventeenth-century Japan. During the twentieth century, however, Asians discovered little agreement on a common East Asian culture that might foster the equivalent of European Unification. The major attempt at such unification, Japan's East Asia Co-Prosperity Sphere, gave such efforts a terrible reputation, and contributed to the current arms race in the region. The three nations all play major global economic roles and lead the world in citizen usage of different types of the new communication media like text messaging (China) and high-speed Internet per capita (South Korea). Accelerated development in the EMC systems has brought about significant regional change since the end of the Cold War as the younger generations attain power.

CONTEMPORARY CHINA: THE IDEOLOGICAL VACUUM AFTER THE CULTURAL REVOLUTION

When the Cold War system disintegrated in 1989, the leadership of the People's Republic of China (PRC) could take some of the credit or blame for bringing about that collapse. After the Sino-Soviet split of the late 1950s, Beijing withdrew from global affairs during the height of the Cultural Revolution. Student Red Guards burned the British embassy in 1967. In the early 1970s, Mao's government adopted a diplomatic position independent of both Moscow and Washington, leading to the Nixon "ping pong" visit and the U.S.-China Shanghai Communiqué of February 1972. Master global strategists Zhou Enlai and Henry Kissinger rejoiced, but Soviet Foreign Minister Andrei Gromyko did not. "Paramount Leader" Deng Xiaoping articulated the rationale behind Chinese diplomatic independence in his speech on the Theory of Three Worlds in 1981 that attacked both "capitalist imperialism" and "social imperialism." The Chinese later set down three conditions for reestablishing the friendly relations with Moscow that had been broken under Nikita Khrushchev at the time of the Quemoy Crisis and the Great Leap Forward. Deng demanded Soviet withdrawals from Vietnam and Afghanistan, and a lessening of Soviet military presence along the Chinese border. Brezhnev rejected all three demands, but by May 1989 Mikhail Gorbachev had accomplished all three of Deng's wishes. Now "the Western barbarian" himself would visit Beijing to sign a new Sino-Soviet Treaty witnessed by an unprecedented gathering of the world's media. However, when the Soviet leader arrived on May 15, Democracy protestors prevented the humiliated Deng from even bringing his illustrious visitor into Tiananmen Square.

This Democracy Movement, which had begun with the funeral of deposed party leader Hu Yaobang, thus upstaged the Sino-Soviet Treaty in the global media. CNN's twenty-four-hour news cycle constantly pushed reporters to find or to create "student leaders" and to file new protest stories pitting the increasingly media-savvy students versus the oppressive government. Dan Rather of CBS went to Beijing to broadcast live. Tiananmen trumped every other story above the fold of the *New York Times* for at least six weeks. That the students held up pictures of Gorbachev as a supporter of democracy mortified Deng. Indeed, Chinese leaders had been watching anxiously as the emphasis of the Soviet government's reform moved from *perestroika* [economic restructuring] to *glasnost* [political openness]. When forced to choose between losing authoritarian political control or delaying economic reform, the Chinese leadership rejected the Soviet path and chose the latter. Deng cashiered party leader Zhao Ziyang and ordered the 27th Army under Yang Shangkun to take the square. Chinese politicians and foreign analysts continue to debate the political roles of various leaders in that crackdown, as illustrated in the release of *The Tiananmen Papers*. When poor aged Zhao finally passed away in January 2005, his funeral became a political issue.

Chapter 4's treatment of Maoist Marxism ended with the Chinese Communist Party's (CCP) general loss of ideological legitimacy following the Cultural Revolution and the death of Lin Biao. The great and much loved premier Zhou Enlai died in January 1976 and Mao followed him in September.Deng Xiaoping then returned from the political wilderness and took his first major step to power by gaining control of the economy at the CCP's Third Plenum in December 1978. Deng and United States President Jimmy Carter established diplomatic relations in January 1979, further opening China to the world and vice versa. Deng then made a wonderfully successful public relations visit to the United States the next month, listening to John Denver's "Rocky Mountain High" at the Kennedy Center, touring Atlanta's Ford plant, donning a ten-gallon hat to slurp chili in Houston, and inspecting Boeing aircraft in Seattle.

Sino-American rapprochement fostered Chinese economic reform. Deng needed global financing and technical expertise to pursue his domestic policy of economic pragmatism. After the cruel debacle of the Cultural Revolution, such economic and social changes generated great excitement in both the cities and the countryside. The new economic rules, however, produced "losers" as well as "winners." Economic "losers" could forfeit their "iron rice bowl" of guaranteed employment and medical care so long provided by the Communist Party. As industrial workers and peasants faced such losses, Confucian *guanxi* [informal connections] regained their crucial importance. Traditional Chinese corruption thus flourished along with Deng's "market socialism." In 1984, for example, Beijing discovered that the Hainan Island Communist newspaper had formed a trading company that diverted scarce foreign exchange to purchase Hong Kong luxury goods for resale to cadres in the rest of the country. China, recently renowned for its "Maoist puritan" ethic, joined countries like Nigeria and Indonesia at the bottom of the international transparency index. Prostitution and the drug trade gradually reestablished themselves, to be followed in the nineties by the AIDS epidemic.

Many Chinese turned to preexisting or new informal social networks, including religious ones, to meet the twin personal goods of community and belief that had been lost with the demise of the credibility of the Communist party. Sometimes these religious practices reinforced other societal groupings like the clan or the village. Sometimes they provided a safe haven for those disadvantaged by rapid economic change or those weakly related to other societal organizations. This religious resurgence included, first of all, the spectacular growth of Chinese folk religion. Columbia anthropologist Myron Cohen comments that, "The growth of popular religion since the so-called reforms is really the resumed expression of something that was never destroyed even though it was terribly repressed."[1] For example, the people in the area around Yulin in northern Shaanxi had built more than fifty major temples, five hundred medium temples, and thousands of smaller temples during the first twenty years of Deng's policies. In Southeast China,

[Local communal religion] involves participation in communal rituals centered in temples dedicated to a variety of gods from a vast pantheon, many of local origin. In addition to participating in communal rites on important annual ceremonies such as Chinese New Year and the lantern festival, or on the birthdays of the gods, individuals can go to village temples any time to worship the local gods by bowing and praying, proclaiming vows, making offerings of food and drink, and burning incense and spirit money. These acts are usually followed by divination of the god's response by dropping divining blocks or consulting divinatory poetry.[2]

There also has been a resurgence of more orthodox, government-approved, Buddhism among the Han Chinese. For the Chinese leadership, state relations with such native Han Buddhism and state relations with Tibetan Buddhism constitute completely different political categories. PRC relations with the world religions among the Han require penetration, regulation, and control by the state Religious Affairs Bureau

---

[1] *Washington Post*, August 24, 1998.
[2] Kenneth Dean, "Local Communal Religion in Contemporary South-east China," *The China Quarterly* 174 (June 2003): 338.

(RAB). In Tibet and in Xinjiang Province, party officials perceive tantric Buddhism and Islam as ethnic and nationality threats. Beijing has also given certain dispensations to non-Han nationalities in social policy, for example, the one-child policy, but recent bombings in Xinjiang and large cities blamed on Islamic extremists have alarmed the leadership. Ethnic groups overlap the Chinese border with Russia and other Central Asian states with their own Islamic oppositions. The September 11 attacks gave Beijing a much freer hand to label all such groups "terrorists."[3]

Chinese Catholicism with its predominantly rural base exhibits many of the same social and political forms as Chinese folk religion. These sectarian forms have protected Catholics against an authoritarian state during times of persecution, but these forms do not encourage Catholics to join an open civil society when that persecution has been lifted, although southern Catholics tend to be more open than northern ones. Government control of religion has always been tighter the closer one gets to Beijing. Madsen's *China's Catholics*[4] focuses on villages in northern Hebei Province and Tianjin City where nineteenth-century missionaries had sought to protect their converts by bringing believers together in Catholic villages, which became a "world of God." In these villages Catholic morality reinforces Confucian filial piety and loyalty to the village. Hebei's Xian County remains very poor and rural, disproportionately Catholic, and for the latter reason, closed to foreigners by the state. National estimates of Chinese Catholics range from ten to twelve million, with four million connected to the state-sponsored Catholic Patriotic Association. The government has manipulated the conflicts between underground and official Catholics to weaken both groups.

Catholics pose a special foreign policy problem because of their loyalty to a pope located outside of, and therefore not under the control of, China. Rome and Beijing fought a fierce battle over the consecration of bishops beginning with the Great Leap Forward in 1957. That conflict moderated somewhat under Deng. According to anonymous and knowledgeable Catholic sources,[5] the Vatican has already secretly recognized almost all government-sponsored bishops like Jesuit Archbishop

---

[3] For persecution in Xinjiang, see April 12, 2005.

[4] Richard Madsen, *China's Catholics* (Berkeley: University of California Press, 1998).

[5] Ren Yanli, Chinese Academy of Social Sciences expert on the Vatican, stated, "We have only nine bishops who are not recognized by the pope [out of 71 altogether]." *Newsweek* (April 18, 2005). Recently, members of the Catholic NGO Sant'Egidio and officials from the Chinese policy research groups have been meeting with the blessing of both leaderships. May 22, 2005.

Aloysius Jin Luxian of Shanghai. Jin, for his part, inserted a "Prayer for the Pope" into hundreds of thousands of prayer books. And the Vatican has never declared the Catholic Patriotic Association to be schismatic. President Jiang Zemin and his economic allies eventually loosened up on state-regulated religion, suggesting that it could contribute to morality and social service. Pan Yue, deputy director of the State Council Office for Restructuring Economic Systems, even advocated recruiting religious persons for party membership "[to] take advantage of the unifying power and appeal of religion to serve the CCP regime."[6] This approach paralleled Jiang's "Three Represents," which welcomed businessmen to party membership.

From the government perspective, all Protestants must join the state-sponsored Three Self Patriotic Movement (TSPM). Contemporary Chinese Protestantism exhibits two main forms. Many urban elite became Protestants as part of their embrace of Western modernity before the founding of the People's Republic of China. That urban Protestant culture, fostered in Chinese universities and welfare institutions founded by British and American missionaries, encourages the international contacts and even occasionally the civil society language of mainline Protestantism. These Protestants also generally belong to the TSPM. On the other hand, the rural "house churches" exhibit many of the same sectarian features as Chinese folk religion and Catholic peasant sectarianism. There are an estimated ten million Protestants associated with the TSPM, and somewhere between twenty and eighty million Protestants who reject any supervision from the government. The government both greatly fears and unwittingly fosters more extreme cases of the latter since when the state makes it difficult for all religion, "more heterodox groups are likely to gain among the uneducated masses. [. . .] China's Great Awakening is just as likely to result in the kind of tumult that happened in the wake of the Taiping Rebellion – which started with a mix of Christianity and native folk practice – as it is to create a liberal revolution."[7] In 1995 Ye Xiaowen, a tough-minded atheist with prior service in the 1994 crackdown in Tibet, became head of the RAB. Ye immediately directed a strong attack on house churches. The party first articulated its post-Maoist policy in

[6] Cited in Pitman B. Potter, "Belief in Control: Regulation of Religion in China," *The China Quarterly* 174 (June 2003): 323.

[7] Joshua Kurlantzick, "Move Over, Confucius," *The New Republic* (September 6, 2004): 41. Kurlantzick is reviewing David Aikman, *Jesus in Beijing: How Christianity is Transforming China and Changing the Global Balance of Power* (Washington, DC: Regnery, 2003), which describes the explosion of Protestant sects.

"Document 19" (1982), which encouraged respect and freedom for the government-regulated five world religions of Buddhism, Daoism, Islam, Catholicism, and Protestantism while discouraging sects. "Document 6" (1991) aimed at increased regulation of all religious activity.

The Chinese government often engages in international public relations on religious issues. After President Jiang Zemin visited Washington in November 1997, he agreed in the following February to an American church delegation to China consisting of National Association of Evangelicals President Don Argue, Catholic Bishop Theodore E. McCarrick, and New York Rabbi Arthur Schneier. In October 2002 just before Jiang Zemin went to Washington, the government changed death sentences to life imprisonment for Pastor Gong Shengliang and two other leaders of the South China Church, banned as a cult.

At the national level, however, human rights challenges to the government have come from elite students and intellectuals only sporadically related to a mass base, with the Third Democracy Movement of spring 1989 resulting in the military crackdown of June 4. The student hunger strike of May 1989 derived its major political significance from convincing the public at large, especially the workers, of student sincerity in their quest for political reform. In the post-Mao period, elite criticism of authoritarianism developed slowly from its tentative beginnings in popular support for Deng's political return in the late 1970s. The first worker-led Democracy Movement of 1978–79 eventually inspired later intellectual-led (1986–87) and student-led movements (1989).

The students in that Tiananmen movement consciously entered into their Confucian elite responsibility. At Hu Yaobang's funeral student leaders knelt as if presenting their memorial to the emperor. They also celebrated the seventieth anniversary of the May Fourth Movement with political gusto. *The Tiananmen Papers* introduces two other characteristics of the Chinese elite dissident tradition that might surprise Americans. Schell comments, "Whereas our own Western notions of 'patriotism' can embrace the idea of a loyal opposition or a patriotic dissidence, in the Chinese worldview patriotism – or *aiguo zhuyi*, literally 'the ism of loving one's country" – is much more confining. . . . Chinese notions of patriotism do not readily extend approval to a citizen who seeks to remain loyal to something other than the ruler, the state, and the larger racial notion of 'being Chinese.'"[8] So the leaker-compiler of the material Zhang Liang

---

[8] Orville Schell, "Reflections on Authentication," Zhang Ling, compiler, Andrew J. Nathan and Perry Link, eds., *The Tiananmen Papers* (New York: Public Affairs, 2001), 472.

(pseudonymn), believing that any meaningful reform must come from within the CCP, would provide the American editors with only computer printouts of the original documents, not the originals. From Zhang's perspective, handing over the originals would constitute treason. Andrew Nathan provides another example: "Zhao's [CCP General Secretary Zhao Ziyang] refusal either to participate in or to resist the [Tiananmen] crackdown can be seen as the response of a principled official in the Confucian tradition, who chooses retirement when he faces a conflict between his obligations to the people and his loyalty to his patron."[9]

In such a tradition, the party-brat zoo electrician Wei Jingsheng, leader of the First Democracy Movement, represents a new type of critical integrity. In his Forward to *The Courage to Stand Alone*, a collection of Wei's letters to Deng Xiaoping and other CCP top leaders from prison, Nathan comments "Wei Jingsheng's prison writings show how much his career as a political prisoner has been a kind of performance art. His tragedy did not simply befall him; he created and shaped it."[10] Few other Chinese dissidents would write the post-Tiananmen Deng from prison: "I've long known that you are precisely the kind of idiot to do something foolish like this, just as you've long known that I am precisely the kind of idiot who will remain stubborn to the end and take blows with his head up."[11] Wei became prominent because of his wall poster "The Fifth Modernization," put up before dawn on December 5, 1978. In plain and simple language he argued that Deng's other Four Modernizations (agriculture, industry, science, national defense) were no good without democracy. The poster states: "What is true democracy? It is when the people, acting on their own will, have the right to choose representatives to manage affairs on the people's behalf and in accordance with the will and the interests of the people."[12] For his democratic zeal, Wei spent more than fourteen years of his fifteen-year sentence in prison. Beijing sent him to the United States for medical reasons in November 1997 just weeks before Jiang Zemin visited Washington.

Wei has been less influential within China than the leader of the Second Democracy Movement, astrophysicist Fang Lizhi. "China's Sakharov" brings the theme of scientific certitude to his treatment of democracy

---

[9] Zhang, *Tiananmen*, xlvi.
[10] Andrew J. Nathan, "Forward," Wei Jingsheng, *The Courage to Stand Alone* (New York: Penguin, 1997), xi.
[11] Wei, *Courage*, 137.
[12] Wei, *Courage*, 206–7.

in the way earlier Western thinkers relied on philosophy. Nathan states, "According to Fang, if democracy were implemented in China, policy would reflect public wishes, decisions would be implemented smoothly, corrupt leaders would be removed from office, government would serve the interests of all classes and nationalities."[13] Largely missing from this predominantly moral debate have been specific discussions of what democratic institutions might best serve China. This situation partly reflects both the elite composition and tradition of most of the debate and the actual political situation where, like Iran, most elite believe that reform can only result from within the dominant political group.

Because of American government lobbying, both Fang and Wei were allowed to go to the West, and eventually to the United States. But these benevolent exiles did not end Sino-American tension over human rights. On October 5, 1998, at the United Nations the Chinese government signed The International Covenant on Civil and Political Rights. It had already signed The International Covenant on Economic, Social and Cultural Rights. This signing followed United States lobbying and a trip to China by the top United Nations human rights official Mary Robinson. On the same day, however, the Chinese government held activist Qin Yongmin for trying to register a human rights monitoring group for the second time in a week.[14] In the cases of both the Chinese Democratic Party (1998–99) and the Falun Gong (1999–2000), the point at issue was not ideology, but CCP control of the organizations.

Chinese governments have also sought to limit the exposure of their populations to Western individualistic "contagion" through control of new communication outlets like e-mail and text messaging. For example, on June 3, 2000, the government arrested Huang Qi, whose Web site was devoted in part to increasing public knowledge of the Tiananmen crackdown. Huang had begun the site two years earlier to help find missing women and children in the chaotic internal migration of the Deng years. Internet cafes currently include cameras to identify users. All traffic must pass through government servers with political filtering systems. In addition, Shanghai requires Internet user cards with national identity numbers. In 2003 Chinese sent more text messages, 220 billion, than the rest of the world combined. On the fifteenth anniversary of the Tiananmen ("6-4" for June 4) massacre, filtering excluded many text messages that

---

[13] Andrew J. Nathan, "Tiananmen and the Cosmos," *The New Republic* (July 29, 1991): 33.

[14] October 6, 1998.

exhibited the two offending numbers in proximity.[15] The major ideological challenge to party monopoly leadership during the last decade came from an obscure religious sect, the Falun Gong, who have used both the Internet and text messaging. Ian Johnson, who won the 2001 Pulitzer Prize for reporting on the Falun Gong, details the internal bicycle and public phone communication structure supporting the protests.[16] The Falun Gong's U.S. Web site continues to provide information and directives in eleven different languages, and devotees have used both satellite and cable to place their message before the Chinese public.

THE FALUN GONG: RELIGION AND POLITICS WITHIN THE ECONOMIC AND COMMUNICATION SYSTEMS

On April 25, 1999, ten thousand members of the Falun Gong thronged Tiananmen Square in front of Zhongnanhai, the highly guarded compound of China's leaders. This demonstration, specifically directed at an anti-Falun Gong article in a Tianjin magazine, constituted the largest and most significant challenge to the PRC leadership since the 1989 student movement. The PRC leadership, especially President Jiang Zemin, reacted furiously to the embarrassment that so many sect members could infiltrate the heart of Beijing without knowledge of the public security forces. A *People's Daily* editorial of July 22, 1999, proscribed the Falun Gong as an "evil cult." (*xie jiao*) Falun Gong (literally, "Dharma Wheel Practice"), also known as Falun Dafa ("Dharma Wheel Great Dharma"), offers a curious blend of traditional Chinese religion and politics set in the contemporary national and global economic and communication systems. The sect claims upward of one hundred million adherents worldwide, whereas the government states that only two million Chinese belong.

Nancy Chen emphasizes that the Falun Gong and other *qigong* sects arose out of the socioeconomic climate of the 1980s reforms: "In the midst of market expansion, alternative healing practices gave meaning to those who were being displaced in the new economic order and who came to embody social disorder."[17] As health care became more and more market-driven, the government faced the challenge of how to differentiate "scientific" *qigong* masters from charismatic charlatans. In the 1980s,

[15] June 27 and July 3, 2004.
[16] Ian Johnson, *Wild Grass: Three Stories of Change in Modern China* (New York; Pantheon, 2004), 185–292.
[17] Nancy N. Chen, "Healing Sects and Anti-Cult Campaigns," *The China Quarterly* 174 (June 2003): 505.

China witnessed an explosion of such *qigong* practices under many different masters, and the government for a time encouraged them to show the scientific value of indigenous medicine. Indeed, most Chinese view *qigong* as a health regime rather than a religion. Master Li Hongzhi, a forty-something former state grain clerk, had developed his particular exercises without any special spiritual or medical training. Li has also written extensively on the laws of the cosmos, another expected characteristic of this type of a syncretistic Chinese sect. The spinning wheel [*lun*], for example, refers both to the fifth exercise of visualizing a centering wheel spinning deep within the abdomen and to planets following the natural laws of the universe.

Many Chinese, both illiterate peasants and educated intellectuals, believe that the unseen forces of *qi* structure the physical world. Again following traditional practice, Falun Gong also preaches moral principles that lead their members to renounce personal vices like drunkenness and philandering. From the religious point of view, Richard Madsen concludes, "Though perhaps near the outer edge of the normal spectrum of Chinese indigenous spiritual practices, Falun Gong does not seem to go far enough over that boundary to be considered a cult."[18] If the Falun Gong represents nothing extraordinary from the religious perspective, why did the government react so negatively, identifying Falun Gong as its primary domestic political enemy? The April 1999 demonstration had directly challenged the CCP's control of religious organizations in an extraordinarily public way at the geographic center of national legitimacy. Although Li had moved to New York in 1998, the government later discovered that he had entered and departed the Beijing airport shortly before that initial demonstration.

Madsen, Chen, and Johnson also refer to the threatening nature of the sect's sociological profile. Falun Gong has attracted not just the rural misfits and marginal urban types prevalent in other potentially less dangerous sects, but also many members of the party, military, and security apparatus. In July 1999 the government arrested over five thousand party members and detained approximately twelve hundred government officials who belonged to the Falun Gong. The CCP sent these officials to North China for required ideological study in preparation for their renunciation of the sect.[19] Falun Gong responded by demonstrating in

[18] Richard Madsen, "Understanding Falun Gong," *Current History* 99 (September 2000): 245.
[19] July 27, 1999.

Dalian, Guangzhou, and twenty-eight other cities. Smaller demonstrations have also taken place sporadically, especially in Tiananmen Square. In the spring of 2000, several dozen of the sect's top leaders, including an air force general and a judge, were publicly sentenced to long prison terms. Li remains free in New York, but understandably difficult to contact personally.

Falun Gong members are also disproportionately middle-aged, that group having been hit hardest by current economic reforms, including loss of their medical benefits. But the organization remains amorphous and difficult to destroy. Lower officials attracted to the sect fear such government campaigns, but the actual exercises are so simple that they can be practiced at home with no outward manifestation. And in true Chinese campaign form, some government officials seem willing to overlook such deviance from lower-level members as long as they have some document of compliance to show their superiors. The Falun Gong also seems to have many connections throughout society and many members willing to sacrifice their freedom at the behest of the leadership. Johnson follows the case of Chen Zixui, beaten to death in Weifang, and her daughter's legal attempts to find out what happened.

The current economic situation offers additional risks for the government. Deng's social and economic policies weakened the party's hold on the nation. Perhaps two hundred million Chinese constitute a "floating population" no longer automatically present at their place of residence by means of the *hukou* [residence permit] system. In addition to these undocumented immigrant entrepreneurs who spend a large portion of their time in large cities, industrial workers, the traditional strength of the party, face increased unemployment as the government seeks to reform the state-owned enterprises (SOE) of the heavy industrial sector. The state fears an incendiary political combination of marginal rural and urban immigrants, religious sectarians, and disgruntled workers. Leadership might come from ex-party, military, and police cadres, and some intellectuals who perceive Master Li's cosmology as more science than religion. The party fears it could be a potent mix.

The government has used its national monopoly of the official media to lambaste the sect continually. For example, by July 1999 a seventy-minute documentary that portrayed the group as a pernicious cult was running almost non-stop on state television. The documentary, among other topics, featured the destruction of 1.5 million Falun Gong publications. By August, Beijing had produced a series of not-so-funny comic books illustrating the nefarious deeds of the "evil cult." The first book,

"Li Hongzhi: the Man and His Evil Deeds," opened with a drawing of Li faking the meditative posture of a traditional holy man, with a caption that reads in part, "His illegal doings seriously disrupted the normal order of society, causing chaos in people's social and moral principles."[20] The campaign's artistic style has approximated earlier denunciations of Madame Mao and "the Gang of Four" at the end of the Cultural Revolution, not a global highpoint in the sophisticated political uses of communication. The state campaign also featured the saga of another cult leader Liu Jianguo, self-anointed "Supreme Deity," who later confessed to his ideological scams after being arrested by the government in June 1998 for rape, extortion, and robbery. Because Falun Gong discourages the use of Western medicine, the Chinese press has trumpeted numerous stories of sectarians and their families dying from the consequent denial of modern medicine and health procedures.

The gruesome photos of the Tiananmen immolation incident on the eve of Chinese New Year, January 23, 2001, also became a staple of state propaganda. First one person, and then four others set themselves aflame in the square. One twelve-year-old girl died from her burns. At the time, a CNN news crew, knowing that New Year holidays tended to encourage protests, frequented the square. They filmed the first immolation from at least sixty yards away. Even before the second group torched themselves, however, police detained the CNN crew, confiscated the film, and then released them. Later government propaganda, however, charged that CNN had prior knowledge of the immolation, and had joined with other Western news agencies in plotting against the Chinese state. On February 4, a PRC-planted article appeared in the Hong Kong *Sing Tao Daily* making the above charges, for which "they [CNN] can be pursued for criminal responsibility under the crime of homicide."[21]

Ceaseless internal media publicity of the immolations did strengthen the government case within China, but even longtime national anti-cult crusaders like Sima Nan,[22] who first attacked Falun Gong in 1995, have been troubled by the ferocity of the attack. The campaign could backfire in generating too many martyrs, they feel, and those same media resources could have been used better in a stronger campaign against corruption. The conflict also caused problems in Hong Kong, as Chief Executive Tung

[20] August 17, 1999.
[21] February 9, 2001.
[22] November 20, 1999.

Chee-hwa sought both to maintain the ex-colony's promised political autonomy and simultaneously to respond to Beijing's heightened concern about Falun Gong activities. In January 2001 the sect sponsored an international conference in Hong Kong to criticize the Chinese government. Tung reacted by warning Falun Gong supporters that the police were monitoring them and that he would not allow the sect "to undermine peace and harmony on the mainland."[23]

JAPANESE SECULARISM AND POLITICS WITHIN THE ECONOMIC AND MILITARY SYSTEMS

Among East Asia's three countries, this nation of four major islands stands out in its religious, political, and economic sensitivity to the global context. Toyoda and Tanaka stress that "[t]he relationship between politics and religion in Japan has been driven, in part, by external, geopolitical forces and the pursuit of nationalist goals."[24] The American victory in World War II led to a parliamentary democracy and the globe's most secular society. Reischauer identified the remaining postwar religious influences as Confucianism and Christianity in ethics, Shinto and Buddhism in popular customs, and "the new religions" in social organization.[25] The latest survey figures for Japanese religious practice show "that only 25 percent of Japanese consider themselves to be religious, and only 4 percent regularly visit a shrine, temple, or church."[26] Nearly all religious Japanese self identify themselves as Buddhists, although their practices combine Buddhist and Shinto elements with, perhaps, a Christian-style wedding. Practicing Christians constitute only 2 percent of the population, but their disproportionately high social standing and global cultural influence magnifies their significance in national life.

Defeat discredited the old military nationalism among the public in general. Remnants of Zen-Bushido values found postwar uses in corporate training programs for "samurai businessmen" and among those conservatives who sought to rearm Japan. Soto Zen monk Victoria comments: "While corporate Zen is the primary manifestation of imperial-way Zen

---

[23] *San Jose Mercury News*, February 9, 2001.
[24] Maria A. Toyoda and Aiji Tanaka, "Religion and Politics in Japan," Jelen and Wilcox, 271.
[25] Edwin O. Reischauer, *The Japanese Today: Change and Continutity* (Cambridge, MA: Belnap, 1988), 203–15.
[26] Toyota and Tanaka, "Japan," 283.

and soldier Zen in postwar Japan, Zen's connection to the Japanese military, and to the sword, has by no means disappeared."[27]

The business use fit well with the reorientation of the entire society toward economic prominence, but Article Nine of the MacArthur Peace Constitution rejected war and a national military force. Traditional loyalty to the group and to the nation, urbanization, high literacy, plus significant U.S. support in the international system enabled Japan to join Germany in becoming one of the world's premier economic success stories. Under the American military umbrella, the conservative Liberal Democratic Party (LDP) and elite bureaucrats cooperated on export-oriented growth. By 1964 Japan had joined the OECD and hosted the Tokyo Olympics. Since the late 1980s, however, the country has experienced political and economic stagnation as it has sought to move from its global leadership in industrial production to the very different demands of postindustrial society. The bureaucratic guidance that proved so helpful in building up automobile and consumer electronics industries has become a stumbling block in the freewheeling competition for software dominance.

The ruling LDP lost its monopoly hold on parliament in 1993 after thirty-eight years of rule, resulting in coalition governments until September 2005. The LDP, however, led most of them. During the Cold War, Japanese Socialists and Communists offered an ideological left that attacked the security arrangements between Japan and the United States. In the 1990s Japanese Socialists ceased to be the second largest party, and they also ceased to offer a leftist ideological alternative. Many new conservative parties, for example, New Frontier, Liberal, New Conservatives, appeared and disappeared around prominent politicians, especially Ichiro Ozawa, which led to many fluid and temporary alliances, almost like the old factional groupings of the LDP. The Democratic Party of Japan, founded by Yukio Hatoyama and Naoto Kan in 1996, has become the principal opposition party. Kan made his name as a reformer as Minister of Health and Welfare when he investigated business and political corruption in Japan's use of tainted blood for transfusions.

The Japanese public demonstrated considerable enthusiasm for the election of LDP Prime Minister Junichiro Koizumi in April 2001. Here was a well-coifed, almost sexy, maverick to shake up the entrenched powers and revive the economy. But Koizumi failed to challenge the economic system while becoming distracted with nationalistic visits to Yasukuni Shrine and foreign ministry corruption. His ratings plummeted by the

---

[27] Brian Victoria, *Zen At War* (New York: Weatherhill, l997), 190.

end of his first year. In September 2002, however, Koizumi made a highly publicized visit to North Korea and in October appointed a new cabinet featuring an academic outsider, Heizo Takenaka, who vowed to settle Japan's huge loan crisis. In September 2003 Koizumi was reelected as party president even though most of the LDP parliamentarians opposed many of his policies and had to vote against their faction leaders to reelect him. Only Koizumi, they reasoned, could lead the LDP to election victory in November. In that election the LDP lost thirteen seats and the Democratic Party gained forty, but Koizumi could still govern effectively with his partner New Komeito and New Conservative parties. When the upper house defeated Koizumi's proposal to privatize the $3 trillion postal savings system, the prime minister called a snap election and recruited young, mostly female, "assassins" to run against those LDP members who opposed him. Koizumi succeeded in keeping the focus on the privatization and the general notion of "reform." The LDP won a landslide victory, increasing its seats to 296 of the 480-seat lower house. The Democratic Party of Japan tried to introduce other issues such as Iraq and relations with China and Korea but failed to generate voter interest. Their seats dropped from 175 to 113.

In Japan's predominantly secular culture, independent religious organizations do not play a significant role in articulating a national vision. Reischauer emphasized that many "new religions" sprang up as postwar migrants to the cities lost their ties to rural religion and found themselves without a suitable social group. Most of these new religions synthesize various Asian traditions with the strongest general influence from Shinto. Soka Gakkai [Value Creating Association] constitutes the largest and the most politically active of the postwar religions. Tsunesaburo Makiguchi founded Soka Gakkai as a lay branch of the Buddhist Nichiren Shoshu in 1930. He died in prison in 1944. His successor Josei Toda led Soka Gakkai's rapid postwar expansion before Daisaku Ikeda succeeded Toda. Ikeda has given more than forty years of official and behind-the-scenes direction to both Soka Gakkai and the political Clean Government Party [Komeito], founded in 1962. Although the political party remains technically a separate organization, Soka Gakkai members constitute its core constituency, which gives it a dependable religious base, but one which limits its appeal to the largely secular Japanese.

Until the political changes of 1993, Komeito generally held the position of the third strongest party after the Liberal Democrats and the Socialists. It always had difficulty, however, in specifying the meaning and policies of "Buddhist politics." Memory of Soka Gakkai's persecution by

the wartime government and Komeito's general stand for peace, however, have served as a break on the LDP right wing's rush to armament.
The original parent religious organization, Buddhist Nichiren Shoshu,
excommunicated Soka Gakkai in 1991. In October 1999, the New
Komeito joined the governing coalition, despite general public and inter-
LDP disapproval. The party had moved to the right in an attempt to
find allies to return to multiple-seat districts since a party with deep but
narrow support runs poorly in Japan's new single-member districts. For
most Japanese, sectlike behavior is associated with the nerve gas attack
in the Tokyo Subway in 1995 by the radical Aum Shinrikyo led by the
charismatic Shoko Asahara, who borrowed from both Buddhism and Hinduism. On the bright clear morning of March 20, Aum members released
the very deadly sarin gas on the Chiyoda, Marunouchi, and Hibiya Lines,
resulting in over five thousand injuries, but fortunately, in only ten deaths.
Japanese novelist Haruki Murakami[28] conducted a fascinating series of
interviews with both sect members and the victims of the sarin attack.

After Japan's defeat in World War II, the nationalistic "imperial-state
Zen" retained influence among rightists who belong to the most conser-
vative factions of the LDP. Victoria points to Japanese Buddhist scholar
Ichikawa Hakugen as the origin of these values in the writings of D. T.
Suzuki and in the Zen line of transmission from the Roshi [Master]
Harada Daium Sogaku (1870–1961) to Yasutani Hakuun (1885–1973),
though neither of the latter mentioned such issues when in the United
States. As Communist China became the major enemy in Asia, American
policy makers focused on preventing leftist power, which gave the nationalist right some breathing room, even if it did not lead to the revision of
the Peace Constitution as the Liberals and the Democrats pledged when
they joined in 1955. Japanese right-wing politics also has a long tradition
of connections with the *yakuza* [underworld], and it is a brave policeman
indeed who will interrupt the nearly ubiquitous high-decibel sound trucks
that preach nationalism in city neighborhoods.

With the breakdown of postwar economic legitimacy, some are calling for the return of prewar nationalism. Shintaro Ishihara, the author of
The Japan That Can Say No, became mayor of Tokyo in 1999. Ishihara
focused his election campaign on a demand that the United States return
Yokota Air Base. As soon as Koizumi was elected in April 2001, the new
prime minister greatly delighted the political right by pledging to visit the
Yasukuni War Shrine on August 15, the anniversary of the end of World

---

[28] Haruki Murakami, *Underground: The Tokyo Gas Attack and the Japanese Psyche* (New
    York: Vintage Books, 2000).

War II. Only Japan's most hawkish prime minister, Yasutani Nakasone, had visited on that day, in 1985. China and South Korea protested immediately and vehemently. When August came, Koizumi changed his visit to August 13, pleasing neither the nationalists nor their critics. The next April Koizumi visited Yasukuni without advance notice, and then stated that he would not visit in August. The controversy over the war shrine is exacerbated by the fact that Japan, unlike Germany, has never conducted a national dialogue nor accepted general responsibility for its wartime aggression. In August 2001, the Korean Foreign Minister Han Sung Joo commented, "The German question has been more or less settled. In Asia, however, Japan remains a difficult neighbor."[29] LDP leaders have sensed that such a discussion might cause conflict, especially within their ruling party, so they have opted for the traditional Japanese virtue of avoiding conflict at practically any cost. Such an avoidance policy carries over into the education of the next generation. For example, a recent government-approved middle school history textbook ignored the invasion of China in 1932, the Nanjing massacre, and the sexual slavery of Korean women during World War II. Foreign visitors to the Yasukuni shrine's Yushukan Military Museum's celebration of suicide bombs, torpedoes, and planes will be amazed to learn that China requested the Japanese invasion and that the defenders of Nanjing were merely "soundly defeated, suffering heavy casualties."[30]

Koizumi reacted to the September 11 attack by promising military support for any US reprisals. In a series of parliamentary debates and decisions on the Special Measures Law for U.S. Military Use (1997), the Revised Guidelines for U.S.-Japan Defense Cooperation (1999), and the Anti-Terrorism Special Measures Law (2001), Japan has positioned itself to act more forcefully in the "areas surrounding Japan" in future situations. However, even on Afghanistan, the SDF did not begin its logistical support until six weeks after the bombing began. "[N]o SDF personnel were deployed for refugee relief, no medical teams were dispatched to Afghanistan, and no weapons or ammunition were transported to U.S. forces. . . . Japanese leaders are pragmatists too concerned with balancing their economic and security interests around the globe to become a full military partner to the United States."[31]

Political trial balloons from the right continue, resulting in some subtle policy shifts. Japan boasts the world's second largest military budget at

[29] August 12, 2001.
[30] Max Boot, *Weekly Standard*, December 1, 2003.
[31] Gregory P. Corning, "Domestic Political Realignment and Japan's Evolving Security Policy," unpublished manuscript, 22–23.

$45 billion, and maintains a larger navy than Great Britain. In addition to the perennial debate about whether or not to revise the Peace Constitution, in June 2002 Koizumi's chief cabinet secretary Yasao Fukuda stated that Japan's three nonnuclear principles (ownership, production, and location on Japanese soil) might also be amended. Fukuda's statement followed by a little over one month opposition leader Ichiro Ozawa's prediction of nuclear armament if China gets "too inflated. [...] We have plenty of plutonium in our nuclear power plants, so it's possible for us to produce 3,000 to 4,000 nuclear warheads."[32] Indeed, Japan's nuclear power program plus missiles from the space program classify the country as a "virtual nuclear power." In July 2003, the Japanese parliament authorized sending one thousand peacekeeping troops to Iraq, but the government heeded public opinion by delaying the deployment until January and then sending only half the troops. The government argued that this deployment did not violate the Peace Constitution because southern Iraq had become a noncombat zone, a fact not noticed by the nearby Dutch and British soldiers. In April the officially favored "press club" Japanese media withdrew to Kuwait after sending back a long procession of cheerful reconstruction photos. When three Japanese aid workers were kidnapped, only two Japanese journalists, both nonpress club, remained. The government billed the three civilian ex-hostages for their flight home, where they received national public opprobrium for embarrassing their country.

THE KOREAN PENINSULA: NORTH-SOUTH COMPETITION IN THE EMC SYSTEMS

Korea makes a crucial case study for this book as all of the major theoretical considerations, from nuclear proliferation to Buddhist-Christian relations, affect politics on this peninsula. The South (Republic of Korea, ROK) and the North (Democratic Peoples Republic of Korea, DPRK), arose from the same historic culture, but exemplify the postwar world's sharpest contrast in political-economic systems. U.S.-ally South Korea remains tightly integrated into the global EMC systems. Until the "sunshine policy" breakthrough of summer 2000, Marxist authoritarian North Korea was the nation least open to the outside world. In fact, those searching for the closest contemporary equivalent of Maoist Marxism would do best to study Pyongyang. The Korean peninsula also offers examples of significant political roles by five major religious traditions:

---

[32] June 9, 2002.

neo-Confucianism, Marxism, Buddhism, Protestantism, and Catholicism. South Korea is 49 percent Christian, 47 percent Buddhist, and only 3 percent Confucian, but the whole culture remains permeated with neo-Confucian values. The Korean dynasties were served by Confucian scholar officials just as jealous of their ideological prerogatives as their Chinese and Vietnamese counterparts. The Yi Dynasty (1392–1910), for example, launched eight major persecutions of Catholics in the nineteenth century, creating a host of Korean martyrs.

Traditionally, the Chinese referred to Korea both as the isolated "hermit kingdom" and as "the Eastern land of civility" for its adoption of Confucian culture within the Chinese sphere of influence. Japanese colonization caused the breakdown of Korean Confucian forms without permitting native alternatives. Japanese officials demanded control over all religious organizations and sought to foster those with Japanese links like Buddhism and Shinto. Although the ROK adopted new and mixed religious and cultural forms under American hegemony, the DPRK inherited the spirit of fierce isolationist independence, albeit under Soviet and Chinese protection. Kim Il Sung and son Kim Jong Il strengthened that isolation by preaching a national ideology of *juche* [self-reliance]. The disappointing economic result has been that this country of twenty-two million, one half the population of the South, has an economy less than one-tenth. And the discrepancy increases yearly. The North does compete militarily, however, thus raising continual concerns in Seoul, Tokyo, Beijing, and Washington. The DPRK fields an army of 1.1 million, which faces the more modern ROK's 690,000 and the US's 37,000 troops on the peninsula.

In the Republic of Korea, a series of authoritarian regimes (Syngman Rhee 1949–60, Park Chung Hee 1961–79, Chun Doo Hwan 1980–88) pursued economic development based on state guidance and governmental support for Japanese-style conglomerates called *chaebol*. The government also clamped down on political opposition, especially on workers and students. On August 8, 1973, Kim Dae Jung, an opposition presidential candidate who had received at least 46 percent of the vote in the 1971 election, disappeared from his Toyko hotel room. The Korean Central Intelligence Agency (KCIA) had already shackled him, mafia style, to a concrete block on a ship when American and Japanese government protests convinced Park Chung Hee to spare Kim's life. In 1980 the new president Chun Doo Hwan, fresh from the massacre of over 200 protestors in Kwangju and a coup d'etat, condemned Kim to death. President Ronald Reagan convinced Chun to trade the "medical" exile of Kim to the United States for a lunch at the White House.

Throughout the Rhee, Park, and Chun dictatorships, Korean students led the democratic protests. For example, a 1960 student uprising overthrew Rhee, with intermittent and qualified support from opposition politicians and religious groups. In the 1950–70s, Christianity, the religion of the hegemonic United States, expanded into the cultural vacuum left by the disestablishment of neo-Confucianism. Korean Christianity did not suffer from being associated with Western imperialism as it did in many other countries. In fact, both Catholicism and Protestantism had come to Korea through Korean laymen prior to any missionaries. Although some Christian missionaries had cooperated with the Japanese, many Christians exercised leadership in the struggle for Korean independence. Following the great sufferings of the Korean War, the great majority of Christians, especially those who had fled persecution in the North, strongly supported the anti-Communist government of Methodist Rhee.

Gradually, however, mainline Protestants and Catholics began to protest government violations of human rights. The breaking point came with Park Chung Hee's Yushin Constitution of 1970 that enabled him to remain in office with Korea's variant of a bureaucratic-authoritarian regime. Christian protests reflected both modern and traditional elements. For example, when Catholics protested in the global Holy Year of 1974, they sang both "We Shall Overcome" and the age-old hymn of the Korean martyrs. Korean Protestants remain more numerous than Catholics and have provided the political system with presidents like Rhee and Presbyterian Kim Young Sam. Individual Catholics have also played roles of significant political influence. For example, Cardinal Stephen Kim Sou Hwan, the archbishop of Seoul, served as the principal ethical spokesperson for the democratic opposition to the dictatorships. President Kim Dae Jung was introduced to Catholicism by his political mentor John Chang, prime minister during a short-lived democratic interlude following the Rhee government. Postwar Korea has thus seen the great expansion of Christianity, the recovery of Buddhism, and the surge of new Korean religions that borrowed elements of Confucianism, Christianity, and native Korean shamanism. Mark Mullins has demonstrated the similar forms and goals of Korean shamanism and the megachurches of Korean Pentecostalism.[33] The Buddhist hierarchy, like conservative Christians, tended to support the government, but 160 progressive monks joined the 2,196

---

[33] Mark Mullins, "The Empire Strikes Back: Korean Pentecostal Mission to Japan," Karla Poewe, ed., *Charismatic Christianity in a Global Culture* (Columbia: University of South Carolina Press, 1994), 87–102.

personages who made up the 1987 Headquarters of the National Campaign for a Democratic Constitution.

The head of the KCIA assassinated President Park in 1979, and Chun Doo Hwan was forced to step down because of regime corruption. Roh Tae Woo,who had been Chun's military colleague, bet that opposition leaders, Kim Young Sam of the Pusan area and Kim Dae Jung of Cholla, could not unite behind a single opposition candidate. General Roh won his bet, and became president with 36 percent of the vote against Kim Young Sam's 28 percent and Kim Dae Jung's 27 percent. Personalism and regionalism have always been strong in Korean politics, even in religious politics. In 1994 the Buddhist leadership, headed by a North Kyongsang monk, was overthrown by a reformist group in which non-Kyongsang and especially Cholla Province Buddhists were numerous. The 1980 Kwangju massacre in Kim Dae Jung's poorer Cholla province, whose inhabitants have traditionally suffered discrimination from other regions, has remained an indelible feature of Korean politics just as the Tiananmen massacre has remained so in Chinese politics. In December 1987, however, the Korean political and business establishment took the risk of a freer election because of Roh's strategy and because democratization fit a modern industrial nation about to be internationally showcased in the Seoul Olympics of 1988. In the 1992 election, the opposition candidate Kim Young Sam, who seemed less radical to the Korean establishment than Kim Dae Jung, became president.

In the December 1997 election, the two frontrunners were Catholic, but they came from very different social and political backgrounds. Establishment choice Lee Hoi Chang led the campaign until the scandal broke that his sons had illegally escaped military service. In addition, the Asian economic flu hit Korea, and the public had become disillusioned with governmental and bureaucratic oversight of the economy. Kim Dae Jung narrowly defeated Choi 40.3 percent to 38.7 percent. Kim then surprised many in the skeptical establishment by moving quickly to reconcile the country. He pardoned dictators Chun and Roh, both natives of Kyongsang region, who had condemned him to death. He reassured foreign investors by pledging Korea's continued economic opening to the international market. The IMF released an additional $3.5 billion to Korean banks the next day. Kim even sought economic advice from the head of the Samsung Group, a *chaebol* that had fervently opposed him for decades.

The crucial test for the Korean political system continues to be the reunification of North and South. Student organizations and progressive Protestants and Catholics have pushed the issue, even when it was illegal to do so. South Korean representatives of the Korean National Council of Churches (KNCC) and North Korean representatives of the Chosun Christian Union gathered in Switzerland in November 1988 to adopt a declaration of peaceful reunification in Korea. The following year saw the arrests of Protestant minister Moon Ik Hwan and Catholic priest Moon Kyu Hyon for visiting the North. On December 2, 2001, twelve priests from the ROK Catholic Priests' Association for Justice concelebrated mass in Pyongyang, with many younger North Korean Catholics in attendance. The secretary of the DPRK-approved Korean Roman Catholics Association (KRCA), Paul Kang Ji Young, became a Catholic after seeing Father Moon on his 1989 visit. However, the earlier Korean War conservative anti-Communist tradition remains, especially among older Christians.

Kim Dae Jung kept up his campaign for a "sunshine policy" until these efforts bore fruit in his June 13–15, 2000, visit to Pyongyang. At the following September Sydney Olympics, Korean athletes entered the stadium arm-in-arm and competed as a single team, producing euphoria across Asia and across the world. In October 2000, Kim Dae Jung received the Nobel Peace Prize for his "great moral strength"[34] in pursuing both democratization and reconciliation over more than thirty years. Called "Asia's Mandela," Kim has, like the South African leader, emphasized nonviolence and reconciliation, and spoken often of the significance of religious faith to his consistent political vision. Kim Dae Jung also reached out to Japan, and Kim's reputation for human rights and reconciliation enabled the Japanese to make a strong official apology for the colonial period when Kim visited Tokyo in October 1998.

Kim Dae Jung's visit to Pyongyang, however, did not solve all of the South Korean, pan-Korean, and global political and economic issues associated with the peninsula. In April 2000, just after the announcement of the trip, the opposition Grand National Party captured 133 of the newly downsized 273-seat parliament, leaving Kim's Millennium Democratic Party a minority of 115. The conservative opposition also criticized stringent IMF terms and the state selling of Korean companies to foreign buyers, as in the case of worker protests over the sale of Daewoo Motors to Daimler Chrysler. In August 2003 the Hyundai business backer of the "sunshine policy," Chung Mong Hun, under pressure for election corruption and $400 million in payments to the North to foster the Pyongyang summit and Hyundai-DPRK joint business projects, committed suicide.

[34] October 14, 2000.

In the December 2002 presidential election, Kim's designated successor, Roh Moo Hyun defeated Lee Hoi Chang of the Grand National Party, 48.9 percent to 46.6 percent. Roh benefited from the support of the younger generation who wished to renegotiate the ROK's relationship with the United States on a more equal basis. Many of these younger voters were located in Seoul a few miles south of the DMZ, and backed a more nuanced approach to the DPRK than that offered by Washington. With Roh winning in a mildly anti-Bush campaign, the year 2002 constituted a trifecta of losses for U.S. diplomacy in three elections of major allies: Germany, Brazil, and South Korea. The election also demonstrated the strength of the Internet and other new media, supportive of Roh, against the old press club system of the major newspapers, supportive of Lee. In fact, Roh gave his first inaugural interview to the online OhmyNews.com and moved to dismantle the press club system left over from Japanese colonization. When the parliament's conservative majority sensed Roh's determination to change Korean politics, they impeached him on March 12, but that conservative "coup d'etat" proved a political disaster. In the April parliamentary elections, Roh's Uri party won 152 of the 299 seats, ousting conservatives for the first time since 1961. The Grand National Party dropped to 121 seats. The national Constitutional Court dismissed the impeachment charges in May.

In summarizing the connections of politics, religion, and economic development on the peninsula, Korean scholar Nyung Kim[35] has focused on the interaction of domestic and international factors. In his comparison with Latin American development, South Korea benefited from its Confucian ethical tradition, but only after the Japanese occupation had disestablished neo-Confucianism. The traditionally prohegemonic Korean political elite switched their alliance from China to the United States, and Christianity, taking advantage of earlier lay missionary work, expanded into the cultural vacuum. Both Confucianism and Christianity faced the dual challenge of economic development and democratization, and both contributed, says Kim, to both authoritarian and democratic strains in Korean society. Kim further comments that the traditional conservatism of Korean Buddhism started to change from the 1980s both in political coalitions with progressive Christians and on issues specific to Buddhists like the treatment of Buddhism in school textbooks and in the communication media. The Buddhist hierarchy, he says, has remained

---

[35] Nyung Kim, "The Politics of Religion in South Korea, 1974–89: The Catholic Church's Political Opposition," Ph.D. dissertation (University of Washington, 1993).

more conservative than the common monks and laity. Both the new religions and later Pentecostalism combined native shamanistic forms with foreign borrowings. All the religious traditions now face the next great challenge for Korea, the reunification of North and South. For example, in June 2004 Inchon local government officials and leaders from seven religions came together under the civic group Solidarity for Reunification for a four-day commemoration of Kim Dae Jung's trip to Pyongyang four years earlier. Bishop Boniface Choi Ki San of Inchon chaired the organizing committee. One hundred representatives from North Korea, 120 from South Korea, and 50 from overseas Korean communities joined in the festival of sports, games, performances, and a procession before a crowd of twenty thousand in the Inchon stadium.[36]

THE FUTURE OF EAST ASIA IN THE EMC SYSTEMS

Hosting international sporting events in the communication system has often signaled the global prestige of a certain stage of economic development and diplomatic acceptance, as in the Olympics of Tokyo (1964), Mexico City (1968), Seoul (1988), and Beijing (2008). The 2002 World Cup, jointly hosted by Japan and South Korea, constituted one of the politically more improbable athletic events of the last one hundred years. Japanese Prime Minister Koizumi, and Akihito's cousin (because the emperor feared being booed), attended the opening ceremonies in Korea on May 31. Kim Dae Jung reciprocated at the final in Yokohama. The South Koreans became the first Asian team to reach a World Cup semifinal, setting off a national delirium among the entire population who suddenly morphed into "Red Devils" with red rooting shirts and red-painted faces. Even the Japanese news media praised the Koreans for proving that Asians could compete with Europeans and South Americans in their traditional game.

East Asian and European nations currently face similar challenges in adjusting to the overwhelming global power of the United States, but the Europeans voice their concerns more insistently, with just a hint of condescension. Such feelings tend to fester in Asia, and then explode. China, Korea, and Japan have all experienced rocky periods with the Bush Administration, making popular nationalist sentiment more likely. For example, within eight days during July 2002, the Pentagon issued a report warning of Chinese militarization on the twelfth, a separate

---

[36] *Asian Focus*, June 25, 2004.

congressional commission concluded that the PRC constituted a security and an economic threat on the fifteenth, and the State Department imposed sanctions on eight Chinese companies and one individual for selling dual-use equipment to Iran on the nineteenth.[37] Although all three actions seemed unrelated – and the Chinese replied softly so as to not disturb preparations for their November party congress – that week's events did point to continued Sino-American tension even after antiterrorism cooperation following September 11. *China's New Rulers: The Secret Files* gives a close look into the opinions of "the Fourth Generation" of PRC leadership. These seven leaders, from Hu Jintao to Luo Gan, all view the Sino-American relationship as the clash of an up and coming power with a hegemonic one. They expect a zig-zag course of more or less tension, but tension that can be managed.[38] The enormous U.S. investment in the PRC gives both countries a strong motive for mutual cooperation. Japan, South Korea, and Taiwan also have significant economic links to Beijing.

In May 2003 U.S. visits, ROK president Roh Moo Hyun and Japanese Prime Minister Koizumi both indicated the desire to find a common solution for tensions with North Korea without radical action. Collapse of the DPRK would cause an economic debacle for Seoul, and even peaceful reunification could cost the South twice what reunification cost Germany. China finds Kim Jong Il troublesome, but it doesn't want the DPRK to collapse, sending refugees across the border. On the other hand, an expanded North Korean weapons program might spark an East Asian arms race, most damaging to Beijing. Since August 2003, China has sponsored a series of six-party talks aimed at defusing the crisis. By September 2005, little progress was reported, but the atmosphere had improved. Pyongyang now has embassies in 41 countries and diplomatic relations with 155.

The ROK has continued to foster links with North Korea while supporting the United States in Iraq. Korean bilateral trade increased to $724 million in 2003 from $400 million in 2000. Since 1999, 700,000 South Korean citizens have visited the Hyundai-run park on the DPRK's Mount Kumgang. In summer 2004 each side opened seven ports to the others' ships, and in the fall a South Korean-run industrial park opened at Kaesong, fifteen miles north of the border. This combines ROK industrial might with cheap DPRK labor, twenty-six cents/hour versus $2.25

---

[37] July 26, 2002.
[38] Andrew J. Nathan and Bruce Gilley, *China's New Rulers: The Secret Files* (New York: New York Review of Books, 2002).

in the South.[39] The Russians desire to build a pipeline through North Korea to supply energy to the entire peninsula, but the strategic considerations remain a nightmare. On the Iraq issue, ROK has continued to support the United States, despite the kidnapping of seven South Korean Arab-speaking Protestant missionaries and the beheading of one.

East Asian political leaders all seek their particular national solution to the ideological challenge of the twenty-first century: How can the government foster a national political community that its citizens will embrace morally and spiritually as well as economically? China's post-Maoist response, Deng's "Four Modernizations," has emphasized economic goals, hoping that economic progress will solidify popular support long enough for the leadership to build new sources of legitimacy. But when the state loses moral legitimacy and substantial sectors of the society face economic hardship, only force and the threat of force remains. Bruce Gilley argues for *China's Democratic Future*, but this author agrees with Kristof that while Gilley makes the case for the demise of the current "appallingly corrupt" regime, there are at least three other possible outcomes (military dictatorship, war with Taiwan and the United States, civil war and chaos), and "there's a good chance we'll both turn out to be wrong"[40] with another unforeseen eventuality. Certainly, it is unlikely that rural religions sects like the Three Grades of Servants and their rivals, the Eastern Lightning, will contribute to a democratic culture.[41]

The *China's New Rulers* dossier presents China's leadership as planning, at most, for a society that resembles contemporary Singapore or Taiwan and South Korea of the 1970s, whose systems combined authoritarian politics and economic development. In November 2002, "the Third Generation" of Jiang Zemin, Li Peng, and Zhu Rongji smoothly handed over power to "the Fourth Generation" of Hu Jintao, Zeng Qinghong, and Wen Jinbao at the 16th Communist Party Congress. The totality of the appointments, however, indicated the continuity of Jiang's influence, the significance of informal power, and the strength of elite consensus. Jiang finally gave up control of the military in September 2004.

Chinese nationalism, especially among the "fourth generation" urban middle classes, presents both an opportunity and a danger to the leadership. These tech-saavy (cell phones and the Internet) thirty-somethings

---

[39] June 26, 2004.
[40] Nicholas Kristoff, "A Little Leap Forward," *New York Review of Books*, June 24, 2004. The book is Bruce Gilley, *China's Democratic Future: How It Will Happen and Where It Will Lead* (New York: Columbia University Press, 2004).
[41] November 25, 2004.

define themselves in opposition to their predecessors of "the Liberal 80s." Although they have grown up in relative affluence, they emphasize what the party has taught them about China's "Century of Humiliation" victimization in fostering strong anti-Japanese and anti-American sentiments.[42] This popular mass anger arose in reaction to Diaoyu Islands incident (1996), the *China Can Say No* controversy (1996–97), the Belgrade Bombing (May 1999), the Spy Plane Collision (April 2001), and the Anti-Japanese Protests (April–May 2005). The nationalistic anger is genuine, but the party is also tempted to foster it to gain political legitimacy and foreign advantage. By contrast, those who protest against the Japanese could turn on the Chinese Communist Party with Cultural Revolution-like fervor and cause major disruptions in trade with these same Japanese. On April 16, Shanghai authorities allowed as many as twenty thousand protestors to ransack Japanese restaurants and cars and to throw rocks at the Japanese Consulate before the city's *Liberation Army Daily* called the protest movement part of an "evil plot" ten days later.[43] In the interim, at the Asian-African summit in Jakarta, Japanese Prime Minister Koizumi apologized for causing "tremedous damage and suffering to the people of many countries, particulary to those of Asian nations."[44] The Japanese government stated that the apology was not connected to recent events in China, and the Chinese government refused to apologize for the damage, thus shielding both governments from their domestic publics. The same day, eighty Japanese Dietmembers visited Yasukuni to express their nationalistic sentiments.

During the postwar period Lee Kwan Yu of Singapore has served as the most prominent international spokesperson for the combination of authoritarian "Asian values" and a modern economy. The single-party state of Singapore has educated its elite in a British-style system, but the government emphasizes neo-Confucian control of the national political ideology. Kim Dae Jung, on the other hand, stands as the foremost Asian critic of the Asian values argument of such leaders. Asian countries supporting the democratic option are Japan, South Korea, Indonesia, Malaysia, the Philippines, Mongolia, and India.

The Chinese press has ignored the decade-long Mongolian democratic experiment, but Hong Kong and Taiwan remain major sources

---

[42] For current nationalism, see Peter Hays Gries, *China's New Nationalism: Pride, Politics, and Diplomacy* (Berkeley: University of California Press, 2004).

[43] April 27, 2005.

[44] April 23, 2005.

of Communist Party concern. Not only are these entities insufficiently integrated into the PRC, according to the CCP, but they stand as refutations of the claim that Chinese culture cannot evolve into democratic political forms. If the stage of economic development is the main consideration for democracy, why cannot the comparatively rich Hong Kong Special Autonomous Region choose its own local leader? In July 2003, the supposedly apathetic citizenry surprised Beijing officials with a massive demonstration estimated at five hundred thousand of fewer than seven million citizens. They protested proposed tightening of Hong Kong security laws, which are supposed to reflect the Basic Law, Hong Kong's mini-constitution that embodies Hong Kong's local autonomy under the principle of "one country, two systems." The perceived long-term threat to religious freedom galvanized Catholics and Protestants, who attended a joint prayer ceremony before the march. Bishop Joseph Zen has been a leading advocate of more democracy, and Christians are the largest voting group (19.5 percent) by religion. Although they only constitute 10 percent of the population, they remain disproportionately influential in business and education.[45] The government's mishandling of the SARS epidemic that year also demonstrated that government secrecy could harm families. Two government ministers resigned, and eventually Governor Tung Chee-hwa withdrew the changes in September. After Chinese President Hu Jintao publicly criticized the Hong Kong executive, Tung resigned on March 12, 2005. The CCP now wants to limit the next executive to filling out the rest of Tung's term lest he show too much independence.

The Basic Law calls vaguely for more democratic means in choosing the chief executive in 2007 and the Legislative Council in 2008, but in 2003 the Standing Committee of the National People's Congress in Beijing ruled that any such bills would have to be submitted to the NPC by Hong Kong's chief executive, and that no changes would be made for 2007 executive and 2008 legislative processes. The subsequent Hong Kong elections would be in 2012. At present, eight hundred prominent citizens, most with Chinese ties and investments, choose nominees for chief executive. Thirty members of the sixty-member Legislative Council are elected by the public, and thirty members come from special interest organizations, most friendly with Beijing. In the September 2004 elections, democracy proponents made gains, but not enough for a majority. That may give Beijing enough security to tolerate the current situation, especially since increased

---

[45] *Wall Street Journal*, September 10, 2004.

authoritarianism in Hong Kong would further alarm the population of Taiwan.

On Taiwan, the Republic of China (ROC) has chosen the democratic solution in a relatively peaceful transition from authoritarian rule. Before fleeing the mainland for the island, the Nationalist Party (KMT) had established an unenviable reputation for authoritarianism, inefficiency, and corruption in losing the Chinese Civil War. On February 28, 1947, Chiang Kai-shek's Mainland army cracked down on the native Taiwanese civilians who were less than pleased with their new guests, even though the Chinese replaced the hated Japanese. The KMT used its authoritarian control to mandate the Mandarin language in education and media and to prevent competing political parties. However, they did encourage the local majority Taiwanese and Hakkas to own land, to get an education (in Mandarin), and to make money (mostly in Taiwanese). Chiang Kai-shek died in April 1975. Gradually, with Taiwanese pressure and Nationalist democratization under Chiang's son, Chiang Ching-kuo, the government suspended martial law and legalized opposition political parties in 1987.

Chiang Ching-kuo died in 1988, and the Taiwanese Lee Teng-hui gained control of the KMT. When some conservative Mainlanders mounted a counteroffensive in early 1990, the students took to the streets to support Lee's mainstream faction and call for popular election of the president. Teresa Wright parallels this movement to the Tiananmen demonstration of 1989 and identifies "the political opportunity structure" as the crucial difference in the outcomes of the two movements.[46] By March 20, over five thousand students had gathered at the Chiang Kai-shek Memorial and sixty had begun a hunger strike. The National Assembly elected Lee on March 21. That evening he met with students in the Presidential Office and agreed to convene a National Affairs Conference to discuss their demands. The students accepted the compromise and the square was largely empty the next day. This fortunate result, says Wright, resulted from the openness of the Taiwan mainstream faction. Both they and the students were very aware that the more the students were perceived to be acting moderately, the better it was for their cause.

In the first ROC presidential election (1996) under the new rules, the voters, Mainlander and Taiwanese, reelected Lee. In the second presidential election of March 2000, KMT voters split when James Soong, a

[46] Teresa Wright, *The Perils of Protest: State Repression and Student Activism in China and Taiwan* (Honolulu: University of Hawai'i Press, 2001).

Mainlander rival of Lee Teng-hui's, left the KMT to run an independent campaign. The leader of the opposition Democratic Progressive Party, Chen Shui-bian, won with 39 percent of the vote. In both elections Beijing campaigned strongly against the eventual winners because of their prior support for Taiwanese autonomy or independence. A few weeks before the 1996 election, for example, the PRC fired missiles over the island into the sea beyond. During the 2000 campaign, the PRC continually denounced Chen. Although the new president had called for Taiwan independence prior to his election, Chen backed off somewhat in postelection remarks that were delivered in Mandarin as a further sign of conciliation to Beijing. In the 2004 campaign, Chen again used Taiwanese nationalism to defeat the combined ticket of Lien and Soong by thirty thousand votes out of thirteen million cast.

Many of the more than one million Taiwanese residents in the PRC returned to vote for Lien, as some American-based Taiwanese came back for Chen. Presbyterian leader William Lo told the island's 230,000 church members that Chen was the "candidate who is closer to the Christian faith."[47] Again, the United States prevailed on Chen to temper his inaugural rhetoric. However, Taiwanese nationalism is still Beijing's biggest foreign policy conundrum. Indeed, the PRC's main goal in its current military modernization has been to put it into the position of being able to counter the United States navy in the area around Taiwan.[48] What it lacks to become a global military power, however, is a defense industry that can produce such sophisticated weapons on a large scale. Taiwan-China economic ties militate against conflict. China is the island's largest export market, and Taiwanese have over seventy billion dollars invested on the mainland. Beijing alternates between threats and inducements in seeking to isolate President Chen. In April–May 2005, Chinese President Hu entertained both of the leaders of Taiwan's opposition parties, Lien and Soong. Lien's trip was especially symbolic (see the perfectly choreographed front page photo in the *New York Times*, April 30, 2005) as he heads the Communist's long-time enemy, the Nationalist Party.

The growth of religious organizations and institutions has contributed to Taiwan's democratization and socioeconomic development. Robert P. Weller states that the Buddhist Compassionate Relief Merit Society (Tzu Chi foundation) constitutes the island's largest civil organization, taking

[47] March 18, 2004.
[48] David Shambaugh, *Modernizing China's Military: Progress, Problems, and Prospeccts* (Berkeley: University of California Press, 2002), 4–8.

an intermediate position between the state and the private individual.[49] Taiwanese Buddhism has become more socially active, and Paul R. Katz[50] documents the strong growth of local temple cults, even offering examples of their participation in presidential campaigns and in tying the island's Mazu temples back to their original temples in China's Fujian Province. The Presbyterian Church, especially Tainan Theological College, has a long tradition of supporting the Taiwanese during their repression by the Mainlanders. Song Choan-Seng, who was president of the seminary during the dark days of 1965–70, became a friend of Taiwan National University Professor, Peng Ming-Min, "Taiwan's Mandela." Song later became president of the World Alliance of Reformed Churches, 1997–2004.

Although Chen Shui-bian's natural Christian allies come from the Taiwanese Presbyterians, the ROC government propaganda office trumpeted the trip of President Chen to the funeral of Pope John Paul II, glorying in the absence of a Beijing representative. The Vatican, not wishing to annoy Beijing, placed Chen between the first lady of Brazil and the president of Cameroon and refused requests for higher-level meetings.[51] Taiwan's disproportionately Mainlander Catholic Church has exercised national influence in education, media, and social work. Buddhism, Christianity, Daoism, Yi Guan Dao, and folk religions all contribute to social cohesion. In addition, adds Katz: "Another striking facet of religion in Taiwan is that economic growth and technological development have not resulted in the decline of religious practice; on the contrary, many educated men and women who surf the web on a daily basis apparently feel no qualms about practicing religion. [...] Religion continues to play an integral role in individual, family and community life, and temple cults in particular have retained their importance as sites for daily worship, community service and massive festivals."[52]

---

[49] Robert P. Weller, *Alternate Civilities: Democracy and Culture in China and Taiwan* (Boulder, CO: Westview, 1999). Tzu Chi was founded in 1966 in Hualien by Master Chen Yen, currently the best-known Buddhist nun in Taiwan. Tzu Chi now has branches in thirty countries, and pursues the Buddhist equivalent of Christian groups such as World Vision and Catholic Relief Services.

[50] Paul R. Katz, "Religion and the State in Post-war Taiwan," *The China Quarterly* 174 (June 2003): 395–412.

[51] Nun and Professor of International Relations Beatrice Leung was not optimistic that the PRC would grant the Catholic Church the necessary administrative independence to make an official rapprochement possible, but stated that Taiwanese Catholics were "psychologically prepared" for a solely religious relationship. May 22, 2005.

[52] Katz, *Post-war Taiwan*, 395.

The major story in East Asian economics over the last ten years has been the shift in power from Japan to China, resulting in Japanese books like *The Day China Surpasses Japan* and *The China That Threatens to Swallow Japan*. Many analysts expect China to replace Japan as Asia's largest economy within twenty-five years. Gradually, China became the region's manufacturing center, then its market center, and finally, it is competing to be the design center. In the case of manufacturing, the Japanese could not compete with the PRC's lower wage costs, but China's great improvements in technology and quality control remind some Japanese of their own country in the 1960s. The shift in marketing results both from China's much greater population, and from Japan's inability to expand its home market. However, the world's second largest economy began to recover in May 2005. The Nikkei stock exchange hit a four-year high in August 2005 on the basis of strong earnings from automotive, steel, and financial sectors. The woes of SUV-heavy U.S. carmakers stimulate Japanese profits.

Japan does control the world's second largest number of patents and now has over $2 trillion, one half of the nation's GDP, invested in foreign markets. Japan will thus move to a "Nike model" where the brand management, the financing, and some of the design remain in the home country, but the manufacturing goes overseas. Japanese relations with China have grown more tense, so that Japan and Russia are getting closer in international affairs.[53] The general East Asian picture, then, is of a rising China who is South Korea's largest trading partner and whose exports to Japan surpassed those of the United States for the first time. Although the United States remains the biggest trading partner in Asia, ASEAN nations and Australia are attracted by the strong growth of the China market. At the October 2003 APEC meeting, Chinese prime minister Wen Jiabao challenged the ASEAN countries to double their current volume within two years, making it almost equal to the United States.[54] China is also becoming a greater economic power in Latin America as it buys more and more resources for its expanding industry.

Even during the first decade of the twenty-first century, whether or not an Asian nation's political-economic solutions have to be democratic depends significantly on that country's integration into the international system and the national creativity for new political-religious ideologies and organizations. Japan is fully integrated and structurally democratic,

[53] February 13, 2005.
[54] October 18, 2003.

but still, like China, suffers from an ideological vacuum that makes xenophobic nationalism a threat to world peace. Although foreign policy was not central to Koizumi's landslide victory in September 2005, the election debacle of the opposition Democratic Party of Japan removes some political obstacles to a more aggressive national stance toward China. Many of the young urbanites who switched to the LDP judge that Japan has been too passive asserting its rights in the East China Sea and in securing its energy lifeline in the area around Taiwan. The much stronger postelection Koizumi stated that he will continue to visit Yasukuni. The advocates of *China Can Say No* and *The Japan That Can Say No* harbor little trust or respect for each other, nor, for that matter, for the United States. South Korea and Taiwan became more democratic as the national societies developed and prospered under United States hegemony. Their religious leaderships made major contributions to political stability and democratization. Korean reunification and development would serve the international community, but Taiwanese nationalism would not. North Korea has become the world's most prominent and most dangerous leftist family dictatorship, but it has begun opening to the ROK. East Asia thus offers tremendous dangers and opportunities for the global political and EMC systems.

7

South and Central Asia

The Legacies of Gandhi and Khomeini and the Bomb

China under Deng had a decade lead over India in opening its economy to the global system. India's Prime Minister Narasimha Rao did so in 1991, following the strategy of Sikh economist Manmohan Singh, who himself became prime minister in 2004. India has thus joined China as one of the faster growing economies in the world. But India, like China, retains a great socioeconomic gap between its emerging urban middle classes and the poverty-stricken urban unemployed and rural peasantry. Many Silicon Valley residents and national campaign consultants have become very aware of India's economic progress from the outsourcing of American technology jobs to that country's Silicon Triangle and from the immigration of Indian professionals to the United States. India lags behind only Mexico in legal immigration, and the United States has more foreign students from India than from any other country.

India attained independence from Britain in 1947 under the leadership of the catch-all Congress Party. Historian Vohra states that "the party was broadly split among the village-oriented Gandhians, the Hindu Conservatives led by Sardar Patel, and Nehru's progressive left wing, all with significantly different ideologies."[1] The English-educated Prime Minister Jawaharlal Nehru's vision of "secularism, socialism, and democracy" won out at the party's highest levels. This secular ideology, aided by family dynastic politics, proved sufficient for the great challenge of uniting the continent's many faiths, cultures, and languages into a single nation, but it could not prevent the establishment of Pakistan or the latter rise

[1] Ranbir Vohra, *The Making of India: A Historical Survey*, 2nd ed. (Armonk, NY: M.E. Sharpe, 2001), 201–02.

of Hindu politics. Both Patel and Gandhi took religion more seriously than Nehru, but from completely different perspectives. Since the opening of the economy to the West, Indians have attempted to build national unity on two very different ideologies: the secular dynastic approach of Nehru's family, and the Hindu nationalism of the BJP. These two visions came head to head in the parliamentary election that upset the BJP in April–May 2004. The political system has been fragmenting progressively since the early 1990s so that all government is coalition government.

THE GANDHIAN VISION

Even from the cynical and corrupt vantage point of India's Congress Party more than fifty years after his death, Mohandas K. Gandhi remains the most significant religious-political figure of the first half of the twentieth century. Gandhi stands out not only for the integrity of his religious life, but also for the national and global political impact of his strategic vision. Later charismatic leaders like Nelson Mandela, Martin Luther King and César Chavez idolized him as their hero and inspiration. Gandhi, who grew up in the Indian state of Gujarat under the British Empire, set off for London to become a proper British barrister. In London he first read the *Bhagavad Gita*, ironically in English, and began to deepen his appreciation of Hindu spirituality. Gandhi eventually embraced the traditional ideal of an "action" karma yogi whose selflessness is fostered by perfect renunciation. In a comment on the *Gita*, Gandhi describes such a yogi: "He is a devotee who is jealous of none, who is a fount of mercy, who is without egotism, who is selfless, who treats alike cold and heat, happiness and misery, who is ever forgiving, who is always contented, whose resolutions are firm, who has dedicated mind and soul to God, ..."[2]

After becoming a lawyer in 1891, Gandhi traveled to South Africa, where he led Hindu-Muslim protests against the pass system and other aspects of *apartheid*. It was through these demonstrations that Gandhi discovered his life's work of nonviolent opposition to the British. He returned to India, where he served as the spiritual conscience of the anticolonial Congress Party led by Nehru. Gandhi thus changed from a poor foreign student aping the colonial British professional elite to a closer and closer identification with what was most liberating in the Indian religious

---

[2] Louis Fischer, *Gandhi: His Life and Message for the World* (New York: Mentor, 1954, 18.

tradition. His tours of rural India led him to establish an ashram where he and his followers sought to exemplify the selflessness that he asserted would be the salvation of his country.

Gandhi embraced *satyagraha* [truth force] to convince the British of the error of their domination. He and his followers dedicated themselves to *ahimsa* [non-violence], preferring to endure the British troops cracking batons over their heads than to engage in violence themselves. Gandhi also proved remarkably clever in imbuing everyday gestures with national symbolism. For example, he advocated the wearing of simple national dress to boycott British textiles. He also led a two-hundred-mile march to the sea to protest British taxation. Arriving at the ocean, with the eyes of India and the whole world on him, he engaged in the "revolutionary" act of making salt without paying the imperial tax. All over India people began making contraband salt. For this and for many other offenses Gandhi and his followers spent many nights and days in prison.

At the heart of the Mahatma's ["Great Soul," a term he disliked] vision lay the traditional Hindu tolerance and respect for all religions. Gandhi spoke highly of Christianity, and he advocated equal treatment for Hindus, Muslims, and all other citizens, regardless of religion, caste, or class. He did not attend the Independence celebrations in 1947 because he was so distraught over the violence between Hindus and Muslims that had led to the separation of the British colony into India and Pakistan. Gandhi fasted to protest British rule, he fasted to protest religious violence, and he fasted to protest the separation of Hindus and Muslims into separate nations.

Muslim demands for a separate state, on the other hand, grew from a very different conception of religious nationalism. Mohammed Ali Jinnah, the founding father of Pakistan, presented this reasoning in a pivotal speech on March 22, 1940: "It is extremely difficult to appreciate why our Hindu friends fail to understand the real nature of Islam and Hinduism. They are not religions in the strict sense of the word, but are, in fact, different and distinct social orders. It is a dream that Hindus and Muslims can ever evolve a common nationality."[3] Gandhi replied to this position with his own deeply held belief: "My whole soul rebels against the idea that Hinduism and Islam represent two antagonistic cultures and doctrines. To assent to such a doctrine is for me a denial of God. For I believe that the God of the Koran is also the God of the Gita, and we are all, no matter by what name designated, children of the same

---

[3] Cited by Sanjoy Banerjee, *San Jose Mercury News*, August 15, 1999.

God."[4] To this day, some Indians and Pakistanis doubt the legitimacy of the other nation. The secular Indian elites judge that a state like Pakistan based on a single religion constitutes an historical anachronism. Pakistanis see India as hopelessly divided by religion, language, ethnicity, and region.

Nathuram Godse, an extremist Hindu associated with the right-wing RSS, assassinated Gandhi in 1948. The RSS perceived Gandhi's irenic approach to Muslims as "appeasement" similar to their judgment that Congress leader Nehru's attempt to treat all religions equally constituted a betrayal of India's traditional culture. Ironically, the RSS agreed with the Muslim political leader Mohammed Ali Jinnah that states must have a dominant religious national culture. The majority of Indians, however, did not agree. The secular Congress became the nation's majority party on the strength of its popular identification with independence and its near monopoly of the Indian elite.

Sectarian strife, however, defeated Gandhi's goal of a united India. One million Indians died and ten million were displaced in the riots between Hindus and Muslims on the eve of independence. In 1947 the British reluctantly acceded to the establishment of two countries: secular India, with a predominantly Hindu population; and Islamic Pakistan, whose western and eastern parts were separated both by Indian territory and by major ethnic and linguistic differences. In 1971 Pakistan further split into its western part, Pakistan, and its eastern part, Bangladesh. The Pakistani army brutally tried to retain control of the entire country. When over ten million Bengali Muslim refugees crossed the border into India, Indian troops invaded Bangladesh and quickly defeated the Pakistani army. Within the Cold War system, the Soviet Union backed its ally India, while Pakistan was supported by China and the United States. The Pakistani debacle thus dealt a defeat to new allies Zhou Enlai and Henry Kissinger.

The Congress party offered India a secular state, which accommodated the most significant religious and regional power bases. Nehru led the party and the nation until he died of a stroke in 1964. His daughter Indira Gandhi (no relation to the Mahatma) succeeded him in 1966 and, with the exception of two years, ruled until she was assassinated by her Sikh bodyguards in 1984. Since the cohesiveness of Independence ideology waned in the absence of British domination, Indira strengthened her

---

4 Ibid. For the pro-democratic aspects of Hinduism, see Pratap Bhanu Mehta, "Hinduism and Self–Rule," Larry Diamond, Marc F. Plattner, and Philip J. Costopoulos, *World Religions and Democracy* (Baltimore: Johns Hopkins University Press, 2005), 56–69.

personal hold on the party apparatus against regional power bosses, even, with the assistance of her son Sanjay, declaring Emergency Rule from 1975 to 1977. Indira then angered Sikhs by sending troops into their holiest shrine in the Punjab capital of Amristar to quell separatist dissent. After the assassination, her son Rajiv Gandhi became prime minister for five years, but he also was swept from office in 1989 amid charges of corruption and incompetence. Rajiv was campaigning to make a comeback two years later when a Tamil suicide bomber, angry that India had sent troops to Sri Lanka to stop the civil war, assassinated him. Cold War India pursued nonalignment in foreign policy, socialism in economics, and a secular cultural policy.

With the disintegration of the Congress-majority political system, many different coalition governments could have arisen. There was no political necessity to the succession of the Hindu nationalist BJP as a plurality party in the 1990s. Rather, writes Thomas Blom Hansen, "the success of the Hindu nationalist movement has to do with the specific ways in which historically produced notions of 'Hinduness' were packaged and recirculated at a particular juncture in the development of democracy and modern governance in India."[5] The middle-class "educated sections," who used to their Congress-based self understanding of "high politics as a virtuous vocation," faced both intensified domestic political competition and, since the 1991 economic and communication revolutions, outside threats from a globalization that seemed not to accord Indians adequate respect. The Congress system had never clarified the relationship between this increasing democratic politicization and the two "antipolitics" of (1) scientific administrative rationalism, from colonial administrators to the National Planning Council; and (2) "cultural nationalists, Gandhian communitarianists... [who] sought to claim the 'inner' life and spirit of supposedly perennial communities as the prepolitical site of the nation."[6] As a result, Hansen states, BJP leaders built the party's success on "the more brutal languages of politics [which] also flourish at the heart of the middle-class world, for instance when broader anxieties regarding the encroachment of the poor and the plebians upon so-called 'respectable' society are translated into discourses on the 'right of

---

[5] Thomas Blom Hansen, *The Saffron Wave: Democracy and Hindu Nationalism in Modern India* (Princeton, NJ: Princeton University Press, 1999), 19. See also Gujarat anthropologist Lancy Lobo, *Globalisation, Hindu Nationalism, and Christians in India* (New Delhi: Rawat Poblishers, 2002) for data and impact on Christians.

[6] Hansen, *Hindu Nationalism*, 58.

the majority,' antiminority xenophobia, and fantasies of an authoritarian state and strong leadership."[7]

INDIA AND PAKISTAN: RELIGIOUS AND SECULAR NATIONALISM AFTER FIFTY YEARS

On August 15, 1997, both Indians and Pakistanis celebrated the fiftieth anniversary of the founding of their respective nations. India's new president K. R. Narayanan, a Catholic *dalit* LSE-graduate married to the head of the nation's YWCA, cited Nehru's 1947 independence speech. Nehru had proclaimed, "Long years ago, we made a tryst with destiny, and now the time comes when we shall redeem our pledge, not wholly or in full measure, but very substantially." Narayanan's address fifty years later set a more circumspect tone. He did laud India's many political and economic achievements: its "distinctly Indian variety of democracy"; and that this country of 970 million had finally succeeded in feeding itself. Narayanan, however, also acknowledged, "I am painfully aware of the deterioration that has taken place in our country and in our society in recent times." He then cited the decline of cultural and social values, the ill treatment of women and low-caste Indians, the government's failure to provide adequately for the health, education, and water needs of its citizens, and the rise of "corruption, communalism, casteism, and criminalization of politics."[8]

In addition to endemic corruption, regionalism, and the penetration of the political system by criminal elements, most analysts have focused on the rise of the Hindu political party, the Bharatiya Janata Party (BJP). From a party that won only 2 of 543 lower house seats in 1984, the BJP attained the plurality of seats in the last three elections of the 1990s: 161 seats in 1996, 182 seats in 1998, and 180 seats in 1999. In 1996 the BJP Prime Minister Atal Bihari Vajpayee formed a government that lasted for only thirteen days, but in 1998 he formed the first relatively stable conservative-rightist government in the post colonial period. Stronger alliances with regional parties strengthened that government one year later.

The immediate precursor of the BJP was the Bharatiya Jana Sangh, founded in 1951. The Jana Sangh sought to transform all India according to Hindu cultural patterns, but it had political clout only in the Hindi heartland, where issues like the promotion of Hindi language,

---

[7] Hansen, *Hindu Nationalism*, 17.
[8] August 15, 1997.

resistance to Pakistan, and the defense of Hindu refugee interests found strong resonance. It won only three, four, and fourteen seats, respectively, in the first three parliaments. Indeed, the party could find no political partners until 1967 when the voters in state elections finally broke the Congress monopoly. In that year the Jana Sangh won thirty-five parliamentary seats nationally and joined coalition state governments in Bihar, Punjab, and Uttar Pradesh. It ended its political isolation by forging relationships with socialist Ram Manohar Lohia in the 1960s, and in the 1970s with Jayaprakash Narayan (known as "JP"), a popular Gandhian who led a protest movement against the Emergency Rule of Indira Gandhi. When Emergency Rule was lifted, it joined three other parties to form the new Janata Party. Janata triumphed in the 1977 election, but proved unable to rule because it lacked ideological cohesion and a common program. The new party suffered a humiliating defeat in the 1980 elections, and the Jana Sangh quit the coalition to reemerge in the newly formed BJP.

The BJP adopted the ideology of Gandhian socialism during its first moderate period, 1980–86. Ironically, at this time Indira and Rajiv Gandhi were slowly distancing themselves from Nehru's secularism by occasionally playing the Hindu card. Following the 1984 assassination of his mother, Rajiv made national unity and Sikh extremism his campaign themes and won an unprecedented victory with 401 parliamentary seats. When Lai Krishna Advani became BJP president in 1986, he launched a two-track strategy for the party. The BJP continued the ex-party president Vajpayee's inclusionist strategy of cooperating with the mainstream anti-Congress opposition. At the same time it gave greater primacy to sectarian activists from the RSS, the Vishwa Hindu Parishad [World Hindu Society (VHP)], and other Hindu nationalist organizations. This two-track strategy worked for the 1991 elections when the BJP won 119 seats in parliament and power in four states – Himachal Pradesh, Madhya Pradesh, Rajasthan, and Uttar Pradesh.

The BJP came to power on the religious-political polarization resulting from the two contentious national issues of the Shah Bano divorce case and the destruction of the Ayodhya mosque. After forty years of marriage, Shah Bano's lawyer husband divorced her according to Islamic law, which had governed personal status issues among Indian Muslims since 1937. Having been left destitute, the wife sued in state court. The high court of Madhya Pradesh awarded her a $23 monthly stipend according to the precedents set in 1979 and 1980 that had cited the Code of Criminal Procedure in awarding maintenance to divorced Muslim women, a ruling that the Supreme Court upheld in 1985. The Congress Party then sought to shore up its Islamic support by passing a 1986 law that denied women the right to seek state redress in divorce cases. The BJP, angered by Muslim law overriding secular Indian law, mobilized nationwide protests. Lawrence stresses that the case itself was not extraordinary, but that "[i]t was the changed climate of religious identity in the mid-1980s that set the stage for the Shah Bano debacle." Indira Gandhi's attack on the Sikh shrine at Amristar and the communal riots following her assassination threatened all minorities. "Personal law became the litmus test of Indian Muslim collective identity, its fragility underscored by the creation in 1972 of an All India Muslim Law Board to maintain and defend its application."[9] When Rajiv caved in to Muslims, over Shah Bano, Hindu public opinion exploded. In the Ayodhya case, in September 1990 Advani announced a ten thousand kilometer *rath yatra* [journey by chariot] to the city to destroy a mosque built by the Mogul ruler Babar in 1528, and to claim the location exclusively for Hindus as the putative birthplace of the Hindu god Ram. The government could not control the situation when Hindu fanatics destroyed the Babri mosque on December 6, 1992.

When the BJP won 182 seats in the 1998 election, it was uncertain whether a coalition government could be formed. The public still associated party leader Advani with Ayodhya, thus making him unacceptable as a prime minister. While Vajpayee, who even admired the Oscar-winning *Gandhi*, was still smarting from the humiliation of having overseen the postwar Indian government of the shortest duration, he finally put together a cabinet. More than one third of his ministers belonged to fourteen regional parties, many of them long-standing opponents of the BJP's doctrine of centralized Hindu supremacy. Such broad coalitions have become a prerequisite for forming any government in a system that is progressively fragmenting along regional, ethnic, caste, socioeconomic, and linguistic lines. The alliance that probably nettled Vajpayee the most was the arrangement with Tamil Nadu's ex-Chief Minister, Jayalalitha Jayaram, who controlled twenty-seven seats. This former movie star, "India's Evita or Imelda," focused on a single concern, escaping jail for her corruption while in office. Such a coalition partner damaged the BJP's reputation for clean government, its main asset with those not devoted to *Hindutva*.

Jayaram precipitated another national election one year later by withdrawing from the ruling coalition so that no majority was possible.

---

[9] Bruce B. Lawrence, *Shattering the Myth: Islam Beyond Violence* (Princeton, NJ: Princeton University Press, 1998), 134.

Neither the BJP nor Congress benefited from the ensuing political chaos, but a more stable governing coalition emerged. Although the BJP itself won two fewer seats (182 to 180), the coalition won twenty-four more (274 to 298). Congress lost thirty-four seats (141 to 107). The BJP had reached its zenith of lower-house votes based on exclusive principles so now it had to find ways to reach out to other social groups. It even lost its strong reputation for probity in March 2001 when tehelka.com journalists released videotapes to national television channels of three major coalition figures accepting bribes for supporting the putative government purchase of fictitious thermal imaging binoculars. As a result of the dot.com sting, Defense Minister George Fernandes, BJP President Bangaru Laxman, and National Security Adviser Brajesh Mishra resigned. This scandal followed in close succession those of Bollywood film lots, fixed cricket matches, the Bombay Stock Exchange, and shoddily built high-rise apartments that collapsed in the Gujarat earthquake.[10]

The year 1997 signaled increased tension between Hindu organizations and Christians, especially in the state of Gujarat. An Australian medical missionary, Graham Staines, who ran a leprosy hospital, and his two young sons (ages six and eight) were burned to death when their jeep was set ablaze by fifty to one hundred people shouting anti-Christian slogans. While the local police assigned collective blame to the Hindu youth organization, the Bajrang Dal (BD), the court held that a single individual, "fanatic" Hindu chauvinist Dara Singh, was individually responsible when he shouted to the crowd that "Christian missionaries were destroying the Hindu religion." When John Paul II visited India in November 1999, the government banned children from attending the only public mass for fear of radical Hindu activists. Security concerns also canceled papal visits to traditionally Catholic Goa and Calcutta, the city of the recently deceased, revered Mother Teresa. President Narayanan told the pope that he had attended a Catholic primary school, and Prime Minister Vajpayee emphasized the religious freedom guaranteed by the Indian constitution, "You know, Holy Father," said Vajpayee, "that India is a land of religious freedom. But we have some intolerant fringes."[11]

Gujarat also served as the location of the large Hindu-Muslim riots in February and March 2002. After a mob firebombed a train carrying Hindu activists returning from Ayodhya that killed fifty-nine, Hindu mobs

---

[10] March 16, 2001.
[11] *San Jose Mercury News*, November 7, 1999.

ravaged the state and killed over two thousand Muslims. The BJP Gujarat chief minister Narendra Modi allowed the riots to proceed unchecked. Modi's aggressive political strategy seemed to succeed as the BJP increased its political control of Gujarat in the state election in December, winning 126 seats in the 182-seat assembly. The hard line Advani commented, "Ordinarily also we would have gotten a renewed mandate. But the renewed mandate coming in this manner has a lesson for the whole country." BJP-ally Bal Thackeray, the Mumbai Shiv Sena strongman who had often used sectarian violence for political gain, claimed that his advice was crucial in convincing the BJP leadership to retain Modi.[12] Indeed, within a year the BJP perceived its political position as so strong that it called national elections six months ahead of schedule. Surveys and pundits all agreed that, in addition to *Hindutva* for its organizational base, the roaring economy and the moderate face of Vajpayee pursuing dialogue with Pakistan would facilitate a great victory, maybe even establish the BJP as the new majority party. The party president bragged about India's "feel good factor," and adopted the campaign slogan "India Shining." As a signal to the base, Vajpayee began his campaign in Ayodhya. The party also sent out ten million phone messages to land and cell users.

No analyst predicted the result, one of the biggest upsets in any post-Cold War national election anywhere on the globe. In hindsight, the BJP had ignored the tremendous economic gulf between the emerging middle classes and the great number of rural poor for whom India was not "shining." The BJP and its allies did not do well in Gujarat and in the major cities, but they lost this national election in the rural states, especially in the non-Hindi south. Unlike Western elections, the poor vote disproportionately more than the rich in India. Rajiv's wife, Sonia Gandhi, led Congress to a plurality of seats, but did not accept the post of prime minister to save the party a bruising battle over her Italian Catholic birth. The Sikh designer of India's 1991 opening to globalization, Manmohan Singh, became prime minister. The election proved a triumph for multicultural, multilingual, multicaste, and multireligious politics. Singh joined India's president, A. P. J. Abdul Kalam, a Muslim from Tamil Nadu and ex-director of the nation's missile program. The new ministerial council contained seven Muslims, two Christians, three *dalit* ["oppressed," preferred term for "untouchable], and two members of tribal groups. Six ministers were women. Most non-Hindu religious leaders, and some Hindu gurus such as Swami Agnivesh, praised the result. Agnivesh also stated

[12] Larissa MacFarquhar, "Letter from India," *The New Yorker*, May 26, 2003, 51.

that the victory would improve prospects for peace between India and Pakistan.[13]

THE BOMB AND SOUTH ASIA

With the emergence of caste, religious, and regional parties, the Indian political system has become a multiparty system with no majority party. The emerging regional and caste parties disagree with the BJP precisely on the centralized elite Hindu vision of India, so any BJP-led majority coalition will have to compromise on such issues. Like the American GOP, the strategic challenge for the BJP concerns maintaining its core constituency with at least the rhetoric of religious nationalism while not taking any action that will completely alienate more moderate regional or class interests. Public nuclear testing of "the Hindu bomb" must have appeared as a low-cost political godsend to satisfy nationalist ambitions. BJP literature is replete with declarations such as, "The Hindu urge to dominate after a thousand years of ignominy and enslavement needs to be understood." Indeed, some BJP cadres now want to build a shrine at the nuclear test site, a global antidote to the Hiroshima peace center.

On May 11, 1998, India detonated three underground nuclear tests in Rajasthan's northwestern desert not far from Pakistan. Pakistan responded with its own tests on May 28. With small arsenals and uncertain planning, this strategic confrontation approximates Soviet-American postures during the early Cold War. However, this South Asian standoff adds the perils of three historic mutual wars (1947, 1965, and 1971), weak intelligence, a less than five-minute flight time for missiles, and fighting in Kashmir since 1989 that has cost sixty thousand lives. Many analysts immediately termed South Asia as the world's most dangerous venue, while the United Nations Security Council and all major powers individually expressed alarm at the testing.

Shortly after the blast, the government announced that it would dramatically increase defense spending, reversing years of reduction. India has refused to sign either the Nuclear Non-Proliferation Treaty or the Comprehensive Test Ban Treaty. Both diplomats and security analysts feared that a single small conventional incident could trigger regional nuclear war. Indeed, India and Pakistan fought a seventy-three-day conflict in 1999 when India discovered that Muslim troops had dug in above a crucial Indian supply line in the Kargil valley of Kashmir. In

[13] *Asian Focus*, May 28, 2004.

his book *Weapons of Peace*, Indian journalist Raj Chengappa states that during this standoff, India went to Readiness State Three, "meaning that some nuclear bombs would be ready to be mated with the delivery vehicle on short notice."[14] Diplomats praised India's measured response to the Kargil incident with conventional arms and only attacking up to the previous "line of control." The fragility of Pakistani command and control was underscored when General Pervez Musharraf staged a coup against then Prime Minister Nawaz Sharif in October 1999. Musharraf's family had lived in New Delhi until he was four, giving him the opposite refugee experience of the BJP's Advani. Generals ruled Pakistan for twenty-six of its first fifty-three years, while the civilian governments of both Bhuttos, father and daughter, and Sharif justly earned reputations for corruption. In April 2002, Musharraf pushed through a national referendum that extended his rule for five years, and gave him the power to dissolve parliament. Then in October, Pakistan held elections for the parliament with no party receiving a majority. The first three parties in the lower house were Musharraf's Pakistan Muslim League-Q, Bhutto's Pakistan People's Party, and the United Action Council (M.M.A. in its Urdu initials), a coalition of six religious parties. Neither Benazir Bhutto nor Sharif, living in Dubai and Saudi Arabia respectively, received permission to participate.

The power of Musharraf, whom most Indians perceived as "the architect of Kargil," rested on the Pakistani army. Indians feared that the weaker Pakistanis would perceive nuclear weapons as an equalizer that would prevent the Indians from responding to situations like Kargil, thus making conventional attacks more likely. The increased participation of Muslim fighters from other countries in Kashmir also worried New Delhi. Islamic fighters have come to Kashmir from as far away as Afghanistan, Chechnya, Saudi Arabia, and Sudan. Pakistan's link to nuclear proliferation became global knowledge in February 2004 when the architect of the Pakistani bomb, Abdul Qadeer Khan, admitted on television that he had sold nuclear technology, gained at the Dutch Uranium Enrichment Company (Urenco), to Iran, North Korea, and Libya. Musharraf immediately pardoned the national hero and stated that the Pakistani army had no knowledge of the transfer.

The state of Jammu and Kashmir, usually referred to merely as "Kashmir," constitutes one of the globe's most difficult diplomatic issues.

---

[14] Raj Chengappa, *Weapons of Peace: The Secret Story of India's Quest to Be a Nuclear Power* (New Delhi: Harper Collins India, 2000).

In 1947 India incorporated this predominantly Muslim state when its Hindu maharajah signed an act of accession, which was the determinate of national status in the British transition system. Pakistan, on the other hand, argues that the final disposition of the state must be determined by popular vote, and that resolving Kashmir is the key to all Indo-Pakistani negotiations. In both 1948 and 1949, India committed itself to a U.N.-sponsored plebiscite, conditional on both armies withdrawing from the state. Those withdrawals never took place. Nevertheless, any plebiscite will be complicated by regional differences within Kashmir. While Muslims make up the majority in the Kashmir valley, Jammu remains roughly two-thirds Hindu, with some Muslim majority districts. Sparsely populated Ladakh is half Buddhist and half Muslim.[15]

In October 2002 elections, the Kashmiri ruling party, the National Conference, lost power for the first time. The winning coalition was made up of Indian National Congress (twenty seats, mostly in Hindu areas) and the People's Democratic Party (sixteen seats), led by Mufti Mohammed Sayeed. His daughter, Mehbooba Mufti, had led a vigorous campaign for the party despite separatist violence against those who took part. Mr. Sayeed became the new Chief Minister, giving hope to those who looked for a negotiated solution to the conflict. The last assembly election in 1987 was viewed by many as rigged and this led to an increase in the fighting. In addition, Sayeed pledged to put pressure on both India and the separatists for negotiation. India had severed all contact with Pakistan as a result of a Muslim terrorist attack on the parliament in December 2001. In May 2003, Vajpayee took advantage of the relatively fair and free Kashmir elections to call for renewed talks with Islamabad. The Indian and Pakistani foreign secretaries met in June 2004. They made no major advances on Kashmir, but both sides recommitted themselves to a "peaceful, negotiated final settlement"[16] and proposed proceeding on various confidence-building measures in trade and tourism. Sports provided further contact the following year. In April 2005 Musharraf used the final match of the monthlong Indian–Pakistani cricket series (Pakistan won the series, 4-2) as a reason to visit New Delhi. His meeting with Prime Minister Manmohan Singh, who also was born in the

---

[15] For suggestions on how religion can play a positive role in the Kashmir conflict, see Ainslie Embree, "Kashmir: Has Religion a Role in Making Peace?" in Douglas Johnston, ed., *Faith-Based Diplomacy: Trumping Realpolitik* (New York: Oxford, 2003), 33–75. Embree is particularly positive on the Hindu Bhakti and Muslim Sufi traditions.

[16] June 29, 2004.

other country before partition, brought further steps in easing tensions, including the discussion of a gas pipeline from Iran across Pakistan to India. Both nations continue their arms buildup, however, now with the blessings of the United States.[17]

AFGHANISTAN: THROUGH THE PASSES INTO CENTRAL ASIA

The tense relations between India and Pakistan influence alliances throughout South and Central Asia. Many of these alliances surround the rugged terrain of Afghanistan, whose mountain passes have always played a crucial geopolitical role. Afghanistan borders on six countries, all of which have ethnic groups on both sides of their respective borders. Afghanistan's population consists of a myriad of ethnic groups, the most important of which are Sunni Pushtuns, Tajiks, Uzbeks, Aimaq, and Shiite Hazara. Although the traditionally dominant Pushtuns, who are split among subtribes, make up 45 percent of the population, all of the above ethnicities make up at least 10 percent of the population. Nuristanis, Panjshiris, Turkmen, Kirghiz, and Baluchis constitute other politically significant, but less populous, ethnic groups.

While Afghani society has long exhibited a propensity for violence among tribal and local units, in 1978 the country also began to play a major role in the Cold War. The Soviet Union perceived the necessity of a friendly government in Kabul as part of its defense against Islamism in Central Asia. When the Soviet client People's Democratic Party of Afghanistan appeared on the verge of losing power to the *mujahidin,* Brezhnev dispatched Soviet troops. In response, the CIA began to join Pakistan, Saudi Arabia, and others in helping to arm the rebels. This ten-year intervention exhausted the Soviet Union and produced a great flow of refugees to neighboring countries: 3.2 million to Pakistan and 2 million to Iran. The concept of Islamic *jihad* not only supported the resistance but also encouraged the refugee flow as the government of Kabul lost its legitimacy with many Muslims. In addition to refugees, over two million Afghans have been killed since 1978, with another six hundred thousand to two million wounded. The war destroyed both prewar society and road infrastructure, turned the economy to opium growing,

---

[17] The U.S. reasoning was that the buildup gives both sides incentive for good behavior. South Asian nuclear armament specialist George Perkovich commented, "It is a risky proposition on its face." April 18, 2005.

and resulted in the general Kalashnikovization (after the Soviet weapon) of society. The American missile strike on bin Laden after the bombing of U.S. embassies in Kenya and Tanzania first drew the world's attention to these connections among the war, its refugee camps, and transnational terrorism. In the development of political Islam, states the Columbia political scientist Mahmood Mamdani, "[t]he influence of the Afghan jihad cannot be overstated."[18]

Successor *mujahidin*, Taliban, and coalition regimes have all demonstrated the significant role of Islam in the politics of Central Asia, where religious fervor travels through ethnic conduits. Afghanistan remains a crucial geopolitical entity situated on the line between Sunni and Shiite Islam and among the disputed national spheres of influence of Pakistan, Iran, and Russia. Iran has traditionally influenced the north of Afghanistan, populated by the minority Shiite groups, while Pakistan remains stronger in the south with ethnic Pushtuns and other Sunni Muslims existing on both sides of its border with Afghanistan. In the struggle against the Soviets, many disparate groups claimed to represent the Afghan people and applied for military aid, but in 1980 Pakistan recognized seven groups (four Islamist and three focused on traditional Afghani values) through which it would channel all aid. With the withdrawal of the Soviets in 1989, chaos ensued, with the Pakistanis seeking to form coalitions among these groups to provide peace under a Pakistani sphere of influence. They failed, and further chaos ensued.

This chaos fostered the rise of the Taliban, a Sunni and Pushtun-based group, with an ideology combining a very radical view of Islamic thought with their traditional code of ethics. From a secular political view, these Taliban foot soldiers paralleled Mao's largely rural People's Liberation Army (PLA) as it prepared to enter China's urban areas in 1949. The Taliban constituted a rural-based movement of uneducated and relatively uncorrupt youth willing to die for their national religious cause. Like the PLA, the Taliban viewed large cities as corrupt centers of power and treated them more harshly than the rural areas. Furthermore, similar to the Chinese Communist Party outranking the state, the Taliban religious movement set the parameters for the policies of the Afghani government. As spokesperson Maulvi Ahmad described the Taliban system: "We have an Emirate system, which means government power is based on a *shura*

---

[18] Mahmood Mamdani, "Whither Political Islam?" *Foreign Affairs* (January/February 2005): 155.

[council], which selects the *amir* [leader of the faithful]."[19] When asked how the movement started, another Taliban spokesman replied:

After the Mujahidin parties came to power in 1992, the Afghan people thought that peace would prevail in the country. However, the leaders began to fight over power in Kabul. Some local leaders, particularly in Kandahar, formed armed gangs that fought each other. There was widespread corruption and theft, and there were road-blocks everywhere. Women were being attacked, raped and killed. Therefore, after these incidents, a group of students from religious schools decided to rise against these leaders in order to alleviate the suffering of the residents of Kandahar Province. We were able to take control of several centres until we reached Kandahar and the former leaders fled from there.[20]

As in many such religious revivalist movements, this one arose under charismatic leadership. Mullah Muhammad Omar, a Pushtun from southwestern Afghanistan earlier associated with one of the traditional *mujahidin* groups, distinguished himself as a brilliant commander against the Soviets. The Taliban now referred to him as Amir, the movement's supreme title. Omar presided over the Kandahar *shura*, which had authority over all the *shuras* in Taliban-controlled areas. Recruits came disproportionately from *madrassas* in refugee camps in Pakistan and from orphanages. Ethnically the Taliban leadership represented the return to power of the traditionally dominant subtribe, Durani Pushtuns. Goodson listed five factors for the Taliban's success: Pushtun ethnicity, the movement's religious piety, the population's war-weariness, Saudi and other financial backing, and Pakistani military and political support.[21]

The Taliban thus constituted an indigenous Sunni movement focused on purifying Afghanistan according to their understanding of Islamic law as modified by their ethnic code. They commanded men to wear turbans, beards, and short hair and women to wear the *burqa*, a garment that covers the entire body. They strongly encouraged men to pray five times a day at the mosque, and forbade women to leave the house except in the company of a male relative. Because women remained responsible for educating the next generation of believers, they should not work, although some exceptions had to be made in the health field so women could treat

---

[19] Larry P. Goodson, *Afghanistan's Endless War: State Failure, Regional Politics, and the Rise of the Taliban* (Seattle: University of Washington Press, 2001), 14.
[20] Peter Marsden, *The Taliban: War, Religion, and the New Order in Afghanistan* (London: Zed Books Ltd., 1998), 60.
[21] Goodson, *Endless War*, 12–13.

women. The Taliban closed all girls' and some boys' schools, and said they would reopen single-sex schools when they controlled the entire country and after religious scholars had designed an appropriate curriculum. Other social decrees attempted to negate the influence of television and movies and banned music, games, and representation of animal or human forms. When the movement reached the capital, it established the Department for Promotion of Virtue and Prevention of Vice to ensure compliance with Taliban social norms. These policies eventually forced United Nations and foreign NGOs to leave the country in July 1998, because of disagreement with the Taliban over its policy toward women and the increasing danger to its workers.

Taliban interpretation of the Islamic prohibition of images led to the destruction in March 2001 of two giant (120 and 175 feet) historic standing Buddhas carved out of the cliff at Bamiyan, one hundred miles west of Kabul. Omar ordered the similar destruction of all statues in the country, including such cultural treasures as housed in the Kabul museum, despite the protest of the United Nations, Pakistan, Iran, Japan, and China. Even the Egyptian Grand Mufti Nasr Farid Wasel objected. The Taliban regime thus became more and more isolated in world public opinion, even among Muslims. As early as October 7, 1996, the Iranian Ayatollah Ali Khamanei declared, "In the neighborhood of Iran, something is taking place in the name of Islam and a group whose knowledge of Islam is unknown has embarked on actions having nothing to do with Islam."[22] When the Taliban needed international support to defend themselves against the American attack following September 11, there would be little.

Afghanistan thus played a major role in the Cold War from the time of the Soviet invasion, but its primary impact on the post-Cold War has been its training of a generation of mobile Islamic fighters who have participated in conflicts as far afield as Kashmir, Kosovo, the Sudan, and Indonesia. Uzbek, Tajik, and Chinese Islamic militants also have returned home to Central Asia. It was this Afghani *mujahidin* experience, of course, that produced the prominence, the transnational organization, and the base camps of the Saudi terrorist, Osama bin Laden. In this sense, what seemed like a clever CIA strategy in the Cold War period turned out to have many deleterious side effects. The Stinger missiles so accurate against Soviet helicopters and the *mujahidin* camps that trained hardened troops against the godless Communists now pose a threat to the United States and its allies.

[22] Marsden, *Afghanistan*, 130.

Afghanistan itself has returned to the partial control of local warlords while it is legally ruled by President Ahmed Karzai under the U.N.-sponsored Bonn accords of December 2001. Reconstruction has been slow, but the *loya jirga* [grand assembly] approved a new Constitution in December 2003. The Constitution declares that the country, the Islamic Republic of Afghanistan, will combine Islam with democratic guarantees. No legislation contrary to Islam may be introduced, but the Constitution does not mention the *shari'a*. Remnants of the Taliban continue to kill Muslim clerics who support the new government, election workers, and NATO soldiers. The United States, then represented by Afghan-born Ambassador Zalmay Khalilzad, increased its security and reconstruction efforts in 2004. National language and ethnic balance remain sensitive issues. In July the Pushtun Karzai took on his defense minister, Muhammed Qasim Fahim, by dropping him as his first vice-presidential running mate. This move favored the new technocrats and challenged the power of the warlords and their armed militias, especially Tajik *mujahidin*. Karzai won a relatively peaceful presidential election in October 2004 with just over 55 percent of the vote, but he generally did poorly in the Tajik, Uzbek, and Hazara north. Taliban remnants also reduced participation in some southern areas.

SHIITE POLITICS IN IRAN: THE AYATOLLAH AND THE PRESIDENT IN THE EMC SYSTEMS

For the contemporary Shiite tradition, Iran remains the great global exemplar. Shiite religious politics offers more organizational strength than its Sunni counterpart, with the leadership of ayatollahs at the national level and the parish-style direction of mullahs at the local level. The traditional majority Shiite ideology has labeled all government as "unjust" until the return of the twelfth Imam. The belief in the possible prior return of the Imam's deputy, however, opens the way for a more just society by direct political action. Zubaida discusses the general weakness of the Persian Qajar Dynasty (1796–1926) that encouraged Iranian Shiite leaders to occupy the political vacuum in expressing popular anticolonial sentiment.[23] In this movement's most famous case, the mullahs led demonstrations and a boycott against the tobacco concession granted by Nasir Ud-Din Shah to the British Imperial Tobacco Company in 1891.

---

[23] Sami Zubaida, *Islam, the People and the State: Essays on Political Ideas and Movements in the Middle East* (London: I.B. Tauris & Co., 1993), 31.

Chehabi also chronicles the rise of Khomeini beginning with the Shah's increased autocracy in 1963, which discredited the moderate opposition and opened the way for political and religious radicals.[24]

Khomeini, *Time*'s "Man of the Year" in 1980, was born into the family of a mullah in the town of Khomein, 180 miles south of Tehran, in 1900. Khomeini's mother and an aunt raised him after his father, according to Khomeini supporters, was killed by the military officer who, as Reza Shah, founded the Pahlavi dynasty in 1925. Khomeini studied Islam at various theological schools, completing his studies at the nation's most famous theological center of Qom. There he became interested in both Islamic mysticism and Plato's *Republic*, the latter of which may have shaped his vision of an Islamic state directed by the clerical equivalent of a philosopher-king. In *Unveiling the Mysteries* (1944), Khomeini attacked the secular modernism and nationalism of the Pahlavis: "God has formed the Islamic Republic. Obey God and his Prophet and those among you who have authority. It is the only government accepted by God on Resurrection Day. We don't say that the Government must be composed of the clergy but that the Government must be directed and organized according to the divine law, and this is only possible with the supervision of the clergy."[25]

The decades leading up to Khomeini's revolution showed signs of secularism, democracy, and authoritarianism. The British forced the pro-German Reza Shah to abdicate in 1941. His son Mohammed Reza Shah succeeded him. Between 1951 and 1953, the Iranian democratic movement reached its high point in Mohammed Mosaddeq's government that attempted to establish a parliamentary democracy. Mosaddeq, however, faced the hostility of the Shah, parts of the army, landlords, the religious establishment, and Britain and the United States. In 1953, a CIA-sponsored coup overthrew Mosaddeq. Mohammed Reza Shah then presided over an authoritarian regime composed of the above elements until he took more personalistic power in the White Revolution of 1963. The new political form, called "sultanistic" by political scientists, was made possible financially by increased oil revenues and diplomatically by the Shah's increased dependence on the United States. His land reform reduced the power of the landlord class, and he also diluted the social power of the religious opposition by bringing major religious endowments

---

[24] H. E. Chehabi, "Religion and Politics in Iran: How Theocratic Is the Islamic Republic?" *Daedalus* 120 (Summer 1991): 72.

[25] Cited in *New York Times*, June 5, 1989.

under state, in practice his own personal, administration. The White Revolution also fostered the emancipation of women and the seizure of clerical lands. Khomeini, preaching to a crowd of one hundred thousand at a Qom mosque, called on the army to depose the Shah. The government jailed Khomeini, later released him, and when he proved unrepentant, finally exiled him in November 1964.

Khomeini first traveled to Turkey, then Iraq, and in early 1978, he moved his headquarters to the suburbs of Paris, an excellent choice for global media coverage. Khomeini continued preaching his anti-Shah message to Iranians through his clerical allies within the country and through thousands of audio tapes smuggled into the country. The political success of the Iranian revolution stemmed from other causes besides Khomeini's charismatic leadership and his creative application of Shiite social thought to the twentieth-century nation-state. Homa Katouzian comments that Mohammed Reza Shah displayed weakness in all three of the major crises of his reign: Mosaddeq's premiership, the popular riots against the White Revolution, and the revolution of 1978–79. Furthermore, as in all sultanistic regimes, the Shah increasingly micromanaged military and bureaucratic decisions, so that the officer corps fragmented. The military proved incapable of united action after its leader went into exile. Most importantly, the corruption of the Shah's family and sycophant hangers-on grew enormously.[26]

Iran simply contained no civic arena for a moderate domestic opposition, so the radical Khomeini inserted himself into the political vacuum from exile. The 1978 celebrations surrounding Shiite Islam's holiest day of Ashura provided a context for great protests against the Shah, "the new Yazid." In addition to the radical clergy that eventually took power under Khomeini, the Islamic revolution of 1978–79 united very disparate elements: liberals, socialist *mujahidin*, open-minded and relatively progressive clergy such as Ayatollahs Motahhari and Taleqani, and constitutionalists such as Ayatollah Shariatmadari. Hatred for the Shah's autocracy and the charismatic personage of Khomeini held the movement together.

The first years of the Khomeini regime saw the deaths, for example, of Ayatollahs Motahhari and Taleqani, and the gradual dismissal of other moderate allies from the government. Khomeini removed the first elected President, Abul Hassan Banisadr, in June 1981. Power devolved more and

---

[26] Homa Katouzian, "The Pahlavi Regime in Iran," H. E. Chehabi and Juan J. Linz, *Sultanistic Regimes* (Baltimore: Johns Hopkins University Press, 1998), 198–205.

more to members of the then parliamentary majority Islamic Republican Party, founded a few days after the revolution by five younger radical clerics, Mohammad Beheshti, Ali Akbar Hashemi Rafsanjani, Ali Khameini, Javad Bahonar, and Ayatollah Abdolkarim Musavi Ardabili. As radical elements under Khomeini took control of the government, and the society polarized over the Iran-Iraq War and the holding of the American hostages, a major struggle began between Khomeini's allies and the socialist *mujahidin*. The latter blew up the parliament building in June 1981, killing Beheshti and four cabinet ministers. The Iranian government's secret police, many of them holdovers from the Shah's notorious SAVAK, responded with torture and terror. But not all went according to Khomeini's plans. Iran had to sign a truce with Iraq in July 1988 after horrendous losses on both sides. Khomeini himself died in June 1989. Then the council named President Ali Khameini to replace Khomeini as the new *faqih*, and Hashemi Rafsanjani became president for two terms, 1989–97. Rafsanjani, dubbed "the Shark" for his political skills, became the leading architect of Tehran's moderately successful attempts to end its international isolation in the 1990s, moves that radicals denounced as "Hashemi's perestroika." By the late 1990s, however, Rafsanjani became part of the conservative coalition attacking the new Iranian president, Mohammad Khatami, who had been elected by a landslide over an Islamist candidate in May 1997.

On January 7, 1998, Khatami gave a forty-five minute interview to Christine Amanpour, CNN's foreign correspondent of Persian extraction, in which he called for increased cultural exchanges as a way to break down Iranian-American mistrust built up over two decades. Many viewed the election of this philosopher-clergyman (In the interview he quoted de Tocqueville's nineteenth-century classic *Democracy in America*) as an opening for moderate politics in Iran and for Iranian-American relations internationally. Khatami's praise for America's ability to balance the religious spirit of its founders with a love of liberty seemed to say as much about his position in domestic Iranian politics as it did about Iranian-American relations.

The religious conservatives under the new *faqih* Ayatollah Ali Khameini, however, prevailed. Tehran's mayor Gholamhossein Karabaschi, was arrested for corruption in April 1998. Karabaschi, mayor since 1989, had distinguished himself both for beautifying Tehran and for strongly supporting Khatami's presidential campaign. Under the current Iranian judicial system, the judge also served as prosecutor throughout the trial, and the judiciary has especially close ties to the *faqih*. Karabaschi was eventually convicted, sentenced to prison for five years, and barred from public office until 2018. Ayatollah Khameini controls the armed forces, the intelligence and security forces, the judiciary, and radio and television, thus wielding much more power than the president. Despite the above political setbacks and a failing economy, in May 2001 the public again elected Khatami president with 76 percent of the vote.

Many students, however, lost faith in Khatami's ability to change social structures or to provide the jobs necessary for the children of the 1980s baby boom. Student protestors in June 2003 chanted against Ayatollah Khameini, but a minority also chanted against what they perceived as the timidity of President Khatami. The 2003 student protests had been fostered by satellite broadcasts from Persian language television broadcasts in California. With the reformist press largely shut down, the quickest way to circulate anti-government news and rumor was to call one of the four Los Angeles stations (National Iranian TV [NITV], Azadei, PARS TV, and Channel One). These stations then broadcast to the illegal but numerous satellite dishes in middle-class neighborhoods. Iranians value these foreign stations as an alternative source of information, but not for their editorial position calling for the return of the Shah's son as monarch.

Only about ten percent of the eligible voters turned out for municipal elections in the major cities in February 2003, demonstrating widespread disenchantment with all politics. This disenchantment provided the conservatives with the opportunity to take back control of the parliament in February 2004. In January, the twelve-member Guardian Council disqualified more than two thousand reformist candidates, including the president's brother and more than eighty other members of parliament. Khameini sought to present himself as above the dispute, but he "failed to persuade" the Council to reinstate more than a few candidates. The Ayatollah then warned against any boycott of the election. The conservatives returned to parliamentary control, and various conservative factions began to gear up for the 2005 presidential election. The political analyst Reza Aslan commented, "I think most Iranians are apathetic about who is in control – as long as anybody gives them a little bit of freedom, they don't care."[27] And the mosques are so empty than many mullahs greatly fear for the future of Islam among the baby boom generation between fifteen and twenty-five. There has been continued clerical criticism of political

[27] February 23, 2004.

Islam from figures like Grand Ayatollah Hossein Ali Montazeri,[28] who was released from his five-year house arrest in January 2003.

In short, there are many similarities to the Chinese political situation. The government, with both force and policy adjustments, maintains control. The liberals, who seem too tame to the students, fear that student protests will give conservatives more excuses to crack down. There is even an Iranian parallel political label to the Chinese "counterrevolutionary turmoil" in "those who fight against Allah." The death penalty may be imposed in both cases.

Unlike China, however, Iranian societal conditions have worsened appreciably since the Revolution of 1979, with high population growth and a per capita income one-fourth that at the end of the Shah's regime. Seventy percent of Iranians are under age thirty, with little memory of the Revolution. The extreme social stratification increases daily. Nevertheless, Dariush Zahedi finds only a low chance of overthrow of the Islamic Republic while "chances for the obliteration or modification of the prevailing order" within the Islamic Republic are moderate. He supports his analysis by comparing the revolutionary situations of 1978 and 2000: "Unlike the previous regime, the theocracy enjoys a solid base of devoted adherents who can readily be mobilized in support of the regime. Intragroup divisions have split the Iranian class structure, producing a social environment less conducive to a revolutionary transfer of power. From the perspective of their survival, Iran's politicized clerics have acted far more wisely than the shah by not dissolving their links with all of the significant components of the nation's civil society.[29]

Whereas the objective socioeconomic situation has worsened, the current theocratic leadership still remains politically more astute than that of the Shah. Above all, it has retained control of the mosques. The theocracy's supporters are stronger, the opposition is much weaker, and there is no Khomeini to lead a new Revolution. The clergy is divided, with the less-powerful majority reformers fearing the long-term damage to Islam from a corrupt theocratic government based on Khomeini's minority vision of Shiiite clerical political leadership. Zahedi states that among the general public and the regime, "the scale of bribery has gone

---

[28] Sussan Siavoshi places Montazeri in the ideological middle on the question of the role of the Supreme Guide. Sussan Siavoshi, "Between Heaven and Earth: The Islamic Republic of Iran," Ted Gerard Jelen and Clyde Wilcox, eds., *Religion and Politics in Comparative Perspective* (Cambridge: Cambridge University Press, 2002), 132.

[29] Dariush Zahedi, *The Iranian Revolution Then and Now: Indicators of Regime Stability* (Boulder, CO: Westview, 2000), 196.

from bad to worse,"[30] a terrifying thought when one remembers the devastating level of corruption under the Shah. Yet, like China, any change in Iran will have to come from within the ruling elites, not from student demonstrators. Sussan Siavoshi judges that "the seculars, if they insist upon a rigid interpretation of humanist republicanism, may be doomed to failure."[31] The best chance of reform would come from a strengthened coalition of Siavoshi's "modern right"(free markets, cultural tolerance, and mixed authoritarian and democratic politics) with Khatami's "modern left" (ambivalence about economic privatization, cultural tolerance, and democratic pluralism). In the first round of the June 2005 presidential elections, the vote fragmented, with five candidates receiving from 13 to 21 percent of the vote. In the second round, Tehran's conservative mayor, Mahmoud Ahmadinejad, surprised most observers by easily defeating Rafsanjani. Ahmadinejad is a verteran of the Iran-Iraq War but not a mullah. He promised honest government and social justice for the poor, many of them war veterans. During the Khatami years, the reformist elite lost connection with these poor, as they could not deliver economically.

SHIITE ISLAM IN THE MILITARY SYSTEM: NUCLEAR WEAPONS AND THE IRAQ WAR

Along with North Korea, which already had nuclear weapons, Iran and Iraq qualified for the infamous "axis of evil" in Bush 43's 2002 State of the Union address. The weapons of mass destruction and the assistance to Al-Queda that the president sought so assiduously in Iraq have a much greater chance of being found in Iran. The Pakistani scientist Khan confessed on television to supplying nuclear technology to North Korea, Libya, and Iran. Libya traded in its weapons program for economic considerations, but the Iranian government has claimed to be interested only in the peaceful uses of atomic energy. On October 21, 2003, Tehran accepted a European plan for stricter international inspections and suspension of the production of enriched uranium for an "interim period." The agreement displeased hardliners in both the United States and Iran. On October 28, however, Deputy Secretary of State Armitage stated that the United States did not seek "regime change" in Iran, signaling an American willingness for further engagement. The leading Bush Administration critic of such agreements was John R. Bolton, then secretary of state for

---

[30] Zahedi, *Iranian Revolution*, 54.
[31] Siavoshi, "Between Heaven and Earth," p. 137.

nonproliferation, who has stated that the Iranian situation might bring about "revolution from below."[32] On November 2, Ayatollah Khameini closed the Iranian public debate by declaring his support for the nuclear agreement. The succeeding relations have been rocky, however, with the Iranians trying to hide what they can and threatening to resume development, and the International Atomic Energy Agency pressing for more disclosure and weapons program termination. Many European diplomats hoped that the June 2005 presidential election of Rafsanjani would provide the hard-nosed Iranian negotiator who could reach a nuclear agreement in exchange for economic support.[33] Rafsanjani lost.

The Iraq War has strengthened Iran's position in the region by eliminating a hated enemy, the "godless" Saddam Hussein. The chaos in Iraq also benefits the Tehran government by keeping the Americans occupied and by emphasizing Iran's traditional Shiite links to southern Iraq. This benefit lasts as long as the Iraqi chaos does not develop into an ethnic and religious regional war that brings in Turkey, Pakistan, Saudi Arabia, and other Muslim states with Russian, Indian, Chinese, and fuller American meddling and/or participation. Since the Ottomans, Iraq's unity has been tenuous. In 1921, the British put together the modern nation from three separate Ottoman provinces: Mosul, whose natural commerce was with Turkey and Syria; Baghdad, which with the Shiite shrine cities of Najaf and Karbala, looked toward Persia; and Shiite Basra oriented to the sea and India. The Sunni Ottomans had placed the minority Sunnis in power in Baghdad, and the British followed suit.

After the first Gulf War, the elder Bush and Colin Powell refrained from deposing the secular Sunni Saddam Hussein because they feared that the country would fragment into a Kurdish north, a Sunni center, and a Shiite south, initiating similar movements throughout the Middle East. For example, a greater Kurdestan would take territory from Turkey, Iraq, and Iran. Following Hussein's subsequent crackdown on his enemies, the Allies established no-fly zones to rein in Saddam while protecting religious and ethnic minorities. The Sunni Kurds thus benefited from eleven years of protection to develop a significant degree of autonomy under the rival factions of the Patriotic Union of Kurdestan (led by Talabani) and the Kurdestan Democratic Party (Barzani). The embattled

---

[32] September 21, 2004.

[33] Kenneth Pollack and Ray Takeyh, "Taking on Tehran," *Foreign Affairs* (March/April 2005), argue that the United States should foster modern Iranian elites choosing economic development over nuclear weapons.

northern city of Kirkuk retains a cosmopolitan population of majority Kurds, Saddam-transplanted Arabs, Turkmen, and Assyrian Christians. Its oil fields contain forty percent of the nation's reserves, currently exacerbating arguments over Kurdish autonomy.

The strong religious connections between Iran and the southern sections of Iraq have influenced both the Iranian revolution and the 2003 Iraqi War. The exiled Khomeini lodged and taught at the impoverished Shiite theological center of Najaf in southern Iraq. Khomeini joined the Hawza, a loosely connected seminary of mosques, houses, and rooms, which provided spiritual leadership for Shiites throughout the world. Khomeini's victory and Saddam's continued persecution convinced many Shiite clerics to flee to Iran. They settled in the theological center of Qom, built around the tomb of the sister of the eighth Imam Reza. Thus, the coincidental rises of Khomeini in Iran and Saddam Hussein in Iraq led to the transfer of global Shiite theological leadership from the Iraqi cities of Najaf and Karbala to the previously religiously less prominent Iranian city under the inspiration of that country's revolutionary Supreme Guide.

In spring 2003, U.S. war planners already knew that Shiites comprised sixty percent of the Iraqi population and that the Imam Husain had been martyred at Karbala, soon to become a battlefield. They were thus not surprised later in April by the great outpouring of religious sentiment for the first government-permitted pilgrimage to the Imam Husain's tomb since 1977. They were shocked, however, by the strong local organizational role taken by various Shiite clerics when the allied forces failed to provide security, sustenance, and electricity. Some Shiite clerics who had remained in Iraq under Saddam, like the Grand Ayatollah Muhammad Sadiq al-Sadr, had been assassinated by the Baghdad secret police. Sadr's son, the thirty-year-old Moktada al-Sadr, became one of the first clerics to seek political power in the wake of the American vacuum. From his mosque in nearby Kufa, Sadr sought to control Najaf and the two million impoverished Shiites who lived in Baghdad's slum of Saddam City, which was newly named for his father. From Qom he received theological support from the fatwas of the Ayatollah Kazem al-Haeri, but the middle-ranking al-Sadr's religious role has been circumscribed by the relatively moderate tone set by the senior Iraqi Grand Ayatollah Sayyid Ali al-Sistani. Two other clerical competitors were killed when the U.S.-supported London-based cleric Sheik Abdul Majid al-Khoei, another son of another revered ayatollah, was shot and hacked to death in the Ali shrine with the cleric Haider al-Rafaei, who had cooperated with the Saddam government.

No wonder the Tehran-based sixty-three-year-old Ayatollah Muham-mad Bakir al-Hakim did not return to Iraq until the United States had approved his two hundred bodyguards. In 1982 al-Hakim founded the Supreme Council for Islamic Revolution in Iraq (SCIRI) and the ten-thousand-strong Badr Brigade militia, armed and trained by the Iranian Revolutionary Guards. Iranian support did not endear al-Hakim to Washington, but in 1999 Clinton designated SCIRI as one of the seven opposition groups eligible to receive American aid. SCIRI has kept its distance from Washington, although after al-Hakim returned to Iraq, he called for a representative, pluralistic government, but one which upheld Islamic values. SCIRI joined the U.S.-sponsored Governing Coun-cil and supported the Interim Government. In late August 2003 a large car bomb exploded at the Najaf mosque, killing Hakim and eighty-one others.

In spring 2004 al-Sadr and his Madhi Army rose against the U.S. occu-pation in central and southern Iraq. They then took refuge in Najaf and Karbala, leading Ayatollah al-Sistani and other senior Shiite clerics to call for all forces, Iraqi and American, to leave the holy cities before they damaged the sacred mosques. Even al-Sadr's sponsor Ayatollah al-Haeri withdrew his support after Sadr's forces damaged the Ali shrine. Al-Sadr, lacking senior religious status, sought to represent the Shiite martyr's tra-dition by often preaching in a burial shroud and talking about his coming death.

Al-Sistani and the other three Grand Ayatollahs, the *marjaiah*, repre-sent the establishment Shiite political-religious view. They oppose an Iran-style clerical political leadership, and have supported the U.S. transfer of power. Al-Sistani vetoed the original U.S. plan for choosing an interim legislature through caucuses, insisting on elections first. These leaders see majority Shiites finally winning fair elections and rightfully taking power after centuries of Sunni domination. Al-Sistani did not even veto the U.S. and U.N. selection of secular Shiite Iyad Allawi as the interim prime min-ister, despite Allawi's prior association with the Baath Party and the CIA. Shiite clerics did object strenuously when the American military reached a cease fire with Sunni rebels in Falluja that allowed the Sunni militias to retain their weapons. The Sunni religious organization, the Associa-tion of Muslim Scholars, is headed by Sheik Hareth al-Dhari, and claims to represent over three thousand mosques. The Sheik has preached fiery sermons against the Americans and the British, but he has also served as the conduit for the release of more than twenty foreign hostages. For-eign Sunni fighters and ex-Baathists have flocked to this insurgency in the Sunni Triangle, especially in Falluja. SCIRI's Shiite Sheik Homam Hamoodi has commented, "He [al-Dhari] represents the Sunni opposition voice in Iraq, and this opposition is supported by outsiders who have no business here [in Iraq]."[34] When the American and Interim Government forces cleared Falluja in November 2004, the Sunni Association's Sheik Qasim al-Hanafi stated, "The clerics believe the Iraqi people are practicing a religious duty and an international right in resisting the occupation, and they bless the holy war being carried out by the people of Falluja."[35] More telling from a military and social perspective, however, was the lack of popular Shiite support for the city's Sunnis in the fall when compared with that Shiite support during the first American attack on Falluja in April.

Great hope surfaced in Iraq following extensive popular participation in the election of January 30, 2005, even though the majority of Sunnis boycotted the election. The new prime minister Ibrahim al-Jaafari, who comes from the traditionally Islamist Daawa movement, has worked very hard to reassure all Iraqis that he has no intension of forcing women to wear veils or imposing an Iran-style *shari'a*. Daawa partisans were impressed that the United States did not try to manage the January elections so that secular Shiite Iyad Allawi would triumph.[36] Sunnis joined the discussions on the new Iraqi Constitution, but in the end, it was proposed without their support. Pressured by the United States to complete their work, the Shiite and Kurdish leadership went ahead, and offered their version for the October referendum. The draft did establish both Islam and democracy as touchstones for law, and deferred extremely difficult decisions on family law and the constitutional court to future negotiations. But Shiite (not just Kurdish) federalism and de-Baathification threaten the Sunni central part of the country, without its own oil revenues. Even the Shiite leader Moktada al-Sadr, whose followers are overwhelming in that central region, opposed the draft. Moktada's followers continue to battle with the Shiite Badr Brigade, and terrorist violence continues, especially in the Sunni Triangle. Sunnis remain a fractured group with no one like Ayatollah al-Sistani to bring them together. Whether the militias or

---

[34] *San Jose Mercury News*, July 11, 2004.

[35] October 21, 2004.

[36] For the background of Daawa, the reasons for its change of worldview, and an interview with al-Jaafari, see *Wall Street Journal*, April 28, 2005. The Communitarian sociologist Amitai Etzioni earlier advocated U.S. support for "soft" Islam. See "Mosque and State in Iraq," *Policy Review* (October/November 2003): 65–73.

the political leader finally determine the future of Iraq remains an open questions.

Religion continues to play a crucial political role in South and Central Asia. India remains the principal political and EMC power. The 2004 Indian election results and Sonia Gandhi's declining of the prime minister's position have opened the country to a possible virtuous cycle, which would combine a more honest multicultural, multireligious democracy, strong and more equal economic growth, and reduced Indian-Pakistani tensions. Vajpayee took risks to pursue the third goal, but he failed to move against the 2002 Hindu rioting in Gujarat, and the BJP forgot about the poor in economic development. Vajpayee also commented that the party had relied too much on a high-tech campaign and that the Gujarat chief minister Modi should have been removed after the riots. The RSS protested the last point vigorously.[37] A return to Nehru's European-style elite secularism and Rao's market economy will not be enough to enable a virtuous cycle. Religious dialogue between Hindus and non-Hindus, leading to Gandhi-like strategic savvy, wisdom, and sacrifice for the advancement of the poor and the underrepresented, and a Kashmiri peace will be required. Unfortunately, the Hindu nationalism of the Sangh Parivar family of organizations remains much more politically effective than any other institutional section of that religion. But many individual *sadhus* [ascetics] such as Agnivesh support peace and human rights within the Hindu tradition.

From Pakistan through the mountain passes to Afghanistan, Iran, and Iraq, various Islamic groups can determine or at least block political arrangements in all four national systems. The Shiite-Sunni split remains crucial everywhere in the region. Continued chaos favors radical elements such as the Sunni Taliban and the Shiite forces of al-Sadr, or fragmentation into a civil war like the Lebanese conflict (1975–91), which featured six major religious groups and led to the rise of the Shiite Hezbollah in the image of Khomeini. Radical religious regimes are thus likely to lead to more national chaos for such countries located in the current global political and EMC systems that are disproportionately influenced by the West.

No moderate political solution is possible, however, without the participation of religious leaders. Shiite religious forms fit this purpose institutionally better than fragmented Sunni ones. For example, the four Grand Ayatollahs of Najaf have played a stabilizing role in Iraq, despite their

[37] June 25, 2004.

distrust of the United States and the history of Washington abandoning both the Shiites and the Kurds. In fact, without the Iraqi Ayatollahs' participation, no political reconstruction is possible. Any permanent Iraqi solution must have Shiite, Sunni, and Kurdish acquiescence, in addition to the acceptance of nearby Sunni states. In all four of the above Muslim countries, military force currently trumps every other consideration. Military force, however, cannot establish a legitimate national leadership nor lead to political and economic reconstruction. The Iranian Islamists, led by Supreme Guide Khameini, maintain control by force, but have lost significant expressive power, thus weakening religious belief among the young majority, those born after 1979. Any Iranian political-economic solution must come from inside the Iranian establishment and be accepted by at least the European Union, if not the United States. E.U.-U.S. cooperation remains crucial throughout the region, to facilitate, for example, a joint negotiating strategy for restraining Iran's nuclear weapons program.

8

The Middle East and North Africa

Jewish and Islamic Politics

ISRAELI POLITICS: JEWISH IDENTITY AND THE ISRAELI STATE

Chapter 7 initially focused on the great religious-political figure of the anticolonial period, Mahatma Gandhi. This chapter begins with the assassination of the most significant political-religious figure of postwar Israeli politics, Yitzhak Rabin. The latter killing in November 1995 exhibited many parallels to the assassination of Gandhi. In both cases the killer came from the extremist right wing of the leader's own religion. Yigal Amir, a yeshiva graduate and student at a religious university, said he assassinated Rabin to stop him from handing over parts of the West Bank to the Palestinians. The killing thus triggered a debate among Jewish Modern Orthodox scholars and leaders as to whether they, too, had some responsibility for the act.[1] The next month the Israeli government refused a visa to a New York rabbi, Abraham Hecht, who, it is said, had given a religious justification for the killing of Rabin only months before the assassination. Rabbi Hecht had apologized to the prime minister for his ruling days before Rabin's death.

Rabin established his security credentials in his lifelong fight for the independence of Israel. Born in Jerusalem in 1922, he joined the Palmach, the elite military strike force of the Hagana underground, in 1941. He later studied at the British military staff college at Camberley and became Chief of Staff for the Israeli Army in 1964. Rabin orchestrated Israel's great victory in the 1967 war. He then replaced Golda Meir as Israel's fifth prime minister in 1974, but he was forced to resign three years later after

---

[1] November 9, 1995.

violating Israel's currency laws. Rabin defeated Simon Peres for control of the Labor Party and returned as prime minister in 1992. He signed the Oslo Accords with Arafat one year later, and all three men received the Nobel Peace Prize. Rabin's guerrilla and regular military successes made him the perfect "bastard for peace" that Friedman called for at the end of the 1989 edition of *From Beirut to Jerusalem*.

In the cases of both Gandhi and Rabin, the assassinations did significant damage to the peace process in a culturally religious, legally secular state. Like Nehru's Congress Party, Israel's founding secular independence party, Labor, ruled uninterruptedly for many years. It finally lost control to Likud's Begin in 1977–84. Then the nearly equal Knesset representation from these two leading political parties produced policy gridlock until the beginning of the Oslo Process in 1993. After Rabin's assassination, Foreign Minister Simon Peres, who had been Rabin's partner in the negotiations, replaced Rabin as prime minister. Unfortunately, Peres did not have Rabin's security credentials. In Israel's first direct presidential elections the following year, Likud's Benjamin Netanyahu ("Bibi") defeated Peres with 50.1 percent of the vote. Israeli popular revulsion to the Hamas spring terrorist campaign tipped the balance to Bibi and Likud, just barely, and the voting illustrated the divided nature of Israeli society. Voting for Peres were 70 percent of Jews of recent European or American descent, 63 percent of secular Jews, and 95 percent of Arab Israelis. Supporting Netanyahu were 62 percent of Soviet immigrants, 60 percent of Jews of recent African or Asian descent, and 96 percent of Orthodox and Ultra-Orthodox Jews. Post–Cold War Russian immigration provided just enough votes to Likud's Netanyahu. Russian voters had become the country's "swing votes," with political advertising in Russian obligatory in all Israeli elections. Russian defectors to Barak would elect him three years later.

Solving the Palestinian question has remained extremely difficult because of the breadth and tenacity of public positions in both Israeli and Palestinian politics. According to Kenneth Wald, more than 80 percent of Israeli citizens are Jews, with approximately 20 percent highly observant, 20 percent nonobservant, and 60 percent "traditional," following a mix of secular and religious customs.[2] The Ultra-Orthodox, who make up half of the highly observant, trace their origins to Eastern European

---

[2] Kenneth D. Wald, "The Religious Dimension of Israeli Political Life," Ted Gerald Jelen and Clyde Wilcox, eds., *Religion and Politics in Comparative Perspective* (Cambridge: Cambridge University Press, 2002), 99–122.

Yiddish revivals in the eighteenth century. These *haredim* wear distinctive
black dress, and seek to establish a communal life separate from the rest of
Israeli society. They view their special call as the protection of the religious
essence of Judaism, the Torah society. None of their women and almost
none of their men serve in the Israeli army, and virtually none of their
yeshivas recognize Israeli Independence Day. This great divide between
the Ultra-Orthodox and the rest of society has been made tolerable, if
annoying, to both sides by the traditional adjustments of the Status Quo.
The state grants the Ultra-Orthodox military exemptions and subsidies
for religious and educational institutions, whereas the Ultra-Orthodox
accept state legitimacy and pay their taxes.

Although these adjustments mitigate the divide over the nature of
Jewish society, they continue to cause major tension when peace gets
close, according to Jewish theologian and conflict resolution specialist
Marc Gopin. "This is due to some of the profound conflicts that Jews
have been having for centuries, and it is also due to the way in which wars
and anti-Semitism have masked basic questions of identity and values until
now."[3] This first divide thus constitutes an institutionalized "culture war."
On February 20, 2002, for example, the Israeli Supreme Court ruled that
Jews converted by Reformed or Conservative movements should be listed
as Jews in official documents. The Interior Minister Eli Yishai, a member
of the Ultra-Orthodox Shas Party, responded that "[t]his is a scandalous,
difficult, and disastrous decision for the Jewish people." Yishai criticized
the court for "strengthening a marginal stream that encourages assimila-
tion and helps to diminish the Jewish people."[4]

The *haredim* also have fragmented into various teaching lines following different eminent rabbis. Many of these rabbis and schools maintain
headquarters or associated synagogues in the United States, especially in
urban New York. Israeli Ashkenazi Ultra-Orthodox have tended to vote
for the United Torah Judaism. The Shas, which won eleven Knesset seats
in 1996, seventeen in 1999, and ten in 2001, is made up of Orthodox and
more traditional Sephardic Jews. Both of the above parties oppose any
legislation that dilutes the authority of the state rabbinate over marriage,
divorce, and conversion, but it is United Torah that has been most insis-
tent on the Sabbath closure of streets in Orthodox neighborhoods and on
other religious-cultural questions.

---

[3] Marc Gopin, *Between Eden and Armageddon: The Future of World Religions, Violence,
and Peacemaking* (Oxford: Oxford University Press, 2000), 116.
[4] February 21, 2002.

The second great political-religious divide over whether or not Israel should turn over any of the land gained in the 1967 war threatens the existence of the state more directly. The strong opponents of trading land for peace are religious nationalists, sometimes called Modern Orthodox. This group combines its religious belief with modern customs and cooperated with the majority secular Zionists in the founding of the Israeli state. Many Modern Orthodox saw the 1967 victory as a sign of God's activity and demand that all of Palestine, including the West Bank, remain Jewish. They have thus led the settlement movement, which Likud enthusiastically embraced when it came to power in 1977. The Modern Orthodox also virulently opposed the Likud-sponsored Camp David Accord that handed back the militarily unimportant but symbolically sacred Sinai area and its settlements to the Palestinians. Since the Ultra-Orthodox have as few dealings with the state as possible, the Modern Orthodox control the state rabbinate. The National Republican Party constitutes their strongest political voice. Because of the increased leverage of minority parties resulting from the minority status of both Labor and Likud, small cohesive religion-based groups have developed political clout in excess of their Knesset seats. So religious Zionism has moved from being an ally of secular Zionists in integrating the new society at the founding of Israel to a separatist threat in the current period.

In May 1999, Labor's Ehud Barak, another "soldier for peace," defeated Netanyahu. Since most voters felt free to vote their ideological choices in the Knesset after voting their compromise choices for president, the new parliament became more fragmented than ever. Fifteen parties received seats, with the three largest parties being One Israel (Labor and Gesher) twenty-seven seats, Likud nineteen seats, and the Shas seventeen seats. Barak chose to ignore the first societal divide by arranging a coalition with the Shas, who were more likely to support compromise with the Palestinians than Likud. But he also brought the National Religious Party into his coalition and gave them the Housing Ministry, which fostered further settlement expansion.

PALESTINIAN POLITICS: PLO VERSUS HAMAS

The major conflict in the Palestinian position has come between the secular Palestinian Liberation Organization (PLO) and the Islamic Resistance Movement (Hamas) and other armed radical organizations. PLO founder Yasir Arafat grew up within the Old Walls of Jerusalem and studied engineering at Cairo University. Friedman called the PLO leader "the Teflon

Guerrilla" for his Reagan-like sense of theatrical timing and his immunity to criticism for failed strategic initiatives. In 1956, when it looked like the Palestinians would disappear as refugees into other national states, Arafat and a group of other middle-class Palestinians living in Kuwait decided to form the organization al-Fatah [Victory] to give Palestinians an independent voice. In 1964 the Arab states sponsored the founding of the PLO as a way to control the chaotic and fragmenting Palestinians. After the Six-Day War, however, Arafat and his supporters got control of the PLO in 1969, thanks to their courageous fighting with Israel. Arafat then demonstrated a genius at keeping the disparate Palestinian groups under his umbrella and at finding a sponsoring Arab state. He built the PLO into both an armed guerrilla force and a social welfare organization, while promoting the Palestinian issue in world public opinion. However, by the end of the 1980s, he seemed terminally unable to deliver on the promise of a Palestinian state. The diplomatic and media skills necessary for his first task did not guarantee the administrative and political abilities necessary for his second.

During this period, the Israelis had not only tolerated, but at times had even nurtured Hamas as a way to weaken Arafat. When Palestinian rage boiled over in the first *intifada* [resistence] of 1987, Hamas became even stronger. It also received increased financial aid from Iran and at least private aid from the Saudis, which enabled it to establish a competing network of hundreds of mosques, schools, orphanages, clinics, and hospitals that permeated almost every village, town, and refugee camp on the West Bank and in the Gaza Strip. These social institutions both increased Hamas' political legitimacy and proved fertile grounds for recruiting terrorists. Suddenly, the secular and moderately corrupt PLO looked like the better option to Israel. After he was elected in 1992, Rabin felt strong enough to begin negotiations with Arafat. These negotiations led to the Oslo Peace Process that rescued Arafat and gave hope to a Palestinian settlement. Hamas constituted the major Palestinian foe of the Oslo agreements, and in seeking to disrupt the process, committed terrorism in Israel at significant junctures. For example, Hamas suicide bombers detonated pipe bombs in Jerusalem and Ashkelon on February 26, 1996, killing twenty-five people and wounding seventy-seven. These bombings broke a six-month lull and turned the Israeli presidential race toward Netanyahu, by a whisker.

How can we account for the final failure of the Oslo Process that began so brightly on the White House lawn in September 1993? The Israeli explanation pointed out that Barak had courageously offered Arafat 97 percent of what the latter demanded, and Clinton strongly criticized the Palestinian leader for refusing to accept Barak's offer. The *New York Times*[5] later offered a more complicated analysis that highlighted mistakes on all sides. From July 11 to 25, 2000, Israeli and Palestinian leaders met at Camp David to reach a final settlement. At the end of two weeks, Clinton announced that they could not reach agreement. Despite the growing violence in the fall, Israeli and Palestinian negotiators continued talking secretly. The American president then unveiled his peace plan, and negotiators for both sides met openly in Taba, Egypt, on January 21, 2001. The talks were suspended by Barak after the killing of two Israelis in the West Bank, then resumed, but suspended again until after the Israeli election. Both Israeli and Palestinian negotiators felt they got very close to a deal at Taba, but Sharon defeated Barak on February 7 with 62 percent of the vote. Sharon, who had a long history of hard line approaches to the Palestinians, terminated the process.

Barak, especially as he represented a faltering coalition, did make a courageous offer at Camp David that included breaking a significant Israeli taboo by discussing a division of Jerusalem. The Palestinians, however, did not feel that Barak's Camp David offer left them a viable state, and Barak himself improved the Israeli offer six months later. The Taba formula started with the Palestinian principle of the return to 1967 borders and then allowed for the swapping of settlement blocs for equivalent land. Arafat never turned down that Taba offer, but the negotiators ran out of time. Some negotiators concluded that Clinton should have released his plan at Camp David in July rather than waiting for Christmas. Of course, the president became more and more of a "lame duck" as the January 20 inauguration of Bush approached. The Palestinians did not feel ready for Camp David in July, but Clinton pressured them to attend.

Ben-Ami, Israeli foreign minister during this period, stated: "At the end of Camp David, we had the feeling that the package as such contained ingredients and needed to go on. But Clinton left us to our own devices after he started the blame game. He was trying to give Barak a boost knowing he had political problems going home empty-handed with his concessions revealed. But in doing so he created problems for the other side." The Palestinians lionized Arafat for having stood up to the Americans over Jerusalem and the refugees. Negotiators state that none of the three big outstanding issues (Jerusalem, Palestinian refugees, and Jewish settlement and future borders) were "deal breakers" at Taba, but

---

[5] July 26, 2001. The following quotations are also from this source.

that they ran out of time as the outside political situation deteriorated. American lead negotiator Dennis Ross offered the following summary: "One of the lessons I've learned is that you can't have one environment at the negotiating tables, and a different reality on the ground." From 1992 to 2001, the Israeli settlement population increased by eighty thousand, the Palestinian standard of living dropped twenty percent, and the PLO became increasingly corrupt. Arafat was losing his political struggle with Hamas and other radical alternatives partially because the Oslo Process was not delivering anything. Rob Malley, the National Security Council's Middle East expert under Clinton, said that the United States was not tough enough on either side, either in discouraging Israeli settlements or criticizing Palestinian incitements to violence. Most of the Jewish public just wanted a cessation of violence and did not sense the urgency of the Palestinians.

When the Oslo Process broke down in 2001, Hamas increased its campaign of suicide bombings and other violent acts. In this they were joined by other terrorist groups such as Islamic Jihad led by Sheik Abdallah al-Shami, the Marxist Popular Front for the Liberation of Palestine, and even the Al Aqsa Martyrs Brigades from Arafat's own movement. Sharon responded with multiple Israeli army incursions into Palestinian Authority territory, several times surrounding Arafat in his Ramallah headquarters. Only United States and European Union protests kept Sharon from capturing and deporting the Palestinian leader. Bush and his foreign policy team had entered the White House convinced that the Palestinian question could produce nothing but headaches, and thus that it should not be a focus of U.S. policy. On June 24, 2002, President Bush finally declared that Arafat must be replaced before the United States would support a Palestinian state. More indicative of the post-Oslo period was Passover 2002, when in a day of raids, a suicide bomber killed twenty-two Israelis and the Israeli army retaliated, killing forty Palestinians. Israeli public opinion also hardened, inducing Labor to enter into a right-wing national unity government. The Israeli peace movement splintered. But most Israelis do not believe that Sharon's policy has delivered either peace or security.

In late October 2002, Labor leader Benyamin Ben-Eliezer led his party out of the "grand coalition" government over his opposition to the funding of Israeli settlements. Yet, in the subsequent Labor primary, Ben-Eliezer lost to popular Haifa mayor, ex-general Amran Mitzna. Mitzna had called for Israeli withdrawal from the Gaza Strip and immediate negotiations with the Palestinians, which, should they fail, would lead to disengagement between two separate countries. Netanyahu challenged

Sharon from the right in the Likud primary, but lost. Sharon retained the prime ministership in January 2003, and Likud increased its plurality in the Knesset to thirty-seven seats versus nineteen for Labor and fifteen for Shinui. This gave Sharon a stronger position, and also demonstrated the weakness of Labor and the continued fragmentation of both the Israeli and the Palestinian political systems. Sharon was already pushing his plan for unilateral disengagement from Gaza when Arafat died in November 2004. As a crucial parliamentary vote on the Gaza plan neared in October 2004, many rabbis, including the former chief Ashkenazic rabbi, Avraham Shapira, told soldiers to disobey the government's orders to remove Jewish settlers from their homes. Both the defense minister and the army chief of staff denounced those statements, and other rabbis agreed that such rabbinical judgments endangered the Israeli state.[6] In January 2005 Sharon formed a coalition of the Likud, Peres-led Labor, and United Torah parties. On Gaza withdrawal, some Likud members defected, but their places were taken on these votes by leftist opposition members from parties such as Yahad. In fact, the leader of the opposition, Shinui's Yosef Lapid, has promised to do everything possible to promote the peace effort, including the Gaza disengagement.[7] When the Palestinian Authority held local elections in May 2005, Abbas' Fatah came in first and Hamas a strong second. The second *intifada* had become a second *nakba* [catastrophe] for both Palestinians and the state of Israel. With the death of Arafat, Abbas and Sharon began a tenuous and prolonged process to construct a new peace process. Sharon's successful pullout from Gaza in August 2005 raised hopes internationally, but it increased the fragmentation of Likud. Netanyahu again challenged Sharon.

THE ARAB ISLAMIC HEARTLAND: SAUDI ARABIA,
SYRIA, IRAQ, AND EGYPT

The failure of the Oslo Process affected not only Israel and Palestine, but the entire Islamic world. Indeed, disagreements among Islamic states have been a regular feature of Islamic and Arab summits from the beginning. These disagreements have disproportionately affected the states of the Arab heartland: Saudi Arabia, Syria, Iraq, and Egypt. Saudi Arabia claims to be the world's oldest Islamic fundamentalist state, but that simple statement belies a much more complicated political-religious situation.

---

[6] October 21, 2004.
[7] January 11, 2005.

The country's twentieth-century founder, Arab chief 'Abd al-'Aziz, did follow the puritanical Wahhabi creed of Islam, but he relied politically on the dominance of his tribe, the house of Sa'ud. By 1929, 'Abd al-'Aziz had made peace with the foreigners and used their weapons to attack the religious zealots among his supporters. In 1932 he signed the Aramco treaty that integrated his petroleum resources into the international economy and ensured long-term support from these powers. The primary religious significance of Saudi Arabia, of course, lies in the fact that the Saudi king is "Protector of the Two Holy Places," Mecca and Madina. This protectorate and active support for Wahhabi Islam internally and for its external missionary activity provides domestic political legitimacy to the ruling family, whereas Western need of Saudi oil has protected the kingdom militarily from its more populous and more powerful enemies in Iraq and Iran. Lawrence comments that the "greatest irony of the Saudi experiment in Islamic statecraft may be that the regime, from 'Abd al-'Aziz to Fahd, played the fundamentalist game without being fundamentalists."[8]

Wahhabism follows the Arabian Islamic reformer-warrior Abdul Wahhab (1703–92), who insisted on a puritanical life, short prayers, undecorated mosques, and the uprooting of holy tombs lest they become pilgrimage sites. In 1925, for example, 'Abd al-'Aziz ordered the wholesale destruction of tombs, graveyards, and decorated mosques in Mecca and Madina. Today Saudi Arabia bans drinking, dating, movies, concert halls, female drivers, and theatres. Because of the affinities of the Taliban and Wahhabism, Saudi Arabia became one of the two major supports for that regime until Riyadh broke diplomatic relations on September 25, 2001. The Saudi kings have always proclaimed their faithful adherence to Islam, and new King Abdullah benefits from his reputation as a pious Muslim. The ruling family also has carefully controlled the ulama in domestic politics. This government trading of overseas missionary support for domestic quiescence has become a more and more difficult political-religious balancing act as radical Islamic terrorism has spread through the global system. Relations between the Saudis and the United States, featured in Michael Moore's anti-Bush movie *Fahrenheit 9/11*, have been strained by recent terrorism. In September 2004, the State Department's annual report on international religious freedom named the kingdom as one of eight "countries of particular concern"

---

[8] Bruce B. Lawrence, *Shattering the Myth: Islam Beyond Violence* (Princeton, NJ: Princeton University Press, 1998), 89.

for its intolerance, particularly against Shiite Muslims.[9] Saudi officials, in response, assert the country's form of governance is "none of their [US] business."[10]

The late 1970s religious challenge to the Saudi leadership came not from the clergy, but from a lay dissident National Guardsman who was the grandson of a Wahhabi killed in 1929. Juhayman ibn Sayf al-'Utayba attacked what he termed the continued religious corruption of the Saudi state for its rejection of Wahhabi morals and proclaimed his brother-in-law as the long-awaited messianic *mahdi*. Some two hundred Saudis, many young theological students, joined al-'Utayba in a daring capture of Islam's holiest mosque in November 1979. The state first obtained the legitimating fatwas from state-approved clergy and then crushed the rebellion, hanging al-'Utayba and sixty-one of the other ringleaders.

The Gulf War increased this latent tension between the Saudi state and Saudi Islamists since the regime was forced to depend militarily on the hated enemy of all Islamists, the United States. Bin Laden and other Saudis returned from their victory in Afghanistan looking for new targets. In November 1995, a Riyadh bombing killed five Americans and wounded thirty-seven. Four Saudis confessed, saying that they had been inspired by bin Laden's call to throw out the infidel military. In June 1996, the bombing at Al Khobar American air base killed nineteen and wounded hundreds. That year bin Laden formally declared war against the United States and two years later proclaimed his "Coalition Against Crusaders, Christians and Jews." The Saudi government finally sought bin Laden's arrest in June 1998.

If some of the Saudi population has been attracted to radical Wahhabism, others, especially the young, watch satellite television and desire a Western lifestyle. Half of the Saudi population is under age eighteen. The recent population gains have lessened the country's feeling of isolation among much more populous Arab nations and worker immigrants, but the population surge has also resulted in dropping per capita GNP. Although their older brothers and sisters clipped stock coupons, this new generation of Saudis must work in the modern global economy. Some Saudi interpretations of Islamic law, for example, that bankers may not charge interest on mortgages, constitute obstacles to modern economic life. The Saudi business class hopes that the country will enter the WTO,

---

[9] *San Jose Mercury News*, September 16, 2004. The others were China, Eritrea, Iran, Myanmar [Burma], North Korea, Sudan, and Vietnam.
[10] October 14, 2004.

thus putting pressure on the government for some further economic adaptations. Political succession also remains an issue. More than twenty sons remain from Aziz's (d. 1953) twenty-two marriages, but these possible successors are gradually dying off. The opposition Movement for Islamic Reform in Arabia broadcast its first call for a street demonstration in October 2003. The Saudi police arrested 350 demonstrators. Saudi Arabia's premier religious leader, the Grand Mufti, denounced the demonstration. Professor Mamoun Fandy of the National Defense University commented "The Saudis are in a tight fix. The Islamists think the Saudis have sold out to the Americans, and the Americans think that they have sold out to the terrorists. Eventually this translates into an erosion of legitimacy – that you are not satisfying the Arabs and Washington, then you're on your own."[11] In April 2005, when the kingdom allowed elections for half of the 178 municipal councils, Islamist candidates prevailed in most contests. The religious "Gold List" originally appeared anonymously as spammed text messages on cell phones. Then religious scholars backed the candidates in speeches and interviews. These candidates, mostly professionals dedicated to traditional Islamic values, generally focused on local issues.[12]

The failure of the Oslo Process has greatly increased political pressure because of the strong support for the Palestinians in Saudi public opinion. For example, in the January 2002 national cultural festival in Riyadh, Crown Prince Abdullah presided over an opening theatre performance. On stage, children threw stones, Israeli soldiers fired into unarmed crowds, dead babies appeared, and finally a voice in Arabic summed up the message, "Jerusalem will be ours again. We will win. We will fight. These are the swords of Saladin, and they must be raised up again."[13] Shortly after this performance, however, Abdullah proposed his peace plan that offered Israel peace and normalization of relations if it withdrew from the 1967 territories. The U.S. attack on Iraq again heightened the tension of the two-pronged policy, even producing two separate types of *jihadis*. Those *jihadis* who slipped out of Saudi Arabia and died fighting the Americans in Iraq have received the approbation of Saudi society at large. Al-Queda-sponsored terrorism within the kingdom, however, has failed to generate wide support, even though the theological justifications derive from the same argument.

---

[11] November 3, 2001.
[12] *San Jose Mercury News*, April 24, 2005.
[13] March 3, 2002.

Unlike the Saudi succession problems, Syria peacefully accomplished its succession from Hafiz al-Assad to his son Bashar al-Assad in June 2000. Although they were mortal enemies, both Assad and Saddam Hussein of Iraq rose as leaders of the secular Baath Party in their respective nations. Both leaders, coming from minority populations, faced significant religious opposition to their increasingly authoritarian rule. Assad came from the Allowite religion, an Islamic variant considered heretical by the majority orthodox Sunnis. Syria also has significant populations of Kurds, Christians, and others. The defining Syrian political-religious event was the elder Assad's complete decimation of the village of Hama in February 1982. Assad responded to the Muslim Brotherhood assassination of members of his government by massacring roughly ten thousand members of the Brotherhood and their families in a horribly ferocious battle and its aftermath. The Twin Towers attack has allowed the Syrian government to repackage this massacre as a successful anti-terrorist campaign and offer the United States some of its considerable security intelligence about Islamist groups throughout the Middle East. Bashar has reduced the number of political prisoners, but political reform is not high on the agenda. Current Syrian priorities are, in rank order, economic reform, administrative reform, and improved delivery of social services, a la the Chinese. The Syrian Soviet-style armed forces, however, are no more competitive than Syria's Soviet-style factories that produced the outdated goods that had been given to Saddam in exchange for contraband Iraqi oil.

The deleterious effects of Middle Eastern religious-political fragmentation can be highlighted in the long Lebanese civil war (1975–91). In the tradition of the Ottoman millet system of assigning social governance to territorially-based religious authorities, the French supported the Lebanese National Covenant of 1943, which assigned political offices to six religious groups (Maronite Catholic, Sunni Muslim, Shiite Muslim, Greek Orthodox, Greek Catholic, Druze) in proportion to their perceived power. The system gave Christians in general a six to five advantage over Muslims in the ninety-nine-seat parliament. The president would always be a Maronite Christian, the premier a Sunni Muslim, and the speaker of the parliament a Shiite Muslim. By 1955, the country became known as "the Switzerland of the Middle East," for its mountain scenery and banking role, and its streets "the parliament of the Arab world" for the frank exchange of ideas. But the system could not withstand both the internal challenge of the increasing Shiite population and the external challenge of the inflow of Palestinian refugees after the 1967 debacle. The Lebanese

Civil War constituted a longer human tragedy and an even more complicated political situation than Afghanistan, but Syria finally established
its sphere of interest over both the Muslim and Christian warring factions. Syria originally intervened to support its Maronite Christian client
Franjieh against the rise of those Christian factions allied with Israel.

Lebanon exemplifies the tenuous political status of minority religions
in the Middle East. Lebanese Catholics and Orthodox, Persian Bahai and
Jews, Egyptian Copts, and others have suffered significantly as Islamist
movements have swept the region. The fact that some of these minority
communities predate Mohammed has not served as any defense. The 1989
agreement that ended the Lebanese Civil War was brokered by the Arab
League in Taif, Saudi Arabia. It maintained each religion's hold on the
chief offices, but revised the six-to-five Christian advantage in parliament
to equal representation. Syria enforced the accord with thirty thousand
troops to guarantee Damascus's control of Lebanese politics. The elder
Assad gave his son Bashar the task of running Lebanon in 1998 as part
of his training for succession. Bashar bypassed the two veteran Syrian
operatives who were close allies of the Sunni Lebanese Prime Minister
Rafik Hariri and appointed Hariri's enemy, Maronite military commander Émile Lahoud, as president, and the Sunni academic Salim al-Hoss, as
prime minister. In the September 2000 election, however, Hariri returned
with a highly financed modern campaign and adroit political horse trading. His supporters won 92 of the 128 parliament seats so that Bashar
was forced to approve the election. In December the Maronite patriarch, eighty-year-old Cardinal Nasrallah Butros Sfeir, criticized Syria's
continued control of Lebanon. The Druze leader Walid Jumblatt agreed
with the cardinal, but many Sunni and Shiite leaders accused him of serving Israeli interests by raising such questions. The moderate Sunni Sheik
Hani Fahs, who serves on the national committee for interfaith dialogue,
responded "Even where I agree with the patriarch's language, I worry
that it could be used by religious fanatics to bring about violence. We
don't want a return to religious conflict in this country. I am afraid for the
Christians of Lebanon."[14] A massive car bomb assassinated the ex-prime
minister Hariri in Beirut on February 14, 2005. Hariri had been more
outspoken in his criticism of Syria in the preceding months. The assassination increased presure on Syria to heed the United Nations Resolution
1559 that demanded its troops leave Lebanon. They left in April, and in
May and June, Lebanon held its first election free from Syrian influence

[14] December 23, 2000.

in three decades. The anti-Syrian coalition of Hariri's son, Saad, and the Druze leader Walid Jumblatt, supported by the Maronite Patriarch Sfeir, won over half of the parliament seats, but probably not enough to unseat Syria's ally, Maronite President Émile Lahoud. The Hezbollah slate won big in southern Lebanon, making disarmament of the militia, also called for by the United Nations, less likely.

As the Oslo Process fell apart and Muslims increased their power in Lebanon, the Lebanese Shiite Hezbollah began to exercise a larger regional role that benefited its main patrons Iran and Syria. Twenty years of attacks finally resulted in the May 2000 Israeli withdrawal from southern Lebanon. The Hezbollah leader Sheik Hassan Nasrallah then journeyed to Tehran to get the advice of Ayatollah Ali Khamenei. The Supreme Guide told him to struggle for the Muslim liberation of Jerusalem. After Sharon's visit to Al Aqsa in September 2000, Nasrallah broadcast on his own channel and on Al-Jazeera a call to all Palestinians to kill Israelis. "If you don't have bullets, who among you doesn't have knives? Hide the knife, and when he comes close to the enemy let him stab him. Let the stab be fatal."[15] Iran began sending missiles to Hezbollah through Damascus so that by September 27, 2002, the *New York Times* cited Western and Israeli sources that Hezbollah had stockpiled eight to nine thousand Katyusha rockets with a range of twelve miles, plus a few longer range weapons. Syria also began supplying 222-millimeter rockets with twelve- to eighteen-mile ranges. Although Syria poses the much greater military threat to Israel with its Scuds, an air force, and chemical weapons, Hezbollah interjects a note of uncertainty since the group does not have the vulnerable assets of a state that might compel more rational behavior.

In Egypt, the "cultural imperialism" of Western secular values has constituted the primary threat in the minds of both the more moderate Muslim Brotherhood and the more radical Islamic terrorist groups. Since the government of Sadat, the Egyptian state has consciously pursued a religious policy which seeks to obliterate those radicals violently attempting to establish a theological dictatorship while simultaneously courting Islamic centrists who have the same beliefs in an Islamic state, but express it in more measured terms. Such a double-edged policy represents a significant political gamble since even supposedly moderate progovernment scholars, for example, Sheik Gad el-Haq, rector of Al-Azhar and Sheik Mohammed al-Ghozali, have branded any arguments in favor of the separation of religion and state as "apostasy," a crime punishable by death

[15] October 15, 2000.

under Islamic law. In the August 1993 trial of the guerrilla organization al-Gamaa al-Islamia for assassinating Egyptian secular writer Farag Fodah the preceding year, Sheik Ghozali declared that "A secularist represents a danger to society and the nation that must be eliminated. It is the duty of the Government to kill him."[16]

SUNNI POLITICS IN NORTH AFRICA: THE AUTOCRATIC STATE AND ISLAMIC OPPOSITION IN THE MAGHRIB

Algeria's National Liberation Front (FLN) triumphed over France, and thus served as arguably the world's most successful anticolonial model of the 1960s. But by 1988, the Arab secular left faced Islamist opposition across the Muslim world. Young rioters trashed, burned, and looted Riad El Feth, the symbol of the Algerian triumph and the sign of how far the country had progressed economically in the twenty-six years since victory. These unemployed urban youth saw this modernistic memorial to the martyrs of independence, with its brilliant neo-Moorish cultural center and surrounding shops, as representing all that they could not attain. Educated in Arabic, they rejected the symbols of the new French-speaking Algerian skilled bourgeoisie who received their news and entertainment from satellite dishes pointed north to Europe. The cultural divide thus exacerbated the socioeconomic gap. Neither the old guard socialist revolutionaries nor the new radical Islamists liked the market reforms of ex-colonel President Chadli Bendjedid. Like Tunisia and Egypt, the burgeoning population and falling oil revenues in Algeria led to mass unemployment. Even for those educated at the university, successful competition for scarce jobs required family influence or bribery. Thus, the immigration to France continued.

In both Tunisia and Algeria, Islam had helped unite the independence movement, but the state did not allow religion to assume a primary political role following victory over France. Tunisian President Bourguiba (1956–87), for example, actively discouraged any public role for Islam, even campaigning publicly against the Ramadan fast in 1960. Lawrence comments on the similarities between Tunisia and Syria in their Francophone legacy and other characteristics. "Politically it [Tunisia] too has the power of the central government vested in one city, the capital city. From Tunis and through Tunis all the mechanisms of the modern nation-state are channeled. Bourguiba, like Assad, defined the state in his image,

---

[16] August 18, 1993.

though Bourguiba even more than Assad might be portrayed as a rank secularist."[17] Ben 'Ali succeeded Bourguiba in 1987 in an army coup.

The judgment of Algeria's Islamic Salvation Front (FIS) – that the FLN had betrayed the Independence Movement by not establishing an Islamic state – was neither shared by many of the competing opposition groups, nor by the Algerian public at large. The bureaucratic strength of the FIS was the "bearded FLN" whose governmental positions made it impossible for the FLN leadership to monitor the vast network of mosques that served as the FIS's base of popular support. Thus, the FLN allowed the formation of the FIS, which promptly won local municipal elections in 1990. The FIS then swept the first round of the parliamentary elections of December 1991, but the government soon outlawed the party. This catalyzed the brutal undeclared civil war of Algeria, which took as many as 150,000 victims on both sides. The guerrillas targeted intellectuals, journalists, and foreigners, even Catholic missionaries.

The FLN, like Egypt's Mubarak, also had to deal with a more radical and violent Islamic group, the Armed Islamic Group (GIA). In the 1999 presidential election Abdelaziz Bouteflika, representative of the FLN military, ran unopposed when all the other competitive candidates dropped out to protest the lack of fairness. Bouteflika then offered amnesty to the Islamic Salvation Army, those guerrillas associated with the FIS. They supported him in the fairer 2004 presidential election, which the government managed by refusing applications from two candidates, rejecting three others on technical grounds, and inviting 120 foreign observers for the balloting. The primary of five opposition candidates was Ali Benflis, rival ex-FLN prime minister with similar military backing. Bouteflika received 83.5 percent of the vote, with hardline Islamists boycotting the election. Rising oil prices had fostered economic growth, but this growth did not solved the unemployment problem for the young. In June the Algerian Army killed Nabil Sahraoli, the leader of North Africa's most dangerous Islamic terrorist organization, the Salafist Group for Preaching and Combat founded in 1998. Sahraoli had taken over the Salafist leadership from Hassan Hattab of the old GIA, whom he opposed as not likely to ally with Al-Qaeda.[18] The military problem seems solved for the moment, except for the long-term psychological effect of so many civil war dead on both sides. The government itself shows no interest in investigating these deaths. After 9/11, Algeria was one of the first Muslim states to

[17] Lawrence, *Shattering*, 76.
[18] June 21, 2004.

offer assistance in the antiterrorist campaign, and President Bush twice welcomed Bouteflika to the White House during 2001.

Both Morocco and Libya exhibit strong personality cults, based in the first case on Islamic tradition, and in the second on a more modern, almost Maoist, cast. In Morocco, the king has retained control of both political and religious discourse. King Hassan II, who carries the title "Commander of the Faithful," claims to be a descendant of Mohammed. Huband comments that "the monarchy's willingness to use terror in the past is what prevents would-be opponents from overstepping the very clearly defined limits of political debate that prevail today."[19] Thus, the Islamist opposition waits in the wilderness, with their main hope in some unforeseen future change. Colonel Mu'ammar al-Qaddafi of Libya has constructed his own nationalistic vision by manipulating various Islamic traditions and joining them to his own personality cult, featuring a "Green Book" instead of Mao's little red one. Groups such as the Muslim Brotherhood have criticized him for revising the Islamic calendar and treating the ulama harshly, but he faces little effective opposition, Islamist or otherwise.

Indeed, Huband's "iron hand of the state" has triumphed over Islamist opposition in all of the Arab countries mentioned in the last two sections. In Saudi Arabia, Syria, Iraq, Egypt, Algeria, Tunisia, Morocco, and Libya, authoritarian states have controlled religious fundamentalism, despite, and partly because of, the states' use of Islamic symbols, cooptation of the clergy, and maintenance of the control of at least some of the mosques. These Islamist oppositions, even in Algeria where the FIS prevailed in elections, have fragmented into "more responsible" and "radical" groups. Still, both leftist and rightist authoritarian governments have neither solved national social and economic problems nor established a legitimate political leadership that could face truly democratic elections. Analysts such as Fareed Zakaria warn against the United States pushing democratic reform too quickly lest it destroy the weak forces of constitutional liberalism. Among Arab states, he says, "if we could choose one place to press hardest to reform, it should be Egypt" as "the intellectual soul of the Arab world."[20] In May 2005, the Egyptian scholar and presidential candidate Saad Eddin Ibrahim made the case for the emergence of Muslim parties "that are truly democratic, akin to the Christian Democrats in Western Europe after World War II." He stressed

---

[19] Mark Huband, *Warriors of the Prophet: The Struggle for Islam* (Boulder, CO: Westview, 1999), 96.
[20] Fareed Zakaria, *The Future of Freedom* (New York: W. W. Norton, 2003), 154.

the organizational strength, socioeconomic and welfare orientation, and popular nature of such parties, and pointed to Jordan and Morocco as successful Arab experiments in partial democratization with constitutional control.[21] When Mubarak sponsored his frist multicandidate presidential election in September 2005, he won over 88 percent of the vote. Twenty-three percent of those eligible voted.

COMPARATIVE NATIONAL POLITICS OF ISLAM AND DEMOCRATIZATION

Chapter Four pointed out that although the Qur'an sets certain parameters for public life, it does not provide a specific political model. The global decline of Islam vis-à-vis the West during the colonial period continued into the twentieth century, when even OPEC in the 1970s could not arrest falling per capita GNPs, increasing social stratification, or political authoritarianism. Authoritarianism derives partially from desert rule. In the absence of a consensus among tribes, both Arab and non-Arab rulers imposed themselves on societies. The resulting authoritarian order contravened the consultative precepts of Islamic law, but it did provide basic stability for the commerce of merchant societies. Middle Eastern authoritarian political leaders such as Syria's Hafez Assad and Iraq's Saddam Hussein attempted to maintain power by balancing the triple political roles of tribal chief, brutal autocrat, and modernizing president. The successful contemporary Middle Eastern ruler, according to Friedman, has the ability "to move back and forth among all three political traditions of their region, effortlessly switching...with the blink of an eye."[22] The presidential role, of course, comes courtesy of the modern nation-state. With the current most likely alternative political systems to such authoritarian regimes coming from Islamist movements, neither minority religious leaders nor secular democrats are apt to advocate risking all in regime change. On the margins of a particular society, however, or in an entire society faced with horrible chaos such as Afghanistan and Sudan, Islam can provide the ideological justification for a *jihad* against infidels like the Soviet Union and the West and against local power holders who are tarred as being irreligious collaborators.

---

[21] May 21, 2005. Those interested in Arab political, social, and economic development should start with the United Nations Development Programme, *Arab Human Development Report 2004* (New York: UNDP, 2005).

[22] Thomas L. Friedman, *From Beirut to Jerusalem*, updated with a new chapter (New York: Anchor Books, 1995), 103.

Current Islamist politics thus derives strong impetus from the failure of prior political initiatives in the face of globalization. In discussing the nature of this twentieth-century response to modernization, Lawrence lists five characteristics: (1) the Islamists see themselves as advocates of a pure minority viewpoint; (2) they confront, not disagree with, their adversaries: (3) they are secondary-level male elites who charismatically reinterpret traditional scripture for modern times; (4) they generate their own technical vocabulary; and (5) although they have antecedents such as the Saudi Wahhabis, they could only emerge in majority Muslim countries after they had become nation states.[23] In addition to these general observations, each region and each nation embodies unique political, cultural, ethnic, and economic variations; for example, the Maghrib's depoliticization of economic issues contributed to the focus on cultural and religious issues in national politics. Neither the FIS nor the Muslim Brotherhood has offered more than a vague utopian plan for socioeconomic policy. Islamist movements all over the world have focused on a single slogan: *al-Islam huwwa al-hal* [Islam is the solution], leaving local politicians and Islamist groups to battle for the definitions of "true Islam" and of the resulting policy proscriptions.

The most favorable location for Islamic political democratization lies in middle level development states where Islam has had to interact with non-Arab cultures, for example, Turkey (HDI [2004 Human Development Index] #88), Malaysia (HDI #59), and Indonesia (HDI #111). Turkey remains crucial to Islamic comparative politics because only Turkey of the post-Ottoman Middle East made the transition to long-lived competitive party politics. Local power elites rallied to Ataturk following World War I to save Turkish independence, and it was this group that switched allegiance to the Democratic Party following World War II. Turkish Islam also produced the Nurculuk Movement, following its founder Bediuzzaman Said Nursi (1873–1960), who emphasized combining multiple sources of knowledge, including those from outside the Islamic tradition.[24]

Chapter 5 discussed the role of Turkey in the future of Europe. The strong role in politics by the Turkish military and Ankara's human rights record have both constituted obstacles for E.U. admission. Since Ataturk, Turkey's army has perceived itself as the primary guarantor of secularism.

---

[23] Bruce B. Lawrence, *Defenders of God: The Fundamentalist Revolt Against the Modern Age*, new preface (Columbia: University of South Carolina Press, 1989), 100–1.

[24] Dale F. Eickleman, "Islam and Ethical Pluralism," Richard Madsen and Tracy B. Strong, eds., *The One and the Many: Religious and Secular Perspectives on Ethical Pluralism in the Modern World* (Princeton, NJ: Princeton University Press, 2003), 168–72.

Following the most recent coup in 1980, the military-backed government imposed the Constitution of 1982, which placed ultimate political-economic power in a National Security Council made up of the president, four cabinet members, and the five top military commanders. Party competition existed, but the National Security Council could intervene at its own discretion. For example, in 1997 it deposed an Islamic-led government, and in 2002 it disqualified the most popular civilian politician, Recep Tayyip Erdogan, from running for parliament. Erdogan, a former mayor of Istanbul and leader of the secular Justice and Development Party, had crafted a moderate pro-Western message to distance himself from his and the party's roots in political Islam. When he was mayor of Istanbul, for example, Erdogan advocated withdrawing from NATO and not applying for the European Union, but in the September 2002 campaign he called talks to join the European Union his first priority. "Secularism is the protector of all beliefs and religions," said Erdogan. "We are the guarantors of this secularism, and our management will clearly prove that."[25] Later the parliament changed the law so Erdogan could become prime minister.

In November 2002, when Erdogan met with European Commission President Romano Prodi, he offered Turkey as a global model of the coexistence of Islam and democracy. "The Turkish population is Muslim, and we are trying to have a positive impact on the way the Muslim world looks at the European Union. We want Turkey to be proof of how we can live side by side."[26] The same day the Turkish broadcasting authority announced it was allowing limited radio and television programming in the once-banned Kurdish language, a demand of the European Union. Islamists also know how crucial Turkey is for Islamic democracy. In November 2003, radicals bombed two synagogues, the British consulate, and a British bank. The day after the synagogue bombings, German Chancellor Gerhard Schröder stated that Turkey's membership in the European Union would make Europe more secure by showing "that the Islamic faith and the democratic values of the European enlightenment need not contradict each other but can coexist."[27] In 2004 Turkey amended its Constitution to reduce the number of posts reserved for the military, and a civilian led the National Security Council for the first time. Negotiations between Turkey and the European Union began in October

[25] November 4, 2002.
[26] November 21, 2002.
[27] November 21, 2003.

2005, with the agreement of all twenty-five E.U. countries, even Cyprus, necessary for setting the rules under which Turkey can enter the European Union. The French and Dutch votes against the E.U. Constitution and the German Christian Democratic stand for a "privileged partnership" rather than full membership have caused some Turks to call for strengthening the nation's relationship with the United States as a balance to the E.U. negotiations. Turkish public opinion still overwhelmingly opposes the U.S. war in the Middle East, but Erdogan has praised Iraqi Prime Minister al-Jaafari as "very keen on achieving democracy in Iraq." Erdogan also stated that Turkey's primary concern is Iraq's "territorial integrity," that is, that Iraqi Kurds do not attempt to join Turkish Kurds in a greater entity. "Turkey has been able to marry democratic culture with Islamic culture," he states, "They can coexist."[28]

Malaysia represents the second case of Islamic democratization. In November 2003 Mahathir Mohammad, seventy-seven, left office after twenty-two years of often autocratic rule. During that time he maintained the country's stability and developed the economy for the over twenty-three million Malaysians. *The 2004 Human Development Report* ranked Malaysia fifty-ninth internationally, the highest ranking for any Muslim-majority state with over four million people. Long a vociferous critic of the United States and of the IMF, Mahathir had fostered a high tech industry featuring Dell Computer, Intel, and other multinationals that survived the Asian flu when Mahathir defied IMF proscriptions. Mahathir denounced both terrorism and the media penchant to make it an Islamic issue. Mahathir's least attractive moment came in his 1998 prosecution of his former successor and Islamic intellectual Anwar Ibrahim for corruption and sodomy. The populace responded by transferring some support to the Islamic Party of Malaysia (PAS) in 1999, and that conservative religious party took over two of the thirteen state governments. The Malaysian high court eventually freed Ibrahim.

While Mahathir used anti-Semitism to burnish his Islamic credentials, his successor Abdullah Badawi, sixty-six, combines an Islamic background with support for the modern economy. Badawi's grandfather and father were religious leaders, and Badawi graduated with a degree in Islamic studies. Badawi now worries most about the transfer of foreign investment from ASEAN countries to China. With Badawi at the helm, the secular United Malay Organization (UMO) returned to its accustomed dominance. Malaysia has thus become the Islamic equivalent of

[28] June 11, 2005.

Taiwan during it early democratization, when the island combined high-tech development, KMT dominance, and fair elections. Malaysia and Taiwan also correspond in terms of the size of their populations.

Indonesia became the first fully democratic Muslim-majority country, even if it retains many more political and economic challenges than Turkey or Malaysia. As Indonesia suffered from the Asian flu in 1998, the population overthrew Suharto. Although Indonesia remains a predominantly (88 percent) Muslim country, and the two moderate Islamic organizations each have more members than the entire country of Malaysia, the revolution did not derive from Islamist ideology nor was it led by Islamist parties. Indeed, Islam in this most populous Muslim country partially owes its popularity to a long tradition of blending with animism, Hinduism, Buddhism, and other preexisting religious and social systems. For example, the Javanese practice *kejawen*, "the syncretistic blend of Hinduism and Buddhism with Sufi-influenced mysticism that characterizes much of Java's spiritual life today."[29] The two largest Islamic organizations, the rural-based Nahdlatul Ulama with about forty million members, and the urban-based Muhammadiyah with about thirty million members, are led by Ahmed Hasyim Muzadi and Syafii Maarif, respectively.

In 1998 the parliament elected the nation's first democratic president, Abdurrahman Wahid, who was head of Nahdlatul Ulama at the time. Wahid espoused a moderate nationalist ideology, but proved inadequate to the presidency. The rest of the fractured political system coalesced to impeach him. The parliament then elected Megawati Sukarnoputri, the daughter of Indonesia's founder, as president and the more militantly Muslim leader, Hamza Haz, as vice president. The perceived lack of success of the somewhat politically lethargic Megawati led to her Democratic Party for Struggle dropping into second place in the April 2004 parliamentary elections, and to her running second in the first round of the first direct presidential elections in July. Voters chose the charismatic General Susilo Bambang Yudhoyono, and rejected the more militaristic General Wiranto, the candidate of the most powerful parliamentary party, Suharto's Golkar. In their attempts to secure Muslim votes, Wiranto chose Wahid's brother as his vice president, and Megawati chose the current head of Nahdlatul Ulama, Muzadi. In the parliamentary election, however, only one Islamic party, Justice at 7.3 percent, overcame the 5 percent barrier for parliamentary representation. Although that party advocates Islamic law, it based its campaign on anticorruption, not on the *shari'a*. General Yudhoyono,

[29] David Pinault, "Indonesia's Buddhist Heritage," *America* 89 (November 24, 2003): 16.

whom the army twice (1976 at Fort Benning, 1990 at Fort Leavenworth) sent to the United States to study, won the presidency in September with 60 percent of the vote.

During the long Suharto period, the Indonesian military ran the country and cracked down immediately on any religious, ethnic, or political challenges to the system. The government argued that only such authoritarianism would maintain "one country, one people, one language" in such a diverse setting. The two major regional challenges came at the two ends of the country, in East Timor and in Aceh. Indonesia had annexed the majority Catholic, Portuguese-speaking former colony of East Timor in 1975, but the United Nations never recognized that annexation. As the Indonesian occupation became more and more brutal, international public support built for the East Timorese. Finally, under a U.N. Mandate, Australian troops entered the area in September 1999 to guarantee the implementation of the people's choice for a separate nation. The local heroes, political leader José Ramos-Horta and Bishop Carlos Filipe Ximenes Belo, had received the Nobel Peace Prize in 1996 as an encouragement for their mediation and non-violent struggle. East Timor's independence did not lead to a "domino effect" throughout the rest of the archipelago because its situation differed markedly from situations in other regions, not least in the support for autonomy by outside nations. In addition, the poverty of this area of less than one million people meant that Jakarta was not losing much financially.

In the case of Aceh's four million citizens, President Megawati offered a greater percentage of the rich natural gas revenues and more local autonomy, even, against secular Indonesia's tradition of restraining public religious influence, letting this most conservative Muslim section of the country adopt sections of Islamic law. As in East Timor, the Indonesian army had used all methods in its brutal crackdown. U.S. Secretary of State Colin Powell, while supporting Indonesian sovereignty over Aceh, told the government that the army must improve its human rights record. Unlike East Timor, Jakarta views holding Aceh as necessary to the preservation of the country and has sent in more troops to battle local guerillas of the Free Aceh Movement (GAM). The local natural gas processing plant, PT Arun, owned 55 percent by Pertamina (state oil company), 30 percent by ExxonMobil, and 15 percent by a Japanese consortium, exports one-third of the nation's natural gas and supplies the Indonesian government with $1.2 billion in revenue each year.

The fall of Suharto plus the September 11 Twin Towers attack changed the dynamics of Islamic politics across Indonesia. During the previous regime, the large Muslim organizations followed the majority local tradition in supporting the government while pursuing moderate social and educational policies. For example, the local Muslim schools, the *pesantren*, had a strong reputation as models in educating mostly poor students for religious practice, democracy, justice, and self-sufficiency. There were a few radical Islamists such as Abu Bakar Bashir, but Suharto jailed him, and then Bashir fled to Malaysia. The fall of Suharto allowed Bashir in 2000 to return to his original Indonesian school in Solo, now decorated with bin Laden portraits and attended by students with bin Laden t-shirts. These Indonesian Islamists envision a pan-Asian Islamic state that would unite Indonesia with Singapore, Malaysia, Brunei, and the Muslim sections of the Philippines.

Most Muslim preachers, however, resemble the nation's popular TV evangelist Abdullah Gymnastiar, who mixes plain advice with moderate Islam. President Megawati invited Gymnastiar to meet Colin Powell when the secretary of state visited Jakarta. Gymnastiar told Powell, "In Christianity the significant word is love. But in Islam it is fair.... You [the United States] don't look fair. Why is it that Israel takes Palestinian land, and why is that the U.S. always helps this?"[30] Even the most moderate Indonesian Muslim preachers support the Palestinians, as have the leaders of Nahdlatul Ulama and Muhammadiyah. When Bush visited Bali in September 2003, he met with Muslim, Hindu, and Christian leaders. The president seemed genuinely surprised that most Muslim leaders considered U.S. policy pro-Israeli and thought that most Americans considered Muslims as terrorists.

ASEAN nations Indonesia and the Philippines constitute excellent political-religious comparative cases with democracy, strong regionalism, similar ethnic backgrounds, large populations, lower medium human development rankings (2004 HDI: Philippines #83, Indonesia #111), and the majority of one of the two most populous world religions and a minority of the other. Nigeria and Sudan offer examples of countries split north-south fairly evenly by Islam and Christianity, so that regional, tribal, and economic issues overlap religious ones, adding tension to politics. Sudan has operated with a radical Islamist government, but the religious and political characteristics of this case are so unique[31] that it would be difficult to draw any general conclusions, other than Sudan (2004 HDI

---

[30] August 23, 2002.
[31] Bill Berkeley, *The Graves Are Not Yet Full: Race, Tribe and Power in the Heart of Africa* (New York: Basic Books, 2002), 195–243.

ranking #139) joins Afghanistan (no 2004 ranking) as a case of terrible
civil war in a very poor country. By contrast, Pakistan, Egypt, and Saudi
Arabia remain candidates for "damage limitation," at least in the near
term. One can easily come up with globally disastrous scenarios beginning with the fall of one of the latter three governments. Pakistan (HDI
#142) adds the danger of a regional nuclear conflict. Shiite-majority Iran
and Iraq constitute countries with both high promise and huge potential
liabilities. Lagging economic development plus high birth rates affect all
of the above countries except Malaysia.

THE POLITICS OF ISLAM AS A WORLD CIVILIZATION

The five Islamic pillars of religious practice support the unity of the global
Islamic community, the *umma*. All the world's Muslims proclaim the same
God and the same prophet, turn five times daily toward Mecca, fast during
Ramadan, give alms, and, if they are physically and financially able, make
the pilgrimage to Mecca at least once in their lives. Indeed, if an analyst
focused only on the seven characteristics of religion discussed in Chapter
Three, s/he would also infer a high degree of international political unity.
Even the casual reader, however, will notice the stark division between
Sunni and Shiite Muslims deriving from the seventh century. The Sunni-
Shiite split retains its extraordinary political significance, both for world
Islam in general and for any country in which both populations reside in
significant numbers such as Iraq and Lebanon. Indeed, the Iran-Iraq war
of the 1980s constitutes the most destructive modern example of a violent
confrontation between Islamic countries.

Nationalism and ethnicity also affect these inter-Islamic struggles. We
have seen that while these two factors reinforce each other in the case
of the Taliban, ethnicity is as significant as religion in the Algerian case
where the Berbers constitute a separate group, and in Iraq and Turkey
where the Kurds at times have sought a nation of their own. Many Muslim scholars assert that Islam as a religion cannot provide authoritative
political unity by itself because it lacks hierarchical institutionalization.
Muhammad Khalid Masud states, "I fully support ... the point that modern Muslims do not support the concept of an 'official' or 'authoritative'
view. They often proclaim with some sense of pride that there is no church
in Islam."[32] In fact, Masud lists seven, often competing, sources of ethics

---

[32] Muhammad Khalid Masud, "The Scope of Pluralism in Islamic Moral Traditions,"
Madsen and Strong, *The One and The Many*, 180.

in Islam. Such diversity, argues Masud, favors pluralism. In earlier times Islamic pluralism was also encouraged by fluid political boundaries and constant interaction with the non-Muslim world. Masud notes, however, that both some Western scholars and some Islamist political intellectuals have sought to reduce the above diversity to their own exclusive interpretations of the Qur'an, the *sunna*, and the *shari'a*.

From its seventh-century beginnings, Islam found political expression in empires established in many preexisting geopolitical power centers. Great cities such as Baghdad, Cairo, Istanbul, Delhi, and Istefan became the capitals for these Islamic empires that covered vast territories and competed with each other and with non-Muslim empires for world leadership. The Sunni caliphate, the putative political leadership of all Sunni empires, endured until 1924 when Ataturk abolished it. In the nineteenth and twentieth centuries these empires, truncated and chopped up by the artificial treaty lines imposed by the West, became one or more sovereign nation states. Would-be Islamic leadership states such as Iran, Turkey, Iraq, Syria, and Egypt also continue inter-Islamic global and regional rivalries. Sunni Islam, like the Protestant tradition, facilitates a broad spectrum of political-religious perspectives, but leaves leadership to the militarily victorious state or empire.

Contemporary competition among Islamic states continues. Central Asian politics currently features the rivalry of six major states over control of the resources and people of that resource-rich region. Turkey, Iran, and Pakistan all seek to gain the hegemony of the region's Islam for their nationalistic purposes. Orthodox Russia, Hindu India, and Marxist China employ other ideologies. The three Islamic states remain so culturally distinct that for this rivalry they have to be treated at least as differently as their non-Muslim competitors. In the Arab world, Egypt and Saudi Arabia both offer strengths and weaknesses in pursuing Arab and Muslim hegemony. Cairo's Al-Azhar University has traditionally led Sunni jurisprudence and religious education. The city also hosts the Arab League. Saudi Arabia protects the Holy Places. Furthermore, the Saudis have used their significant financial resources to spread their Wahhabi variant of Islam. With such a diverse group of would-be leader Islamic states, we can conclude: (1) it is unlikely that any Muslim state can establish hegemony over fellow Islamic states; and (2) any state that does so, even regionally, will have to solve the conundrum of how to embrace Islam and modernity simultaneously if such influence is to endure.

What about international or transnational Islamic organizations? One leadership possibility would be the fifty-five-nation Organization of

Islamic Conference (OIC). In December 1997 following Khatami's first electoral victory, for example, Iran hosted the OIC, demonstrating its rehabilitation among even its harshest Islamic critics such as Saudi Arabia, whose heir apparent Crown Prince Abdullah attended. The consensus final resolutions condemned Israeli "state terrorism," but did not condemn the Oslo Process since Arafat and other delegates still supported it. Internal disagreements also stymied any response to the United Nations sanctions of Iraq. The OIC did comment on recent terrorist killings in Algeria, Pakistan, and Egypt, by stating that "the killing of innocents is forbidden in Islam." OIC political and diplomatic action depends principally on negotiated agreements among the fifty-five individual nation states. At the October 2003 OIC meeting, retiring Malaysian prime minister Mahathir received strong applause for a speech which included the following statements, "The Europeans killed 6 million Jews out of 12 million, but today the Jews rule the world by proxy: They get others to fight and die for them. . . . Even among the Jews, there are many who do not approve of what the Israelis are doing."[33] As in the nearly simultaneous statement of U.S. Lt. Gen. William Boykin that termed the war on terrorism a Christian crusade against Islam, the global communication system immediately turned local rhetoric into global political incidents. In fact, many U.S. newspapers ran the stories side by side, and compared them in editorials. In another example, Iranian conservative radio and TV stations unceasingly played George W. Bush's recent criticism of the country's presidential election system to motivate conservative voters to get to the polls in June 2005.

Even greater political fragmentation afflicts the twenty-two-member Arab League, a possible regional focus for Islamic unity. However, not all Arabs are Muslims, nor are the majority of Muslims Arabs. The League even delayed its March 2004 meeting for two months when the host Tunisia, representing smaller countries such as Jordan and Bahrain, called for more specific language on democratic reform, the Palestinian question, and the U.S. occupation of Iraq. The League's secretary general Amr Moussa has pushed organizational changes that would enhance his and Egypt's role.

If the Islamic world exhibits such tenuous political links, internationally, state to state, and within the religion itself, why call it a "world"? What is the best way of conceptualizing "the Islamic world" within the new paradigm? Compared with the religious unity of Christianity

---

[33] October 21, 2003.

and the political unity of the West, for example, contemporary Islam exhibits significant weaknesses in the political, economic, and military systems and a strengthening role in the communication system. We can understand global Islam best if we focus on the communication system and its connection to contemporary political-religious identities and values. With the disappearance of the political caliphate, Muslims are most strongly held together by their self-identity as Muslims and by the reinforcement of that identity and those values by the contemporary communication system, from *madrasses* to Al-Jazeera to the Internet. Chapter One related the argument that mass education and the new communication system have led to an Islamic nongovernmental sphere analogous to the historical growth of Western voluntary organizations. As many national, ethnic, and tribal identities seem politically, economically, and militarily ineffective for contemporary Muslims, their self-identities as Muslims are enhanced primarily in the communication system, especially since they perceive all four global systems as prejudiced against their religion. They believe the outside world threatens their identity and their values. Xenophobic Chinese or Japanese nationalisms of less powerful countries in the early twentieth century constitute a secular analogy.

The most relevant present Islamic *jihad*, then, occurs in the global communication system, not in the political, economic, or military systems. United States misconduct at Iraq's Abu Ghraib Prison made little difference politically, economically, or militarily, but it was an American debacle in the communication system. Islamists believe that Islam will recoup its political, economic, and military power of five hundred years ago, but only in a long, staged struggle in which the communication system now dominates. Islamist theorists discuss the stages and the timing of the struggle as the Marxists debated similar issues one hundred years ago. For these theorists, the eventual worldwide caliphate has taken over from the stage of perfect Communism as the end product. At the present time, chaos benefits Islam by showing the bankruptcy of competing secular and religious ideologies. So far the political and economic development of most Islamic states has been shameful, although Islamists would argue that the *shari'a* has never really been adopted completely. In the contemporary military system, weakness in state-versus-state conventional war has driven Islamist leaders to pursue two very different strategies: (1) weapons of mass destruction; and (2) nonstate terrorism. The West, China, Japan, and India most fear the linking of the two, an Iranian bomb in the hands of Hezbollah.

The U.S. military victory in Iraq meant that U.S. forces were located on both sides of Iran, and Washington began to pressure Tehran, especially over more intrusive inspections of the Iranian nuclear program. Washington has also criticized Iran for its support of the Palestinian Hamas and Islamic Jihad, and of the Lebanese Hezbollah. Khatami visited Beirut in May 2003 as part of Tehran's response to increased U.S. pressure in the region. Fifty thousand Lebanese Shiites welcomed Khatami in Camille Chamoun Stadium, with Hezbollah's leader Sheik Hassan Nasrallah receiving the second largest cheer. Khatami called for a rapid American withdrawal followed by an inclusive government representing all ethnic and religious groups. Khatami represented a source of pride for Lebanese Shiites, but also a reformist trend within their religion.[34] On the Palestinian question, Iran has opened itself to accepting whatever the Palestinian people accept, even if Ayatollah Khomeini had earlier called Arafat "a traitor and an idiot" for being too compromising with Israel.[35]

Within the communication system, who shapes the discussion? The religious prestige of Al-Azhar University remains among traditional moderates, and it does exercise some expressive power throughout Islam. Many of the leading Southeast Asian Muslim scholars studied in Cairo. There are also non-governmental global meetings such as "Islam in the Era of Globalization," held July 10–12, 2003, by the World Conference of Islamic Scholars in Kuala Lumpur, Malaysia. Nine hundred attendees from thirty-three countries heard the keynoter, Malaysian Prime Minister Mahathir, call for Muslims worldwide to restore the glory of Islamic civilization and for ulama to guide their followers in both religious and secular knowledge. Mahathir shares this emphasis on reform of the ulama with leaders like Wahid, versus those Islamists who have largely written off most of the local legal scholars as too traditional for remaking society.

Iranian ex-President Khatami has attempted to speak not only for Islamic civilization, but also for nationalistic Iranian political influence and Persian culture. For example, he addressed the United Nations on September 21, 1998, presenting himself as a philosopher-statesman, "a man from the East" from "a great and renowned nation."[36] He asked the United Nations for help in resolving the Afghanistan problem peacefully, but did not criticize the United States, and offered only a muted criticism

---

[34] May 14, 2003.
[35] November 10, 2001.
[36] September 22, 1998.

of Israel, calling neither to free Jerusalem from Israeli rule nor attacking the Oslo Peace Process in general. Rather, Khatami called for international dialogue, quoting the New Testament, the Qur'an, and thirteenth-century Persian poetry. In March 1999, while Iran held the chairmanship of the OIC, Khatami visited Pope John Paul II in the Vatican, generating a *New York Times* front-page photo.[37] Any Shiite leader will lack fuel legitimacy among majority Sunnis, however, and Khatami has lost significant support among younger, more secular Iranians.

In the absence of any widespread legitimacy of a caliphate system incorporating traditional ulama, of contemporary national political leadership based on secular visions such as those of Nasser or Ataturk, of effective Islamic global organizations, and of widespread international personal legitimacy of political leaders such as Khatami, Islamic scholars John Esposito and John Voll focus on the activist Muslim intellectuals of the last fifty years as likely to provide the key to the ultimate direction of the Islamic resurgence: "While they [activist intellectuals] are all well informed in Islamic traditional studies, they are not traditional ulama. Although they are real intellectuals in their general interest and work in defining and expressing concepts and symbols, they are activists in that they are directly involved in political and social affairs rather than standing aloof as intellectual critics."[38] According to Esposito and Voll, the first generation (Ismail al-Faruqi, Khurshid Ahymad, Maryam Jameelah) articulated new ways of joining religion and modernity after the perceived failure of both traditional ulama and secular theorists. The second generation (Hasan al-Hanafi, Rashid al-Ghannoushi, and Hasan al-Turabi), who wrote and led during the 1960s and 1970s, became important theorists for Islamist movements in Egypt, Tunisia, and Sudan, respectively. Finally, in the 1990s, Abdolkarim Soroush (Iran), Anwar Ibrahim (Malaysia), and Abdurahman Wahid (Indonesia) attempt to combine democracy, nationalism, and Islamic culture in their efforts to articulate what Islam means for the twenty-first century.

Despite the rise of Islamism, there is no imminent threat of a united Islamic political regime. The concept remains a bogeyman to scare Western readers and voters. Such Muslim unity would only occur in the extremely unlikely worst case scenario of total global diplomatic meltdown. The breakdown of the Oslo Process, however, has provided a

---

[37] March 12, 1999.
[38] John L. Esposito and John O. Voll, *Makers of Contemporary Islam* (Oxford: Oxford University Press, 2001), 21.

central political issue that galvanizes the entire Islamic world. In October 2000, for example, the Islamic Defenders Front of Indonesia, carrying flags reading "Jews are killers," led a demonstration of ten thousand outside the parliament building to protest planned Israeli participation in an international parliamentarians' conference in Jakarta. Then Front members in white uniforms and green scarves patrolled the airport and hotels looking for Jews to beat up. When the Israeli government was informed that it could not send Mossad agents to safeguard the delegation, the Israelis remained in Tel Aviv. The international communication system has modernized and diversified so that not only do devout Muslims hear about Palestine issue in their mosques (ulama and political leaders know that Israel is a surefire "no cost" local topic to increase Muslim identification with their religion), but modern Middle East media provide almost instant coverage of any Israeli human rights violation and set the cognitive frame for the popular adulation of "heroic" suicide bombers. As long as the Palestinian tragedy continues, such media coverage will continue to be a source of global Islamic unity and national political polarization toward Islamism.

For the West, this "Jerusalem dynamic" will only continue to be morally troubling and economically annoying, but not geopolitically crucial, as long as the "iron hand of the state" retains its hold in Muslim countries. However, relying on such autocratic regimes remains a global "bet" that makes less sense than the U.S. war in Iraq. If these authoritarian states, few of which inspire their disproportionately young populations, suffer even more grievous economic problems, and the political leadership becomes even more corrupt, there might be more successful Islamist revolutions. Such regime changes, like the Iranian revolution and Afghani chaos, would provide "free spaces" for military training and financial support for terrorist activity. The end result in a worst case scenario could be a brutal war between the West and an Islamist coalition in which both might employ weapons of mass destruction. The West would probably "win," and maybe the war could be fought by proxies along the Muslim-Christian dividing line from Nigeria to Sudan, a la the 1980s Beirut Green Line writ large. In reality, of course, all humanity would lose.

The September 2001 attack may have resulted from Islamist political ideology and economic desperation, but it took place in the communication and military systems. Al-Qaeda chose the Twin Towers and the Pentagon precisely for their symbolic value, and the aftermath featured Al-Jazeera, CNN, Fox News, and the Internet. In the military system, the attack pointed to a new type of warfare integral to the post–Cold War world when both Iran and Hezbollah can constitute a threat. Western military planners must yearn for the simplicity of an earlier era when they could count on a well-defined enemy, set battles, and effective command and control on both sides.

9

Latin America

Indigenous Religions, Christianity, and Globalization

This fifth regional chapter covers Latin America. As in the previous four chapters, the text must both demonstrate the usefulness of the paradigm and explain the regional characteristics of political-religious identities, ideologies, and institutions. In terms of the paradigm, a Latin American analyst should focus on the contemporary interactions of the political and economic systems. Regional and national economies maintain overwhelming political significance. The communication system takes secondary importance. Global publicity about human rights violations and politically oriented *telenovelas* both remain relevant. Since Argentina and Brazil renounced nuclear weapons in the 1970s, the military system has consisted of "low-level" civil wars and uprisings against authoritarian regimes.

At the beginning of the post–Cold War period, most Latin American countries found their political-economic equilibrium in democratic politics and integration into the global market under United States hegemony, best symbolized by the North American Free Trade Agreement (NAFTA) of 1994. In the last decade, however, this "Washington Consensus" has failed to produce security and development, so that a majority of Latin Americans favor economic efficiency over political democratization, even if it means authoritarian leadership.[1] National political chaos has increased in the region, especially among the Andean countries, while the "Big Three" ABC (Argentina, Brazil, and Chile) nations have all opted for center-left governments and more distance from the United States. All analysts are struck by the tremendous social stratification on the continent.

---

[1] UNDP report in April 22, 2004.

Chilean President Ricardo Lagos, who has signed a free trade pact with the United States, still commented that "This [Latin America] isn't the poorest continent, but it might be one of the most unjust."[2] And most Latin American societies can hold their own with those of Africa, Central Asia, and the Middle East in any comparisons of national corruption.

IBERIAN POWERS, INDIGENOUS RELIGIONS, AND THE LATIN AMERICAN POLITY

In an attempt to stop feuding between their Catholic Majesties of Spain and Portugal, in 1493 Pope Alexander VI divided up the globe between the two Catholic powers. Spain received all of Latin America except Brazil. Portugal received Africa and all of Asia except the Philippines. No one consulted the inhabitants or the later sixteenth-century Protestant powers of England and the Netherlands. The Spanish immediately began Latin American colonial expansion from their base in the West Indies. By 1521, Cortés, with some courage and considerable luck, had conquered Tenochtitlán (Mexico City), the great Aztec lake capital in the valley of Mexico. The conquistadors and the friars that accompanied them focused on whether or not the native people physically joined the Catholic Church, while integrating many preexisting religious forms. The Spaniards destroyed temples, but built churches on the same holy spots, thus creating a new hybrid of Iberian and indigenous civilizations. In Mexico, for example, the Indian Juan Diego had a vision of the Blessed Virgin. After overcoming his initial skepticism, the bishop of Mexico City built a great cathedral to house Juan's miraculous cape which remains the object of continuous pilgrimages. Under the title of Our Lady of Guadalupe, the Blessed Virgin became "Patroness of the Americas," and since the apparition, she has symbolized the pro-indigenous form of Latin American Catholicism.

In Brazil, the largest Catholic country in the world, the relationship of African-derived religions and Catholicism has become even more complicated. Candomble and variants such as Macumba and Umbanda arrived with the slave trade. The Church originally designated some African spirit healers as catechists, provided they and their flocks declared themselves Catholics. Recently, however, the Catholic hierarchy has sought to separate, for example, Catholic saints such as St. George from Ogum, the Candombe god of war. In 1987, Cardinal Archbishop Lucas Moreira

---

[2] January 14, 2004.

Neves stated that such syncretism, understandable during the period of slavery, must be overcome with religious education. Candombe leaders have taken various stances in response, from agreeing that separation of beliefs and mutual respect should be the goal to denying that any separation is possible or desirable after all these years.

Latin American colonial governments constituted social pigmentocracies, with race determining social status. *Peninsulares*, Caucasians born in Spain, received the highest status. Over time the *peninsulares* became a minute fraction of the population, less than one percent in Mexico in 1810. *Criollos* (pure Spanish blood, but born in Mexico) resented the fact that they could not ascend to the highest state and ecclesiastical positions. The *criollo* priests Hidalgo and Morelos became the first two leaders of the Mexican Independence movement (1810–21). Neither could attract much lay *criollo* support, however, because the priests advocated both independence from Spain, which was in *criollo* interest, and social reform, which was not. Most *criollos* had no interest in overturning a system that guaranteed their dominance over *mestizos* and indigenous peoples. After the Spanish execution of Hidalgo and Morelos, Mexican independence *sans* reform eventually prevailed under General Agustín de Iturbide, who then set himself up as emperor. Thus began a dolorous half-century for Mexico under *caudillo* leadership, the most notorious of whom was General Santa Ana. The United States took advantage of Santa Ana and Mexico's political weakness to grab the great Southwestern territory in the Mexican-American War (1846–48).

Race remains a major determinant of social class in most Latin American countries. The bitter and bloody civil war in Guatemala partially derived from the fact that the majority of Guatemalan citizens are indigenous, and that they exercise very little influence in national politics. But Latin American Catholicism continues to play the dual roles of legitimizing social reform and supporting elite dominance. Thus, both church and state reprised their Iberian roles in Latin America. Although the relationship of *peninsulares* and *criollos* to native peoples and *mestizos* was that of powerful patron to subservient client, the colonial relationship of the two major institutions, church and state, differed significantly in the various countries and periods. Margaret Crahan summarizes the tension inherent in the situation:

Analysts have focused on this [supporting] role of the church with some justification but at the expense of comprehending the degree to which the church and church people pursued goals that sometimes undercut royal interests. The very structuring of the empire, with its complex system of vertical and horizontal checks and overlapping jurisdictions involving both civil and ecclesiastical officials, helped to generate tension and conflict. In addition, from the outset of the colonial enterprise some church leaders, most notably the friars Bartolomé de Las Casas and Bernardino de Sahagún, enunciated objectives that diverged from those of metropolitan and colonial elites.[3]

The first ideal type of historic Latin American church-state relationship, the traditional authoritarianism of the state, relied on the triple alliance of landowners, military, and higher ecclesiastics. Colonial wealth came from land, and the political control of the establishment was reinforced by the coercive power of the military. The church played a dual role. It articulated ideological support for the state system, and it also provided the educational and social welfare institutions for the society. Experiences in the latter role sometimes led clergy to protest the mistreatment of the native people. Leaders of all three institutions tended to come from the same great families, and in the colonial period, the highest officials had to be born in Spain. In this model, the relative power of church and state could vary enormously. From its beginning, the Colombian church exercised enormous influence vis-à-vis the state, not so the Venezuelan one. In his comparative study of the two churches, Daniel Levine emphasizes that Colombia constituted a significant colonial political center and that after Independence the Conservatives won the nineteenth-century civil war, so that "the power of such institutions – most notably a strong central state, a unified economic and social elite, and a powerful Church – would be carried over into the twentieth century, bringing as well the styles of action and the axes of conflict characteristic of earlier times."[4] In the nineteenth century, almost every Latin American country faced this *kulturkampf* between Liberals and Conservatives. The Liberals under Benito Juárez won in Mexico, thus preparing the way for banishing the Church from the public sphere in the Mexican Revolution.

The second type of church-state relationship is illustrated in Brazil up to the beginning of the twentieth century. In this model of ecclesiastical diffusion, Catholicism pervaded the culture, but the Church had little direct institutional influence. Indeed, so extensive were the ecclesiastical privileges of the Portuguese state in Brazil that Thomas Bruneau states that "during the whole colonial period (1500–1822) it is probably misleading

---

[3] Margaret Crahan, "Church and State in Latin America: Assassinating Some Old and New Stereotypes," *Daedalus* 120 (Summer 1991): 31.

[4] Daniel H. Levine, *Religion and Politics in Latin America: The Catholic Church in Venezuela and Colombia* (Princeton, NJ: Princeton University Press, 1981), 58.

to talk about a Church."[5] In both Brazil and Mexico, the suppression of the Jesuits greatly weakened the church versus the state. Bruneau comments that "The Jesuits were not only the most effective clergy in Brazil, but they were also the largest order."[6] Brazilian church-state relations did not change after Independence. In 1847 the Brazilian Emperor Pedro II even turned down the prestige of having Latin America's first cardinal to "avoid subtleties which constantly prevail in the Roman Curia." In this diffused system, rural priests depended on landowners, and urban clergy on merchant guilds. The Brazilian government oversaw the seminaries and controlled ecclesiastical appointments. Until the fall of the Emperor Pedro and the establishment of the Republic in 1889, the state limited the church to one archbishopric, six bishoprics, and two prelacies. The First Republic separated church and state, thus freeing the church while removing state subsidies. The Brazilian elite, nurtured on the ideological traditions of the European Enlightenment, waited for the church to collapse.

The newly independent Brazilian church did not collapse, but expanded rapidly with the assistance of European missionary personnel. In less than thirty years, Rome had divided the country into fifty-eight ecclesiastical jurisdictions. By 1930, according to Bruneau, the Brazilian church "had become a large and organized body"[7] based on the most successful ecclesiastical model of the time, which relied on the bourgeois for societal influence. The Brazilian church built parochial schools, established various ecclesiastical organizations, and emphasized the frequent reception of the sacraments. This set the stage for the third Latin American church-state model, Neo-Christendom. Less than fifty years after the state left the church for dead, ecclesiastical leaders forced the Brazilian government to recognize Catholicism as the religion of the country. The great practitioner of this strategy, Dom Sebastião Leme, led the Brazilian church from the time he became bishop (later archbishop and cardinal) of Rio in 1921 until his death in 1942. He cooperated with his close friend, the agnostic president Getúlio Vargas, by trading ecclesiastical support for Vargas's rule for substantial privileges for the church.

The late 1950s and early 1960s brought tremendous political, social, and economic changes to Latin America. By 1961 only one military

[5] Thomas C. Bruneau, *The Political Transformation of the Brazilian Catholic Church* (Cambridge: Cambridge University Press, 1974), 16.
[6] Bruneau, *Transformation*, 19.
[7] Bruneau, *Transformation*, 40.

government, in Paraguay, remained on the continent, and after 1959 the example of Castro's Cuba electrified leftist politics throughout the region. The Catholic Church faced these new developments with two new models, the fourth and fifth of this section. The fourth model, Christian Democracy, came from Europe. The heyday of Christian Democracy in Europe, 1945–60, attracted and influenced the entire Catholic world. Many Latin American ecclesiastical elites who studied in Rome during this period came to believe that it offered the best political form to integrate democratic institutions with Catholic values. The Chilean Christian Democrats came to power in 1964 when their presidential candidate Eduardo Frei received 55 percent of the vote. Brian Smith explains this victory as a result of the unique political religious history of Chile:

Social Catholicism in Chile between 1935 and 1958, however, was the most significant movement of its kind in Latin America. This was due to the socially progressive orientation of Catholic Action programs, the small but committed nucleus of lay leaders these structures trained over time, and the perdurance of a reformist party of Christian inspiration in competitive multiparty politics throughout this entire period.... Such conditions, coupled with the continued officially neutral position of the Church in partisan politics after the mid-1930s, laid important groundwork for major advances by the Chilean Christian Democratic Party in the 1960s.[8]

Six years later the Chilean Constitution prohibited Frei from running for a second term. The electorate split into three nearly equal blocks with the largest two polarizing on the right and the left. The socialist Allende became president with 36.2 percent of the vote, and the political stage was set for the tragedy of the Pinochet coup in 1973. In the 1960s, Christian Democracy fit the rising middle class well, both in Europe and in Latin America. It failed, however, to solve the problem of the rural poor, who were much more numerous in Latin America than in Europe.

Brazil contained whole regions of mostly poor peasants, such as Northeast, and Brazil's urban areas exhibited some of the world's greatest income disparities. The Brazilian military seized power in 1964 and established a powerful national security state (1964–85) of military-bureaucratic control focused on making Brazil a global power. Progressive Catholicism, the fifth church-state model, began in the early 1950s under the leadership of the Brazilian bishops conference (CNBB) and Catholic

[8] Brian H. Smith, *The Church and Politics in Chile: Challenges to Modern Catholicism* (Princeton: Princeton University Press, 1982), 105.

Action. Monsignor Giovanni Battista Montini (later Pope Paul VI) of the Vatican Secretariat of State supported Dom Hélder Câmara in his formation of the CNBB. The CNBB Secretary Câmara, some progressive bishops from the Northeast, and a small group of clergy and laity constituted the entire organization, but they managed to give the impression that the entire church supported social change. These efforts constituted a new Church strategy focused on peasants and urban workers. Brazilian Social Catholicism, however, remained an elite rather than a mass movement, and the reorganization of CNBB to include all the bishops deprived Câmara of his position. The National Security State of 1964, unlike its predecessor progressive government, strongly opposed the new Catholicism. The generals could not resurrect Neo-Christendom, so they sought to remove all church influence from society. The poor would be better off, they thought, attending *fútbol* [soccer] games on Sunday rather than the Catholic liturgy where they might pick up subversive ideas.

The second meeting of the Latin American Bishops (CELAM II) at Medellín in 1968 combined elements of reformist Christian Democracy, the more sweeping critiques of Brazilian progressive Catholicism, and the Latin American Catholic radicalism that contributed to the Allende victory of 1970. The more conservative bishops from countries such as Argentina, Colombia, and Mexico balanced the Chilean and Brazilian hierarchies. Following CELAM II the Vatican appointed the young Colombian Alfonso, López Trujillo as CELAM secretary in an effort to "moderate" the organization. López Trujillo hoped to make CELAM III (1979), situated at the grand Palafox Seminary in one of Mexico's most conservative cities of Puebla, a significant turning point to the right for the Latin American episcopate. The recently elected John Paul II, however, made his first foreign trip to Mexico City and Puebla. The Pope's presence changed a planned bureaucratic event into one in which charisma played a significant role. John Paul's speeches pleased both conservatives and liberals by stressing the necessity of social justice while condemning Marxism. The bishops' final report encouraged Basic Christian Communities [*communidades eclesiais de base*, or CEBs] and stressed the political role of the laity to improve the life of the poor. The bishops also sent a shorter "message to the Peoples of Latin America," which stressed Divine Liberation and human rights. From the 1960s to the early 1980s, the Catholic Church at the international, regional, and some national levels, fostered progressive inclusion of the poor and human rights.

After Latin American democratization, Anthony Gill[9] points out that the Latin American Catholic Church drew back into a more institutional strategy of "spiritual retrenchment" for several reasons. First, Pope John Paul II began appointing more and more theological and political conservatives in an attempt to consolidate doctrinal control of the global church. Second, the emergence of democratic governments and civil society meant the exodus of social activists into newly legal secular organizations. Finally, Protestant denominations experienced an explosive growth. Once the Methodists, Baptists, and nondenominational faith missions began to proselytize among the rural and urban poor and to indigenize their movements, evangelical Protestantism took off. As an indicator of this sixth model, Religious Interest Group in a Democratic State, the fourth meeting of the CELAM in Santo Domingo (1992) issued a final document that, while reaffirming Social Catholicism's commitment to the poor, focused almost completely on spiritual matters. As a result, the Latin American Church has more than tripled its native seminarians, but most national churches have still not attained one-to-one replacement ratios for current parish staffing.

CENTRAL AMERICA DURING THE COLD WAR: UNITED STATES INTERVENTION AND LIBERATION THEOLOGY

Since the nineteenth-century Monroe Doctrine, the United States has considered all of Latin America, but especially Central America, within its sphere of influence. That hegemony has been maintained, even if it has been necessary for Washington to support an "at least he is *our* bastard" type of authoritarian government. Economically, the region has traditionally supplied basic market crops, as in El Salvador's progression from cacao to indigo to coffee. Cultivation of international market crops encourages concentrated land ownership and the creation of an economic elite. Klaiber states that the Central American nations of El Salvador, Nicaragua, and Guatemala "all shared common characteristics: highly stratified social structures; the absence of a large middle class; the persistence of long dictatorships; and unequal land distribution."[10] In addition,

---

[9] Anthony Gill, "Religion and Democracy in South America: Challenges and Opportunities," Ted Gerard Jelen and Clyde Wilcox, eds., *Religion and Politics in Comparative Perspective: The One, The Few, and The Many* (Cambridge: Cambridge University Press, 2002), 195–224.

[10] Jeffrey Klaiber, S. J., *The Church, Dictatorships, and Democracy in Latin America* (Maryknoll, NY: Orbis Books, 1998), 164.

says Klaiber, the three had a long history of North American intervention, a high percentage of foreign church personnel, and great polarization between conservatives and progressives in the church. Until the 1970s, El Salvador most closely approximated the above traditional authoritarian model of church-state relations. Montgomery points out that the cyclical economic patterns produced their political counterpart after the 1932 army massacre of thirty thousand peasants:

> Each political cycle followed a consistent pattern. First, a group of progressive, young military officers who pledged to break with the past and institute needed reforms overthrew an increasingly repressive regime. Next, the most conservative elements of the army, influenced by members of the oligarchy, reasserted themselves and let the reforms lapse. This produced civil unrest which, in turn, led to increasing repression by the regime. This often repeated relapse became known in El Salvador as *"derechizacion,"* or a drift to the right. Following this drift, a group within the army became disaffected once again, ultimately producing yet another coup.[11]

Montgomery lists six such cycles between 1932 and the young officer's coup of October 1979. The cycles stopped when the army proved incapable of defeating the opposition militarily, leading to the bloody civil war of 1980–91. In the late-1970s, the beginning of this battle for human rights coincided with the tenure of United States president Jimmy Carter. Carter delivered his most famous speech on human rights at the University of Notre Dame in June 1977 before graduates and three human rights bishops. Cardinal Stephen Kim, Cardinal Paulo Arns, and Bishop Donal Lamont had resisted authoritarian governments in Korea, Brazil, and Rhodesia, respectively. When Ronald Reagan became president in 1980, it touched off a struggle between many U.S. Catholics and a U.S. administration supporting the right in Central America. Washington would have chosen a stable centrist democratic government (read Christian Democratic), but better "our bastard" dictator than a leftist leader who might ally with the Soviets.

The Vatican played different roles in each Central American country. When John Paul II visited in March 1983, he focused on human rights in Guatemala, internal church matters in Nicaragua, and used the late Archbishop Oscar Romero's theme of "reconciliation" in El Salvador. In Guatemala City, the Pope reprimanded the Protestant dictator Rios Montt for executing six opponents after the Vatican made a special plea

---

[11] Tommie Sue Montgomery, "El Salvador: The Descent Into Violence," *International Policy Report* (March 1982): 3.

for their release. "When you trample a man, when you violate his rights, when you commit flagrant injustices against him, when you submit him to torture, break in and kidnap him or violate his right to life, you commit a crime and a great offense against God."[12] John Paul II also encouraged greater solidarity among Guatemalan Indian tribes as a means of strengthening their resistance against exploitation. In Nicaragua, where the Sandinistas had gained power from the dictator Somoza, the pope refused to let Ernesto Cardenal, a Liberation Theologian who had joined the Nicaraguan government in defiance of Rome, kiss his ring. He called on all clergy to avoid too political a stance.

In the El Salvador conflict, strong American Catholic support existed for both the center and the center-left. José Napoleón Duarte, the Christian Democratic president from 1984 to 89, had studied engineering at the University of Notre Dame where President Theodore Hesburgh encouraged him to enter politics. Missionary priests and nuns who worked with the poor had friends and colleagues at Catholic universities and in the American Congress such as Tip O'Neill. These contacts often came through the U.S. missionary society, Maryknoll, and the Jesuits. Three times during this period the Salvadoran right committed atrocities against church workers that incensed United States Catholic opinion against the Reagan and Bush administrations. In March 1980, a professional gunman assassinated Archbishop Oscar Romero during mass. In December 1980, army personnel raped and killed four American church women. In November 1989, the Salvadoran army massacred six Jesuits and two women at the Catholic University of Central America (UCA). The UCA Jesuits performed the triple functions of advocating human rights and socioeconomic development, providing the best academic research on Salvadoran public opinion, and mediating the war.

When the FMLN guerrillas launched their final offensive, a tactic the Jesuits predicted would fail for lack of popular support, the army massacred the Jesuits. Finally, both the military and the rebels realized that neither could win militarily, so they signed the peace treaty of 1991. Over seventy thousand Salvadorans had died in the Civil War, 85 percent of whom had been killed by the right according to the March 15, 1993, *United Nations Report of the Commission on the Truth* established by the treaty. Many hundreds of thousands more had fled to the United States and neighboring countries. Like Afghanistan, the Central American case of the 1980s was much more significant globally than the number of

---

[12] March 4, 1983.

people involved. Both wars involved the Cold War superpowers fight-ing to maintain their traditional geographic influence by supporting old allies in the traditional military manner. Unlike Afghanistan, however, the countries of Central America became democracies in the 1990s, and their conflicts did not produce an international terrorist movement.

LATIN ASIA: THE PHILIPPINES

Like the case of Central America, the church-state struggle in the Philip-pines combines many of the domestic and international analytical con-cerns of this book. The Philippines has the added significance of a projected 2050 population of 154 million, larger than the projected populations of either Russia or Japan. Because the pope assigned the country to the Spanish colonial sphere in 1493, its traditional culture combines Malay and Hispanic elements, and its form of church-state relations remains Latin American. Indeed, Filipino political scientist Jose Magadia[13] ties his current analysis to Latin American treatments of "associative networks" in postauthoritarian states. Following nineteenth-century "Manifest Destiny," the Protestant United States annexed the islands so that Americans could "Christianize their little brown brothers." The little brown brothers proved ungrateful, however, which resulted in a long and ferocious conflict full of blood and tropical illness for the troops on both sides. This failed war of independence also left scars on the Filipinos, physically, psychologically, and politically. Many analysts have referred to a recurring "crisis of sovereignty" in the Philippines, so long captive to Spanish, American, and even briefly Japanese, military and cultural spheres.

After recovering independence in 1946 the Philippines became a multi-party democracy, albeit with strong patron-client characteristics. In 1972 the democratically elected President Ferdinand Marcos changed the coun-try to a type of authoritarian government termed a "sultanistic regime." The nation returned, via a nonbloody coup, to an electoral democracy in 1986. Following in this political path, the Philippines constitutes a unique case globally during the entire Cold War period. Sultanistic regimes such as Pahlavi's Iran, Somoza's Nicaragua, Mobutu's Zaire, and Batista's Cuba ended with violent national revolutions that resulted in subsequent authoritarian regimes. Even in the cases of Trujillo's Dominican Republic,

---

[13] Jose J. Magadia, *State-Society Dynamics: Policy Making in a Restored Democracy* (Manila: Ateneo de Manila Press, 2003), 9–11.

Duvalier's Haiti, and Ceausescu's Romania, no preexisting multiparty democracy existed, nor has it been easy to construct one following the flight of the dictator. The weaknesses of this political form seem to survive the demise of any particular government. "Sultanistic regimes," according to Chehabi and Linz, are governments based on a personal authority figure supported "by a mixture of fear and rewards to his collaborators. The ruler exercises his power without restraint, at his own discretion and above all unencumbered by rules or by any commitment to an ideology or value system."[14]

Sultanistic governments usually combine both personalism and dynasticism. Families, especially wives, play significant roles, as did Imelda Marcos, who combined the mayorship of Metro-Manila with a cultural czarinaship reminiscent of Madame Mao. Instead of the seven canonical Maoist theatrical events, Manila got the Miss Universe Pageant and the "Thrilla from Manila" Frazier-Ali fight. The Marcos "conjugal dictatorship" eventually split into "his and hers" hangers-on, warring over political influence and business bribery, for example, $700,000 from Westinghouse for a nuclear plant contract. Imelda also objected to Ferdinand's frequent affairs, with assignations such as third-rate American starlet Dovey Beams. Relatives and cronies took control of most of the country's large corporations, a la the Shah's Iran.

How, then, do we account for the globally unique political path of the postwar Philippines? The corruption and chaos of Philippine politics in 1972 provided a rationale for Marcos's declaration of martial law. Although the competing Liberal and Nationalista parties each had held the presidency three and four times respectively, these very similar parties did not represent voters, but functioned as elite cliques. When one party won the presidency and its enormous resources, many from the losing party would join it. As time went on, the ruling party would lack enough resources to satisfy the rapidly multiplying claimants, and an elite opposition would form for the next election. The system was kept from a national authoritarian regime by the relatively uncorrupt armed forces, Committee on Elections, and Supreme Court, and by the fact that the permanent power remained with regional powerbrokers who acted as "little sultans" in their own domains, for example, the Marcos family in Ilocos Norte. The war hero Ferdinand Marcos, who had married the elite beauty queen Imelda from Cebu, argued that only a strong central

[14] H. E. Chehabi and Juan J. Linz, eds., *Sultanistic Regimes* (Baltimore: The Johns Hopkins University Press, 1998), 23–24.

authoritarian government could save the Philippines. In the Vietnam War climate, the Nixon Administration embraced anticommunist order, and many Philippine elite feared Marxist revolution. In fact, Marcos manufactured the leftist threat and employed the spendthrift use of "guns, goons, and gold," even during his first term.

When Marcos declared martial law in 1972, the Philippine Catholic Bishops Conference (CBCP) remained cautious for the first two years. Opus Dei technocrats could appreciate Marcos's call for efficiency. However, even Cebu's Cardinal Rosales, a bishop so conservative his brother Paraguayan bishops refused to meet with him when he attended an anticommunist conference in their capital Asunsión, protested the detention of Filipino priests and the deportation of foreign, mostly American, clergy and religious. In late 1976 a series of police raids plus a government document designating 155 clergy and laity, including four bishops, for arrest prompted sixty-six of the seventy-four Philippine bishops, even those usually supportive of Marcos, to sign a strongly worded statement against government interference in church evangelization.

The juxtaposition of the 1981 visits of John Paul II and George H. Bush to Manila illustrates the divergence of Philippine policy between the Vatican and the United States. While the pope challenged the dictator to improve his human rights' record, the Vice President gushed, "We love your adherence to democratic principles and democratic processes."[15] What finally pushed the church into the active political, as distinct from moral, opposition was the realization that normal political forces could not save the country. The leading opposition figure, Benigno Aquino, was assassinated at the airport as he returned to Manila from "medical exile" in the United States. Cardinal Sin then began to construct a coalition of noncommunist popular movements, traditional political elites, legitimate business interests, and the Reform the Armed Forces Now Movement (RAM) organized by passed-over Generals Juan Ponce Enrile and Fidel Ramos. The Church thus provided an alternative source of legitimacy versus Marcos's authoritarianism, alternative media distribution versus the state media, and alternative parish-based grassroots organization versus Marcos's political party and local cronies. When Marcos called a "snap election" in February 1986 to bolster his democratic credentials with his American patrons, the coalition chose as the opposition candidate Corazon Aquino, Benigno's widow, whose moral appeal would be unquestionable. The cardinal also wore a NAMFREL (vote monitoring group organized by businessman-president of the national Council of Catholic

---

[15] July 1, 1981.

Laity) cap, and used Catholic Radio Veritas to call out people to protect the forces of Enrile and Ramos in the few hours in which the revolution hung in the balance. The television pictures of unarmed priests and nuns halting the Marcos troops, offering them flowers and leis, made wonderful international public relations. The United States finally embraced this almost ideal coalition of regime soft-liners and the moderate opposition. The political interests of the reformist military, the political opposition, the Catholic Church, legitimate business, and the international patron all coincided. The Marcoses left for Hawaii, with Ferdinand returning only in his coffin.

Cardinal Sin also supported the 2000 campaign to impeach ex-movie star President Joseph Estrada after it became clear that Estrada had received massive bribes. Sin and other bishops led "protest Eucharists" attended by Catholic social and labor organizations and Catholic university faculty and students. Many Pentecostal churches also supported the anti-Estrada campaign. Estrada's major Catholic backing consisted of his spiritual adviser, the religious media superstar Mariano Velarde, the founding leader of the country's largest charismatic movement, El Shaddai. In November 2003 Velarde hosted a fifteen-hour "national prayer and fasting for national reconciliation" in Manila's Rizal Park attended by eight hundred thousand, including President Gloria Macapagal-Arroyo and Archbishop Fernando Capalla of Davao, then soon to be installed as the president of the Philippines Bishops' Conference. Arroyo prayed for reconciliation between those who denounced and those who supported Estrada. Capalla asked for God's help in talks with both communist and Muslim rebels, and said that in the Estrada case, that "once again" the nation had "plunged into a crisis largely of our own making."[16] The ex-economist Arroyo won the presidency outright in a contest against another taciturn ex-movie star. Fernando Poe Jr. was backed by Estrada, business magnate Eduardo Cojuangco of San Miguel beer, ex-defense minister Enrile, and Imelda Marcos. Like Indonesia, the Philippines faces tremendous political, economic, and terrorist challenges. In July the bishops again called for unity after the May 10 election, and intensification of "our fight against corruption."[17]

During the Cold War period in Latin America and the Philippines, many national Catholic hierarchies fostered democratization. Klaiber lists

---

[16] *Asian Focus*, November 14, 2003.
[17] *Asian Focus*, July 16, 2004. When some of Arroyo's former supporters such as Cory Aquino called for her resignation in July 2005, the bishops did not join the campaign. Arroyo supporter Ramos suggested that the country adopt a parliamentary system.

five ways: they deprived dictatorships of legitimacy; they used religious symbols and liturgy to support opposition groups; they founded national offices for the protection of human rights; they legitimized the opposition; and they served as mediators between the government and the opposition, especially during civil wars.[18] Pope John Paul II backed these initiatives in his pastoral visits to countries such as the Philippines, Haiti, and El Salvador. Different religious actors played different political roles. The cardinal primate of the capital city, for example, Cardinal Sin of Manila, or the president of the national conference of bishops, for example, Cardinal Lorsheider of Brazil, stated the moral position of the national church, the nation's "primary ethical broker." Such cardinals also protected those clergy and laity who took more radical positions. One or a few bishops, for example, the Igorot [indigenous tribe] Francisco Claver in the Philippines, expressed the most radical position acceptable within the episcopate. Claver spent much time under house arrest during the Marcos regime, but killing him would have been counterproductive. Church academic institutions, for example, the UCA Jesuits, provided social scientific analyses of national issues. During the Philippine crisis, Jesuits Bishop Claver, Provincial Ben Nebres, and Ateneo President Joaquin Bernas wrote important letters and speeches for the bishops, Sin, and Aquino. Many graduates of Catholic grassroots organizations such as the CEBs joined the political opposition. Even staunchly middle-class Christian Democrats, for example, Duarte in El Salvador, denied the government the traditional ideological cover of the landowner-army-church alliance.

During the Cold War such human rights struggles took place within the United States sphere of influence. Both the United States and the Vatican could cooperate in supporting a Christian Democratic government. Where that solution did not exist, and it did not in most developing countries, Washington opted for the authoritarian state. The Catholic Church then became more and more involved in human rights. The most relevant church actors became the Vatican, the U.S. Catholic Church with its contacts to Congress, the national episcopal conference, the cardinal primate, government-leaning bishops, human rights bishops, religious orders, associations of clergy and nuns, and Catholic lay organizations. The demise of a personalist, sultanistic, traditional Latin American authoritarian, or a more modern National Security State did not necessarily mean that a democratic government would succeed. Sometimes no straight path exists to political consensus and a functional civil society.

[18] Klaiber, *Dictatorships*, 7–11.

CONTEMPORARY MEXICO: A NEW PARADIGM
FOR RELIGION AND POLITICS?

The Mexican Catholic Church lost the Conservative-Liberal struggle of the mid-nineteenth century. The Liberal period of Juárez was followed by the positivist period of the *porfiriato* (Porfirio Diáz, 1875–1910), whose *científicos* bureaucracy saw its model in the French Enlightenment and state. However, these rational planners ignored the poverty of *campesinos* in the rural areas, especially on large northern ranches. In 1910, shortly after being reelected in a "managed" process, Porfirio Diáz fled to Paris as the various *caudillo* leaders of the Mexican Revolution (1910–21) began their uprisings. The Revolution also attacked those elements of the church that had sneaked back into public life during the *porfiriato*, so the triumph of the Revolution brought about the even further marginalization of the church. Such a strong anticlericalism proved counterproductive, however, when it stirred up the Cristero Rebellion of the late-1920s. Finally, President Calles reached an agreement with the Catholic Church that it could have relative security in the private sphere if it stayed completely out of the public sphere. By this time the Revolutionary generals had eliminated leftist leaders such as Emilio Zapata and had formed the Institutional Revolutionary Party (PRI) with its vision of stability through the corporate political participation of all social sectors, except the church.

The Mexican state encouraged strong leadership without dictatorship by instituting a powerful presidency, but limiting the office to one six-year term. The outgoing president chose the PRI's next office holder, and then retired. Including all sectors in policy decisions meant that different sectors increased their political influence or had it decreased in different administrations. For example, the accession of Lázaro Cárdenas in 1934 meant that the relatively disadvantaged urban workers and rural peasants had more policy input. From the accession of Cárdenas's successor, Camacho, the business community gained influence at the expense of the military and the poor. Finally, in the 1980s, the political technocrats took charge and made decisions based on the neoliberal economic integration of Mexico into the world market. This system, called *salinistroika* after President Carlos Salinas de Gotari (1988–94), reached its apex in Mexico's participation in the North American Free Trade Agreement (NAFTA) with the United States and Canada.

On January 1, 1994, the date for the implementation of NAFTA, the peasant Zapatistas surprised everyone with their rebellion in the southern poverty-stricken and predominantly indigenous state of Chiapas. The

Zapatista rebellion patterned a new type of Latin American politics, more oriented toward the global communication system than the national military one. Including the initial attack there were only twelve days of combat and 145 killed. Subcommander Marcos and his troops then withdrew to the forests, from which they waged an international public relations campaign via the Internet, various celebratory conferences, and finally a national march to Mexico City. Their unique blend of Catholic Liberation Theology, Mayan organization, and leftist politics surprised Mexican elites. The Zapatistas did not attain the Congressional ratification of the San Andres accords that increased indigenous rights, but they kept the plight of Mexico's ten million indigenous citizens in front of public opinion and contributed to the end of the PRI's political monopoly.

In March 1994, Salinas's chosen candidate, the respected Luis Colosio, was assassinated at a Baja campaign stop. The PRI then selected Ernesto Zedillo, but Salinas's early failure to face the nation's economic downturn and his reckless campaign spending forced Zedillo to devalue the peso in December. Then the corruption of the Salinas regime, in which the president's brother Raúl excelled, emerged publicly. The police arrested Raúl, and Carlos fled to Ireland to escape prosecution. These political and economic disasters contributed to the PRI's loss of control of the Chamber of Deputies in July 1997. Three years later the PRI lost the presidency for the first time.

Although the PRI remains the strongest party, there are now two viable opposition parities, the National Action Party (PAN) and the Revolutionary Democratic Party (PRD). Each of these three parties maintains a unique relationship with the majority Catholic Church. The PRI tried to shed its anticlerical past under Salinas when the government and the Vatican signed a concordat in December 1991 which gave legal recognition to religious institutions. The concordat also permitted priests and nuns to vote, but not to hold office. The PRD, coming out of the Cárdenas left wing of the PRI, retains the strongest anticlerical tradition. This can be illustrated by the Senate cries of "Viva Juárez, Viva Zapata" that protested the PRI's regularization of relations with the Church. However, on social justice issues like the government's treatment of indigenous peoples, bishops like Samuel Ruiz of San Cristóbal would seem to have been natural allies in advocating social services and education for the poor. But trust between PRD activists and clergy remains difficult.

The PAN remains the Catholic party culturally, with strong roots in traditionally religious states such as Jalisco, in which the PAN won the governorship as early as 1995. The PAN hopes to become the majority through businesslike economic efficiency, Catholic cultural social probity, and a global economic vision supportive of NAFTA and open borders with the United States. Vicente Fox Quesada, ex-PAN governor of Guanajuato, won the presidency in July 2000. The handsome rancher ran a Kennedyesque campaign for revolutionary change and against PRI corruption, holding his core business and Catholic support, while projecting an image of inclusiveness to all Mexicans. When Fox was inaugurated in December 2000, he found that campaigning was easier than governing. He already knew he would face a difficult legislature split among the three parties with PRI pluralities and no majority in either house. In the lower five-hundred seat Chamber of Deputies the seats were 211 PRI, 207 PAN, and 52 PRD. During the period between the election and the inauguration, Fox's good friend, fellow rancher George W. Bush, became president of the United States. The global economy, however, worsened, making new political initiatives significantly more difficult for this administration elected on promises of reform. Then came September 11, which diverted Bush's attention elsewhere. Fox discovered how difficult it was to get measures adopted in the single-term Chamber of Deputies from a minority party position. The PAN lost heavily in the 2003 lower-house elections, dropping to 151 seats as the PRI rose to 225.

ARGENTINA, BRAZIL, AND CHILE: RELIGION, POLITICS, AND ECONOMICS

The Catholic spiritual retrenchment of the 1990s seemed to fit the continent's political democratization and economic integration into the global market. Conservatives rose in the church hierarchy and neo-liberals took over national economies. Argentina, with its conservative hierarchy, most closely fit this ecclesiastical and economic model, instituting the most aggressive privatization of federal agencies of any Latin American state. Local businessmen hoped to benefit greatly from these policies most associated with President Carlos Saul Menem, who drove a red Ferrari and flew in his private Tango 01 jet. Despite the nation's increasing social stratification, the Argentine economic experiment seemed an overall success into 1998. The value of the Buenos Aires Stock Exchange rose exponentially in eight years, whereas per capita income quadrupled to $8,970, twice that of Mexico at the time.

During the halcyon days of expansion, however, the government ignored both economic fundamentals and the poor. The state privatized many federal agencies, but it failed to provide for the laid off workers or to guard against high utility and transport costs. Private owners, often with U.S. partners such as Citibank, sought a high profit on their "public" investment. Most of the hoped for low- and medium-skilled jobs for the newly unemployed never materialized, since that sector departed for low-wage countries in other regions. The United States government disengaged, as illustrated by Treasury Secretary Paul O'Neill's comment in summer 2001: "They [Argentina] have been in trouble for 70 years or more. . . . They don't have any export industry to speak of at all. And they like it that way. Nobody forced them to be what they are."[19] When the crash finally did come, the IMF eventually criticized its own performance.

Whole provinces such as San Salvador de Jujuy went into deep recession, causing social unrest. After a chaotic period marked by five presidents, in January 2002 the country devalued the peso and defaulted on its debts under a new president, Peronist Eduardo Duhalde. This resulted in huge losses to overseas investors, especially from the United States and Spain. It also ushered in a period of tough negotiations with the IMF. In 2003 the center-left Néstor Kirchner was elected president for a regular four-year term when Menem dropped out of the race. Washington could no longer count on Buenos Aires' "automatic alignment" in foreign policy on issues as diverse as the war with Iraq and human rights violations in Cuba. All of this economic chaos hurt doubly because Argentina, rich in resources, literacy, and European immigration ("a piece of Europe that broke off and landed in South America") had had the continent's highest standard of living for much of the first half of the century.

The free trade and democracy decade of the 1990s produced greater social stratification in Latin America, already the most skewed in the entire world. At the beginning of the decade the top 10 percent of the population earned thirty-eight times the bottom 10 percent. By the end of the decade, it had increased to forty-seven times. Poverty rates soared in Argentina, Mexico, Venezuela, and most other countries that carried out neoliberal economic reforms. Chile did much better, with only a marginal increase in social stratification. Chile, however, had a long tradition of a middle class and a middle-class political party, the Christian Democrats. From the beginning of the Pinochet dictatorship, Cardinal Raúl Silva Henríquez of Santiago led the Chilean fight for human rights. His successor, the more conservative Cardinal Juan Francisco Fresno, united the eleven-party opposition to Pinochet in the National Accord for the Transition

---

[19] December 25, 2001.

to Full Democracy (1985) and worked hard for a large turnout in the 1989 plebiscite that defeated the dictator. In the last Chilean election, both leading candidates fought for the center, emphasizing both economic growth and programs for the poor. The Socialist Ricardo Lagos barely defeated the Christian Democrat Joaquín Lavin in March 2000. Lagos, a member of the Latin American new left resembling European Social Democracy, had suffered under Pinochet, but he had also received his doctorate in economics from Duke and spoke fondly of Wall Street.

During the Argentine crisis of late 2001, currency speculators next bet against the Brazilian real. The United States and the IMF then organized the same type of economic full-court press that they had exhibited in the Mexican crisis of 1994. In August 2002, the IMF provided a $30 billion lifeline, but $24 billion was marked for disbursement the following year after a new Brazilian president was elected. Many foreign investors worried that the leading candidate, Luiz Inácio Lula da Silva of the Workers Party (PT), might change Brazil's free market orientation. Lula, however, had given up his workers' clothes for three-piece suits and spoke soothingly to Wall Street. The Brazilian voters elected Lula on October 27, 2002, with over 61 percent of the vote. This metalworker with less than a sixth-grade education, whose family came to São Paolo from the poverty-stricken Northeast, won on his fourth try. The Brazilian poor expected much from their hero Lula, but the new president followed a moderate economic policy that actually shrank the GNP slightly in 2003. Finally, by July 2004 the economy seemed to be improving with surging exports, increased capital spending, and rising retail sales. Job creation was also better, but slower than the other indicators. In October the PT doubled its hold nationally on city halls, but the PT's idiosyncratic Marta Suplicy, a divorced Stanford-educated psychologist, lost São Paolo. And the level of corruption in the Brazilian government continued at high levels, for example, paying opposition members for their support.

President George W. Bush began his presidency by pledging a "fundamental commitment" to Latin America, but the Bush-sponsored Free Trade Area of the Americas (FTAA), Alaska to Argentina, has failed to materialize. Indeed, Lula warned that the October 2002 form of the FTAA agreement would be "tantamount to an annexation of Brazil by the United States."[20] At the November 2003 FTAA negotiating meeting in Miami, Brazil led the opposition to U.S. proposals. U.S. farm subsidy bills undercut the American position because Congress demands protection for

---

[20] October 30, 2002.

those U.S. markets of "sensitive" agricultural products such as sugar, cotton, orange juice, and textiles, which would be most beneficial to Latin American countries. In June 2004, the WTO ruled for Brazil against the cotton subsidies of the United States. Brazil has become the fifth largest grower of cotton in the world and would benefit significantly if the world price strengthens as a result of a more expensive U.S. product. It is a new era in U.S.-Latin American relations with center-left governments in all three of South America's major countries. Venezuela, a major U.S. energy source, chose an even more leftist government under populist President Hugo Chávez, elected with 60 percent of the vote in July 2000. Uruguay elected a center-left Broad Front, from Christian Democrats to Communists, on October 31, 2004. In countries such as oil-rich Venezuela, the U.S. business community has read the national situation much more correctly than the Bush Administration. Social stratification and economic decline has tarnished the reputation of U.S.-style free trade, and only a center-left regime can pursue moderate economic policies, provided it is not perceived as being too close to the Americans. So far the continent's anti-Americanism has mostly benefited China, which has greatly increased its economic contacts.

In summarizing the current political-religious-economic situations of South America's ABC countries, Brazil (2004 HDI ranking #72) stands out for the size of its economy, a history of slavery until the end of the nineteenth century, the mixed racial nature of the population, its social stratification, and the potential richness of its resources. Argentina (#34) shares with Chile (#43) a middle-class tradition of European immigrants. Unfortunately, Menem bet Argentina's economic house on globalization in the 1990s. All three countries have adopted center-left governments after a decade of neoliberalism. The Chilean political system definitely emerged in the best shape for continuity and stability. Brazilian and Chilean national Catholic hierarchies have maintained their national reputations because they opposed authoritarian dictatorships during the 1970s and 1980s. The Argentine state and church are still dealing with the fallout from the "Dirty War."

Pentecostal churches have also interacted very differently with each of the three countries. Argentina's secularism with its strong Peronist movements among the poor has not offered a very hospitable environment for either charismatic movements or Catholic Liberation Theology. In Brazil and Chile, according to David Martin, "evangelicals have tended to belong to the politically voiceless, and their pastors, for the most part, have acquiesced to the demands of military government or even offered qualified support." Pentecostals in the two countries, however, offer very different social profiles. The vast majority of the Chilean Methodist Pentecostal Church come from "marginal people with limited education, engaged in insecure employment and living either in the rural areas or on the peripheries of the larger cities."[21] They vote center or center-left, thus corresponding with their expected socioeconomic place in the system. The Brazilian Assemblies of God, however, comprise both lower and middle classes. There is not much data on how they vote, but they are represented by over thirty national deputies and they also play a role in regional politics.

CATHOLIC RETRENCHMENT, PENTECOSTAL GROWTH, AND GLOBALIZATION IN LATIN AMERICA

The Catholic retrenchment of the 1990s resulted partially from Pentecostal competition. As Jenkins ruefully observed, "the Catholic Church has chosen the poor, but the poor choose the Pentecostals, and the choice rankles."[22] Protestantism first came to Latin America when mainline Protestants, British Anglicans and German Lutherans, came to Argentina and Brazil, where they still form a significant portion of the Protestant population. These churches made sporadic attempts to convert the middle and upper classes during the late nineteenth century, but in general they failed. This changed when Pentecostals began targeting the urban and rural poor and indigenizing their movements along evangelical lines. Mainline Protestant and Pentecostal congregations have tended to serve different social constituencies with little tradition of working together. One could also distinguish between Pentecostals and neo-Pentecostals such as La Familia de Dios, and El Shaddai, which stress that God rewards the good with material advancement. Protestantism has been most successful in Guatemala, Brazil, and Chile, and least successful in Argentina, Colombia, Uruguay, and Venezuela.

Some national Catholic hierarchies responded by trying to limit the activities of the new religions or make it more difficult organizationally.

[21] David Martin, "Evangelical and Charismatic Christianity in Latin America," Karla Poewe, ed., *Charismatic Christianity as a Global Culture* (Columbia: University of South Carolina Press, 1994), 81–82.

[22] Philip Jenkins, *The Next Christendom: The Coming of Global Christianity* (Oxford: Oxford University Press, 2002), 63. Such competition between churches is crucial for Religious Market theorists, for example, Roger Finke, Rodney Stark, and Lawrence Iannaccone. For Latin America, see Anthony Gill, *Rendering Unto Caesar: The Catholic Church in Latin America* (Chicago: University of Chicago Press, 1998). For the argument against these theorists, see Pippa Norris and Ronald Inglehart, *Sacred and Secular: Religion and Politics Worldwide* (Cambridge: Cambridge University Press, 2004), 11–32.

Hence, the 1887 Vatican-Colombia concordat forbade non-Catholic religions from proselytizing in 75 percent of the territory, required children to present a Catholic baptismal certificate to enter public schools, and limited recognition to civil or Catholic marriages. Since Constitutional legislation eliminated these arrangements, Protestant evangelization has taken off. Colombian evangelicals provided important swing votes for presidents César Gaviria and Ernesto Samper, as they had for Peruvian President Alberto Fujimori in 1990.[23] The Chilean Catholic Church supported legislation in the early 1990s that would have prohibited legal registration of churches with fewer than two hundred members, street preaching, and excessive noise outside religious buildings. More than ten thousand evangelicals marched in Santiago, and defeated the legislation. Recently, however, the continent's Catholic bishops have moderated their approach. Comparing the documents and statements at CELAM in Santo Domingo (1992) and Quito (1999), the Pentecostals have changed from "the rapacious wolves" of an evangelical "invasion" to a stimulus for the church's own efforts with the underevangelized. Catholic bishops have also stressed two issue areas of ecumenical cooperation: advocacy for the poor and defense of traditional moral values.

Latin American Catholicism also gradually adopted the Catholic Charismatic Renewal (CCR), which, like Pentecostalism, came from the United States and focused on the healing gifts of the Holy Spirit. In fact, the CCR has become the continent's largest lay Catholic movement, gradually winning the support, or at least the cautious approval, of the episcopate. Chesnut describes the movement of the CCR from the February 1967 "the Duquesne weekend" at Duquesne University in Pittsburg to Latin America in the 1970s, retracing the Pentecostal journey of fifty years previous. The first CCR members were disproportionately middle-class, female, and previously active in Catholic organizations. During the economically "lost decade" of the 1980s, however, CCR became active among the poor:

In contrast to its [CCR's] Protestant competitor, which was conceived among the Latin American poor and began to work its way up the social scale, the CCR started to descend from its rarified origins into the hotly contested marketplace of the popular classes. The Renewal's emphasis on divine healing during a decade of severe economic depression gave it great possibilities for expansion among the

---

[23] Peruvian Catholicism demonstrates significant social splits. It is the native country of the first articulator of Liberation Theology, Father Gustavo Gutiérrez and of the first Opus Dei member who became a cardinal, Juan Luis Cipriani Thorne. Cardinal Cipriani has become much more controversial than his predecessor, Cardinal Juan Landázuri Ricketts. May 8, 2005.

swelling ranks of the disprivileged, but it was only through pastoral outreach and evangelization efforts that the CCR was able to realize its potential of becoming a mass movement.[24]

One major CCR difference with Pentecostals has been the Catholic emphasis on the traditional role of the Blessed Virgin, especially Our Lady of Guadalupe. CCR has become strongest in Brazil and its Brazilian television network, Redevida, competes head to head with the leading Pentecostal media outlets like Rede Record run by The Universal Church of the Kingdom of God.

Why did the Pentecostal churches spread so rapidly in Latin America? Certainly, North American aid helped. Protestant analyst Martin comments, "The United States irradiates an image of power and prosperity; there is much American money behind the electronic church and other modern modes of communication; there are thousands of missionaries, more particularly in the smallish faith missions; and evangelical relief work draws heavily on North American generosity."[25] But Martin, Hallum, and others agree that local factors have been even more important. In addition to the above Catholic state failure to serve the poor, the lower educational threshold for Pentecostal pastors, for example, has fostered inculturation and the decentralization of the movement so that it fits into local political and social structures. Pentecostalism also offers natural affinities with some already existing Latin American religious traditions. "Pentecostalism expels evil spirits, engages in miraculous healing, offers ecstatic release, insists on ascetic discipline, and arouses millenarian expectation. Brazil, in particular, has harbored millenarian movements and Afro-Brazilian movements for spiritual health and healing." In the end, says Martin, Pentecostalism "marks above all a walkout from the structure and from the culture as at present constituted, and, as such, from the Catholic church. It is a walkout from the local fiesta, with its web of entangling relationships. It is a walkout from the male personality, with its violence and familial irresponsibility."[26] To illllustrate the appeal of Pentecostalism in a Brazilian favela, Martin proposes a stereotypical wife faced with poverty and the disintegration of her family. To solve the problem she can join any of three groups professing Pentecostalism, Catholic

---

[24] R. Andrew Chesnut, "A Preferential Option for the Spirit: The Catholic Charismatic Renewal in Latin America's New Religious Economy," *Latin American Politics and Society* 45 (Spring 2003): 72.

[25] Martin, "Evangelical," 77.

[26] Martin, "Evangelical," 85.

Liberation Theology, or the African spirit cult Umbanda, respectively. All three groups recruit a majority of working class women. What Pentecostalism offers the wife, argues Martin, is the opportunity to remove her family from the regular neighborhood network into a detached zone where she can find financial and emotional support while a reformulation of family links takes place.

The Mexican village of San Juan Chamula in Chiapas presents an even more complicated picture of the relation of indigenous, Catholic, and Protestant religious values. Tzozil Catholicism, presided over by local leaders called "mayordomos," includes pre-Hispanic customs such as the drinking of [alcoholic] posh. In fact, years ago local Catholics expelled some diocesan priests from the village for objecting to their traditional customs. Protestantism has appealed to other villagers because of its advocacy of abstinence that would strengthen their families. Posh-drinking local Catholics drove the evangelicals from the village, but the Chiapas ecumenical Human Rights Commission helped facilitate their return and the building of the Prince of Peace Temple.[27]

In the northern part of Chiapas, Protestants have been associated with the paramilitaries, on the pattern of the U.S. evangelical linkage to Guatemalan ex-president Rios Montt who joined the Pasadena-based "El Verbo" movement and became Guatemalan president in a 1982 coup. His "Rifles and Beans" campaign distinguished itself for ferocity and cruelty, even in Central America. Guatemala has the region's largest indigenous (55 percent) and largest Protestant (between one-fifth and one-third) populations. Neo-Pentecostal Jorge Serrano Elias became Latin America's first elected evangelical president in 1990, but attempted an *auto-coup* when the populace resisted his neoliberal economic policies. Later discovery of Serrano's embezzlement of $14 million convinced the ex-president to leave Guatemala for Panama. The cases of neo-Pentecostals Montt and Serrano, say Pentecostals, demonstrate that Christians should stay out of politics. The Guatemalan Catholic Church, by contrast, has been active in human rights, leading to the Project for the Recovery of Historical Memory, which detailed 422 massacres during the civil war, 401 committed by the army or rightist paramilitaries. Auxiliary Bishop Juan Gerardi Conedera was assassinated in his garage in April 1998 after he released a report on wartime atrocities, *Guatemala: Never Again!*

Will the expansion of Pentecostalism into Latin America foster the values of the Anglo-European "Protestant ethic"? So far, according to

[27] August 13, 2000.

both Brian Smith[28] and Gill, this does not seem to be the case. On survey data, notoriously difficult to obtain in Latin America, Catholics and Protestants exhibit similar political and cultural profiles at similar societal levels. Latin Americans seem not to have adopted either the laissez-faire Protestant economics or the Pentecostal withdrawal from society. Protestants do exhibit more diversity than Catholics, but the major value cleavages among all Christians derive from the frequency of churchgoing, regardless of denomination. Frequent churchgoers are more conservative and have more trust in societal and governmental organizations, even when socioeconomic level is controlled for. Because of this, Gill argues that the current religious pluralism will lead to a greater civil society in Latin America. The competition between Catholics and Protestants, he states, means that even the lower classes will be served religiously, learning civic skills in their religious organizations. Smith is not quite as optimistic, but he believes that in the most probable scenario, neither Catholic nor Pentecostal activists will choose a "flight from the world" mentality, which would reinforce authoritarian political culture and exacerbate social gaps. Thus, Latin America retains its Catholic worldview, but on any given Sunday there may be as many Protestants in church as Catholics. The mutual cooperation of these Christian activists in support of the poor and in building democratic values would be the best hope for the continent.

WORLD CHRISTIANITY IN GLOBAL POLITICS

This section discusses the international political impact of Christianity, thus paralleling the last two sections of Chapter 8 on national and world Islam. At the millennium, the *World Christian Encylopedia* provided global population figures of 215 million Orthodox, 342 million Protestants, 79 million Anglicans, 386 million independents (Pentecostals and others), 26 million "marginal Christians," and 1 billion, 57 million Roman Catholics.[29] Orthodox political influence in Russia and Eastern Europe has already been discussed in Chapter 5. Over the last thousand years, Orthodoxy has suffered the most from Islamic geographic expansion, so it is no accident that the relations between these two traditions remain tense.

---

[28] Brian H. Smith, *Religious Politics in Latin America: Pentecostal vs. Catholic* (Notre Dame: University of Notre Dame Press, 1998).
[29] *World Christian Encyclopedia* (Oxford: Oxford University Press, 2001).

Chapter 4 cited Marty's Reformation division of what became mainline Protestantism into Lutheran, Reformed-Presbyterian, and Anglican traditions. These churches remain very important politically in North America and Northern Europe. In July 2002, the Anglican Communion chose its first Archbishop of Canterbury from outside of England. The fifty-two-year-old Welsh cleric Dr. Rowan Williams seemed a good fit to bridge the religious concerns of the developed and the developing worlds. For progressive Anglicans of the developed world, Williams supported gays and women as clerics and attacked the Walt Disney Company as one of the media's worst offenders in the premature sexualization of children. For the developing world, Williams criticized the United States for withdrawing from environmental treaties and denounced the military strike against Iraq. The Anglican Communion retains both the opportunities and the challenges of a "bridge church" that combines both the Catholic and the Reformed traditions.

Less than a year after his appointment, Williams faced a crisis that has threatened to split the Anglican Communion. The Episcopal Church USA voted to consecrate its first openly gay bishop, Canon V. Gene Robinson, for the Diocese of New Hampshire. The leaders of Anglican provinces in Africa, Asia, and Latin America opposed the selection, as did conservative U.S. Episcopalians, Orthodox bishops, and John Paul II. Williams called Anglican bishops from all over the world to a special meeting in London in October 2003. "The estrangement of churches in developing countries from their cherished ties with Britain is in no one's interests," said the archbishop, "It would impoverish us as a church in every way."[30] In October 2004, an Anglican commission headed by Archbishop Robin Eames of Armagh, Northern Ireland, called on the Episcopal Church USA to apologize for causing pain and division in the Communion, and to refrain from consecrating gay bishops and blessing same-sex unions until "until some new consensus in the Anglican Communion emerges."[31]

Mainline Protestant churches created their post–World War II global paradigm in the World Council of Churches (WCC). The critical mass for the formation of the WCC arose in the late-nineteenth- and the early-twentieth-century social and educational cooperation of mainline missionary churches. Two British-based ecumenical traditions, Life and Work, and Faith and Order, with ninety member churches, constituted

[30] October 12, 2003.
[31] October 19, 2004.

the WCC at its founding First Assembly in Amsterdam in 1948. The WCC later included the International Missionary Council (IMC), which joined at New Delhi in 1961. Assemblies of the leaders of what are now over three hundred member churches with four hundred million believers have been held in Evanston (1954), New Delhi (1961), Uppsala (1968), Nairobi (1975), Vancouver (1983), Canberra (1991), and Harare, Zimbabwe (1998). The ninth will take place in Porte Alegre, Brazil in February 2006. The WCC Central Committee, composed of 150 members elected by the Assembly, meets yearly to review staff, budget, and programs. The administrative center, led by a General Secretary, resides in Geneva. The current General Secretary is Samuel Kobia, a Methodist from Kenya with wide ecumenical experience. Since the WCC welcomed the official Orthodox churches from Eastern Europe in its initial years, it has become the international NGO that most prominently represents both mainline Protestantism and Orthodoxy.

Throughout the Cold War, the religious, social, and political stances of the WCC generated controversy in the United States and in Western Europe. To fundamentalists, cooperation in such a "superchurch" (a term the WCC explicitly rejects) seemed bound to undercut evangelical emphases on the individual and the Bible. From the political perspective, the WCC strongly attacked colonization and apartheid with initiatives such as its Programme to Combat Racism. Three Dutch Reformed Churches from South Africa withdrew over WCC stands on racism in the early 1960s. The Salvation Army and the Presbyterian Church of Ireland withdrew in the 1970s over WCC humanitarian funding for liberation movements in Southern Africa. For a detailed criticism of the WCC at the end of the Cold War, see the Freedom House book of the Dutch journalist J. A. Emerson Vermaat: "The Council's concern for Third World poverty, economic debt, hunger and racism, for example, is a valuable addition to the international attempts to aid millions of people. But to blame reflexively the West in general, and democratic capitalism in particular, for problems in the Third World is both unworthy of a worldwide church organization and unproductive toward resolving Third World ills."[32] Of course, the WCC is first and foremost an ecumenical union of 3,417 national churches in 120 countries, whose basis was redefined at New Delhi as "a fellowship of churches which confess the Lord Jesus Christ as God and Saviour according to the scriptures, and therefore seek to fulfill

---

[32] J. A. Emerson Vermaat, *The World Council of Churches and Politics* (New York: Freedom House, 1989), 102.

together their common calling to the glory of the one God, Father, Son, and Holy Spirit."[33]

Statistical data on the world's 386 million independents and the 26 million "marginal Christians" remains unreliable on two accounts. A majority of these believers come from the poor for whom accurate statistics do not constitute a priority. Most also belong to a myriad of small, independent churches whose size militates against keeping the detailed records that in larger movements would foster central planning. Pentecostals and African Independent Churches are the most globally significant sectors of this group. Pentecostalism dates back to Holiness preacher Charles Fox Parham's (1873–1929) revival in Topeka, Kansas, in 1901, and William Joseph Seymour's (1870–1922) preaching in Azusa, California, in 1906–09. The overwhelming majority of those 386 million Christians listed as independent reside in the United States, Latin America, and Africa. This chapter has already treated Latin American Pentecostalism.

Jenkins[34] describes a common pattern for the creation of independent African churches. An enthusiastic convert to one of the mainline mission churches gradually becomes estranged over the tension between native culture and church practices. S/he then receives a vision in which God calls the believer to preach the "real African meaning" of Christianity. The new church emphasizes visions and charismatic gifts. Independent churches, which have been generally leery of entering national political systems, still face political challenges in both Africa and Latin America. For example, "Apolitical or not, evangelical populations, once established, find themselves drawn into the patronage politics and polarizations of Latin America."[35]

In terms of global independent missionary impact, Karla Poewe mentions Americans Pat Robertson, Paul Crouch, the Bakkers, and Canadians George Hill, David Mainse, and Bernice Gerard.[36] These evangelists fostered the explosive international growth of charismatic Christianity by global televised messages, augmented by North American megachurch financial outreach and fellowship networks. The 1970s also witnessed popular and scholarly writing by charismatic Christians like those of Jimmy Carter's sister, Ruth Carter Stapleton (1897–1983). In August 2000, the Billy Graham organization brought together over ten thousand

---

[33] http://www.wcc-coe.org
[34] Jenkins, *Christendom*, 48.
[35] Martin, "Evangelical," 84.
[36] Poewe, *Global*, 2–4.

evangelical activists from 209 nations at Amsterdam 2000. This assemblage listened to a recuperating eighty-one-year-old Graham (by satellite from Rochester, Minnesota) and others such as the seventy-eight-year-old retiring founder of Campus Crusade for Christ, Bill Bright, pass on the wisdom of fifty years of evangelical expansion. The conference's ten-page statement emphasized that Jesus is the exclusive way to know God, but said little about relations with fellow Christians. Graham invited an observer from the WCC. Ghanan Greek Orthodox priest Kwame Labi expressed disappointment in the lack of sociopolitical discussion because he believed that matters of justice and poverty "belong to the very essence of the Gospel."[37] Graham and like-minded evangelists have neither called for a broader evangelical organization to compete with the WCC nor expressed a desire to join one. In Christianity, as well as Islam, overseas missionary financing has disproportionately supported conservative theologies in the postwar period.

Papal visits constitute the major Catholic communication events, but Catholic mission funding cannot keep pace with their Protestant brethren. The German church tax remains a most important financial source for both mainline Protestants and Catholics. The Catholic Church in the developed world also faces a crisis in priestly vocations. Ireland, a traditional source of missionary personnel, ordained fewer than ten priests nationwide in 2004. For twenty-first-century Catholic global politics, the most significant fact remains its newly majority southern population. On February 21, 2001, Pope John Paul II made cardinals of forty-four Catholic clergy from twenty-seven countries and five continents. The Pope thus enlarged to 135 the number of cardinal electors, those under age eighty eligible to vote for his successor. Although Italians maintained their position as the largest national group, the century-long process of diluting their presence continued, with 41 percent of those electors now coming from the developing world. One-fourth of the new cardinals came from Latin America versus three from the United States. One new Venezuelan cardinal, Ignacio Antonio Velasco Garcia, commented, "I think that the center of Catholicism – not the government of the church, which is still in Rome – but the real center of the Church is moving from Europe to Latin America. This may be why the pope named so many Latin American cardinals."[38] In October 2003 John Paul II appointed an additional thirty-one new cardinals, of whom only one was American. Nineteen were

---

[37] *San Jose Mercury News*, August 19, 2000.
[38] February 22, 2001.

residential archbishops from areas as diverse as Ghana, Guatemala, India, Vietnam, Sudan, and Nigeria.

World Catholicism thus links the West with the developing world, especially Latin America, Africa, and the Philippines, as Islam links its traditionally Arabic lands with Central, South, and Southeast Asia. Vatican Council II's *aggiornamento* [updating] constituted Catholicism's most significant change during the last five hundred years, reorienting Catholic thought from a classical approach to one based on historical consciousness and interaction with modern ideas. During the Cold War, the Catholic Church acted as "expressive leader" for the West as the United States acted as the "instrumental leader." From Pius XII to John Paul II, the papacy articulated a strong denunciation of atheistic Communism, even while seeking a modus vivendi with the Soviet bloc from the mid-1960s in the Vatican policy of *Ostpolitik*. The Polish John Paul II added a certain national diplomatic toughness, and in his three Cold War visits (1979, 1983, 1987) to Poland, inspired the "solidarity" of his countrymen in their resistance to Communist rule. While Reagan and John Paul cooperated on Eastern Europe, however, Vatican and American policy often differed over human rights in the developing world. In the post-Cold War period, the Catholic Church must balance the unchallenged military and economic power of the United States with ethical statements about the moral responsibilities of the rich nations. John Paul II continued Paul VI's emphasis on the Southern Hemisphere in Vatican formulations of international social justice, a point well made by J. Bryan Hehir in his 1990 *Foreign Policy* article.[39] Hehir details the movement from Vatican identification with the West under Pius XII to a position independent of both Washington and Moscow crafted during the pontificates of John XXIII, Paul VI, and John Paul II. The Vatican thus finds itself in some very lonely ethical positions globally, as in its early criticism of sanctions against Iraq.

U.S. President Clinton and the Pope, however, both focused their efforts on the Palestinian issue in the Millennium year. In March 2000, John Paul II made his first visit to the Holy Land. Israelis called for John Paul to apologize for Pius's silence during the Holocaust, whereas the Palestinians wanted the Pope to endorse explicitly the refugees' right to return to their homes in Israel. At Yad Vashem Holocaust Memorial, the Pope bowed his head before a granite slab symbolizing the graves of unidentified victims. "Silence," he said in a later speech, "because there are no words strong enough to deplore the terrible tragedy of the Shoah." The previous

[39] J. Bryan Hehir, "Papal Foreign Policy," *Foreign Policy* 78 (Spring 1990): 26–48.

day he had visited the Palestinian Dehaisheh refugee camp and called the conditions "degrading" and "barely tolerable." That event, his tenth meeting with Arafat, constituted a state visit in everything but name. In such a highly contentious environment John Paul made no diplomatic faux pas, so that the *New York Times* used the front-page headline, "A Pilgrimage Avoids Slips."[40] For example, both Israeli President Weizman and Arafat referred to Jerusalem as the eternal capital of their states, but the Pope refrained from commenting on either statement. Clinton brought together the principals that summer at Camp David, but the results disappointed both the president and the Pope.

Compared with Islam and evangelical Protestantism in the communication system, the Catholic Church suffers in the partially secularized West because of its believers' less total religious self-identification. Catholicism's comparative global advantage lies in the political system, its strong institutional presence simultaneously at international, national, and local levels. The Vatican, according to Cleary, takes its place "among the more important world actors,"[41] based on the number and quality of the nation states maintaining diplomatic relations with the Vatican and the usefulness of its global information network, especially in the rural developing world where even major nations face significant obstacles in obtaining any information at all. Development work in dangerous situations at the local level adds credibility to the Holy See. The United Nations and other international organizations constitute the Vatican's natural sphere of action. Over many years, the Catholic Church has developed a sophisticated social theory on global issues such as social justice, peace, and human rights. The Catholic principle of subsidiarity (political decisions should be made at the lowest effective level) lowers the level of political competence for many issues, thus fostering decentralized decision-making, but it also raises the level for those problems such as nuclear proliferation and global warming which can only be solved internationally. The more crucial the ethical issue, and the more chaotic the political situation, the more welcome are "extraordinary" interventions from unique transnational organizations such as the Holy See.

Popes exhibit different leadership styles toward the world and the Vatican bureaucracy, the bishops, and Catholics worldwide. Vatican specialist John Allen describes John Paul II's relationship with the curial

---

[40] March 25, 2000.
[41] Edward L. Cleary, "Vatican in World Politics: View from Europe," paper for APSA 1998 Annual Meeting, 5.

bureaucracy as "he felt that God had a logic for his election. It included addressing the Cold War split between the Soviet empire and the West, persuading Europe that it needs to 'breathe with both lungs,' East and West, reawakening the pastoral and evangelic dimensions of the papal office through travel, and pursuing a dialogue with the broader culture through his encyclicals and other writings. The price of pursuing these objectives was leaving much ordinary Church business in the hands of his aides."[42] When John Paul II died on the evening of April 2, there was a great outpouring of grief, affection, and media coverage from all over the globe. For example, the *New York Times* led with the papal story for over one week. Many national and religious leaders attended the funeral, praising him for religious integrity and diplomatic initiatives. When the cardinals met to choose a successor, they chose policy continuity and a short papacy, but a non-Italian European with a very different church-oriented background from his predecessor. The seventy-eight-year-old German Cardinal Joseph Ratzinger is a theologian who had spent the last twenty-three years as head of the Congregation for the Doctrine of the Faith. In that role he had disciplined theologians as diverse as the Swiss Hans Küng,[43] the Brazilian Leonard Boff, the American Charles Curran, and the Sri Lankan Tissa Balasuriya. Benedict XVI's first statement stressed the greatness of John Paul II, the need for theological dialogue, and pledged to pursue "the promising dialogue that my predecessors began with various civilizations."[44] He immediately sent a friendly message to the Chief Rabbi of Rome, and Jewish commentary was generally favorable. The cardinals all stressed his humility and warm, if shy, personality. Benedict XVI does

---

[42] John L. Allen Jr., *All the Pope's Men: The Inside Story of How the Vatican Really Works* (New York: Doubleday, 2004), 69. Allen, 95–140, lists the ten most important curial values as authority, *bella figura*, cosmopolitanism, loyalty, objectivity, populism, realism, rule of law, time, and tradition. Scholars of Chinese bureaucracy will recognize much in this book. Allen also shows the effects of the Vatican's location in Rome, Italy, and Europe. His source book for the choice of the next pope was *Conclave: The Inside Story of How the Vatican Really Works*, rev. and updated (New York: Doubleday Image, 2004).

[43] For the Küng side of this story, see Hans Küng, *My Struggle for Freedom: Memoirs* (Grand Rapids, MI: Eerdmans, 2002). There is a superb intellectual and cultural biography to be written (in German, of course) about Küng and Ratzinger, the most intelligent and pious boys from their small German-speaking villages who collaborated during the first parts of Vatican Council II, then went on to oppose each other vigorously after the social movements of 1968. Ratzinger's memoirs are *Milestones: Memoirs 1927–1977* (San Francisco: Ignatius Press, 1998). See also John L. Allen, Jr., *Pope Benedict XVI: A Biography of Joseph Ratzinger* (New York: Continuum, 2005) and a plethora of other books.

[44] April 21, 2005.

not have the charisma or the diplomatic experience of his predecessor, so he reappointed the Vatican Secretary of State Cardinal Angelo Sodano and the other heads of congregations, at least for the initial period.

The Church's most important institutional decision, of course, concerns papal succession, but the selection of local bishops can also have major religious-political effects in the nations involved. Government officials often attempt to influence the selection of bishops, as in the cases of the Salvadoran Romero, the Mexican Ruiz, and the Park government's failed request for a second conservative cardinal to balance the Korean progressive Cardinal Kim Sou Hwan. One of the key positions in the Roman Curia, then, is Prefect of the Congregation of Bishops, which recommends such appointments to the pope.

Religious orders such as the Franciscans and the Jesuits also link Rome to the local level since they combine centralized direction from Rome with strong national and local ties throughout the globe. Often these orders compete with the Curia and with local bishops over issues and works they perceive as part of their special vocations. Opus Dei and its institutions constitute a conservative counterweight to the Jesuits. John Paul II has supported Opus Dei with the incredibly speedy canonization of its founder, the Spanish priest Josemaria Escrivá de Balaguer (1902–75), in October 2002. The foundation and growth of national episcopal conferences like the Brazilian CNBB and the American NCCB constituted the major Catholic institutional change in the postwar period. These national conferences served as defenders of human rights and promoters of world peace during the Cold War, but John Paul and the Curia lessened their influence in the post–Cold War period. Church decentralization (the religious term is "collegiality") is not just an American but also a developing world issue. Cardinal Varkey Vithayathil of Kerala, India has called for a reform of canon law to strengthen these national bishops' conferences, which "hardly have any authority now," but "they should become powerful bodies."[45]

In summary, world Christianity reflects diversity and internal tension as does global Islam.[46] Like Islam, Christianity also offers some societal patterns as Christian traditions interact with the political and EMC systems. The Vatican and the WCC, the populations of which are predominantly in the southern hemisphere, have embraced both international social justice

[45] *Asian Focus*, November 21, 2003.
[46] For an African perspective, see Lamin Sanneh, *Whose Religion Is Christianity? The Gospel beyond the West* (Grand Rapids, MI: Eerdmans, 2003).

and religious dialogue. Independent Christianity offers a more charismatic and less institutionalized face, with North American evangelists devoting significant financial resources to preaching the gospel through the global communication system and to worldwide charity. South Korea has sent the second largest group of Christian missionaries after the United States. Christianity is no longer a merely Western phenomenon.

10

Religion and Politics for the Next Millennium

This chapter brings together conclusions from throughout the book to recommend future international political-religious policy. First, since no paradigm has ever offered the definitive understanding of even natural science, let alone global politics, what are the advantages and the limitations of the paradigm employed by this text? Second, the interaction between religion and politics constitutes the second plane of the paradigm. How do the three factors of the level of interaction, the nature of the religion, and the regional or national form of political-religious interaction help explain current international politics? Third, the book divided seven world religions into three types: religions of the book, religions of meditative experience, and religions of public life. How do these types influence each other religiously and politically, especially at the regional and global levels? Fourth, what are the most crucial international political alliances which could best serve world peace, justice, and order in the twenty-first century? What interfaith dialogues would be helpful for these alliances? Finally, "Is religion good or bad for politics?" If, "Both," the more specific question becomes, "Under what circumstances does mostly good result?"

THE NEW PARADIGM FOR CONTEMPORARY POLITICS: ADVANTAGES AND LIMITATIONS

Few foreign affairs pundits predicted the rise of democratic forces in Poland, Czechoslovakia, Hungary, and East Germany that led to the fall of the Berlin Wall. Academics more easily foresee relatively minor adjustments in the political and EMC systems. On the other hand, occasionally ideologues and policy makers predict major political changes, for example, Iraqis immediately embracing democracy in spring 2003, where none occur. In both the above Polish and Iraqi cases, analysts significantly underestimated the political and social impact of religious identities and institutions. They discounted the political repercussions of the Polish religious and social responses to John Paul II and Lech Walesa. They also failed to foresee the attachment of Iraqi Shiites to their religious leadership. That Iraqis would follow the secular exile Ahmed Chalabi was a U.S. Defense Department fantasy! Taking religion seriously offers a much broader spectrum of political possibilities. For both the greater good and the worse evil, humankind at times acts in ways that cannot be anticipated according to political and EMC rational calculation.

In contrast with the Westphalian and Cold War paradigms, this book's approach stresses rapid change and uncertainty in the global political and EMC systems. This paradigm also focuses on religion as an autonomous sphere of human activity, but not a global system. Islam, Buddhism, and Maoist Marxism do *not* constitute a global religious system any more than Arabic, Basque, and Chinese form a world linguistic system. The advantages and limitations of the new paradigm are as follows:

Advantages

Speed Through Technological Innovation. The first plane of the paradigm focuses on change, not continuity. The increasing speed of technological innovation means that no decision maker can call up even half of the political and EMC data needed for the five-year impact of any single policy decision. Even the most conscientious analyst must expect mistakes and negative fallout. The public must learn to tolerate such mistakes, provided the decision fits a long-term broad vision that inspires public trust. In such a rapidly changing social environment, however, public trust becomes scarce. People losing their cultural moorings opt more rapidly for the polarizing positions of rigid fundamentalism or ethical relativity. A political-religious idenity that combines both traditional and modern elements can maintain some social stability.

Uncertainty. The paradigm explicitedly states that it expects innovations in both technology and spirituality that can completely revamp the political situation. Imagine yourself as a Japanese defense analyst on July 14, 1945, the day before the Trinity nuclear test, or a Roman general in Syria at the time of the death of Mohammed. Expecting random innovations means that the decision maker will be constantly asking oneself about the possible sources of such innovations, and about the special local or national forms these innovations might take.

Relational Emphasis. The paradigm pays as much attention to the mutual influences among the political and each of the EMC systems as it does to the changes within those systems. This can prevent political leaders and analysts from being blindsided by EMC events. Chapter Seven, for example, cited the influence of Indian nationalism on the BJP's 1998 testing of the atomic bomb. Pakistan responded, to ensure Musharraf's hold on Pakistani politics. The unanimous global response threatened economic harm to both countries.

Globalization Emphasis. This paradigm reflects increasing global integration by focusing on the political and EMC systems. These four *are* global systems. Any major national political or EMC event affects the entire globe. For example, the Internet immediately ties all sorts of groups together, from immigrants to terrorists to believers. In such complicated environments, often only one political solution exists, which requires at least the simultaneous acquiescence of many political, religious, and EMC actors. The most general form of international affairs thus approximates the Palestinian question with the most probable outcome being a partial solution or more chaos. However, even partial solutions of such political difficulties will benefit many other actors in their solutions to other political issues. If the religious concepts of the Muslim *umma* and the Christian Communion of Saints did not exist, current political analysts would have to invent them!

Historical Content Through Self-Identity. The first advantage listed above pointed to the inherent limitation of information for any decision. What will influence every decision, however, is the self-identity of the decision-maker and his/her constituency. It is through this identity, for example, Serbian Orthodox, that hundreds of years of Serb battles with Croatian Catholics and Muslim Ottomans become relevant to contemporary politics. However, unlike Huntington's thesis, this paradigm expects that personal and social identities will constantly evolve, thus offering both hope and new challenges. "The West" could disintegrate if Americans and Europeans no longer viewed themselves as united by common values.[1]

---

[1] Ronald Inglehart has provided a mapping of the World Values Survey along the two axes of traditional to secular-rational values, and from survival to self-expression values. Catholic Europe sits right in the middle. The chart, from Ronald Inglehart et al., *Modernization,*

Continuity, Not Quick Fix. Attention to these personal and social identities in the second part of the paradigm will save decision makers and negotiators from "quick fix" decisions that look good in "rational" political-military-economic terms, but ignore the human, communication, and historical elements of the issues. Such accelerated decisions usually solve the immediate problem by making the long-term situation worse, or at least extremely troublesome, as in the CIA arming of the *mujahidin* against the Soviets in the Afghan War.

Religion Focuses on All Four Systems. Contemporary analysis of religion and politics that does not give equal weight to the relationship of religion to the EMC systems remains fatally flawed. In addition to obvious issues of survival in the military system, religious leaders and believers often care more about economic and communication issues than political ones. Increasing economic stratification and "obscene" global poverty offend the deepest held communal beliefs of all major religious traditions. The current global communication system in many ways also threatens the survival of religion. As such, this paradigm calls into question the current autonomies of the global EMC systems according to the individualistic mantra: "free market, free arms sales, free broadcasting."

Limitations

Categories, Not Answers. Any leader who counts on the definitiveness of a paradigm will make major mistakes. This paradigm offers categories for analysis, not answers to specific policy questions. If the categories are useful, better (not "correct") political answers will be easier, but never simple. Better solutions will always require prudent analysts with expertise in the relevant cultural and technological areas.

Policy, Not Leadership. Even when the leader chooses a better policy decision, the paradigm offers no guarantee that it will be carried out effectively. The leader can fail to organize well and/or fail to inspire others to support the decision. U.S. leaders failed in both ways during the initial months of the Iraq reconstruction.

Cultural Change and Democracy (Cambridge: Cambridge University Press, 2005), can be found in Timothy Garton Ash, *Free World: America, Europe, and the Surprising Future of the West* (New York: Random House, 2004), 237.

Definitions and Methodology. This paradigm relies on a host of academic studies that use many different definitions and approaches to both "religion" and "politics." For example, in most survey research the religion is self-described by the interviewee. The definitions necessary for the breadth of the paradigm would be exceedingly difficult to operationalize in some of these studies. This book takes pains not to falsify the results of such research, but differences in definitions reflect the complicated nature of human consciousness with regard to religious belief, belonging, and degree of attachment to religious organizations. The reader's final question should be: Does the paradigm add intelligibility in Chapters 5–10?

Danger from "Political Monks." The prominence of religion in this paradigm could bring out the worst in religious leadership. The temptation to use religion for political and EMC advantage over other religions, or even over rival leaders in the same religion, has a long and inglorious history.

Danger from "Pious Politicians." The prominence of religion in the paradigm could also bring out the worst in political leadership. The politician's temptation to play the religious card is ever present, as is the temptation to posture one's pious demeanor to attract political support from fellow believers. However, the many similarities in the distinct religious and political leadership positions should give these leaders some empathy and tolerance for each other. Political and religious leaders have autonomous vocations, but, in the twenty-first century, their successes and failures have become inextricably linked.

RELIGION IN INDIVIDUAL, LOCAL, NATIONAL, REGIONAL, AND INTERNATIONAL POLITICS

The paradigm's second plane consists of various geographic sets of political-religious identities responding to the rapidly evolving global political and EMC systems of the first plane. Political-religious identities depend generally on three factors: the level of interaction, from local to global; the nature of the religious tradition, from Christianity to Buddhism; and the regional or national form of political-religious interaction, from secular Japan to the Islamist Taliban. Chapter 3 ended with a brief analysis of the combined impact of the first two factors, the level of interaction and the nature of the religious tradition. Chapter 4 then differentiated among and within the seven religious traditions. Finally, Chapters 5–9 discussed the regional and national forms of political-religious interaction. This section will discuss the individual, local, national, regional, and global levels, adding considerations from the nature of the religion and the national and regional forms.

Individual. Studies of the influence of religion on politics should begin by focusing on the individual since it is at this personal level that the unpredictable Other calls the believer, even if the call occurs in an institutional context. For example, Mahatma Gandhi's conversion from British-trained lawyer dandy to spiritual leader took place as he interacted with the poor in South African and Indian cities and villages. Focusing on personal conversion also emphasizes the crucial political influence of some religious individuals. There is no escaping the harmful political impacts of the assassinations of Romero, Gandhi, and Rabin by right-wing fanatics from their own religions. In fact, the failure of the Oslo Process and the success of the Iranian Revolution remain unintelligible without weighing the absence of Rabin in the former and the presence of Khomeini in the latter.

Berkeley[2] demonstrates how local leaders such as Mayor Jean-Paul Akayesu consciously played the ethnic card in the Rwanda genocide that produced over five hundred thousand deaths. Tribal identity in politics, abetted by the communication system's virulently anti-Tutsi Radio-Télévision Libre Mille Collines, triumphed over the common Catholic religious identity, though not completely. Some Hutu Catholics did risk death to save their Tutsi fellow believers. An estimated three hundred priests died, either because they were Tutsi or because they tried to save Tutsi. Twice before, in 1959 and 1963, the Rwandan churches had become recognized sanctuaries during ethnic violence, but not in 1994. Hutu Archbishop Vincent Nsengiyumva's close identification with the government contributed to the atrocities. He had headed the Rwandan church for 21 years, and for most of his tenure, served on the central committee of the ruling Hutu political party. Tutsi rebels assassinated him in 1994.

Some Hutu priests and nuns joined the rampaging militia, or failed to help Tutsi Catholics. Author Christian Terras remarked, "As many

---

[2] Bill Berkeley, *The Graves Are Not Yet Full: Tribe and Power in the Heart of Africa* (New York: Basic Books, 2002), 245–84.

as 100 pastors, priests and nuns played an active role, siding with the Hutu militias."[3] In the end, states Haitian-American U.N. prosecutor Pierre-Richard Prosper, such horrendous genocide occurs at the end of a long national descent into moral darkness, and requires three types of people: "the ideologues *and* the opportunists *and* the thugs. Otherwise, it just won't happen."[4] Mayor Akayesu acted as the rationally calculating opportunist who responded to the call of national ideologues by organizing his village's thugs to slaughter the Tutsis. The centralized efficiency of this process throughout Rwanda belies the claim that such genocide results inevitably from tribal irrationality in "failed states." Berkeley and Gopin agree that the time to stop the genocide came during the previous hundred-year descent into modern tribalism and moral civil depravity.

Local. All religions in all political-religious forms play a significant cultural and political role by fostering the basic identity of the individual within the cohesion of local society, as expressed in the traditional saying "the religion of the village is the life of the village." It is easy to grasp the local political significance of spirituality, ritual, scripture and prophecy, cultural worldview, and morality in traditional society. Women remain disproportionately significant in local religion, as in Chapter 9's description of Latin American women choosing from among Catholic Liberation Theology, Pentecostal, and Afro-Brazilian religions. At the local level the impact of various religious traditions exhibits the most similarity, whether the local religious leadership consists of a mullah, a minister, a monk, or a mandarin. Chapter 6 described how local temple cults have recently surged in both Taiwan and the Chinese Mainland despite different political systems.

The local level also introduces the distinction between those religious-political phenomena which result principally from hierarchical action and those which well up from the grass roots. Susanne Rudolph and James Piscatori[5] organize their entire book on this distinction. The four cases of globalizing Catholicism, world religions and national states in East Asia, Catholic philanthropy in Central and Eastern Europe, and the religious aspects of Saudi foreign policy illustrate the former dynamic. Trans-state Islam and security, Muslim missionaries in African states, Latin American

---

[3] May 12, 2002.
[4] Berkeley, *Graves*, 262.
[5] Susanne Rudolph and James Piscatori, eds., *Transnational Religion and Fading States* (Boulder, CO: Westview, 1997).

Liberation Theology, and French Catholic transnationalism document the latter. All eight cases involve changes at all levels from the local to the international, but the causality in each case flows primarily either from the top down or from the bottom up. Long term local religious success demands both local initiative and higher-level sponsorship.

National. Chapter 2 proposed four general categories of the relationship of religion and politics at the national level: (1) dominant religions have traditionally provided a "sacred canopy" legitimizing state power; (2) governmental and religious organizations can battle for institutional and expressive power within the national society; (3) various religions can compete for influence within the nation; and (4) religious groups can seek to control the national culture or to defend their group from a threatening national or global culture. Chapters 5–9 offered many cases of all four types, but especially the second type of conflict between political and religious organizations. Although European states and the church no longer struggle over the appointment of bishops, the contemporary Chinese state does seek to penetrate, regulate, and control all religious organizations. The principal post–World War II global cases of church-state conflict have focused on human rights. Anglican Bishop Tutu led the criticism of the South African government and Cardinals Sin, Silva, and Lorscheider led the attacks on the Marcos, Pinochet, and the Brazilian National Security State, respectively. The absence of such a primary ethical broker or an agreed upon process to come to national ethical consensus signals fragmentation of the entire nation or region, as in Africa's "First World War."

Regional. In comparison with other regions, the West tends to separate religious and political institutions, which provides a semisecular public square. Both the secular state and the religious family have strong interests in education, so that issue constitutes one good, but not infallible, indicator of the degree of secularity in a Western society. Asia does not represent a single regional form. Rather, China, Japan, Korea, and India present four separate national political-religious forms. China maintains the institutional arrangements of Confucian Marxism absent the belief. Japan constitutes the world's most secular society. South Korea blends a neo-Confucian societal form with Christian and Buddhist belief. India witnesses the struggle to define the political-religious future of Hinduism among the spiritual disciples of Gandhi, the secular disciples of Nehru, and the BJP. In the Islamic world, the two most crucial divisions exist between Sunni and Shiite, and between Arab and non-Arab. Latin America combines the traditional Catholic societal forms of the Iberian Peninsula with indigenous, African, and Pentecostal traditions. Each nation and each locality modifies these broad regional indicators.

Global. At the international level, the four primary international political-religious issues derive from the EMC and political systems, respectively: (1) social justice in the economic system; (2) peace in the military system; (3) religious and cultural identity and values in the communication system; and (4) democratic human rights in the political system, including the right to religious belief and activity. Because of the interaction of the four systems, progress on one of these four issues fosters progress on the others, for example, the interaction between democracy and economic equality. The main theme of the U.N. *Human Development Report 2002* was the necessity of democratization for human development. Nobel Prize-winner Aung San Suu Kyi stated that "[g]overnance for human development must be democratic in substance and in form."[6] Chapter One cited the World Bank's 2003 political-economic stance that only with a broad distribution of assets could a nation construct unbiased and effective coordinating institutions.

Russett and O'Neal have demonstrated statistically that states are much more likely to live at peace with each other if they are both democracies, if they practice economic interdependence, and, with a smaller impact, if they share membership in a dense network of International Governmental Organizations.[7] IGOs provide a framework conducive to lobbying by religious and secular NGOs. Most religious NGOs are multi-issue organizations deeply immersed in local cultures. They thus have an advantage in making prudential judgments where values compete, for example, peace versus justice and human rights in Sierra Leone, where the Muslim-Christian Inter-Religious Council immediately demanded the restoration of democracy. This is especially true when a dominant religion, or religious coalition, serves as the nation's primary ethical broker. From 1990 to 2000, total international NGOs grew from 31,246 to 37,281 (up 19.3 percent), and global religious NGOs grew from 1,407 to 1,869 (up 32.8 percent).[8]

[6] Cited in United Nations Development Program, *Human Development Report 2002* (Oxford: Oxford University Press, 2002), 52.

[7] Bruce Russett and John R. Oneal, *Triangulating Peace: Democracy, Interdependence, and International Organizations* (New York: Norton, 2001).

[8] UNDP, *Human Development Report 2002*, 103.

GLOBALIZATION AND RELIGIOUS RESTRUCTURING

The contemporary globalization of economics and communication and the enhanced political role of religion have fostered the partial restructuring of all three types of religion. Accelerated globalization and immigration mean that all religions tend to learn from each other and to develop across the entire spectrum of the seven types of religious expression, from spirituality to organization. This dynamic has fostered a renewed emphasis on spirituality in religions of the book and a new emphasis on ethics and moral activity in religions of meditative experience. Such restructuring does not eliminate the specific characteristics of the original tradition, however, because even when a religion copies directly from another it does so in its own unique way.

Ecclesiastical organization and media coverage, both positive and negative, have become more important as global communication and immigration increase. Within the religions themselves, the need for new multilayered personal identities adds significance to both scriptural interpretation, to ground these identities in the modern world, and to ritual practice, to experience those identities. The speed of technological innovation also constantly forces religious leaders to adjust their worldviews, doctrines, and moral stances, even if their response consists merely in reaffirming previous positions. That reaffirmation itself constitutes a new position because the social and religious contexts have changed.

Religions of the book most naturally step into political and societal roles, but recently religious leaders from Sufi masters to Jewish rabbis, from Evangelical ministers to Catholic monks have challenged believers to reexamine such roles lest adherents lose their religious integrity in "the false idolatry" of external projects. Religions of meditative experience have developed more concrete systems of social ethics and ecclesiastical organization, for example, Buddhist social ethics and Hindu political and social organizations, so that these religions seem to be converging structurally with the religions of the book. The religions of public life maintain their hold on the cultural and political leadership of China and Vietnam, but the respective populations have generally lost contact with both Marxist and Confucian spiritualities. It is difficult to see what organizational apparatus possesses the ideological legitimacy to support spiritual renewal, but Confucian culture traditionally has looked to scholars for moral leadership. The current expansion of world religions and native sects in China and Vietnam highlights the spiritual vacuum in neo-Confucian Marxism.

Both the contemporary restructuring of Buddhism and the Chinese state's traditional attempt to assert political-religious control are exemplified in the twentieth-century relationships of Tibetan Buddhism with the Chinese state. The Dalai Lama's religious-political leadership of Tibetans also illustrates both the great significance of a single individual and political-religious interaction at and among all geographic levels, from the very local to the global. Since fleeing Tibet in 1959, the Dalai Lama has campaigned from Dharamsala, India for increased political autonomy for the Tibetan population. Han Chinese occupy most of Tibet's high political positions, and defend their hegemony in terms of socioeconomic development, for example, constructing modern roads and hospitals. When President Clinton visited Beijing in June 1998, he and Chinese president Jiang Zemin debated Tibet and other issues in a public forum broadcast live to the entire country, providing the most candid exchange on Tibet ever heard by a Chinese mass audience.[9] The Dalai Lama, as a major religious figure in the global communication system, addresses social issues that he never would have encountered had he stayed in Tibet. Since 1959 he has remained outside the control of Beijing.

Up to January 2000, however, the PRC had physical control of the second (Pachen Lama) and the third (Karmapa) most important Tibetan religious personages, traditionally rival leaders to the Dalai Lama of the Yellow Hat sect. The Karmapa's spectacular flight to India thus became an unmitigated foreign policy disaster for China.[10] On the night of December 28, 1999, the fourteen-year-old boy pretended to begin an eight-day solitary retreat, but in reality he sneaked out of Tibet's Tsurphu monastery. After a dangerous journey of eight days by SUV, horse, foot, train, and taxi, he arrived at the Dalai Lama's residence in Dharamsala. The Karmapa's warm reception by the Dalai Lama, plus the consensus decision to educate him in all four Buddhist traditions, points to the possibilities of less internal tension among Tibetan Buddhist sects and of a single national leader from the less important Red Hat sect, at least during the next childhood of the reincarnated Dalai Lama. Such religious, political, and communication changes would never have occurred without globalization.

Religious restructuring helps different religions to understand each other, but it does not signify the development of a global religious system. Nor, contrary to the ambitious visions of some religious leaders, is

---

[9] June 29, 1998.
[10] Isabel Hilton, "Flight of the Lama," *New York Times Magazine*, March 12, 2000.

there likely to be one in the near future. Ever since the World Parliament of Religions at the 1893 Columbian Exposition in Chicago, there have been various global public conferences of religious leaders to advocate world peace. Such gatherings, however, face multiple political and religious challenges, from differences over the nature of religion itself to the guest list. Just as some religious leaders find the very concept of a "parliament" of religions amusing, others state that their traditions vigorously object to any kind of religious systemization. However, political leaders such as ex-U.N. Ambassador John Danforth have called for a new religious forum to help solve world conflicts.[11]

Hundreds of religious leaders met at the United Nations in September 2000 to discuss their "special responsibility for the well-being of the human family and peace on earth."[12] Although this four-day Millennium World Peace Summit did not qualify as an official meeting of the United Nations, Secretary General Kofi Annan opened the gathering that held its first two days in the General Assembly chamber and its final two days in a hotel across the street. China objected to the Dalai Lama's coming to the United Nations, so the organizers invited him for the last two days only, drawing a letter of rebuke from Desmond Tutu. Nonprofit donors, including Ted Turner's U.N. Foundation and the Better World Fund, paid the bill. Bawa Jain, a veteran organizer of interfaith meetings, brought together representatives of, as listed in the final declaration, Bahá'í, Buddhism, Christianity, Confucianism, Hinduism, Indigenous Peoples, Islam, Jainism, Judaism, Shinto, Sikhism, Taoism, and Zoroastrianism.

In January 2001 Pope John Paul II invited 250 religious leaders to Assisi, the birthplace of St. Francis, the Catholic patron of peace honored by many religious traditions. Representatives of twelve world religions, led by the Orthodox Patriarch of Constantinople, pledged themselves to reject violence. In addition to such interfaith meetings, individual prelates such as the Episcopal Bishop of California William E. Swing have founded projects such as his United Religions Initiative. Swing quoted Swiss Catholic theologian Hans Küng "that there would never be peace among nations without peace among religions, and there would be no peace among religions without dialogue."[13]

---

[11] September 13, 2004.
[12] September 5, 2000.
[13] September 23, 2000.

Küng, never the Vatican's favorite theologian, began his world initiative with a 1991 book *Global Responsibility: In Search of a New World Ethic*, which combined the above two phrases with a third: "No Survival without a World Ethic."[14] The World Parliament of Religions endorsed Küng's text in 1993. In 1996–97, Küng and his collaborators wrote, and the InterAction Council proposed "A Universal Declaration of Human Responsibilities" to parallel the U.N. Declaration of Human Rights. The InterAction Council (IAC) is composed of ex-chiefs of state, at that time twenty-six including Schmidt (Germany), Fraser (Australia), Arias Sanchez (Costa Rica), Giscard d'Estaing (France), de la Madrid (Mexico), Carter (United States), Miyazawa (Japan), Peres (Israel), and Trudeau (Canada).[15] The IAC document generated little excitement at the United Nations, however, and received criticism from some human rights activists who feared it would be used by governments to stall progress on human rights. In contrast to the Enlightenment's exclusive emphasis on rights, the IAC framers responded that global religious thought has usually also stressed the responsibilities of believers toward fellow believers and toward society at large.

GLOBAL RELIGIOUS DIALOGUE AND
POLITICAL-RELIGIOUS ALLIANCES

Although the twentieth century witnessed many horrible events, from the Holocaust to the Cambodian Killing Fields, it also experienced four major global successes: the allied victory in World War II, the postwar rapprochement of France and Germany leading to the European Union, the end of Western colonialism, and the peaceful end of the Cold War. "The Greatest Generation's" defeat of Germany and Japan took place in the global military system, with the Allies employing the Judeo-Christian tradition and liberal democracy as alliance links and ideological motivators. The second success, European unification, used all four systems and resulted in the closer unity of reconciliation. Christian Democracy offered a motivating vision and Christianity advocated the forgiveness of past wrongs. The end of colonialism represented the political victory of Enlightenment

---

[14] Hans Kung, *Global Responsibility: In Search of a New World Ethic* (New York: Crossroad Publishing, 1991).

[15] Other similar organizations include the Global Leadership Foundation, Collegium International, the Council of Women World Leaders, and the Club of Madrid. Some leaders belong to multiple organizations, with Mary Robinson a member of four.

principles of equality and democracy among peoples and nations world-wide, with Gandhi's use of *satyagraha* in India as the most salient religious contribution. Political independence, however, did not do away with exploitation in the very unequal EMC systems. The peaceful conclusion to the Cold War also remains unfinished socioeconomically in the liberated nations, but humankind has again escaped Armageddon. Religion contributed to the unity of the Western alliance, counseled moderation in military action, and withheld political legitimacy from Communist states.

What are the most important contemporary global political links for world progress on social justice, peace, personal identity and values, and human rights? This book emphasizes the strengthening of two major international relationships: Europe with the United States, and the West with the non-West. Both solidifying the Western alliance and expanding it further, from Los Angeles to Brussels to Istanbul and Vladivostok, would provide the world with a center of global stability and socioeconomic progress that could positively affect all other parts of the world. The future E.U. admission of Bulgaria, Romania, Russia, Belarus, the Ukraine, and Turkey would provide Orthodox and Muslim links to the rest of the world.

In fostering the Atlantic Alliance, and in moving the West to its fullest expanse, interfaith dialogue among the religions of the book could play an indispensable role in creating a common societal identity and in fostering a common willingness to sacrifice for broader goals. The fully expanded West would have to be built ideologically on the common vision of the religions of the book within liberal democracy and a mixed economy. At each step, the European political, economic, military, and communication systems must define at least a quasi-religious identity that inspires the people to support the commonalities of the larger unity over national and/or local self-interest. In May 2001 John Paul II signaled this when he visited Athens to apologize for Catholic wrongs against the Orthodox and then went on to Damascus to become the first pope to enter a mosque. The West together must articulate a broader vision of its responsibility toward the international common good, based on the ethical traditions of the religions of the book and Enlightenment rights. The alternative would be an international system that has returned to the great power rivalry model with the United States, the European Union, China, Japan, India, Brazil, and other nations as major actors, all pursuing their own interests and swapping allies indiscriminately.

In addition to the U.S.-European relationship, the second globally significant link brings together the West with the rest of the globe. In this case, Islam and Christianity play indispensable roles, either in facilitating the North-South connection or, if that mediation fails, in replacing the Soviet bloc as the other international pole resisting American or Western dominance. In 2000, Christianity and Islam represented 33 and 19.6 percent, respectively, of the world's population. Given current demographic rates, those percentages will be 33.4 and 22.8 percent in 2025 and 34.3 and 25 percent in 2050. The percentage of the global population belonging to one of these two religious traditions thus will rise from roughly 50 percent to roughly 60 percent in the next half century. Both religions will be heavily weighted in the Southern Hemisphere. In 2025, even Christianity will have only one of its six largest national populations in the economically most advanced countries, the United States. The other five will be Brazil, Mexico, the Philippines, Nigeria, and the D.R. Congo. To add political significance, the following countries with large populations will be divided between Muslims and Christians: (A) mainly Muslim: Indonesia, Egypt, Sudan; (B) mainly Christian: the Philippines, D.R. Congo, Germany, Uganda; and (C) more evenly divided: Nigeria, Ethiopia, Tanzania.[16]

If the current two most important political links are between Europe and the United States, and between the West and the non-West, what religious dialogues could support those links? Islam and Christianity play pivotal roles. Chapter 8 concluded that: (1) it is unlikely that any Muslim state will establish other than regional hegemony over fellow Islamic states; and (2) any state that does will have to solve the conundrum of how to embrace Islam and modernity simultaneously. The same chapter emphasized the impact of the communication system and offered a list of possible national and international sources of global Islamic leadership: restoring the caliphate and ulama influence, specific nation states, Islamic or Arab political organizations, activist intellectuals, and terrorist groups. The individual spectrum ranges from Indonesian ex-president Abdurrahman Wahid to Saudi terrorist Osama bin Laden. The only future absolutes about Islamic politics are its uncertainty, the crucial significance of the communication system in its future, and its orientation toward the southern hemisphere and developing countries.

Wahid, the first democratically chosen president of Islam's most populous state, defended the separation of church and state in Indonesia and pursued Liberation Theology dialogues with Latin American Catholic

---

[16] Philip Jenkins, *The Next Christendom: The Coming of Global Christianity* (New York: Oxford, 2002), 167.

prelates such as the late Oscar Câmara in Brazil. Muslims and Christians can coalesce around issues of religious toleration and global social justice. For example, Cardinal Julius Darmaatmadja of Jakarta praised the anti-corruption campaign launched by the Muslim organizations Nahdlatul Ulama and the Muhammadiyah, "We [Catholics] must join and support their anti-corruption movement and make it a joint movement of brotherhood to build the nation."[17] The Indonesian Catholic bishops also issued a pastoral letter for the 2004 national elections encouraging Catholics to vote for candidates who would narrow the country's social inequality. Other cardinals with expertise and experience in Islamic-Christian dialogue are Francis Arinze of Nigeria, Carlo Martini of Italy, Anthony Okogie of Nigeria, Bernard Panafieu of France, Polycarp Pengo of Dar-es-Salaam, and Gabriel Zubeir Wako of Khartoum.[18] In August 2003 the Bishops-Ulama Conference of the Philippines sponsored the Asian Gathering of Muslim Ulama and Catholic Bishops, which met in Pasay City. More than one hundred Catholic, Protestant, and Muslim participants came from Bangladesh, Hong Kong, Japan, India, Indonesia, Libya, Malaysia, Myanmar, the Philippines, Singapore, Sri Lanka, Taiwan, Thailand and Uzbekistan. The final statement affirmed that "our faiths, Islam and Christianity, are religions of peace which worship the One Merciful and Almighty God."[19]

The death of Pope John Paul II brought an outpouring of grief from Islamic religious and political leaders. King Abdullah II of Jordan praised "tangible contributions and positive stands towards the legitimate Arab cause"[20] and the fact that his values often coincided with Islamic values. Egypt's Hosni Mubarak declared three days of mourning. Jordan and the Arab League lowered their flags to half staff. Most Arab governments sent expressions of condolence. Al-Jazeera and Al-Arabiya covered the vigil for the dying Pope and his funeral, providing talk shows and documentaries about his global contributions, especially on Middle East issues. After the election of Benedict XVI, some Muslim commentators worried about Ratzinger's prior emphasis on the rechristianization of Europe and his opposition to including Turkey in the "cultural continent" of Europe. However, analysts such as the Jordanian political scientist Muhammad al-Momany stated that they didn't "expect a radical turn in the church."[21] On the first day following his installation as Pope, Benedict XVI thanked

---

[17] *Asian Focus*, November 21, 2003.
[18] For the backgrounds of the current cardinals, see Allen, *Conclave*.
[19] *Asian Focus*, August 29, 2003 included the full text.
[20] April 4, 2005.
[21] April 21, 2005.

Muslims for their presence at the ceremony and called for a "growth of dialogue between Muslims and Christians."[22]

Chapter Nine summarized the current political-religious position of Christianity as its population and leadership becomes more and more oriented to the developing world. Since World War II, the mainline WCC has promoted national liberation and social justice issues, often under religious leadership from the developing world. The evangelical, Pentecostal, and independent Christian churches have expanded rapidly in Latin America and Africa. In the 1960s, the Catholic Church combined the religious *aggiornamento* of Vatican Council II with a global political position more independent of the West. This new position became diplomatically significant for mediating between the East and the West during the Cold War, and for supporting developing nations in the global economic system. The crucial deficit in current global Christian dialogue, however, lies in the paucity of contacts between mainline Protestants and Catholics on the one hand and evangelical Protestants on the other, especially Pentecostals in Latin America and independent churches in Africa.[23]

As relations among Orthodox, Catholics, and Protestants remain strained in Russia and the Ukraine, the tension between evangelical Protestant missionaries and Muslims also continues. This was evidenced when the Taliban arrested Western Christian aid workers in Afghanistan and in the November 2002 murder of American missionary nurse Bonnie Penner Witherall in Lebanon. The local acting archbishop of the Roman Catholic diocese, Bishop George Kwaiter, criticized what he termed the Protestant mission's emphasis on conversion in such a hostile and fragmented political environment. The new media complicates the situation even further. The evangelical Web site, hoping to draw financial support, reported, "Dramatic conversions are being reported. And nearly 600 women have received prenatal care and heard the good news of compassionate Healer, Jesus Christ."[24] Evangelical Protestants and Muslims, however, hold the most strongly negative opinions on the impact of the global culture industries on religious life, at least setting up the common interest of protecting all believers from the "corrupting and secularizing" influence of the unregulated global communication system.[25]

---

[22] April 26, 2005.

[23] In November 2004, twenty-three churches formed Christian Churches Together in the USA, made up of Catholics, Orthodox, and evangelical and mainline Protestant denominations.

[24] November 25, 2002.

[25] See Canadian Liberal Muslim Irshad Manji's comments on the differences between North Americans who take religion seriously and Europeans who do not. November 18, 2004.

The most personally demanding of the significant religious dialogues occurs among Christianity, Judaism, and Islam. The breakdown of the Oslo Process exacerbated that difficulty. For example, Rome's Catholic Sant'Egidio Community convened a meeting of Muslim and Christian religious intellectuals in October 2001, one year into the second *intifada*. The Muslim scholars all represented moderate Islam, but the political and military actions of "arrogant Zionists" became a principal theme almost immediately. Yusuf al-Qaradawi, director of the Sunna Research Conference in Qatar, stated, "We go to sleep at night and get up in the morning in a Palestine transformed into a continuous funeral. We refuse terrorism but don't consider it terrorism to defend one's own home." All could agree with Syrian Orthodox speaker Mar Gregorios Iohanna Ibrahim, however, that "[t]here is no one civilization superior to the other, because every civilization has its particular character."[26] The Sant'Egidio community has a simultaneous long history of dialogue with both Islam and Judaism. Two weeks later, it commemorated the Roman Jews killed by the Nazis during World War II.[27]

Dialogue between Islam and Judaism presents significant advantages and significant challenges. In form, rabbinic Judaism and Islam remain the closest of major religions with their common emphasis on the interpretation of God's law, the *halakhah* and the *shari'a*. Both traditions maintain a strong sense of the Oneness of God, and there is considerable overlap in their recognized prophets. However, sometimes the very closeness of religious form complicates dialogue since the same types of claims are at stake. Gopin uses Judaism and Islam as paradigms for what is missing from religious approaches to war and peace. He advocates "that in order to truly understand war and peace in these religious traditions and, most important, to understand this murky space in between war and peace where peoples and civilizations really make the fateful decision to humanize or dehumanize the Other, it is vital to learn the broad range of interpersonal and communal ethical ideals that have served as the cohesive force of sustainable communities since their beginnings."[28]

---

[26] October 5, 2001.

[27] For the controversial issue of Pope Pius XII in Jewish-Catholic relations, see Pierre Blet, S.J., *Pius XII and the Second World War: According to the Archives of the Vatican* (Mahwah, NJ: Paulist Press, 1999); James Carroll, *Constantine's Sword: The Church and the Jews* (Boston: Houghton Mifflin, 2001); and John Cornwell, *Hitler's Pope: The Secret History of Pius XII* (New York: Viking, 1999).

[28] Marc Gopin, *Between Eden and Armageddon: The Future of World Religions, Violence, and Peacemaking* (Oxford: Oxford University Press, 2000), 84–85.

In a contrasting interfaith dialogue embodying very different forms of religion, the Muslim activist intellectual and Malaysian deputy prime minister (1993–98) Anwar Ibrahim sponsored and keynoted a seminar on "Islam and Confucianism" at Kuala Lumpur in 1995. Ibrahim often called for a new consensus of Muslim-Confucian "Asian values" that would foster Asia's dialogue with the West.

The five politically most significant religious dialogues for global politics are, in order of importance: first, among the religions of the book, focused on the developing world and its relationship to the developed world; second and third, multireligious dialogues centered geographically and culturally on China and on the Indian subcontinent;[29] and fourth and fifth, multireligious North American and European dialogues mediating relationships between the religious traditions long held in these regions with those of the new immigrants. Success or failure in each of the dialogues influences the outcomes of the other four. On the geographic and religious boundary of China and India stands Tibetan Buddhism. Thomas Merton provides an excellent example of monastic dialogue between Tibetan Buddhism and Christianity in his 1968 visits to the Dalai Lama and Chatral Rimpoche.[30]

This section's emphasis on future Christian-Muslim cooperation might seem strange to most political analysts. After all, this book has documented the long historical enmity between believers in these two global missionary religions. However, Muslims and Christians do share a common concern about global inequality and, at least among Muslims and Catholics, an anti-Westphalian political tradition. In the last fifty years, both religions have suffered from United States support for autocratic regimes. It is no accident that the first major postwar CIA coups overthrew democratic regimes in Shiite Iran (1953) and Catholic Guatemala (1954). The subsequent religious suffering under U.S. autocratic clients in the Middle East, Latin America, and Africa has been horrendous.

Topics for Muslim-Christian dialogue can start with social theory and a global ethic and then gradually include more religious themes such as the relationships of global humanity to the *umma* and the Communion of Saints, the stages of religious sanctity, fasting and pilgrimages, the discernment of God's will in concrete situations, and monastic and Sufi practice.

---

[29] See Francis X. Clooney, S.J., *Hindu God, Christian God: How Reason Helps Break Down the Boundaries between Religions* (New York: Oxford, 2001).
[30] *The Asian Journal of Thomas Merton* (New York: New Directions, 1973): 100–25, 142–45.

The last topics to discuss, in this author's judgment, would be the controversial historical periods that involved warfare. There is enough killing, mayhem, and blame for all traditions, and these topics, such as the history of the Reformation for Catholics and Protestants, require partners who have already established trust to be successful. In the dialogues within a single religious tradition like Christianity, the theologian Andre Gounelle[31] has recommended focusing not on conflicting doctrines, nor on the contrasting ecclesiastical structures, but on the religions as opposed, but complementary attitudes. This strategy works best within single religious traditions, as in theologian Paul Tillich's "the Protestant principle" and "Catholic substance," or within Islam between Sunnis and Sufis, but not between Christianity and Islam. One encouraging example within Christianity has been the International Mennonite-Catholic dialogue on peace and conflict resolution.[32]

During the next fifty years, then, relations between Christians and Muslims offer to global politics both a promising upside and a horrible downside. There is no question that Islam, unified predominantly in the communication system, will remain a strong global actor taking its positions from a developing world perspective. Will these Muslim religious-political forms foster or discourage dialogue? The most crucial political question about the possibility of an alliance of the religions of the book, however, hinges on the political stance of the West and Christianity in the next fifty years, as discussed in Chapter 9. Will Catholics and Protestants, taking their positions from the Vatican, the World Council of Churches, and missionary evangelism, remain connected to both the developed and the developing worlds, or will they embrace nationalism and global polarization?

The current rapidly integrating international political and EMC systems demand a deeper spirituality than the Westphalian and Cold War periods because each major political challenge includes many more stakeholders all over the world, all in instantaneous communication. Solutions

---

[31] Andre Gounelle, "Paul Tillich: A Vision of Protestantism Today," Frederick J. Parrella, ed., *Spirit and Community: The Legacy of Paul Tillich's Thought* (Berlin and New York: Walter de Gruyter, 1995), 158–66.

[32] Drew Christiansen, S.J., " 'No, Never Again War': The Evolution of Catholic Teaching on Peace and War," Lecture at Santa Clara University, April 28, 2004, 3–4. Fr. Christiansen traced the evolution of the John Paul II's position to one closer to Mennonite concerns. "We [the Catholic Church] are neither a pacifist church, nor a just-war church. We are a peacemaking church and peacemaking involves much, much more than non violence."

to explosive global issues such as Palestine, Kashmir, the Korean peninsula, and the Taiwan Strait require unique solutions, with chaos and
mayhem the only alternative to that one singular compromise solution.[33]
Although it may have been safer after the Thirty Years' War to privatize religion, in the current political and EMC systems, today's incredibly interconnected global society can only escape its obscene economic
stratification and the ever threatening Armageddon with public religious
activity supportive of these singular solutions.

IS RELIGION GOOD OR BAD FOR POLITICS?

Doesn't the material presented in this volume show that twenty-first-
century religion remains such a noxious element in the international political and EMC systems that humankind would be better off devoting significant resources to eliminating it or at least to privatizing it all over the
globe? Wouldn't the world be much better off if John Lennon's lyrical
line of "and no religion too" described global secularization? Such was
the ethical vision of Enlightenment thinkers who sought to separate religion and politics and to confine religion to the private sphere. This book
presents ample material to support both the malevolent and the beneficial
impacts of religion in current world affairs. A deeper understanding of the
political and social effects of religion will serve both believers and nonbelievers by clarifying the influence of different types of religious ideology,
organization, and activity. Even if such effects result as unintended consequences, religious and political leaders should face them with integrity.

Religion both unites and divides. Belief can sponsor a universal consensus about the inherent dignity of each person or it can demonize
an opponent for slaughter. The three principal positive political effects
of religious practice are: (1) the fostering of widespread support for
the inherent dignity of each individual and for the solidarity of all
humanity, regardless of creed, race, or gender; (2) the inspiration for
continued positive action in seemingly hopeless social and political situations; and (3) the maintenance of personal and societal identity and
values in the contemporary ever-changing "Fast Track" world. The first
effect derives from the simultaneous personal experience of unity with

---

[33] My favorite image of such international challenges is a ten-tumbler slot machine in which
the only diplomatic solution requires the simultaneous appearance of the same symbol
(a bell or a dove?) while the lever is being pulled every few seconds.

the Other and global humanity. Religion creates international, regional, national, and local communities, linking the believer to all humankind. Even at its shallowest, common belief provides a linkage among dissimilar national backgrounds and class interests. The description of the paradigm at the beginning of this chapter emphasized the ever increasing assault on public trust in a world of rapidly changing political and EMC systems.

Twentieth-century religion thus played a very beneficial role in bringing about reconciliation between former enemies in France and Germany, in lessening the war in Cambodia, and in ending apartheid in South Africa. Religion sanctifies forgiveness through offering iconic role models who have forgiven their enemies, whether it be Jesus on the Cross or Mohammed when he entered Mecca. Anglican Archbishop Desmond Tutu's *No Future Without Forgiveness* articulates this rationale and describes the experience of South Africa's Truth and Reconciliation Commission (TRC), which aimed at bridging the gap between the nation's whites and blacks following the election of ex-prisoner and African National Congress candidate Nelson Mandela as president in April 1994.[34] Tutu chaired the TRC in his purple cassock, opened and closed each session with a prayer, and sponsored two retreats for the commissioners, the second in the notorious prison on Robben Island. Four of the seventeen commissioners had been ordained. When perpetrators and victims testified, a ritual candle lighting commemorated those who had died as victims. Forgiveness is certainly no global panacea, but when promoted carefully and treated as a *process*, not a single event, it has contributed to political solutions in Northern Ireland, the Balkans, and South Africa.[35]

For the second effect, religion provides a reason for perseverance in the midst of the incredible hardships that are so often the lot of human life in the twenty-first century. It gives the believer hope that enables significant sacrifices, even of life itself, for the good of the community and the progress of humankind, understood in such religious identities as the *umma* and the Communion of Saints. Neither Nelson Mandela nor Kim Dae Jung could rationally have hoped to succeed in their early democratic struggles.

---

[34] Desmond Tutu, *No Future Without Forgiveness* (New York: Image Books, 1999).

[35] For seventeen lessons learned about forgiveness, see William Bole, Drew Christiansen, S.J., and Robert T. Hennemeyer, *Forgiveness in International Politics* (Washington, DC: United States Conference of Catholic Bishops, 2004), 182–85. These lessons summarize five years of discussions on the topic by prominent practitioners and analysts.

For the third effect, religion provides a centering personal and social identity and values amid the ever-faster-changing communication environment. This paradigm offers the person's political-religious identity as representing that person because both religion and politics signify ultimate values. Religion is that pattern of beliefs and activities that expresses ultimate meaning in a person's life and death. Politics grants to rightly constituted authority legitimate coercion of that person, even unto death. Political leaders, for example, send soldiers into harm's way without their volunteering. The religious part of the paradigm thus maintains the long historical view versus the contemporary political, political-economic, and political-military decision-making that tends to pursue a "quick fix" within the twenty-four-hour news cycle. If contemporary religious leadership, exempted from frequent elections and the twenty-four-hour news cycle, cannot maintain the long-term view of the global common good, who can?

The final advantage of religion is a preventive one. Religious leaders such as Desmond Tutu or Trich Nhat Hanh provide a challenging religious option for people who feel called to express ultimate values more fully in their total lives. In the absence of such healthy options, demented charlatans can occupy the empty public square as the only alternative for idealistic young people who wish to change the world. It is no coincidence that Aum Shinrikyo released sarin gas in the Tokyo subway in the world's most secular country.

The principal negative effects of religious belief, on the other hand, derive from the widening of divisions among regional, national and/or local groups. Religion can provide the rationale for demonizing competing groups and applying extreme measures, either in the defense of one's own political-religious community, or in an attempt to obliterate the other community. With the current state of military technology, a religious rationale for hatred can lead to unspeakable suffering. So religion becomes most dangerous when it "sanctifies" political divisions, either within polities as in Northern Ireland and Sri Lanka, or between states as in the Iran-Iraq War.

Mark Juergensmeyer's *Terror in the Mind of God: The Global Rise of Religious Violence* documents and seeks to explain the terrible killing, bombing, and maiming done in the name of religion during the last decades of the twentieth century. His book presents separate chapters on Protestant America and Catholic Ireland, Israel, Islam, Indian Sikhism, and the Aum Shinrikyo. Juergensmeyer seeks his explanation in the unique contemporary intersection of "the current forces of geopolitics and in a strain of violence that may be found at the deepest level of the religious imagination."[36] Although most of the terrorists he studies belong to "the lunatic fringe" of religious traditions, they maintain significant ideological connections to mainstream religion. These terrorists articulate social and political concerns widely held in the surrounding cultures and selectively focus on specific religious elements present in the mainstream faith, for example, transcendent morals, a cosmic war between good and evil, long historical time frames, and the necessity of embracing the difficult demands of the religion as it existed at its foundation.

Some analysts such as Rodney Stark and Lester Kurtz suggest that monotheistic religions remain disproportionately liable to such terrorism since they have less room for doctrinal compromise and syncretism. The religions of the book and the religions of public life produce evil principally by connecting religion to partisan crusades, from Holy War to the Cultural Revolution, whereas the religions of meditative experience do so by employing religious discipline in the service of evil ends, thus disconnecting meditative practice from social and political ethics. Consider, for example, Brian Victoria's *Zen War Stories*[37] on Buddhism or the 2002 Gujarat religious riots on Hinduism. Global religious restructuring has meant that all types of religion learn both evil and good practices from each other.

At the end of his book, Juergensmeyer offers five scenarios for the future relationship of religion and politics, with the most positive being "Healing Politics with Religion": "when secular authorities embrace moral values, including those associated with religion." He points to the irony that, although "the governments of modern nations have so often been perceived as being morally corrupt and spiritually vacuous since, the Enlightenment concepts that launched the modern nation-state were characterized by a fair amount of moralistic fervor."[38] Bringing religion and politics closer together does present a risk, but at the beginning of the twenty-first century, that risk is less than that posed by the secular status quo.

Hollenbach[39] takes another tack in demonstrating that the autonomy of national self-interest plus Enlightenment tolerance cannot provide a

---

[36] Mark Juergensmeyer, *Terror in the Mind of God: The Global Rise of Religious Violence*, updated (Berkeley: University of California Press, 2000), 6.

[37] Brian [Daizen] Victoria, *Zen War Stories* (London: Routledge Curzon, 2003).

[38] Juergensmeyer, *Terror*, 238–43.

[39] David Hollenbach, S.J., *The Common Good and Christian Ethics* (Cambridge: Cambridge University Press, 2002), 47–56.

satisfactory intellectual framework for solving contemporary global problems. Hollenbach begins with the incoherence of four dimensions of U.S. public opinion on international issues: (1) the high concern for issues that directly affect U.S. quality of life such as drugs and terrorism; (2) moderate concern about issues that affect the whole world, and thereby the United States, such as global warming; (3) moderate concern about strategic allies, such as U.S. troops in South Korea; and (4) low concern about global altruism, such as human rights in Africa, especially if U.S. troops would be involved. Such a broad spectrum in national public opinion, termed either "guarded engagement" or "tempered internationalism" is based principally on American interests.

This framework articulated by Alvin Richman, says Hollenbach, runs into three inherent contradictions that it cannot solve. First, environmental problems and poverty in developing countries are connected with each other, but the U.S. public will only support environmental action, and that minimally. Second, the failure of the "Washington Consensus" to improve developing world economies has failed to stimulate demand for American products, and also has led to policy revolt by U.S. labor and agriculture. Third, the framework's central concept, national state sovereignty, is being attacked by multinationals from above and by chaos and civil war from below. Hollenbach concludes that an understanding and acceptance of the global common good is necessary. This text argues that such public acceptance of a global common good is only possible today if it is perceived by most of the world's inhabitants as a religious responsibility, whether the global political leadership is consciously religious or secular.

From these examples and others, what rules should guide the global interactions of religion and politics if one is seeking to maximize the good effects of religion and minimize the bad? For an answer, the text will employ Thomas Merton, the book's expert on spirituality. Up to this point, Merton's objective descriptions of spirituality and its characteristics have contributed to the analysis. Now, his personal normative perspective provides further insight. The answer thus seeks to relate Merton's analysis of personal religious experience to the institutional significance of religion in global politics. The current speed of technological innovation means that a correct understanding of the rapidly accelerating political and EMC systems, based only on those systems, is doomed to failure. Any worthwhile paradigm must also employ a correspondingly correct anthropology of the human spirit. What kind of religion would lead to a better political world?

Nine Global Religious-Political Rules

1. A refusal to advocate religious violence in any situation remains
    the first political hallmark of religious depth. Gandhi was right!
    Political leaders must sometimes make difficult judgments about
    the legitimacy of coercion in protecting the human rights of the
    weak, but religious leaders should sacrifice their own lives before
    advocating violence. Even the language of violence against other
    religions must be banished. The September 2004 Islamist suicide
    butchering of school children in Russia justly generated significant
    criticism among Muslim commentators.[40] In addition to this com-
    mon religious ethical support of respect for life (Do not kill), Kung
    adds dealing honestly and fairly (Do not steal), speaking truthfully
    (Do not lie), and respecting and loving one another (Do not abuse
    sexually) as the four touchstones of his formulation. These four eth-
    ical directives are based on the principles that every person must be
    treated humanely and according to the Golden Rule in its various
    religious formulations.[41]

2. Religion should promote rational discussion of religious convic-
    tions and freedom of religious belief and unbelief. As soon as
    a religious principle is offered as a reason for political or legal
    action, it enters the public arena. In commenting on the desire
    of the politicians Mario Cuomo and Mark Souder to introduce
    their different religious convictions into public policy, Richard Fox
    states, "Thankfully, they both say they cherish continued dialogue.
    The importance of that dialogue cannot be overestimated. Political
    evangelicalism of the Souder variety and political liberalism of the
    Cuomo stamp are going to have to coexist for a long time to come,
    and both sides will benefit from clarity about what they do and do
    not have in common."[42] The fostering of religious pluralism will
    be a delicate balancing act, but neither religious intolerance nor
    secularism is a substitute.

[40] September 9, 2004.
[41] See Kung, *Global Responsibility*.
[42] Richard Wightman Fox, "The Politics of Religion in a Sinful World," E. J. Dionne Jr., Jean
Bethke Elshtain, and Kayla M. Drogosz, eds., *One Electorate Under God: A Dialogue
on Religion and American Politics* (Washington, DC: Brookings, 2004), 97. For the
many possible forms of these relationships, especially in the European context, see Alfred
Stepan's discussion of the "twin tolerations" in Larry Diamond, Marc F. Plattner, and
Philip J. Costopoulos, eds., *World Religions and Democracy* (Baltimore: John Hopkins
University Press, 2005), 3–23.

3. Religion should promote interfaith and ecumenical dialogues. In practical terms, all believers have much to learn both from those who practice other faiths and from those who profess no religious faith. The deeper the spirituality, the more intimate the connection between belief and unbelief. To prepare for religious dialogue, a person must first establish significant depth in his/her own tradition. Neither "generic religion" nor "spirituality lite" will accomplish anything.[43]

4. In political crises, the public should generally support the senior cleric over junior leaders. A longer life, deeper spirituality, and religion-wide support generally lead to greater tolerance. The world needs more religious leaders such as the Grand Ayatollah al-Sistani and fewer such as Moktada al-Sadr.

5. A religious primary ethical broker strengthens a nation in times of political and social crises. However, his political intervention is by its nature extraordinary and a sign of that crisis. Cardinal Jaime Sin rightly refused a position in the successor Philippine government.

6. When the world is viewed as a whole, each person and each nation has a specific political and religious calling. For example, Ukrainian Catholic and Orthodox leaders need to focus on advancing mutual reconciliation in Eastern Europe. Western Christians and Jews should deepen their spirituality in fighting Western consumerism, as Christians and Muslims in developing countries should join in attacking political and economic corruption. Americans need not prepare to be either U.N. Secretary General or Pope.

7. The world lacks an international primary ethical broker to articulate and to focus attention on the most crucial international moral issues. Such a body could be composed of six ex-religious leaders with political crisis experience and six ex-politicians with high ethical standards. Winners of the Nobel Peace Prize and other globally prominent leaders would make excellent candidates, for example, in a list of one nominee per country: Desmond Tutu, Jimmy Carter, Mary Robinson, Kim Dae Jung, Amartya Sen, Carlo Martini, Abdurrahman Wahid, Oscar Arias Sánchez, Mohammed Yunus, Elie Wiesel, Corazow Aquino, Mohammed Khatami, Zhu Rongji, Aung San Suu Kyi, Anwar Ibrahim, Trich Nhat Hanh, and Mikhail Gorbachev. Lack of enthusiasm from the home government, for the

---

[43] In Bangkok, Thomas Merton offered five rules for such dialogue among contemplatives. Cunningham, *Merton*, 235–36.

last four names, constitutes a global recommendation. The Dalai Lama, the pope, and current presidents and prime ministers remain too involved with their own institutions to accept this calling. A retired WCC General Secretary would be a natural selection.

8. The unchecked EMC systems pose the greatest threats to politics and to religion. A global religious alliance, *not* system, could be built, then, on economic development, social justice, peace, and human rights in the economic, military, and political systems and on the maintenance of religious identity and values in the communication system. The enemy would not be any specific government or economic organization, but the runaway concentrations of power in the three global EMC systems and any government's emphasis on unilateral national interest. Religious and political leaders would thus become allies against the takeover of the world by transnational corporations, arms merchants, and media moguls, and in opposing hegemonic nationalism.

9. Finally, another person's spiritual life, especially if that person belongs to another religion, is the last concern of a politician. Yet each of us, says Merton, has a stake in the spiritual growth and the political wisdom of the religious leaders and believers of all denominations. All religions testify to confusion within the self and the necessity to sort out this confusion to be open to the depths of union with the Other. Fostering religious depth in all its manifestations thus partakes of the international common good.

If the new paradigm is useful, and if the above nine general rules are valid, what education would best prepare our young people to participate in this world and to better it for their own children? The education must be interdisciplinary, from the arts to humanities to social science to natural science to technology, for the future leader must analyze all four global systems to arrive at better policies. The education would be religiously pluralistic, not secular. The ideal graduate would constantly ask questions about and formulate personal answers about his/her identity and his/her communities. When Thomas Merton was asked by his alma mater Columbia University for an essay on the meaning of education, he wrote the following: "The function of a university is, then, first of all to help the student discover himself: to recognize himself, and to identify who it is that chooses."[44] An education for the twenty-first century would

---

[44] Cunningham, *Merton*, 358.

foster intelligence and spirituality, global and local visions, technological and traditional forms of expression, and lifelong learning for service and for its own sake.

No pedagogical system, however, can guarantee that the student will exercise his/her opportunity and actually become a wiser person. Education, like life and politics, is always an act of faith. Statesman, teacher, and student must wait in solitude and gratitude for the coming of the mysterious Other, when the individual's "spirit sees God precisely by understanding that He [or She] is utterly invisible to it."[45] That intuitive leap, devoid of content, constitutes the basic foundation for, among other gifts, political service and a strong defense against the terrible ravages of false religion anchored in the false self of ourselves and others. Such a leap leaves us spiritually "naked." Merton adds, "Spiritual nakedness, on the other hand, is far too stark to be useful. It strips life down to the root where life and death are equal, and this is what nobody likes to look at. But it is where freedom really begins: the freedom that cannot be guaranteed by the death of somebody else."[46] May the next generation learn to embrace such nakedness, find their spiritual depth, and thereby in true political wisdom contribute to more just and peaceful societies all over the globe!

[45] Cunningham, *Merton*, 236.
[46] Cunningham, *Merton*, 360.

Appendix I

Thirty Years of Nobel Peace Prizes, 1975–2004

The following list includes the book chapters in which they appear.

2004: Wangari Maathai (Chapter 1)
2003: Shirin Ebadi (Introduction)
2002: James Earl Carter (Introduction, Chapters 5, 9, 10)
2001: United Nations, Kofi Annan (Chapters 2, 10)
2000: Kim Dae Jung (Chapters 6, 10)
1999: Médecins sans Frontières (Chapter 2)
1998: John Hume, David Trimble (Chapter 5)
1997: International Campaign to Ban Landmines (ICBL), Jody Williams (Chapter 2)
1996: Carlos Filipe Ximenes Belo, José Ramos-Horta (Chapter 8)
1995: Joseph Rotblat, Pugwash Conferences on Science and World Affairs
1994: Yasser Arafat, Shimon Peres, Yitzhak Rabin (Chapter 8)
1993: Nelson Mandela (Chapters 7, 10), Frederik Willem de Klerk
1992: Rigoberta Menchu Tum
1991: Aung San Suu Kyi (Chapter 10)
1990: Michael Sergeyevich Gorbachev (Chapter 5)
1989: The Fourteenth Dalai Lama (Tenzin Gyatso) (Chapter 10)
1988: United Nations Peacekeeping Forces (Chapter 5)
1987: Oscar Arias Sánchez (Chapter 10)
1986: Elie Wiesel (Chapter 4)
1985: International Physicians for the Prevention of Nuclear War (Chapter 2)
1984: Desmond Mpilo Tutu (Chapters 2, 10)

1983: Lech Walesa (Chapter 10)

1982: Alva Myrdal, Alfonso Garcia Robles

1981: Office of the United Nations High Commissioner for Refugees (UNHCR)

1980: Adolfo Perez Esquivel

1979: Mother Teresa (Chapter 1)

1978: Mohamed Anwar al-Sadat (Introduction, Chapter 2), Mechnachem Begin

1977: Amnesty International (Chapter 1)

1976: Betty Williams, Mairead Corrigan

1975: Andrei Dmitrievich Sakharov (Chapter 6)

Appendix II

Paradigm Chart and Category Questions

1. Political: Who will be the Democratic and Republican candidates for president in the next election?
2. Economic: What percentage of an investor's portfolio should be in global bonds?
3. Military: What technologies are most apt for a National Missile Shield?
4. Communication: What percentage of television programming is devoted to reality shows?
5. Political-Economic: What African policy will best assure the United States of Western access to Nigerian oil?
6. Political-Military: What responses should the United States take if North Korea tests a nuclear weapon?
7. Political-Communication: What communications policies would be in the best interest of the American public?
8. Economic-Military: What amount of U.S. aid would be necessary to compensate Ankara for Turkish economic losses in the U.S. attack on Iraq?
9. Economic-Communication: What should be the theme of Nike's new advertising campaign?
10. Military-Communication: How long would the Russian people support a war in Chechnya under different degrees of media coverage?

POLITICAL   ECONOMIC
SYSTEM   SYSTEM

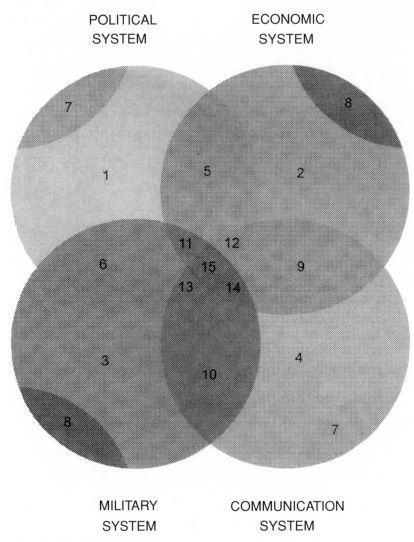

MILITARY   COMMUNICATION
SYSTEM   SYSTEM

Chart by Kara Hanson

11. Political-Economic-Military: Can the United States induce Iran to forego nuclear weapons for economic goals?
12. Political-Economic-Communication: What U.S. presidential visits would foster the formation of a Latin American Free Trade Area?
13. Political-Military-Communication: What military and communication roles should the British play in Iraq?

14. Economic-Communication-Military: Considering both the terrorist threat and the need for oil, what armed forces should the United States station in Europe and the Middle East?

15. Political-Economic-Military-Communication: What response should the United States have taken to the September 11 attacks?

Index